The First World War and its Aftermath

The Shaping of the Middle East

Edited by T. G. Fraser

GINGKO
LIBRARY

First published in Great Britain in 2015 by
Gingko Library
70 Cadogan Place
London SW1X 9AH

ISBN 978 1 909942 752
eISBN 978 1 909942 769

Typeset in Optima by MacGuru Ltd

A CIP catalogue record for this book is available from the British Library.

Printed and bound in Spain by Liberdúplex.

www.gingkolibrary.com

Contents

ROMANIA

Danube

Black Sea

BULGARIA

○ Sofia

SERBIA

Salonica

Edirne
(Adrianople)

Istanbul
(Constantinople)

○ Bursa

Ankara ○

Kizil Irma

GREECE

O T T O M A N

Athens ○

Izmir
(Smyrna)

○ Aydin

○ Konya

Antalya (Adalia)

Adana
○
Mersin ○

Chania ○

DODECANESE
(to Italy)

CYPRUS
(British)

Mediterranean Sea

Beirut ○

Acre ○
Haifa ○

Jaffa ○

Jerus
○

Tripolitania &
Cyrenaica (Libya)
(Ottoman)

EGYPT
(British-ruled)

Alexandria
○

Gaza ○

Nile

○ Cairo

Ak
○

The Ottoman Empire 1914

Introduction: the political transformation of the Middle East 1914–1923

T.G. Fraser[1]

The political map of the Middle East in 1923 could not have been more different to what it had been ten years before. Through no wish of their own most of the peoples of the region were under the rule of Britain and France. There were three exceptions to this. Under the commanding hand of Mustafa Kemal the Turks were emerging from the wreckage of their empire to forge a new national identity in their Anatolian heartland and the Egyptians, who had rebelled against British tutelage in 1919, had been granted sovereignty in 1922, albeit as yet limited. In the Arabian peninsula after a series of military successes against his rivals, Ibn Sa'ud was poised to take over the Hijaz. Otherwise, the areas which had formed part of the Ottoman Empire were part of an Anglo-French *imperium*, disguised as Mandates from the newly-formed League of Nations. What had brought about this transformation of the Middle East had, of course, been the First World War, the defeat of the Ottomans,

1 Much of the discussion which follows is based upon T.G. Fraser, with Andrew Mango and Robert McNamara, *The Makers of the Modern Middle East* (Gingko Library, revised and expanded edition, London: 2015). I have not sought to burden the reader by repeating the extensive footnotes and bibliography that the book contains. Leila Tarazi Fawaz, *A Land of Aching Hearts: The Middle East in the Great War* (Harvard University Press, Cambridge, Massachusetts; London, England: 2014) and Eugene Rogan, *The Fall of the Ottomans: The Great War in the Middle East, 1914–1920* (Allen Lane, Penguin Books, London: 2015) should also be consulted. I wish to thank Professor Alan Sharp for his comments on my drafts.

and the attempts at a peace settlement which followed. Of the victorious Allied and Associated Powers, the United States, which had never been at war with Turkey, showed no inclination to become directly involved in the region, neither did the Japanese whose focus was elsewhere, while the Italians and Greeks tried but failed. With their overwhelming military strength, that left the leaders of Britain and France free to dispose of the Middle East as they saw fit, or so they thought.

The Ottoman Empire on the eve of war in 1914 presented many paradoxes, prime amongst which were its prospects of survival. From the time of the capture in 1453 of Constantinople, the last faint echo of the Roman Empire, the Ottoman Turks had created an empire which at its zenith embraced territories and peoples across three continents. It was only with their failure at the siege of Vienna in 1683 that the remorseless advances of Prince Eugene's Habsburg armies pushed the Ottomans farther and farther into the Balkans, so that by 1914 the capital of Istanbul seemed uneasily positioned close to the new states of south-eastern Europe which had emerged in the course of the 19th century. Together with the atrophy of their position in Europe went the erosion of their rule in North Africa. From 1882 Egypt was *de facto* ruled by the British who were concerned to safeguard their vital imperial life line of the Suez Canal. While the country was still under the suzerainty of the Sultan in Istanbul, this fiction was ignored by the British who brooked no challenge to their rule. In 1911, the remaining Turkish possessions in North Africa, Tripolitania and Cyrenaica, were seized by Italy.

By 1914, then, the Ottoman Empire had become in real terms a Middle Eastern polity, but it must not be thought that this was necessarily a position of weakness, still less that it was facing the prospect of final collapse and dissolution. There was a secret organisation, mostly composed of young army officers schooled in fighting in the Balkans, who were determined to restore the empire's fortunes. Known as the Committee of Union and Progress, or Young Turks, they secured a form of constitutional rule in 1908, ousted the autocratic Sultan Abdul Hamid II the following year, and in 1913 mounted a coup d'etat. Led by two army officers, Enver and Cemal, and a civilian, Talat, they sought to reverse the empire's record of military defeat, turning to the Germans to reorganise the army, while entrusting the navy to the British and the paramilitary gendarmerie to the French. Although the army's equipment and infrastructure generally could not match the standard of the major European powers, it was equipped with modern Mauser repeating rifles and 198 batteries of Krupp artillery. Above all, the courage and toughness of its soldiers were of a high order, as the British imperial forces were to find out. But the military reforms had barely got under way when the army had to face a war against three of the leading armed powers of Europe and in the resulting conflict the empire was to be tested beyond its limit.[2]

Of the empire's estimated population of some 26,000,000, 10,000,000 were Turks and 7,000,000 were Arabs, mostly Sunni Muslims. What united Sunni Turks and Arabs was their common allegiance to the Sultan as Caliph of Islam, although sections of the latter would have preferred an Arab Caliph. More marginalised were the Shi'a Arabs of the Tigris and Euphrates and the large Christian minorities, most obviously the Armenians whose aspirations found an echo across the Russian border, with tragic consequences for them in 1915 once the two empires clashed. Long-standing Jewish communities existed in their Holy Cities of Jerusalem, Safed, Tiberias and Hebron, but also in Baghdad and Mosul. There were, in addition, the Zionist settlements in Palestine which had grown up in the wake of anti-Jewish persecutions in Russia from the 1880s and the formation of the Zionist organisation by the Austro-Hungarian journalist Theodore Herzl in 1897. Other minorities were the Greeks, with their ancient settlements along the Aegean coasts, the Kurds, Maronites, Copts, Alawites, Druzes, Yezidis, Circassians and Chaldeans. Cosmopolitan Istanbul was a microcosm of the empire as a whole.

There were important predominantly Arab cities with a long heritage, Damascus, Aleppo and Baghdad, and, however nominally, Cairo, but Arab society was largely agricultural, looking for leadership to the local a'yan, or 'notables'. As the war was to demonstrate, there was a level of discontent with Turkish rule, but this sentiment should not necessarily be conflated with Arab nationalism. Even so, a nascent Arab nationalism was in existence prior to the outbreak of war. Largely an urban expression of Arab identity, in Egypt it was directed against the British and elsewhere against a Turkish domination which was, if anything, hardening under the Young Turks. Whether these groups were looking to independence from Istanbul or would have settled for an increased voice in the empire's affairs is hard to judge. The principal weakness in the empire in 1914 was not so much the national question as an economic system which was ill-equipped to withstand the strains of a war against three of the major European powers. This was still a pre-industrial economy, crippled with debt and with an inadequate infrastructure in the

---

2 See Hew Strachan, *The First World War*, Volume I, *To Arms* (Oxford University Press, Oxford: 2001), chapter 8 'Turkey's Entry'; also reference 3 below.

face of which only the tenacious bravery of its army stood between the empire and defeat.[3]

On 29 October 1914 Turkey entered the war bombarding Black Sea targets of their hereditary Russian enemies and on 5 November Britain declared war on the side of her ally. Four days later, speaking in London's Guildhall, the British Prime Minister, Herbert Asquith, raised the future of the empire. The 'Eastern Question', the subject that had been debated by the statesmen of Europe for much of the previous century, now entered the lists of possible war aims, with Britain, France and Russia each having something to gain from Turkey's defeat. That the peoples of the empire might see opportunities and nurture hopes of their own cut little ice in the corridors of London, Paris and Petrograd, except when they suited the needs of the hour. With the Bolshevik Revolution of 1917 the Russians ceased to count for a time until they re-emerged under a different cloak three years later and the French were far too preoccupied in Europe to devote major resources to the Middle East, which left Britain, by 1918 the overwhelming military force in the region, the decisive voice. One immediate consequence of the war was that Britain declared Egypt to be a Protectorate, a unilateral act which, combined with the high-handed actions of imperial forces in the country in the course of the war, stoked the fires of anti-British nationalism.[4]

Few aspects of modern Middle Eastern history have been picked over quite so minutely as the promises and agreements that British officials and political leaders made in the course of the war. The military dominance enjoyed in 1918 with Sir Edmund Allenby's decisive battle of Megiddo was not so apparent earlier in the war with the disastrous failure at Gallipoli in 1915 and the humiliating surrender of General Charles Townshend's Anglo-Indian force at Kut in April the following year. The initial campaign in Mesopotamia, as it was then called, was so mismanaged that it became a national scandal. It was inevitable that the campaigns against the Turks had to rank well below the unprecedented military effort that the army was mounting against Germany and hence hardly surprising that the British would look for local support wherever they could find it. The chosen instrument of British policy was Sharif Husayn, head of the Hashemites, and Guardian of the Muslim Holy Places of

---

3 See the entry for 'Turkey', in *Encyclopaedia Britannica*, 11th edition (Cambridge University Press, Cambridge: 1911), Volume XXVII.

4 T.G. Fraser, 'Egypt in 1919: the founding year of the American University in Cairo', in Aran Byrne (ed), *East-West Divan: In Memory of Werner Mark Linz* (Gingko Library, London: 2014): pp 21–35.

Mecca and Medina. His interests and ambitions coincided with those of the British, or so it seemed. By allying with the British, he could assert the claims of his family and the Arabs at any peace conference, while an Arab army under Hashemite leadership offered Britain the prospect of a new means of harassing the Turks at the outlay of a monthly subsidy and the supply of arms. The crucial inducement to Husayn to lead a revolt against the Turks came in a letter from Sir Henry McMahon, High Commissioner in Cairo, on 24 October 1915 in which he was assured that: 'Great Britain is prepared to recognise and support the independence of the Arabs in all regions within the limits demanded by the Sherif of Mecca'. There was, nonetheless, an important caveat which excluded 'portions of Syria lying to the west of the districts of Damascus, Homs, Hama and Aleppo'.[5] What exactly this proviso meant has been the subject of endless debate, with McMahon subsequently claiming that Palestine had been excluded from his promise. Whether this was the case or whether the exclusion was aimed at the area of what became Lebanon where France claimed established interests remains obscure. The essential point is that Husayn and his family, trusting in what they believed McMahon had promised, kept their part of the bargain. On 5 June 1916, the Arab Revolt began, led by Husayn's son, Faysal. The Hashemite campaign was to catch the imagination of a war weary British public because of its association with the exploits of T.E. Lawrence, the archaeologist turned gifted soldier who was to become Faysal's trusted adviser.

At the same time as these approaches to Husayn, the British government had started to explore possible options for the post-war structure of the region. A committee chaired by Sir Maurice de Bunsen in 1915 recommended that in the event of the Ottoman Empire's disintegration, Britain should acquire Mesopotamia with a link to the Mediterranean port of Haifa. The Mesopotamian districts of Baghdad and Basra were increasingly seen as a vital British concern because of their proximity to the facilities of the Anglo-Persian Oil Company across the border. The key to this thinking was the Royal Navy's decision in 1912 to change from coal-burning to more efficient oil-burning ships.[6] The Royal Navy was, after all, the ultimate guarantor of Britain and her

5 McMahon to Sharif Hussein, 24 October 1915, *Correspondence between Sir Henry McMahon and the Sharif Hussein of Mecca, July 1915-March 1916* (Cmd 5957, Her Majesty's Stationery Office, London: 1939).
6 Elizabeth Monroe, *Britain's Moment in the Middle East 1914–1956* (Chatto & Windus Ltd, London: 1963) pp 98–9.

world empire. France's interests would be recognised in the districts around Damascus and Beirut, Russia would be granted the long-cherished Straits, and the interests of all three powers, Protestant, Catholic and Orthodox, in Palestine would require agreement. Here, in embryo, was the drift of British thinking about the region, which was soon to acquire more concrete form, particularly since the French were anxious that their interests and ambitions in Syria were not ignored.

The detailed negotiations were entrusted to two men who could claim first-hand knowledge of parts of the region. Charles Francois Georges-Picot, son of an eminent historian, had been consul-general in Beirut prior to the war. His British counterpart was the Conservative Member of Parliament, Sir Mark Sykes, traveller and author of two books on the Ottoman Empire, the second of which was published in 1915. If the French were looking to Syria, Britain's priority was the safeguarding of Mesopotamia. The results of their delibera-tions were formally conveyed by the Foreign Secretary Sir Edward Grey to the French ambassador Paul Cambon on 16 May 1916, although the terms had been agreed earlier in the year. Britain secured control of the key districts of Baghdad and Basra in Mesopotamia while France was assigned the coastline of what became Syria and Lebanon. The two countries were to recognise an independent Arab state or confederation of states in two other areas, marked (A) and (B) on an accompanying map, in which they were to be permitted to establish their own direct or indirect administration, spheres of influence in effect. There was to be an international administration for Palestine. Arabia was not mentioned in Grey's letter and here, it seems, was to be the inde-pendent Arab state that Husayn was being offered.[7] In retrospect the Sykes-Picot Agreement, as it came to be called, clearly foreshadowed the future Anglo-French partition of the Arab territories of the Ottoman Empire. This projected division of these territories, as yet theoretical and negotiated away from the public eye, took no account whatsoever of the possible wishes of the people who lived there, but simply reflected the priorities which London and Paris had at that time. Everything turned on Britain and France winning the war, in 1916 seemingly a remote prospect, but if that victory came then reality would have to be faced.

In the event, 1917 was a dismal year for the Allies, relieved only by the American entry into the war on 6 April. With the impending collapse of the

---

7 For a text see C.H. Dodd and Mary Sales (eds), *Israel and the Arab World* (Routledge & Kegan Paul Limited, London: 1970) pp 59–63.

Russian front, unsuccessful offensives, mutinies in the French army, the successes of the German U-boats, and the Austro-German victories in Italy, the overriding question was whether Britain and France could hold on long enough for American power to be mobilised and deployed in Europe. This depressing prospect encouraged British politicians and officials to look favourably on Zionist aspirations over Palestine, in the hope that such an initiative might encourage Russian and American Jews to throw their weight behind the war effort. The British Zionist leader, the Russian-born chemist at Manchester University, Dr Chaim Weizmann, had become well acquainted with leading political figures, including David Lloyd George, Arthur Balfour and Alfred Lord Milner, as a result of his contribution to war production. Various drafts of a pro-Zionist declaration were thrashed out in the course of 1917 until the final text was released on 2 November in the form of a letter from Balfour to Lord Rothschild, which committed Britain to 'view with favour the establishment in Palestine of a national home for the Jewish people', with the proviso 'that nothing shall be done which may prejudice the civil and religious rights of existing non-Jewish communities in Palestine'.[8] With the Balfour Declaration Britain had completed her portfolio of promises over the shape of a post-Ottoman Middle East. How these could be reconciled remained to be seen.

The war with Turkey ended on 30 October 1918 with an armistice agreement signed on board the rather appropriately named British battleship *Agamemnon* anchored at Mudros on the Greek Aegean island of Lemnos. By then Allenby's imperial forces, and Faysal's Arab army which had operated on his right flank, were in Damascus. Before negotiations over a peace settlement for the Middle East could get under way, the region was being affected to some degree with ideas which were coming from unexpected quarters, but which reflected how the world was changing. The new Communist government of V.I. Lenin in Russia needed to address the issue of the Muslim areas which had been trying to break free from Moscow's control. Once they had succeeded in defeating the anti-Bolshevik forces in 1919, the Communists could turn their attention to these areas, regaining control of Azerbaijan and Dagestan in the spring of 1920, and trying to assert a community of interest between Communism and Islam in a common anti-imperialism. Their efforts were to have been crowned at the Baku Congress in September 1920, but the avowed atheism of the government in Moscow, as well as its ruthless repression of Muslim discontent in the Caucasus and Turkestan, crippled any attempt to

---

8 Dodd and Sales (eds), *Israel and the Arab World* p 63.

harness Islamic sentiment in the Middle East.[9] More seductive was the idea of self-determination which the American President Woodrow Wilson had thrown into the public arena in a speech on 11 February 1918. Wilson was talking in the context of Europe, and national self-determination came to be a major feature of how the continent emerged from the Paris Peace Conference, but the idea was understandably taken up with alacrity in other parts of the world, including the Middle East. A claim for self-determination was to feature in Egyptian demands for an end to the Protectorate in 1919, but, of course, the roots of Egyptian nationalism were much older and deeper than that.[10]

The signing of the Mudros armistice proved to be a straightforward affair compared with the complex process of settling the post-war Middle East, which had to take its place behind the conclusion of a peace treaty with Germany and the reconstruction of central Europe after the implosion of Austria-Hungary. On the invitation of the British, Faysal, advised by Lawrence, came to the Paris Peace Conference to assert his father's claim to be the leader of the Arabs and for the establishment of the independent Arab state in the area that he believed had been promised. The French, for their part, understandably regarded him as too close to the British and were determined that their position under the Sykes-Picot Agreement be adhered to. Faysal came to Paris in the knowledge of Sykes-Picot, the terms of which had been put in the public domain by the Bolshevik authorities in Russia. The British introduced the concept that the Arab areas of the former Ottoman Empire be placed under Mandates held under the proposed League of Nations. France's response was that the two areas that had been assigned to her under Sykes-Picot be made into a single Mandate. With Britain and France at odds on the question, Wilson proposed that an Allied commission be sent to Syria to ascertain the views of the population. Its brief was expanded to include Mesopotamia. Convinced that there was nothing more to be gained in Paris, Faysal left for Damascus where a gathering of notables rallied to him, demanding full independence under his leadership.

Faysal's was not the only presence in Paris with Middle Eastern interests, since the Lebanese also had a delegation. On 27 February 1919, a Zionist delegation led by Weizmann and Nahum Sokolow appeared before the Council of Ten. The British Empire's representatives were Balfour and Milner, both

9 L.F. Rushbrook Williams, *India in 1920* (Superintendent Government Printing, India, Calcutta: 1921) pp 1–3.
10 Fraser, 'Egypt in 1919'.

intimately associated with the Declaration of 2 November 1917. The Zionists' request was very simple. It was that sovereignty over Palestine should be assigned to the League of Nations, with Britain holding the Mandate with a view to securing the Jewish National Home. The French government issued an immediate statement that it would neither oppose this proposal nor a Jewish state, a term which the delegation had not used. As later developments were to demonstrate, the meeting proved to have a decisive impact on the future of Palestine, but others were not permitted the same opportunity to present their case. The most obvious omission was that of Egypt where nationalist opposition to the Protectorate had grown apace and whose aspirations were articulated by the *El-Wafd* or Delegation Party led by Sa'ad Zaghlul Pasha. Zaghlul's demand that Egypt's case be put to the Peace Conference was rejected out of hand by the British, a stinging riposte since Egyptians had reason to feel that their country was much more developed than that represented by Faysal. When Zaghlul and three of his principal colleagues were deported to Malta, widespread revolutionary outbreaks occurred across the country. Faced with the scale of violence, Britain appointed a Commission under Milner, who had previously served in Egypt. On 28 February 1922, Milner and his colleagues recommended an end to the Protectorate with Egypt as a sovereign state, even though a British military presence was to remain and the country's foreign policy had to conform to that of Britain.[11]

With the signing of the Treaty of Versailles with Germany on 28 June 1919, followed by the Treaty of Saint Germain with what little remained of Austria on 10 September, the attention of the victorious powers could turn to the Middle East, although, for reasons already noted, the United States and Japan were largely bystanders. Away from the lush surroundings of the Ile-de-France, the peoples of the Middle East were aiming to set their own agendas, as the recent events in Egypt and Syria had clearly indicated. Confirmation of this development came on 28 August 1919 when the commission of inquiry which Wilson had triggered earlier in the year reported to the Peace Conference. The two commissioners were the Americans Dr Henry C. King, President of Oberlin College in Ohio, and the Chicago businessman Charles R. Crane, who toured extensively in Syria and Palestine for some six weeks in June and July. While their report was shelved, their findings should not be dismissed since they broadly reflected what was emerging from other sources. They reported that the overwhelming opinion in Syria was against a French Mandate and that

---

11 Fraser, 'Egypt in 1919'.

nine tenths of the population of Palestine was opposed to Zionism. Thinking in elite British official circles was very different. On 26 June, Balfour set out for Lloyd George his view that all the Arab territories should be detached from Turkey, that France should get the Mandate for Syria, Britain that for Mesopotamia, and that Palestine should become the responsibility of Britain or the United States, the latter an unlikely event. By 4 August, the government had decided that Britain would accept a Palestine Mandate which would embody the substance of the Balfour Declaration. The Arabs were to be reassured that they would not be despoiled of their land, forced to leave the country or put under the rule of a minority, but told that agitation would be useless since the establishment of a Jewish National Home was a *chose jugee*.[12]

This parcelling out of the non-Turkish areas of the former empire was formally agreed in April 1920 when the Principal Allied Powers met at San Remo with the American ambassador to Italy in attendance. Britain was confirmed as the Mandatory Power for Mesopotamia, or Iraq as it became the following year, and was also chosen to have the Mandate for Palestine charged with implementing the Balfour Declaration. The French were granted the Mandate for Syria, clearing the way for them to deal with Britain's erstwhile ally, the increasingly isolated Faysal. Their imperious proconsul in the region, General Henri Gouraud, was steadily building up his forces so that by the summer they vastly outnumbered Faysal's army, in addition to which he had at his disposal tanks, heavy artillery and aircraft, which the latter did not. After negotiations over a series of French demands, Gouraud ordered a march on Damascus which fell to his forces on 25 July. The previous day the French had overwhelmed an Arab army led by the minister of war, Yusuf al-Azmah, at the battle of Maisaloun. Killed in the battle, al-Azmah, a gallant former Ottoman officer, became a national martyr for the Syrians.[13] Fleeing south to British-controlled territory, Faysal left Haifa for Europe. Gouraud did not await the formal start of the Mandate to stamp France's authority, on 1 September announcing the creation of a Greater Lebanon based on Beirut and including Mount Lebanon, Tyre, Tripoli and the Bekaa valley. Yet another political boundary had emerged, but one which contained a

---

12 Mr Balfour, Paris, to Earl Curzon, 2 July 1919, Enclosure 'Memorandum for' Lloyd George; Earl Curzon to Colonel French, Cairo, 4 August 1919, E.L. Woodward and Rohan Butler (eds), *Documents on British Foreign Policy 1919–1939* (Her Majesty's Stationery Office, London: 1952), No 211, pp 301–3; No 236, 329.

13 Tabitha Petran, *Syria* (Ernest Benn Limited, London: 1972) pp 59–60.

potentially unstable population of Christians, Druzes, as well as Sunni and Shia communities.

The Egyptian revolution of 1919 was not the only source of unrest that Britain had to face in the Middle East, or elsewhere for that matter, since India was in turmoil under Mahatma Gandhi's emergent leadership and in January the Irish War of Independence had broken out. The granting of the Mandate for Mesopotamia at San Remo was followed by a revolt which broke out in July 1920. In a letter to *The Times* on 23 July Lawrence made the obvious point that the Arabs had fought the Turks for their independence not to change masters. Substantial reinforcements from both the British and Indian Armies had to be sent at a time of financial stringency, forcing the Cabinet to consider making their former *protege* Faysal king of Mesopotamia in an attempt to appease nationalist sentiment. This option appealed to the new Colonial Secretary Winston Churchill who assumed office in January 1921 and pursued it at the Cairo Conference in March. The Hashemites were finally to be rewarded. Transjordan was to be separated from Palestine with Faysal's brother Abdullah as its amir. Faysal was to indicate his willingness to be king of Iraq. Arriving in the country in June 1921, on 23 August, having been confirmed by the Council of Ministers and in a referendum, he became king.

There was no such neat solution for Palestine, where opposition to the Zionists and to the proposed Mandate had been steadily growing since the summer of 1919. On 4 April 1920 there were demonstrations in Jerusalem in support of Faysal in which five Jews and four Arabs were killed. The following year more serious disturbances broke out in May with attacks on Jewish settlements in which 47 were killed, while 48 Arabs were killed by the security forces. An enquiry into these events chaired by the Chief Justice of Palestine, Sir Thomas Haycraft, concluded that the root cause was Arab fears prompted by increasing Jewish immigration with the consequent threat to their economic and political position. The reassessment of British priorities came in what was termed the Churchill White Paper of 3 June 1922 which attempted a redefinition of the Balfour Declaration in the light of the forthcoming Mandate. The National Home was to be a centre in which the Jewish people could take an interest and a pride, and immigration into Palestine would depend upon its absorbtive capacity. Accepted by a reluctant Weizmann, the formula was rejected by the Arabs

On 10 August 1920, the Turkish representatives followed the path already travelled by their former German, Austrian, Hungarian and Bulgarian allies to the suburbs of Paris to sign a peace treaty. The Treaty of Sevres, based upon the San Remo agreements, confirmed Turkey's loss of all of her former Arab territories. Armenia was recognised as an independent state, while Kurdistan was to have an autonomous government. The port of Izmir, Smyrna to the Greeks, together with its hinterland was to be administered by Greece for five years after which a plebiscite was to be held. The country was in effect to be disarmed, its military forces restricted to a gendarmerie of 35,000 for internal security reinforced by 15,000 troops, although the Sultan was to retain his bodyguard. Finally, the Straits were to be internationalised, the Turks retaining Istanbul, but hemmed in on the European side by the Greeks who were to acquire Eastern Thrace. Further provisions, such as an insistence that excavations in the country could only be conducted by qualified archaeologists and that the brakes on railway carriages had to be in order, were at best demeaning and at worst gratuitously insulting to the Turks.

Such terms could only have been imposed upon a country which was prostrate, but by then a movement of national revival had begun galvanised by an army officer, Mustafa Kemal, who had first made his name at Gallipoli. Realising that Istanbul was too vulnerable to foreign military intervention, as the Allies demonstrated in March 1920, he made his base at Ankara in the interior of Anatolia where, on 23 April, a Grand National Assembly convened. Elected as its President, Kemal was effectively head of a rival government to that of the Sultan in Istanbul. On 19 August, the Assembly declared that the Ottoman representatives who had signed the Treaty of Sevres had been guilty of treason. The Kemalists had now issued two challenges, one to the Allies and the other at the Ottomans who had Kemal sentenced to death. In fact, the latter had pathetically little authority left, their forces no match for the Kemalists, but the Greeks whose troops had landed at Izmir in May 1919 and who enjoyed the support of Lloyd George were another matter.

The war between the Kemalists and the Greeks was bitter. At one point the latter's army seemed to threaten Ankara but at the decisive battle of Sakarya in September 1921 their offensive in Anatolia was thrown back. Despite Lloyd George's partiality for the Greeks there was no appetite in London or Paris to come to their aid nor, indeed, to confront the new spirit of Turkish nationalism. In August 1922 Kemal's army routed the Greeks. On 9 September, Izmir was taken, and the historic Greek Smyrna came to an end. Much of the city was destroyed by fire with over 200,000 Greeks and other Christians being evacuated in Allied ships. The extent of Kemal's victory then threatened the British military enclave on the Asian side of the Straits at Canakkale, or Chanak, but when it became clear that of the British dominions only New Zealand

and Newfoundland would support a renewed war with Turkey the crisis was defused and the way opened for a settlement to be negotiated. An armistice was signed at Mudanya on 11 October by which Greece agreed to evacuate eastern Thrace. Turkey was at last at peace. Formal confirmation that this was the case came with the Treaty of Lausanne which was signed after prolonged negotiations on 24 July 1923. The losers at Lausanne were the Greeks, who had to forfeit eastern Thrace and some Aegean islands, not to mention the loss of their ancient presence in Anatolia, the Armenians whose forces had also been defeated by the Kemalists, and the Kurds who did not rate a mention in the Treaty. The new Turkey had been secured. By then the Ottomans had departed, the last Sultan, Vahdettin, sailing into exile on a British battleship on 17 November 1922. On 29 October 1923, the ninth anniversary of the country's entry into the war, the Assembly proclaimed Turkey to be a republic with Kemal as its President, from 1934 uniquely honoured with the name of Ataturk, or Father of the Turks.

However the nature and extent of nationalism in the region by the early years of the 20th century may be judged, the events of the First World War unquestionably accelerated the pace of its development. That nationalism, as the doyen of Middle Eastern historians Albert Hourani explained, embraced elements both secular and religious. Kemal may have forged a secular republic but the Turks were still Muslims and few Arabs were inclined to follow his path, Arab nationalism being grounded in an Islamic past.[14] The complex intellectual and political interactions which resulted may be seen in the contributions of Michael Erdman, Bruno Ronfard and Alp Yenen, while Amany Soliman explores the subtle relationship between Egyptian nationalism and the diverse foreign community which had settled in the country. While much has been written about the impact of the war on women's lives and roles in Europe and the United States, the chapters by Noga Efrati and Sevinç Elaman-Garner analyse the changes that were also stirring amongst the women of the Middle East.

The war touched people's lives in areas seemingly remote from the main battlefronts, but here, too, in ways that had long-term implications, as Jason Pack explores in his analysis of the Anglo-Sanussi war. It need hardly be said that the conflict also had disastrous personal consequences, not just for those who suffered on the fighting fronts. The catastrophic demographic effects of the influenza epidemic are well known, but equally the food shortages

---

14 Albert Hourani, *The Emergence of the Modern Middle East* (Macmillan, in association with St Antony's College, Oxford, London and Basingstoke: 1981) pp 185–7.

and famines which had devastating consequences for Germany in the Turnip Winter of 1916–1917 and parts of India were matched by the famine in the Levant which is the subject of Najwa al-Qattan's chapter, with all the human suffering that it entailed.

The catalyst was the war itself. Once the leaders of the Young Turks had staked the empire's fate on an Austro-German victory, the British, French, and for a time the Russians, could plan for its future disposal on their own interests. Despite encouraging the Hashemites' revolt against the Turks, their intended structures, the shape of which had been secretly negotiated by 1916, ignored the wishes of those affected on the ground. In an analysis on 11 August 1919 Balfour conceded that they had made 'no declaration of policy, which, at least in the letter, they have not always intended to violate'.[15] Steven Wagner details how British Intelligence interacted with Arab nationalism in this crucial period. Even before the war, the decision to adopt oil-burning ships for the Royal Navy had brought oil to the forefront of British concerns, but the mechanisation of warfare, not least the exponential development of air forces, made the commodity an even more pressing consideration as the conflict went on and this continued into the post war years. The centrality of oil in thinking and policy-making about the Middle East and how its production affected those involved are analysed by Jonathan Conlin and Kaveh Ehsani.

In 1919 the victorious Allied and Associated Powers convened in Paris with much of the world, including the former territories of the Ottoman Empire, seemingly at their disposal, but Andrew Arsan explains that other discourses were at work in the Middle East which need to be taken into account if the workings and consequences of the peace settlements can be fully appreciated. Key aspects of the new political dispensations which were emerging out of the novel concept of League of Nations Mandates are discussed in the chapters by Mark Farha, John McHugo, Harrison Guthorn, and Laila McQuade and Nabil Al-Tikriti, while those by Louise Pyne-Jones and Aaron Y. Zelin explore the religious implications for the region of the war and its aftermath.

Sufficient has been said in this sketch of how the Middle East evolved between the outbreak of war in 1914 and the proclamation of the Turkish republic exactly nine years later to demonstrate how the region's political shape had been determined by the wartime policies and imperial ambitions of the European powers, most obviously those of Britain and France. This

---

15 'Memorandum by Mr Balfour (Paris) respecting Syria, Palestine, and Mesopotamia', 11 August 1919, *Documents on British Foreign Policy*, First Series, Volume IV, No 242, pp 340–9.

was a process in which the aspirations and identities of those who lived there went largely ignored until they were able in a changing post-war world to assert them, as increasingly they did. In the chapters that follow scholars from a range of countries and academic perspectives explore many dimensions of this critical period of Middle Eastern history, shedding light on how the region was emerging in the ways that it did – and with consequences which a century later were still being worked out.

ROMANIA

KINGDOM
OF THE SERBS,
CROATS AND
SLOVENES

Danube

Black Sea

BULGARIA

◦ Sofia

Edirne
(Adrianople)

Istanbul
(Constantinople)

Salonica

Ankara ◦

Kızıl Irm

GREECE

T U R K E

Izmir
(Smyrna)

◦ Konya

Athens

Adana

Antalya (Adalia)   Mersin ◦ ◦

ISKENDE

DODECANESE
(Italian)

TERRITORY
THE ALAW

CYPRUS
(British)

LEBANO
(French mand.

Beirut ◦

M e d i t e r r a n e a n   S e a

Acre ◦

PALESTINE
(British mandated)   Haifa ◦

Tel Aviv/Jaffa ◦

Jerusalem ◦

LIBYA
(Italian)

Gaza ◦

EGYPT
(British-ruled)

Alexandria ◦

Nile

Cairo ◦

A

Turkey and the Near East 1923

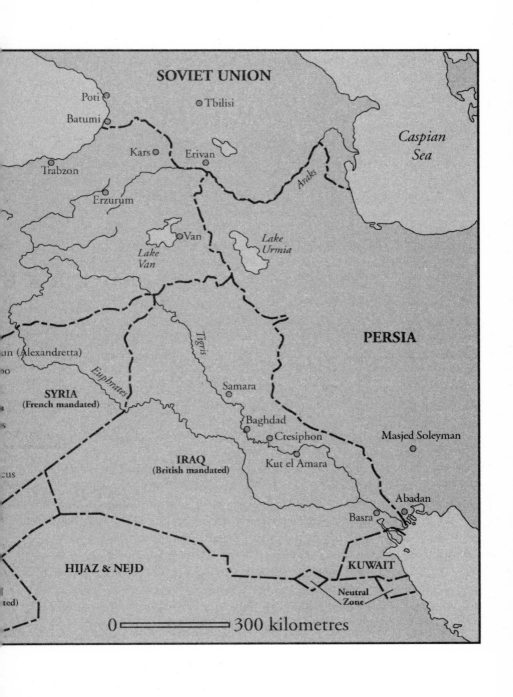

1

The rise of Egyptian nationalism and the perception of foreigners in Egypt 1914–1923

Amany Soliman

This chapter argues that the perception of foreigners in Egypt was influenced by the rise of Egyptian nationalism. The protection of foreigners by the British occupation, as well as the long standing privileges of the Capitulations, made the *khawagat* (foreigners) a major concern against the hoped-for Egyptian independent nation state for many of the nationalist activists. However, this chapter tries to show that the negative perception against the foreigners in Egypt, when found, was not due to xenophobia. It was the result of two factors; first: foreign economic dominance and exploitation, and second: the political activities of many foreigners who expressed a stance against Egypt's nationalist movement.

Cosmopolitanism in Egypt from the late 19th century until the 1950s has been romanticised by many writings in the West which described the foreigners' life in Egypt as almost perfect. Writings such as Lawrence Durrell's *Alexandria Quartet* and poems of the Greek poet Kafavis are considered references on this period as they were written by Europeans who lived an amazing life in Egypt and in Alexandria in particular. If the nostalgic literature is a popular genre, nostalgia for Alexandria and cosmopolitan Egypt is a very frequent topic appearing in this genre's works.

On the other hand, writings by most Egyptian historians about this era always show a sense of resentment towards a time when the fortunes of Egypt did not belong to the Egyptians. Egyptian writings would bring new elements to the discussion including; foreign domination of the Egyptian economy and how the foreign communities were alienating themselves from the native middle and lower class Egyptians and were looking down on them. It is true that the foreigners who came to the country in the third wave during the First World War did mingle with the Egyptians; however, they had to mingle with the Egyptians because they were poor and they had to live in modest affordable neighbourhoods and work in artisan professions as the common Egyptians did. On the other hand, the writing of history in Egypt during the 1950s and the 1960s was dominated by the Nasserite Pan-Arabism ideology and the battles that President Nasser was always going through with the West made Egyptian historians, novelists and cinema makers lean towards demonising the foreign presence in Egypt before 1956. Even after the time of Nasser, the doctrine was sustained in historical writing that still used the same narrative. The dilemma comes also with other Egyptian writings about the same issue, which mourn the cosmopolitan era and describe them often as 'the good old times'. Those writings tell stories about how multicultural and open to the world Egypt was. This latter argument has been heavily used since the 1980s to resist the radical views of fundamentalists and the religious fanaticism movement that escalated in the Egyptian society.

In a confused manner, while the majority of writers attempt to assert their nationalist loyalty, those who write about this period – in literature or history – can not ignore certain cultural and societal bright sides, though their nationalist ideology drives them to highlight the evils of the 'rotten old time' – el a'ahd el ba'ed, and its evil trio – the monarchy, the British occupation and the greedy foreigners. Between the writings of euphoric nationalist Egyptian writers and romantic Europeans who lost their dreams in Egypt, most of the writings about this period show an exaggerated one side of the story.

It is not suggested that the rise of Egyptian nationalism and its most recalled event, the 1919 uprising, was a reaction or a result in response to foreign economic dominance, or even the involvement of foreigners in anti-nationalist activities. However, other demands and forms of injustice were widely studied in Egypt and elsewhere. Hence, this chapter does not investigate the perception of foreigners to prove that their presence or dominance ignited the uprising. It is an investigation of a bilateral process of action and reaction between the common people and the opinion leaders in Egypt from one side and the foreigners from the other, which can be translated into recording the then current perception as well as the role of mass media of this era in pushing people to conceive certain views towards the foreigners.

This chapter is not an attempt to support either of the two exaggerated sides of historic writings. Demonising the foreign presence in Egypt is not the full story and neither is exempting the foreigners from an obvious economic exploitation of the country as well as undermining its legitimate aspirations for sovereignty. However, since writings in the West are mainly focused on the dreamy views of a harmonious co-living between the foreigners and the Egyptians, this chapter tries to show that there were moments in which human interactions took place and which resulted in tension between the Egyptian natives and foreign residents.

On 11 June 1882, near the district of El Hammamil in Alexandria, a Maltese passenger and an Egyptian donkey man argued about the fare that the Maltese owed the Egyptian. The argument escalated into a fight and the Maltese stabbed the Egyptian with a knife. A call was vigorously spread within minutes that the Egyptians were attacking the foreigners, and vice versa, in the European quarter of Alexandria. By the end of the day, 50 Europeans and 250 Egyptians had lost their lives in addition to hundreds of injured. Within one month, British warships started the bombardment of Alexandria and the British occupation in July 1882 was the result of the so called 'Alexandria massacre'.

The Egyptians used to blame these violent events between the natives and the Europeans on the occupation of their country. Many commentators and nationalist leaders, as well as the masses, thought that the British had their eyes on Egypt since 1807[1], and even earlier since the time of the French expedition (1798–1801). However, Egyptians thought that the Alexandria massacre gave a perfect opportunity for the British to play the role of the saviours who came to Egypt to protect and save the Europeans and the minorities from the savage fanatic Egyptians. If it was not for this heavy presence in numbers and interests of foreigners, Egyptians thought, the British Empire would not have found a justification to take over the country.

The historiography of the foreign presence in Egypt during the 19th and 20th centuries highlights the main waves of European and foreigners, *el Khawagat*, coming to Egypt. During Muhammad Ali's reign (1805–1849), due to his economic reform plans and the exemptions and facilitations he granted the

1 In 1807, a British expedition tried to invade Egypt through Alexandria and the Mediterranean port of Rosetta. The Royal Navy and the British army tried to take over the northern Egyptian Mediterranean coast as part of their war against the Ottoman-French Alliance. The British forces stayed in Alexandria from March to September 1807 until orders were given to withdraw from Egypt.

investors, he succeeded in attracting European capitalists to Egypt. The city of Alexandria that he had restructured as a modern European-styled business centre was the most important new attraction in the region for investors and investment opportunities.

In the second half of the 19th century, Ismail pasha (1863–1879), followed his grandfather's legacy in attracting foreign capital. With the development of the Suez Canal project, the railways and new urbanising plans of both Cairo and Alexandria, another wave of Europeans arrived in Egypt, giving a new economic and intellectual face to the country. The sectarian clashes in the Levant and Palestine pushed the Levantines, especially non-Muslims, out of their countries. Many of the Levantine immigrants favoured Egypt as a destination. They have, as well, contributed to the revival of the cultural, artistic and media awakening of Egypt. Many of the Levantine immigrants were businessmen and merchants who came to Egypt with investment plans.

Despite the aggression in 1882 between the Egyptians and the foreigners and the British occupation afterwards, foreign migration to Egypt continued to make use of the new economic opportunities in Egypt, especially the Suez Canal and the cotton trade. However, the four years of the First World War experienced a paradigm shift as many of the Europeans and other immigrants into Egypt were poor refugees without capital to invest or profits to collect. These immigrants were living in proximity with housing and livelihoods with common Egyptians.

The census of 1907 showed that only 2% of the population (almost 11.2 million in total) were foreigners; of whom the Greeks were the biggest foreign community. The census showed that 78% of the foreigners in Egypt were Greeks, Italians, French and British nationals.[2]

Greeks	62793
Italians	34926
French	14591
Other European and US residents	38900

2 Mahmoud Soliman, (1996) *alaganeb fi Misr 1922–1952 derassah fe tarikh misr elegtemaie* [The foreigners in Egypt 1922–1952: A Study in Egypt's Social History (Ein for human and social studies, Cairo: 1996), pp 59–60

The following census in 1917 showed that the Greeks were still the biggest community. However, the total number of foreigners in the country dropped due to the involvement of Egypt in the First World War. The census showed that only 1% of the population (12.8 million people in total) were foreigners.

Greeks	56731
Italians	40198
French	21270
Armenians	7760
Other European and US residents	26791

For the argument in this chapter, analysing the perception towards British citizens in Egypt will not be explored. The perception towards the British would be mainly affected by the occupation and hence it cannot be analysed based on the two factors mentioned previously; economic dominance and political activity. The word 'foreigner' is used in this chapter to describe any foreign resident in Egypt between 1914 and 1923, which includes Arab residents as well as the Europeans and all other nationalities. The first law to organise the granting of Egyptian citizenship was issued in 1924; hence, the description of a resident as a foreigner was due to how these individuals identified themselves. The censuses that were done by the Egyptian government starting from 1882 took into consideration that the foreign residents were keen to register themselves with foreign communities in order to guarantee the financial and judicial privileges of each foreign community.

The analysis of the perception towards the foreigners will focus in this chapter on the popular views either in popular culture or in the mass media. Analysis of political views, writings and speeches will be done only if these were unofficial stances, representing the views of non-ruling politicians. It will not analyse official or state behaviour and/or decisions of the Egyptian government or the British administration unless they directly influenced the people's perception.

The impact of the First World War and its coming was considerable:

'... These days are black for Egypt, white for the others who come to our country to take advantage of our fortunes and to manipulate our naïve simple people. They made themselves rich by pulling the money out of the people of this country into poverty.'[3]

Turkish, German and Austrian residents were the earliest and formed most of the foreigners who left Egypt even before the actual start of the First World War. The 1907 census recorded 7,700 Austrians and 1,850 Germans living in Egypt. In August 1914, their numbers dropped to only 2,800 Austrians and 257 Germans. AlAhram was monitoring the fleeing of the German and Austrian citizens from Egypt. News on 4 August 1914 mentioned that high profile German foreigners were leaving Egypt including Mr. Shadah, the chief librarian of the Khedivial Library and a known cultural figure, as well as two Austrian vice consuls. Younan Rizk wrote that Austrians took the risk and stayed in Egypt in large numbers, despite the British occupation, due to their heavy involvement in tourism and the hotel industry. He wrote that they were worried about the financial gains they would make if they stayed in Egypt that expected military, media and diplomatic people to arrive from Europe and elsewhere.[4]

The Egyptians had a deep resentment towards the economic dominance that the foreigners enjoyed in Egypt. Whether through the British occupation, international companies or the foreign individuals, most of the economic activities in Egypt were dominated by Europeans and foreigners. Sayings like the above quote, in 1911, shows how this resentment was present even before the First World War. Vaudevilles, plays, colloquial poetry and proverbs often expressed how the Egyptians always felt subordinate to the foreigners when it came to the economy.

However, the foreigners who fled to Egypt from Europe and the Levant during the war were suffering economically, which was obvious since they lived in the same neighbourhoods as the Egyptian middle and lower class and competed with the them around the limited livelihoods in traditional districts of Cairo and Alexandria as well as other small towns in the Delta and upper Egypt. On 13 November 1916, the Germans targeted Cairo with an air raid. All the targeted districts were residential middle and lower class neighbourhoods. Al-Ahram newspaper reported that 20 persons were killed of whom eight

---

3 Tala'at Harb, (1911) Elag Misr Eleqtessady [Economic remedy of Egypt], a series of Speeches and a project for the bank of the nation or bank of the Egyptians, http://dar.bibalex.org/webpages/mainpage.jsf?PID=DAF-Job:159084&q , last accessed 26 March 2015.
4 Younan Labib Rizk, Diwan El Hayah El Moa'esera [Diwan of contemporary Life] (Al Ahram History Center, Cairo: 2003) Vol 8, pp 136–137

were foreigners, including Armenians, Greeks and a Jewish woman.[5] These casualities referred to a new phenomenon of the foreign presence in Egypt; that foreigners were no longer confining themselves to high class districts. The foreigners were everywhere, sharing life concerns and limited livelihoods with common Egyptians.

In a colloquial poem (zagal) that was published in *Al-Masamir*, the poet accuses the Egyptian and foreign wealthy men of not just stealing the fortunes of the country and exploiting the nation, they are not even giving respect or proper behaviour to the poor whom they are depriving.[6]

This resentment was not just towards the Europeans; but also towards other residents who enjoyed privileges due to the war circumstances including Arab nationals as well. The Syrian employees and their influence on the government and administration in Egypt during the war have been mentioned on several occasions. They were fluent in Arabic and capable of managing governmental and administrative affairs. Moreover, they accepted working with the British authorities. The Egyptian historian Latifa Salem thinks that the occupation favoured them, especially the Christian Levantines, because they did not support the Ottomans and did not sympathise with the Ottomans as the Muslim Egyptians would do. They were clever civil servants, Salem asserts, but they were less annoying to the British administration in general.[7] They came to Egypt fleeing from the persecution of Cemal Pasha and they joined the British in their enmity to the Ottoman Empire.

The foreigners were heavily accused of contaminating Egyptian society with immoral commercial activities starting with bars and gambling all the way to fashion and producing garments that did not respect the value system of the Egyptian conservative society.

The Greeks controlled the industry of alcohol and liquor related activities in general. Kotsika, the famous Greek alcohol millionaire, was the wealthiest man in Egypt in the first quarter of the 20th century. Egyptian poets used to criticise the Greeks and Armenians for owning and running bars. One of the

---

5 *AlAhram* newspaper, 14 November 1916, p 1

6 Mal'un abu sa'atak [your eminence can go to hell] A translation by Ziad Fahmy may be found in his book Ziad Fahmy, *Ordinary Egyptians: Creating the Modern Nation through Popular Culture* (Stanford University Press, (Stanford: 2011), p120. The original poem is published in *AlMasamir* satirical newspaper on 18 September 1918, p 1

7 Latifa Salem, *Misr fi el harb el 'alameya el awla* [Egypt in World War One] (Egyptian General Book Authority, Cairo: 1984) p 191.

most famous zagals by AlTunsi was 'Manolis' Bar'[8] was written to criticise a bar in Abdeen in central Cairo owned by a Greek man called Manolis:

> Manolis' Bar is every night full...
> Muslims of all kinds are there.
> Until 1 or 2 Am it is open...
> Until Abdeen Police orders them to sleep.
> He [Manolis] divides it to two halves...
> One is for artisans and thieves.
> While the other half is for the wealthy fat people...
> With a "private" sign on the door.

Metaphorical and common names of certain nationalities were widely used in satirical newspapers, vaudevilles and musicals in reference to certain Europeans. In the following excerpt of a musical called Ish or (wow) an Egyptian naïve peasant called Kiskish bey sold his cotton and then a Greek bar owner called Kharalambo deceived him and took both the money and the farmland:

> Kharalambo saw that my pocket was full...
> He immediately stood still (mesmerized)
> His eyes were on my farmland ...
> He told me, let's play some poker ...
> Made me drink Johnny Walker
> I played, got drunk and lost ...
> Until I fell into the Abyss[9]

By the end of the war, foreigners were usually criticised for making fortunes out of the war. Egyptians were already suffering injustice because of the forced labour they were pushed to in hundreds of thousands, either in military or civilian activities, a suffering that the foreigners in the country did not go through although many of them belonged to nationalities or the protection of countries that were main parties in the war, like the British and the French. The Egyptians felt that they suffered for this forced labour and conscription,

---

8 Bayram ElTunsi, Zagal: 'hanet Manoli [Manolis' Bar]', in Diwan of Bayram ELtunsi (Maktabet Misr, Cairo: 1948) Vol. 2, p 13 (translation is done by myself).
9 Translation is done by Ziad Fahmy in Ordinary Egyptians, p 126.

in addition to the fortunes accumulated in the war years and were not in their pockets, despite being made on their land.

On 11 January 1919, Muhammed Abdelrasoul wrote a zagal in *Al-Masamir* newspaper entitled 'Oh Nile!! I love you'[10]:

Oh, Nile!! I love you
You Egypt, the paradise of Life and afterlife
Your people are noble and sophisticated
And they are all I want to see evolving
When would I see your people healed from their continuous wounds?
When will we beat the enemies?
All peasants must then unite and stop imitation and relaxation
We have to survive the evil of **Yanni**, and **Saddah**
Those who stole the money of the peasants' and we will keep repeating
    the song until we have our rights back

Yanni was the preferred name for Egyptians to call a Greek while Saddah is a Levantine or Syrian name. The poet in this poem is bluntly accusing the Greek and Levantine capitalists of stealing from the peasants and he thought that there would be no evolution in Egypt unless the country survived the evil of these two foreign groups and their like.

The women's struggle was taking momentum in the country that would escalate with the role women played during the 1919 uprising. Most of the conservative or even sceptical commentators in the Egyptian popular media were accusing foreign women for having a bad influence on Egyptian women.

The influence, according to the critiques, varied from missionary and foreign schools to the taking off the veil and even to mixed marriage between Egyptian men and foreign women. Some poems even criticised the foreign female tailors who made dresses that did not respect Egyptian traditions and were encouraging women to wear indecent apparels. Muhammed Abdelrasoul wrote a poem in *Al-Masamir* addressing a girl called Hend who started to ruin her future by a dress made by a foreign tailor that she would in the end ride a bike in the alley where she lived and bring shame to her family[11]:

---

10 Muhammed Abdelrasoul, Zagal: 'Ya Nil Ana fi hobak dayeb [Oh Nile!! I love you]', *AlMasamir* newspaper, 11 January 1919, p 1 (translation is done by myself).
11 Muhammed Abdelrasoul, 'Bent Elbalad Rakabet A'galah [The Egyptian girl is riding a bike]', *AlMasamir* newspaper, 23 February 1919, p 1.

The Egyptian girl is riding a bike!!
Oh Hend, Go to the Kotab (Quran school)…
The sheikh should be teaching now

…

Oh Daddy!! My mum said that I should go to a Khawagaya tailor…
Who can sew a dress that reveals much with sparkle and embroidery.
Oh Hend, your religion should come first and it will protect you…
Stop wearing embroidered clothes…don't follow fashion
Decency and saving are always better

…

The girl is in quite a mess and she's making effort to ruin her own life
With the flowers on her chest…she wonders from one place to another

…

And it took me by surprise a scene that was shameful and disgraceful
This local girl [bent elbalad] is riding a bike…
and the kids are running and cheering after her.

The nationalist movement and its emerging leaders in El-Wafd[12] realised the sensitivity of the issue of the foreigners and minorities and how it would jeopardise the nationalist cause in general. That proved how the memory of the Alexandria massacre of 1882 influenced their way of planning their movement and prioritised their discourse, especially that many of the El-Wafd leaders were members of the Urabi movement and knew how this matter was played off by the British.[13]

On 10 January 1919, almost seven weeks before the exile of El-Wafd members, Sa'ad Zaghlul and his partners issued a statement entitled 'Statement to the foreign residents', signed by Zaghlul who wrote his title as 'deputy of the parliament and chairman of the Egyptian Wafd'. Zaghlul wrote:

---

12 El-Wafd (the delegation) was formed in late 1918 and it was led by Sa'ad Zaghlul and other deputies of the people's assembly who wanted to represent Egypt in the Paris conference to demand the end of the British occupation. When the British authority refused to let El-Wafd participate in the conference, the members started to collect the signatures of the Egyptians on a petition that delegated El-Wafd members to represent them in Paris. The British Authorities confiscated the petition then caught Zaghlul and his colleagues and exiled them to Malta in March 1919. The Uprising spanned Egypt from Alexandria to Aswan calling for the return of El-Wafd members home and for the British to end the Occupation.

13 Sa'ad Zaghlul was involved in the Urabi movement and he was tried and acquitted as a member of the 'Revenge' clandestine society that was formed in 1883 to resist the British occupation.

...We are assuring you, that while we are representing the goals of the Egyptian people, we (Egyptians) deserve, as well, this freedom that will enable our home country of retrieving its ancient position to pay off our duty in serving humanity. We are aiming to lead our own country by forming a constitutional government to manage our affairs and fix what the foreign rule of our country had sabotaged, deliberately or not, and hence to reach the goals we have been preparing ourselves for. In order to do that, we have to keep the trust of the foreigners by facilitating to them ways to keep their activities in our country sustained; in business and industrial affairs as we take the best care of their capitulation agreements... In conclusion, we seek our full independence away from any foreign sovereignty without affecting the rights and financial privileges of the foreigners either in legislation, judiciary or in protecting their homes, personal freedom and all matters related to security. These are our hopes and goals. Any act that does not conform to this vision (towards foreigners) is considered nothing but an act against the nationalist cause...[14]

Three days later, Zaghlul addressed *El-Wafd* members in a non official meeting[15]:

... We should cordially offer the foreigners ways and guarantees to their stay in Egypt. We should facilitate their work and residency and they would freely compete in fields of education, agriculture and industry... these foreigners are our link to sources of science and modern discoveries. Independent Egypt must engage in the universal completion, and this is why we should welcome the newest accomplishments to our land... however, our engagement in this competition depends on the sustainability of the foreigners who keep coming to our country which will be a response to how generous we are to them...

Support for the uprising by foreigners was not a mere act of individuals; a supportive stance was repeatedly shown in the foreign press in Egypt. Several

14 Abdulrahman Fahmy, *mothakkerat Abdulrahman Fahmy: yawmyeat Misr Elsyasyiea* [Memoires of Abdulrahman Fahmy: Egypt's Political Chronicles] (Egyptian General Book Authority, Cairo: 1988) Part I, pp 82–83.
15 Abdulrahman Fahmy, *mothakkerat Abdulrahman Fahmy*, pp 95–96.

journalists and correspondents aligned with the nationalist movement and were persecuted by the British forces.

M. Vassie was a French journalist and editor in chief of the French newspaper *Journal Du Caire*. Due to his writings in support of the nationalist movement, the British administration deported him and stopped his newspaper from being published. M. Vassie was annoying enough to the British that General Allenby and Arthur Balfour were exchanging telegrams discussing whether he could be sent back to Cairo or not.[16] Eventually, it was agreed that Vassie could return to Cairo and reopen his newspaper on one condition which was 'conducting his paper in complete harmony with the British authorities.'[17]

The Italians were heavily taking the side of the nationalist movement as well. The first book ever written about the uprising was written by Emanuel Baldi in 1921. During the events, Italians were killed in the protests and names like the martyr Marangoni were mentioned in the alleys of Cairo. Maltezi was an Italian teacher who was deported by the British in 1919 over accusations of igniting the students to protest. Italian journalists took sides with the uprising in many cases. Max de Colatto was the editor in chief of the Italian newspaper *Roma*. He was deported to Italy in September 1919 by martial law following accusations of visiting Al-Azhar and coordinating activities with Azhar students and sheikhs.

Egyptian historians used to highlight the role of Europeans in supporting the nationalist movement in 1919. Mahmoud Soliman wrote that in addition to the Europeans who supported the uprising for being a legitimate and just act for independence, there were also pragmatic reasons for this support such as: that the Italians and the French were worried about their investments in Egypt; that the British did not compensate the Europeans properly on their losses during the war; that the British granted their citizens privileges in the public sector jobs while not treating Europeans equally. [18] For these reasons as well as real support and belief in justice, many Europeans stood hand in hand with the Egyptians in their call for justice and independence.

The political activities that were overtly against the Egyptian nationalist movement were always related to the main foreign communities; the Armenians and the Greeks. Before analysing the tensions that they have experienced

---

16 Balfour to Allenby, Telegram no. 49, 17 May 1919, FO 608/2/14, The National Archives in Kew, London (hereafter TNA), p 19.

17 Ibid.

18 Mahmoud Soliman, *The foreigners in Egypt*, p 144

with the Egyptian, it is important to mention a brief note on their presence in Egypt in modern times.

The Greeks: The ties between Egypt and Greece can be traced back to the time of Alexander the Great in the 4th century BC and the establishment of Alexandria which resulted in the migration and settlement of thousands of Greeks in Egypt. In modern times the Greeks started coming to Egypt in major numbers starting form 1821 when their ties with the Ottoman Empire were dissolving and Egypt was economically flourishing, under Muhammed Ali, at the same time.

The 1917 census showed that 56,731 Greeks lived in Egypt. However, this figure cannot be accurate as other records show that the Greeks were the most foreign community most inclined towards registering themselves under other communities to enjoy better Capitulations and judicial consular service[19]. Thousands of Greeks registered themselves as British, Italian or French.

The Greeks acted according to their large numbers and heavy presence. They empowered themselves in Egypt and started to establish their community associations as early as in 1843 in Alexandria. They established 32 community associations that spanned Egypt from Alexandria to Sinai. These associations established and managed churches, schools, clubs and charities. They were the most integrated with the Egyptian population unlike most of the other foreign communities.[20] However, the numbers of the Greeks in Egypt cannot be recorded according to the censuses only. Several Greek families registered their members under other communities which enjoyed better Capitulation agreements or more powerful consular courts. It is estimated that at least 8 % of the Greeks in Egypt registered themselves as British or Italian citizens.[21] One of the best known examples of this phenomenon is the Greek poet Constantine Kavafis whose family was registered as British citizens.

The Armenians: Several waves of Armenian immigrants resided in Egypt to make use of the economic incentives that Muhammad Ali (1805–1841) applied to the Egyptian economy and the environment of business. Hence, most of the Armenians chose freely to come to Egypt during the 19th century. However, in 1896 and onwards, most of the Armenians who came to Egypt were seeking refuge. It is estimated that 100–200 Armenians were arriving at

---

19 Ibid., pp 88–89.
20 Ibid.
21 Ibid.

Alexandria every day in 1896 on Egyptian, Austrian and Russian ships.[22] The Armenians kept coming to Egypt, from Armenia and the Levant, until their biggest wave that arrived to Egypt in 1915 following the Ottoman persecutions of that year. Most of the Armenians who came to Egypt during the First World War were poor families and most of them were vocational workers, artisans and farmers.

It is estimated that 12,458 Armenians lived in Egypt in 1917, representing 7.02% of the foreign community in Egypt.[23] However, this figure cannot be precise for three main reasons:

- Many of the Armenian families who resided in Egypt for a long time, no longer presented themselves as Armenians. Many of them proclaimed an Egyptian identity or registered themselves with one of the strong foreign communities to enjoy the privileges of the Capitulations.
- The Levantine or Syrian Armenians who started fleeing to Egypt since the mid of the 19th century to avoid the Ottoman persecution or sectarian tensions came to Egypt and registered themselves as Ottomans, Levantines or, likewise the previous category, registered themselves in a protected European community.
- The refugees who came to Egypt starting from 1896 and afterwards were afraid of the pro-Ottoman or the Pan-Islamists in Egypt. As being enemies or at least casted from the Ottoman Empire, they refrained from registering themselves as Armenians, or at least did not announce their identity publically.

What applied to Armenians in terms of real identity vis-à-vis the identity of fear applied also to many other foreign groups in Egypt. However, it was clearly more confusing when it comes to issues of registering or counting the Armenians in Egypt in the early 20th century.

As a result of their continuous suffering from the Ottoman authorities, the Armenians in Egypt were sceptical about the Egyptian nationalist movement and they thought that it was pro the Ottoman Empire's control over Egypt and it did not target sovereignty or independence. Several Armenian writers in Egypt promoted an analysis that the Egyptian nationalist movement was an

---

22 Muhammed Rif'at ElEmam, *Al Armen fi Misr 1896–1961* [The Armenians in Egypt] (Cairo Armenian General Charity Association, Cairo: 2003) p 117.

23 Muhammed Rif'at ElEmam, *Al Armen fi Misr 1896–1961*, p 247.

Islamic extremist movement. A writer called Yervent Odian wrote in 1908'...
it's a fundamentalist and extremist movement against the Christians and the
Armenians.'[24]

The so called anti-Armenian movement in Egypt that started in 1919 represented a case where foreigners of Armenian origin were facing a negative
perception in Egypt due you to their stance towards the Egyptian nationalist
claims for independence.

In an official letter written by General Allenby to Lord Curzon on 13 April
1919, the General said that he was not sure that Al-Azhar spiritual leaders
ignited this movement, but they were taking advantage of the whole situation
and offering the Armenians help on one condition; not to accept help from
the British authorities in Egypt.[25]

These clashes between the nationalists from one side and the Armenians
and Greeks on the other worried the nationalist leaders who could not deny
it and tried to show how the majority of the Egyptians refused to take part and
condemned any attacks on the foreigners. Abdulrahman Fahmy[26], the secretary-general of El-Wafd, barely referred to them in his chronicles. He tried to
mention these events without distorting the romantic narrative of the uprising:

> It is sorrowful that few Armenians gunshot the protesters in certain
> neighborhoods of Cairo which resulted in the peoples' attack on the
> Armenians in A'bdeen and ElKhaleeg street. However, the people themselves
> stopped their attacks that would harm the nationalist movement.[27]

The satirical newspapers and the popular opinion leaders realised suddenly
that their uprising was being perceived by the world as barbarian riots and

---

24 Ibid., p 460.

25 Allenby to Curzon, Letter no. 168, 13 April 1919, FO 608/213/5, File 662/1/8, Peace
Conference, (TNA), p 340

26 Abdulrahman Fahmy (1870–1946), An Egyptian politician. Graduated as a military officer
and then worked as a high ranked civil administrator. He was famous for objecting the
Khedive A'bbas Helmy 2nd try to buy an endowed farm and he was forced to retire in 1913
at the age of 43. He then joined the nationalist movement and became the secretary general
and treasurer of secret service in El-Wafd. Fahmy was tried and imprisoned by the British
occupation in 1923 for establishing and managing the clandestine nationalist activities of
El-Wafd. He was also known as the founder of several workers syndicates and as an elected
deputy in the Egyptian parliament.

27 Abdulrahman Fahmy, mothakkerat Abdulrahman Fahmy, p 153

looting mobs which were targeting the foreigners and the refugees who had come to find a safe home in Egypt. Even the most radical anti-Capitulations patriots were worried about the atrocities against foreigners; including the poets who used to write zagals to attack the wealthy Europeans in Egypt. Muhammed Abdulnabi wrote in *AlMasamir*, that was specialised in anti-foreigners zagal, this poem:

> Muslims, Copts or Greeks
> Jews or Armenians…
> All are long time brothers united under a cross and a crescent …It's an
>   unbreakable bond
> Ahmed, Moses and Jesus.. All were prophets of God…
> The nation is calm and in peace…all who did harm, and caused conflict
>   are the mobs and the raffish and mean men
> May all the foreigners be in peace.In Egypt and everywhere else[28]

The rational opinion leaders realised the gravity of the situation and they tried to intervene. The report of the Armenian Pope on the 1919 events mentioned an Egyptian Muslim affluent man called Ahmed bey Fathy who hosted most the Armenians of Fayoum town (almost 31 in 1917) in his own house.[29]

It should be noted that the students and Azhar Sheikhs who tried to calm down the masses used frequently the term 'guests' to refer to the foreigners though many of them had lived in Egypt long enough or were already carrying the same Ottoman citizenship as the Egyptian at this time. It could be related to the large numbers of refugees who poured into the country for five years, or perhaps the more experienced opinion leaders were trying to call a sense of manners and hospitality to tame down the anger of the young nationalists.

By the mid of May 1919, the economic loss of the Greek community in Egypt was estimated at £600,000 in addition to ten casualties and approximately as many injuries[30]. The Greek minister in Egypt asserted that this loss is approximate and he can not be sure especially regarding the material damage.

---

28 Muhammed Abdelnabi, 'Zagal: untitled', *AlMasamir* newspaper, 18 May 1919, p1
29 ElEmam, *Al Armen fi Misr 1896–1961*, p 468.
30 Allenby to Balfour, Decypher of telegram (unnumbered), 16/5/1919, FO 608/2/14, (TNA), p 8.

The Italians too were panicking and they asked for help from the British military as a precaution.[31]

On 22 May 1921, violence erupted again in Hammamil district in Alexandria between the Egyptians and the foreigners, specifically the Greeks. Tension levels were escalating due to an internal dispute in the *El-Wafd* party as well as the events in Turkey where Mustafa Kemal was engaging with the British and the Greek troops. Many Egyptians especially young students were confronting the Greeks in the streets of Cairo and Alexandria and raising posters to salute Kemal. When the properties of the Greeks were threatened on the night of 22 May, at least 76 lost their lives 50 of whom were Egyptians shot dead; in addition to hundreds of injuries and loss of properties.[32] The Colonial Secretary in the British cabinet, Winston Churchill, made a public statement that granting Egypt its independence would only result in chaos and the mass killing of the Europeans and minorities in the country.

The gravity of the situation can be asserted when one thinks about Zaghlul's decision to ask the Egyptian people to stop the protests. His best and perhaps only card to put pressure on the British was to push the people to take to the streets and his ability to maintain that for more than two years. However, the second Hammamil clashes in 1921 and the following statement by Churchill made him abandon his best card. It was clear that the entire nationalist movement was threatened and the efforts of more than three years were jeopardised. In an echo of the 1882 massacre; threatening the foreigners was a perfect justification to oppress the nationalist movement in Egypt.

On 10 July 1923, three gun shots were fired in the Savoy hotel in London taking the life of Ali Fahmy, a wealthy Egyptian young womaniser. The murderer was his wife Marguerite Albert Fahmy whom the deceased had married one year earlier in Cairo. Sir Edward Marshall Hall, the famous British attorney, convinced the court to acquit Madame Fahmy, despite her admission of committing the murder, due to the uncivilised way that her Egyptian husband was insulting her. The proceedings of the trial focused on how the men of the East were savage against their wives; and how Muslim men were always violent and inconsiderate towards them. Mrs. Fahmy was found not guilty after a one week trial.

The Egyptian media reached for what was published in the European press, especially in London and Paris, and informed Egyptian readers on how the

---

31 Ibid.
32 Minutes of proceedings and Report of the Military court of enquiry into the Alexandria riots, May 1921, http://catalog.hathitrust.org/Record/011590260 , last accessed 30 April 2015.

Europeans were justifying the murder by insulting Eastern culture and Eastern people in general. In response, the Egyptian press started to accuse the foreign women of being indecent and only seeking the fortunes of Egyptian men while refusing to conform to the conservative lifestyle of Egyptian spouses.

Several Egyptian mass media and opinion leaders started to highlight this incident to show the public that economic exploitation can take other forms rather than occupation and Capitulations. They were asserting to the public that the foreigners *Khawagat* were still taking advantage of Egypt and the Egyptians, despite the nominal independence, by inventing new methods of exploitation that included banks, companies and even marrying the wealthy Egyptians. They wrote that the nominal independence was not the end of the story or the suffering of the Egyptians by *el Khawagat*.

The *Abo el-Hole* (Sphinx) newspaper issued several op-ed and readers' letters to support these accusations against foreign women in Egypt in particular. *Abo el-Hole* newspaper published a satirical cartoon with a comment as a dialogue between an Egyptian husband and his European wife on its first page[33]:

Egyptian husband: why are you wearing a night-out dress? I'll be back home at 8 pm.

European wife: those who wear a coat never come back until dawn. I'll only believe you if you take me with you.

Abu Elhole: and this is how she is upsetting him. He deserves that.

A new *zagal* by 'Ezzat Sakr was written on this occasion to shame the greedy wife and to blame the husband who chose her against his family's will:

You charmed your husband then you took his life...
May God punish you and punish him too
Punished he would be for marrying you...
Against his family's will, he the ignorant...
Why oh you beautiful and smart...
You could have avoided this story
Or was that only a fake mask...

---

33 *Abo el-Hole*, Issue 156, 30 October 1923, p1.

at some point you had to reveal[34]

This murder of the rich Egyptian Fahmy on the hands of his own foreign wife increased a sense of resentment that was already escalating in Egypt against marrying foreign women and against the presence of foreign women in the country in general. Foreign women were usually taking the blame for 'polluting' the minds of Egyptian women by showing them a lifestyle and telling them liberal ideas that did not conform to their culture and religion.

A famous vaudeville that was widely popular *'dah ba'af meen?'* or 'who is that jerk?' was used to condemn the young men's marriage to foreign women:[35]

Pardon Effendi [Mr.] please tell me…
What's wrong with the Egyptian (woman)?
Are your choices very limited…
So that you are marrying a foreigner.
Understand…
Be reasonable…
You fool…
Why should we let the others separate us from one another..
Let's keep what's ours to ourselves .
While the Egyptian woman would be your source of pride…
A foreign woman is only after your money.
Oh man !!

However, the resentment against the exploitation of the *Khawagat* to Egypt's fortune did not stop as the socio-economic order in Egypt did not change. Bayram ElTunsi wrote in 1923 his famous zagal 'Kheirema receives and collects'[36]:

We Thank Allah the greatest for the nothing we have…

---

34 E'zzat Sakr, Zagal: 'Diwan Amir Elzagal E'zzat Sakr' [Diwan of the prince of zagal E'zzat Sakr] (Misr Publish House, Cairo: 1933) p 192.
35 Written by Badi'e Khairy and composed by Sayed Darwish *'dah ba'af meen?'* or who is that fool? A poem/song in the play *Kololoh* [tell him], http://www.mawaly.com/music/Hayat+Sabry/track/77605 , last accessed 31 January 2015
36 Bayram ElTunsi, Zagal: 'Kheirema yeqbadh we yehassal [Kheirema Receives and Collects]', in *Diwan of Bayram ELtunsi* , Ibid., p 41. (translation is done by myself).

Luxury and independence and Allah gave us all that.
We are done with the (British) authority and exiles to Malta…
And moved to days where we cannot make a penny.
The Cotton still belongs to Mizrahi [Jewish] and Kurdahi [Levantine]…
And the Egyptian has nothing, as an orphan in his own country.
He (Egyptian) planted and harvested these cottons…
But when he sells them, he makes zero profit.
Which means that the foreigners loot us in our own homeland…
They deceive us and want to ruin our lives…
And they live heavenly luxurious.

The foreigners and their communities in Egypt stayed for long enough to have human interaction with the Egyptians, which means that there were moments of tension and many other of civil peace. Their presence had its advantages and disadvantages to the Egyptian people. It is not the record of history that relations were always peaceful, for the Egyptians clashed with foreigners in times and cooperated with them in many others. Over-romanticising this period or demonising it is neither correct nor just to either of the two sides.

However, these clashes and tensions should not be regarded as xenophobic as several British records suggest; especially with the incidents during 1919–1922. These incidents reflected how the Egyptians resented that the foreigners were not only exploiting the country economically; moreover, they denied the Egyptians their right of independence and the establishment of a sovereign nation-state of their own. These clashes and tensions were often led by non-Egyptians who shared with the natives their rejection of economic and political foreign dominance. The leaders of the workers' movement who ignited strikes and sit-ins against European capitalists were often non-Egyptian workers. Many of the poets, journalists and actors who criticised the foreigners in Egypt were not Egyptians i.e. the Syrian actor Naguib ElRihani and the Tunisian poet AlTunsi. The founders of the communist party and other communist groups in Egypt, who fiercely attacked the foreign, and native, capitalists were French, Greek or Italian leaders. Many of the journalists who supported the Egyptian uprising in 1919 were French and Italian journalists who were either banned or deported following accusations of supporting 'turmoil' and encouraging the Egyptian 'extremists'.

It is important to notice that, in this era, the Egyptian people suffered an illiteracy rate of almost 97%. However, zagal and satirical poems were well rhymed and in Egyptian colloquial which made it easy for the Egyptian commons to memorise and repeat the zagals of AlTunis, Sakr and AlQadhy among others. Those poets admitted themselves that they wrote their poems while they listed to the concerns and dreams of the peoples on the cafés of Cairo, Alexandria and other major cities and towns in Egypt. Zagal was not to educate the people; it was a reflection of what they suffered or had gone through. When composers started to process zagal into songs (vaudevilles or colloquial light songs); it was flowing easily from one street to another and from one café to another. During times of crisis, i.e. the 1919 uprising, a unique supply chain would take the words from the people to the poets who would, in turn, give zagal poems to composers. Within hours, what started as a sarcastic remark or a sorrowful comment from a common man walking in the street was sent back to him as a song he could either sing on a café or shout in a protest.

These representations of popular resentment and rejection against injustice which the people suffered in Egyptian society were an expression of refusing the foreign dominance either by the occupier or the European and foreign interest groups that stood in the face of the nation's legitimate dreams of independence and sovereignty. Violence would never be justified, but it can be understood as a mutual act in a certain context or specific set of conditions that would inevitably lead to civil tension.

2

The antecedents and implications of the so-called Anglo-Sanussi War 1915–1917

Jason Pack

This chapter examines the background to – and fallout from – the First World War in Cyrenaica, the former Ottoman province comprising modern day Eastern Libya.[1] Within the vast western language historiography of the First World War, this micro-conflict constitutes one of the War's least studied theatres. In Arabic, there does not seem to exist a single book-length treatment of the subject. From the British vantage point, this theatre was either understood as the war in the Western Frontier Desert or as 'the Anglo-Sanussi War'. Over the last century the details of the conflict have only been treated in one scholarly book:

---

1 Although indigenous Cyrenaican resistance to the ongoing Italian colonisation and pacification efforts raged throughout the years 1914–1918 and these struggles were indirectly affected by developments in the global war (e.g. the withdrawal of Italian troops to fight in Europe or the dispatch of more German armaments and Ottoman military trainers to the Cyrenaican and Tripolitanian theatres), this chapter does not treat this ongoing indigenous resistance to Italian colonisation of Libya as part of the First World War. It was a simultaneous yet separate conflict. This is because these anti-colonial struggles antedated the global conflict and were not catalysed by it. Nor were they understood as a separate front in the First World War by any of the major participants. The 'Anglo-Sanussi' confrontation in Egypt's Western Desert from 1915–17, however, is clearly different: it was catalysed by the First World War, it was not a direct continuation of a pre-war conflict, and it was understood by both the Central and the Entente Powers as representing the opening up of a novel front in the global conflict.

Russell McGuirk's *The Sanusi's Little War: The Amazing Story of a Forgotten Conflict in the Western Desert, 1915–1917.*[2] The paucity of scholarly research notwithstanding, the First World War undoubtedly reshaped Egypt's and Libya's borders, rooting a certain form of 'indirect rule' imperialism into the very fabric of this sub-region. Moreover, the events from 1915–1917 can be seen as the focal point of Britain's engagement in Cyrenaica for the next five decades. For this reason alone this mostly forgotten conflict deserves our attention.

It is also worthy of study due to its many unusual features: 1) the two adversaries actively sought to avoid hostilities – in fact, they carried out a 'cordial' correspondence during the hostilities; 2) once the war haphazardly began, unlike normal Clausewitzian adversaries, they did not seek to inflict maximal damage or precipitate a decisive battle; and 3) militarily it was a deeply anachronistic conflict – filled with cavalry charges and supply chains run by camels. Fascinatingly, in this war of manoeuvre in the 19th century style, the use of Model T Fords by the British helped to contain the Sanussi offensive and interdict their supply routes.[3] In fact, the outcome of the conflict was as paradoxical as the means used to wage it: the erstwhile adversaries were quickly reconciled and embarked on a fifty-year long alliance to rule Cyrenaica together in an informal partnership.

This chapter seeks to problematise the prevailing scholarly narrative which tends to see the events in the Western Desert as the Sanussiyya temporarily expanding their decades long 'jihad' against the French and Italians to include the infidel British in Egypt, as well as seeing British officials as motivated by negative attitudes of the Sanussi as religious 'fanatics'.[4] Potentially, the very

2 Russell McGuirk, *The Sanusi's Little War: The Amazing Story of a Forgotten Conflict in the Western Desert, 1915–1917* (Arabian Publishing, London: 2007).
3 Model T Fords were the most durable and easily repairable car available to British forces. They were essential to the Light Car Patrols which were launched in the summer of 1916 and successfully contained Sanussi forces in Egypt's central oases until the end of the war in February 1917. Although the patrols rarely engaged in combat with the Sanussi they were highly effective at charting the desert, finding all the caravan routes, wells, etc. which was essential to interdicting the Sanussi supply chain and preventing any break out towards the Nile. This amazing story is comprehensively treated in Russell McGuirk, *Light Car Patrols 1916–19: War and Exploration in Egypt and Libya* (Silphium Press London: 2013) and Andrew Goudie, *Wheels Across The Desert: Exploration Of The Libyan Desert By Motorcar 1916–1942* (Silphium Press London: 2008).
4 For the view that the British saw the Sanussi as fanatics see John Slight, 'British Understandings of the Sanussiyya Sufi Order's Jihad against Egypt, 1915–17', in *The Round*

terminology of an 'Anglo-Sanussi War' should be abandoned in favour of the rhetoric used by the participants themselves. They tended to see the conflict as yet another front in the Anglo-Ottoman war – one in which the sanctity and administrative structures of the Sanussiyya[5] were temporarily hijacked by Ottoman agents.[6] A final reason for interest in this episode is what it reveals about one of the themes of this volume: identity formation and British Imperial ambitions in the Middle East.

Detailed study of this war shows that Imperial ambitions were not purely about securing geostrategic interests but also involved acting upon the emotional/ideological connections to favoured allies.[7] The British connections to preferred collaborators decisively favoured Cyrenaican identity over emerging conceptions of Libyanness, and attachments to tribal and Sanussi affiliations over more 20th century forms of national identity.[8]

Prior to the entry of British tanks into Libyan territory in the Second World

---

Table, 103.2 (2014) pp 233–242; For the view that the pre-existing jihad was extended to include the British in Egypt see Claudia Gazzini, 'Jihad In Exile: Ahmad Al-Sharif Al-Sanusi 1918–1933' (Princeton, MA thesis, 2004) and Lisa Anderson, 'The Tripoli Republic, 1918–1922', in *Social & Economic Development of Libya* (ed), G. Joffé and K. MacLachlan (Wisbech, Cambridgeshire: 1982) pp 44–62.

5 From the foundation of first Sanussi *zawiyya* (lodge) in North Africa at Bayda in 1843, the Order quickly became established in the mid- to late-19th century as the paramount social and political force in non-coastal Cyrenaica. It was an inter-tribal arbiter, a builder of roads and mosques, and the creator of an educational and tax-collecting bureaucracy that existed outside of the Ottoman state – to which it was opposed ideologically, but nonetheless forged *de facto* accommodations with both the Porte and the Khedive that allowed the Order to function and expand relatively unmolested. The Sanussiyya constructed a network of lodges and a bureaucracy to maintain them so as to propagate its largely exoteric and orthodox form of Islam. Its use of the organisational trappings of a Sufi Movement to spread a revivalist and literalist form of Islam is termed by certain scholars (and by this thesis) 'neo-Sufism' and is seen as a uniquely 19th-century response to the decline of the Ottoman Empire and the incursions of the European powers into the Islamic heartland.

6 Chanler report and assorted correspondence from 1915, FO 371/2354, The National Archives, Kew, London, (hereafter TNA).

7 A point long ago understood by the famous Imperial historians of Oxford and Cambridge Ronald Robinson and John Gallagher but largely forgotten since.

8 Examples of the difficulty of forging a coherent trans-regional Libyan identity via a nationalist narrative during this period are discussed in depth in Anna Baldinetti, *The Origins of the Libyan Nation: Colonial Legacy, Exile and the Emergence of a New Nation-State* (Routledge, Abingdon, UK: 2010).

War it is conventionally assumed that the British did not have pressing interests in internal Cyrenaican politics.[9] My research[10] demonstrates that contrary to the traditional presentation, the British had been internal players in Cyrenaican politics since the 1880s and that Britain's First World War interlude in Libya was simply the first point at which Britain used arms rather than diplomacy to secure her longstanding imperial and ideological interests in Cyrenaica.

In the 1880s and 1890s, both British and Sanussi power were growing in non-coastal North-eastern Africa. Both deployed their expanding capabilities to forge alliances with local potentates and regional powers.[11]

In the intense, short-term political game of the 1880s and 1890s, the British and Sanussiyya faced the same enemies: the French[12] and the Sudanese Mehdists.[13] It is for this reason that British intelligence officers in Khartoum and Cairo invested heavily in cultivating intelligence about the Sanussiyya Sufi Order[14] and in feeding it into their higher ups intense deliberations (reaching

---

9 As such, study of Britain's pre-First World War interests in Cyrecaica does not constitute a focus for those scholars who have conducted deep and perceptive studies of Libya's geopolitical importance to Britain during and after WWII, without investigating if British strategic interests at that time were rooted in prior entanglements. Wm. R. Louis, 'Libya: The Creation of a Client State', in Wm. R. Louis and P. Gifford (eds), *Decolonization and African Independence: The Transfers of Power 1960–80* (Yale University Press, London: 1988) pp 503–528; Scott L. Bills, *The Libyan Arena: The United States, Britain and the Council of Foreign Ministers, 1945–1948* (Kent State Univ Press, Kent, Ohio: 1995); Saul Kelly, *War & Politics in the Desert: Britain and Libya during the Second World War* (Silphium Press , London: 2010); Saul Kelly, *Cold War in the Desert: Britain, the United States, and the Italian Colonies, 1945–52* (Palgrave Macmillan, London: 2000).

10 Jason Pack, *Britain's Informal Empire in Libya? The Anglo-Sanussi Relationship, 1889–1969* (Hurst/OUP, London: forthcoming 2017).

11 Looked at from a game theoretical perspective, these two expanding "empires" might eventually collide as adversaries. Alternatively, they could forge a tacit alliance to respect each other's spheres of influence or even openly collaborate in certain instances. In reality, the ultimate decision to forge an alliance had to do with an admixture of ideology and pragmatic calculation.

12 The Sanussiyya had been fighting the French since their incursions against the Sanussi-aligned Sultanate of Wadai and Emirate of Bornu in modern Chad started in the 1880s and came to threaten key Sanusi strongholds in the 1890s.

13 Fergus Nicholl, *Gordon, Gladstone, and the Sudan Wars* (Pen and Sword , Yorkshire: 2013). Evelyn Baring (later Lord Cromer) frequently mentioned in dispatches that he felt the Mehdiyya could be a buffer against French incursions from the South.

14 See, for example, Reginald Wingate's mapping of the geographical spread of the

all the way up to the office of the Prime Minister Lord Salisbury) about how best to conduct diplomacy with the Order.

As time passed and both sides acquired knowledge and comfortability with each other, the British and the Sanussiyya came to consider each other trustworthy, reliable, and ascending powers; they consequently began a tacit, hands-off collaboration that evolved into more active cooperation as it was driven forward by various 'activist Arabists'[15] from the British side and Anglophilic Sanussi leaders such as Idriss al-Sanussi, who, even when his uncle Ahmad al-Sharif was head of the Order, visited Cairo and forged alliances with key British Egyptian officials like General John Maxwell and Henry McMahon.[16] In many ways, these officials were simply inheriting the legacy of pre-British Khedival Egypt.

Since the creation of the modern Egyptian state under Muhammad Ali after 1805, Egypt's Bedouin subjects were subject to different laws as well as in taxation and corvée exemption as a way for the Egyptian state to placate those outlying constituencies that it could only rule indirectly with their consent.[17] Therefore, when the British conquered Egypt in 1882 they inherited the distinction between pure Arabs (i.e. bedu) and the settled peoples. This 'positive' prejudice towards the Bedouin and the Sanussi could be seen as a Khedival Egyptian inheritance that the British built upon and developed even further.

As the British were trying to expand Egyptian sovereignty into this borderland, the Bedouin held de facto authority and the ability to undermine any attempts to encroach into their fiefdom with its separate tribal law and privileges. Hence, to deal with issues like smuggling, tribal feuds, etc., British

---

Sanussiyya in 1889 as preserved in Wingate Papers 155/5/57 in the Sudan Archive housed at Durham University, UK.

15 'Activist Arabist' is used in this chapter to refer to Imperial functionaries who with increasing familiarity of Islam and the Arabic language became emotionally attached to the people they governed (particularly Bedouin Arabs) and sought to use their positions of authority to forward Arab interests and 'traditional' modes of authority (as they understood them). The term overlaps with a particular subcategory of Robinson and Gallagher's 'man on the spot' – one in which the Imperial functionary was not motivated by personal gain or wishing to expand Britain's sphere of influence but rather by an ideological attraction, emotional affiliation and sometimes missionary zeal.

16 E.A.V. De Candole, The Life and Times of King Idris of Libya (Special Issue, 1990).

17 Similarly to the privileges granted to the Bedouin, with the death of the founder of the Sanussi Order in 1859, the Khedive sent money for a golden dome over his tomb in Jaghbub and cultivated a special relationship with the Order granting them various tax exemptions.

policy was not to confront the Bedouin head on or impose new and unpopular rules on them but to empower local actors and work through local power structures to cope with these issues. In short, to continue the long Egyptian tradition of indirect rule through the Bedouin and Sanussi social structures that had been in place for decades.

Instrumental in Britain's decision to deepen the Egyptian states traditional alliance with the Beduoin and the Sanussi were a coterie of philo-Sanussi British officials based in places like Cairo, Khartoum, Benghazi, and Marsa Matruh. Officials based out of the latter named place, were likely to be Coast Guard officials dealing with the thorny governance issues of the amorphous border between Egypt and Ottoman Cyrenaica. They had to cope with tribal raids, smuggling, the lack of a functioning justice system, and the inability of any state structure to exercise sovereignty over this borderland. Into this undemarcated zone many actors were competing to build institutional and commercial frameworks to exercise sovereign functions over the local population of nomadic herdsmen and oasis date farmers.

From 1841–1900, the Sanusiyya Sufi Order became the preeminent power broker throughout the whole nebulous region known as the 'Western desert', filling in the de facto authority vacuum that had arisen at the margins of Ottoman and Egyptian sovereignty. After 1900, new players erupted onto the scene and intensified the competition for control over this semi-governed borderland.

On the one hand, the Egyptian Khedive Abbas Hilmi II sought throughout the period to bolster his own personal authority in the Egyptian West against the wishes of the British government in Cairo by implementing an array of development projects and buying prime farm land, as well as by cultivating tight political bonds with key local notables in the oasis of Siwa.[18]

On the other hand, the Italian Government set its sights on an eventual colonial occupation of the Ottoman Libyan provinces and began to assert a stronger presence in the region from both the Ottoman and the Egyptian sides through commercial and cultural projects. This together with Ottoman attempts to collect taxes from recalcitrant Cyrenaican tribes and establish border posts in turn drew the British deeper into the fray. In short, the Ottomans, the Italians, the Khedive, and the British (via the institutions of the Egyptian state), all contested the laws, norms, and borders in the Western desert.

---

18 Matthew Ellis, 'Between Empire and Nation: The Emergence of Egypt's Libyan Borderland 1841–1911' (PhD thesis, Princeton: 2012) pp 25–32.

Each attempted to build sovereign capabilities and ties to local actors in this area that was still a no man's land disputed between Egypt and Cyrenaica. The British trump card to extend the sovereignty of the Egyptian state to this patch of territory was an alliance with the de facto quasi-state power holders: the Sanussi.

As Bedouin unrest and tribal movement challenged this process from 1902–1911, the 'Egyptian Coast Guard steadily came into its own throughout this period, transforming itself from a small scale quasi-state institution into the paramount arm of the Egyptian state authority in the West.'[19] The Coast Guard outperformed its Ottoman competitors because it was the arm of the Egyptian bureaucracy which maintained the Anglo-Sanussi link.

Going back into the 1880s, British officials connected the dots between their problems of establishing governmentality in Egypt's western border with issues they faced on its southern border. They put forth many justifications for an Anglo-Sanussi connection, one of which was the idea of the Sanussiyya as natural leaders of an authentic and noble (i.e. Sharifian) Islamic movement against the base and plebeian Sudanese Mehdiyya of Muhammad Ahmed. Reginald Wingate, the chief British Intelligence agent stationed in the Sudan, combined the ideological with the strategic in his political reporting as he believed an alliance with the Sanussi was key to keeping Egypt and the Sudan safe and promoting British influence throughout North-eastern Africa. The most striking illustration of the emotional logic of an alliance comes from an 8 May 1889 letter from the consul in Benghazi, Captain Cameron, written to Evelyn Baring in Cairo in which Cameron defended the 'activist Arabist' position against his non-Arabist colleagues who had read the French alarmist anti-Sanussi scholar Henri Duvreyeir[20] and as such opposed the initiation of the Anglo-Sanussi relationship on the grounds that the Sanussi were a menace to European civilisation likely to wage a pan-Islamic jihad across North Africa. Cameron wrote:

> Senoussi's [sic] spiritual supremacy is complete in this province [i.e.
> Cyreniaca] … Turkish misrule and high taxation has made all Arab
> [sic] follow him, but there is no trace of a Jehad… [Hence…] It may be

---

19 Ibid., p 298.
20 The definitive work about the origins of the alarmist school of viewing the Sanussi is Jean-Louis Triaud, *La Légende noire de la Sanûsiyya. Une confrérie musulmane sous le regard français 1840–1930* (Fondation Maison des sciences de l'homme, Paris: 1995).

advisable to regard [Mahdi al-] Senoussi not from Mount Atlas, but from Cairo, i.e. from a purely English view.... Like all other Shereefs, he has scorned the idea of a plebeian Soudanese Mehdiism.[21] For a time he was threatened. We fought his battle on the Nile. Where we could not help him, he appears to have beaten back the Dervishes.[22]

Cameron's linking together of strategic and social tropes foreshadows British administrators during both world wars who advocated not only for the strategic advantages of ruling Cyrenaica through the Sanussiyya, but also that the Bedouin were the 'aristocrats of the desert' and the head of the Sanussi Order was 'the natural leader' of the Bedouin.[23] Cameron also subtly implies a unique kinship between the Sanussiyya and upper-caste Britons. By referencing the Sanussi's 'noble' status as opposed to the Mehdi's base status, he sought to evoke trust in the Sanussi as a personage and the advantages to Britain of having his doctrine spread and dominions expanded. This perspective reinforces the descriptions of the sociological tropes of late 19th and early 20th century Arabism put forth by Priya Satia and Katherine Tidrick.[24] It also reveals the extent to which David Cannadine's idea of 'Ornamentalism' – the practice of 'seeing' British style social hierarchies in other societies and hence choosing policies which reinforce them – played out in the Activist Arabists' views of the Sanussiyya and their relationship with Bedouin society.[25]

From its true genesis in 1889 the Anglo-Sanussi relationship grew into a

---

21 To avoid any possible confusion this chapter adopts the antiquated British spelling 'Mehdi', 'Mehdiyya', or 'Mehdist' for the Sudanese Mahdi, Muhammad Ahmed ibn Abdalla al-Mahdi, while retaining the proper IJMES spelling of 'Mahdi' for Mahdi al-Sanussi. This decision can also been seen as reflecting the differences between Egyptian and Sudanese Arabic with its preference for Kasra-ization (the conversation of short 'A' vowels into 'I' or 'E' vowels) with the absence of Kasra-isation in Cyrenaican Arabic which is closer to Fushaa or Classical Arabic.

22 Sheikh Senoussi, EGYPT & TRIPOLI: Information, FO 881/5845, (TNA).

23 The evolution of British attitudes toward the Sanussi and how they influenced policy making toward Cyrenaica will be treated in Jason Pack, *Britain's Informal Empire in Libya? The Anglo-Sanussi Relationship, 1889–1969* (Hurst/OUP, London: forthcoming 2017). This chapter (p)rehearses the main arguments which will be developed and illustrated there.

24 K. Tidrick, *Heart Beguiling Araby* (Tauris, Cambridge: 1981); P. Satia, *Spies in Arabia: The Great War and the Cultural Foundations of Britain's Covert Empire in the Middle East* (Oxford University Press, Oxford: 2008).

25 David Cannadine, *Ornamentalism : How the British Saw their Empire* (Oxford University Press, London: 2001).

collaboration over borders, smuggling, policing, custom duties, and local administration.[26] British officials in the Egyptian Coast Guard came to interact with the Sanussiyya as counterparts in a shared governance enterprise, as both were trying to extend their control onto previously ungoverned regions and tribes in the triangle between Marsah Matruh, Siwa, and Tubruq – and beating the Ottomans to the punch throughout this region.

To recap, from 1887 to 1911 the Sanussiyya and the British were part of the same alliance bloc in North-eastern Africa as both were staunch opponents of French and Mehdiist expansion. They both also sought to aggrandise their domains at Ottoman expense. As sketched above, the Anglo-Sanussi relationship became entrenched for reasons of a) geopolitics, b) ideology, and c) a pragmatic approach to expand Egypt's sovereign capabilities over the Western borderland via indirect rule through the Sanussi.

After the Italian invasion of Libya in 1911 things became more complicated. The Anglo-Sanussi relationship faced grave challenges at the level of high politics as diplomats in London increasingly faced pressure to prioritise the Anglo-Italian relationship which now ran at cross purposes to the Anglo-Sanussi relationship. In 1902, Britain gave Italy various private assurances that they would not oppose the Italian conquest of the remaining parts of Ottoman North Africa 'if territorial changes were required by extraordinary circumstances' or if Italian interests were being unfairly prejudiced. This arrangement was attractive to the British prior to the *Entente Cordial* because placing Italy physically in between Algeria and Egypt was thought to buffer the potentially destabilising Franco-British rivalry in North Africa.[27] Nonetheless, the

---

26 For the importance of the Egyptian Coast Guard as a point of interaction with the Sanussi in order to combat smuggling see McGuirk, *The Sanusi's Little War.*

27 *Affairs of Tripoli, Anglo-Italian Relations, 1903,* FO 101/94, (TNA). When the British Ambassador to France was discussing the possibility of an Anglo-Italian secret treaty concerning Ottoman North Africa with Count Giuseppe Tornielli the Italian Ambassador to France on 23 January 1902, the Count told his British colleague, facetiously, that if Libya were offered him on a silver platter he would keep the plate and return the province. Tornielli noted that the key beneficiary of shooing the Italians into Libya would be the British: "The establishment of Italian domination in Tripoli [Modern day Libya] would put an end to that possibility of transporting a *corps d'armee* from Algeria by land to Egypt, which he imagined, must have always presented itself as a disagreeable contingency to HMG. Tripoli in the occupation of Italy would be a buffer between the French North African Dominions and the Valley of the Nile, into which latter it would never be likely that the French would enter with the connivance of Italy."

British did not formally or publicly support Italian claims to Ottoman Tripoli or delimit a border,[28] but they wanted to perform a balancing act so as to maintain working political alliances with the Italians, Ottomans, and Sanussis all simultaneously.

Given these complex pre-existing alliance systems, when hostilities broke out between the Sanussiyya and Italian troops attempting to pacify all of Libya after 1911, the Italians demanded not only neutrality from London, but British assistance in preventing the flow of supplies to the Sanussiyya from Egypt. Pro-Italian Whitehall-based officials[29] instructed British functionaries in the Western Desert of Egypt to abandon their long term alliance with the Sanussiyya and close the border to the movement of supplies and armaments to the Sanussiyya which were being used in the anti-Italian resistance. Nonetheless, local pro-Sanussi officials deliberately allowed supplies and volunteers to reach the Sanussi against the wishes of higher-ups in London. For example, they claimed that monetary donations coming from Egypt were charity and not contraband even though it was well known they were being used by the Sanussi to buy weapons and supplies to fight the Italians.[30] In short, in many documented cases, British functionaries in the desert chose their emotional and pragmatic attachment to their Bedouin 'friends' over their professional obligations to London.[31] This is understandable for both emotional and practical reasons. Bolstering the global Anglo-Italian alliance did not help a given Coast Guard official to prevent tribal hostilities in his district, but a good relationship with Sanussi potentates did.

Similarly, officials in Cairo had many reasons to support the Ottomans over the Italians and moulded Egyptian policy in that direction: the British happily took over the Ottoman military border post at Sollum in 1911 to prevent it from falling into Italian hands. When an Italian syndicate tried to buy the Khedive's Maryut railway in 1912 which would have allowed Italy to project

---

28 Ellis, 'Between Empire and Nation', pp 331–354.

29 For a long time since the Risorgimento, Italy was Britain's only consistent ally on the European continent. In fact, just as Britain promoted the unification of Italy on the international scene, some scholars have spoken of an aristocratic English love affair with the political nation of Italy from 1861 onwards which mirrored the English attraction to Greece which began forty years earlier with Greek independence from the Ottomans. A. J. P. Taylor, *The Struggle for Mastery in Europe 1848–1918*, (Oxford University Press, Oxford: 1954).

30 Situation in Cyrenaica: Italy and The Senussi. Engagements between Italians and Arabs at Sollum, FO 141/653/1, (TNA).

31 Ibid.

commercial and military power into Cyrenaica via Egypt's Western desert, Lord Kitchener stopped the scheme as he feared it would lead to the Sanussi's defeat via Italy and the loss of Egyptian (i.e. British) sovereignty over the key borderland area. These actions show that the Anglo-Ottoman and Anglo-Sanussi alliances were stronger than the Anglo-Italian one on the ground in Egypt, even though at the high politics level the Italians were definitely seen as more important allies for His Majesty's Government.

British willful prevarication in dealing with their Italian allies requests allowed the positive personal relationships with the Sanussiyya to endure during the tough years of 1911–14. It was during this time that presents were exchanged between Sanussi princelings and British Coast Guard officials and joint efforts were also made to apprehend tribal raiding parties.[32]

When the First World War began, the Sanussis were not formally aligned to their old overlords, the Ottomans, who were the only power that could seriously aid the anti-Italian resistance.[33] Prior to Italy's entry into the war in mid-1915, the Ottomans attempted to capitalise on this leverage by making military supplies to the Sanussi contigent upon the Sanussi attacking Egypt. Ottoman fatwas also proclaimed in late 1914 that resistance against the Italians could not be considered part of the Ottoman Sultan's global jihad, as the Italians were neutral in the global conflict. These actions reveal the consistent

---

32 McGuirk, The Sanusi's Little War; Senussi-Italian Relations 1913, WO 106/1532, (TNA). Not only were the British ingratiating themselves with gifts, but they were intercepting Sanussi letters to see if the strategy worked. One letter sent by Ahmad al-Sharif stated, 'When my brother Hilal was in Siwa, the Governor there, Mr. [Leopold] Royle, gave him 600 GBP as a grant of hospitality. May God Bless him…'

33 Relations between the Ottomans and the Sanussiyya had always been tempestuous, yet Ottoman training and arms were essential for any Sanussi jihad to be successful. Although the Sanussi inherently rejected the Ottomans' claim to sovereignty over non-coastal Cyrenaica and disagreed with the centralising and secularising tendencies of the Ottoman tanzimat, starting in October 1911 when Enver Pasha was dispatched to Libya to fight the Italians, the Ottomans and the Sanussiyya reached a modus vivendi to collaborate in the common anti-Italian jihad. Yet, the early enthusiastic partnership quickly faded. Ahmad al-Sharif felt that the Ottomans failed to live up the mantle of Islamic leadership when they signed the Ouchy peace treaty with Italy in the autumn of 1912. Despite this disappointment, however, he continued to maintain warm relations with Ottoman volunteers and envoys who arrived in Cyrenaica to provide high level support for the Sanussi war effort. Rachel Simon, Libya between Ottomanism and Nationalism: The Ottoman Involvement in Libya during the War with Italy (1911–1919) (K. Schwarz , Berlin: 1987); Nicola Ziadeh, Sanūsīyah; a Study of a Revivalist Movement in Islam (Brill, Leiden: 1958).

logic undergirding Turkish actions during the First World War in the Libyan theatre. The Ottomans' sole aim was to redirect the Sanussi fighting machine in Cyrenaica away from its traditional Italian opponents and onto the Ottomans' British adversaries.[34]

Conversely, prior to the Italians formally entering the First World War, the British wished to remain strictly neutral in Libya so as to avoid extending the Anglo-Ottoman conflict to a new front. This strategy allowed them to remain allied to the Sanussi covertly while courting the Italians overtly. When the Italians formally entered the War on the Allied side on 26 April 1915, many in London anticipated that a conflict with the Sanussi was inevitable, even if HMG would exert maximal efforts to avoid it.

Nonetheless, British officials in Cairo continued to write dispatches praising the Sanussiyya and promising that Ahmad al-Sharif, the Sanussi leader, would not make war on Egypt. Just as Henry McMahon saw in the Hashemites a natural ally against the Ottomans, he viewed the Sanusiyya similarly and implicitly blamed the Italians for the Sanussiyya's siding with the Ottomans.

In short, he held the Order in quite a different perspective than his Italian allies did. Unsurprisingly, the British were sending letters containing warm 'salamaat' to Ahmad al-Sharif in late 1914. And, in January 1915 they were giving him presents through Captain Leopold Royle. From the British perspective, such actions sought to prevent or forestall a Sanussi attack on Egypt at a time when all energies were tied up in Gallipoli. Yet, British efforts led to Italian accusations of encouraging Sanussi rebellion against Italy.[35] After the Italians joined the Allies via the Treaty of London, Henry McMahon wrote to Rennell Rodd in Rome:

> The Italian Ambassador maintains that his Government regard Senoussi
> as a rebel while the British authorities treat him as an independent ruler.
> I understand that Senoussi has never made his submission to Italy and
> that our dealings with him are chiefly prompted by a wish to secure
> the goodwill of an important spiritual personage who is in a position to

---

34 W. Roderick Dorsey Consul at Tripoli to American Embassy Rome, 10 November 1914, 'Records of the Department of State Relating to Internal affairs of Italy, 1910–29', RG 59, 865c, M569.R7, College Park, Maryland, US National Archives II.
35 Situation in Cyrenaica: Italy and The Senussi. Engagements between Italians and Arabs at Sollum, FO 141/653/1, (TNA).

restrain the fanatical zeal of his followers and prevent them from joining in a Jehad [sic].[36]

Lord Kitchener, now Secretary of War, also had pro-Sanussi sensibilities left over from his days in the Sudan and in Egypt.[37] To Kitchener, Ahmad al-Sharif was seen as a venerated leader of British Muslims as so many of his followers were in Egypt and the Sudan and he lived at the Order's base in Jaghbub, a location that Kitchener claimed as Egyptian territory. Kitchener wrote to Grey, 'We have already restricted Ahmed al-Sharif's supply of arms and food, meeting Italian demands and risking our position with him.'[38]

In short, Cairo understood that limiting supplies to the Sanussiyya was likely to cause war as starving the Bedouin tribes would necessitate the Sanussi to take action on their behalf. They felt that such a blockade would further push Ahmad al-Sharif into the Turko-German camp. Therefore, the British government did the bare minimum needed to preserve Italian belief in British goodwill while letting goods flow from Egypt to the Sanussiyya – attempting to maintain the two mutually contradictory Anglo-Italian and Anglo-Sanussi relationships simultaneously. This phenomenon is best understood by analogy. Just as elements in London favoured the Zionists and some in Cairo were ideologically attached to the Hashemites, while others in India inclined to the House of Saud, the pressure of the Gallipoli crisis and Britain's subsequent manpower shortage repeated this dynamic in the war in the Western Desert: London 'wanted' to support Italy, while Cairo 'wanted' to back the Sanussiyya.

In short, both Kitchener and McMahon understood that limiting supplies to the Sanussiyya or ceasing their generous subsidy was likely to cause war and serve Turko-German interests. Attempting to square the circle and remain allies to both sides in the conflict inside Libya, they partially restricted the flow of arms and volunteers to the Sanussi; this was the bare minimum needed to preserve the Italian belief in British goodwill. This British policy can be explained by a combination of ideological attachment to the Sanussi, the need to avoid opening up another front while troops were stretched thin elsewhere, and the geostrategic fact that the British position in Arabia, Egypt, Sudan,

---

36 McMahon to Rennell Rodd, Memorandum of the French Embassy in London to the British FO, 12 February 1915: FO 371/2353 PRO, (TNA).

37 For Kitchener's 'Activist Arabist' tendencies see Philip Magnus, *Kitchener: Portrait of an Imperialist* (Dutton, London: 1958).

38 Kitchener to Grey, March, 1915, FO 371/2353 PRO, (TNA).

elsewhere would suffer greatly from a Sanussi attack if it would drain the religious legitimacy of the British to rule in their Muslim dominions.[39]

McMahon telegraphed to the Foreign Ofice on 30 July 1915 that the Italians appeared to be deliberately letting Ahmad al-Sharif get weapons from the
coast and enter into collaboration more and more with the Turks out of the
idea that this might drag him further into hostilities with Britain and cause the
British to fight the Italian's enemies in Cyrenaica. Amazingly to modern sensibilities, such was the commitment of British Arabist officials to their Sanussi
protégés that they sought to push their colleagues in London to ask if the Italians could be asked to abandon their position in Cyrenaica and be compen-
sated with some territory in Asia Minor at the war's end.[40] This proposal was
linked to efforts coming out of the Cairo Office to set up a Sanussi emirate
under British patronage at the War's end and treat the Sanussi similarly to the
Hashemites. This dynamic of seeking Sharifian allies against a resurgence of
anti-imperial pan-Islamism shows a way in which currents of thought throughout the First World War pre-conditioned British officials to relate to the Sanussi
via the then popular indirect rule paradigm.

However, despite the fact that British Arabist sensitivities clearly lay with the
Sanussi – and Ahmad al-Sharif's sentiments lay, not with the Ottomans who
he personally detested and with whom his Order had been rivals for decades,
but with the British – neither were able to prevent the outbreak of war, as
Turkish and German agents paid and trained various Sanussi commanders and

---

39 Milne Cheetham to Clayton, *Situation in Cyrenaica: Italy and The Senussi. Engagements
between Italians and Arabs at Sollum*, 3 July 1915, p 209, PRO 141/653/1, TNA. The implicit
existence of the Anglo-Sanussi relationship and the potential implications of transgressing
it are understood by Cheetham as follows: If the British ever even began to prepare for
war against the Sanussi or took any actions to strengthen themselves for that eventuality 'it
would be an unwarrantable breach of faith.' This reveals the way in which the existence of
the alliance in the minds of Cairo-based officials coloured their perceptions of what was
happening between the British and Sanussi until the actual assault began. This argument is
strengthened in a 13 July 1915 letter of the Adviser of the Interior to Cheetham. Stating that
'[if we were to engage in] hostilities against a religious chief such as the Senussi ... we should
suffer, the moral effect of our treatment of a religious chief of so much importance would
be far reaching and would affect the cause of the Allies not only throughout North Africa
but in Arabia, India and elsewhere, where the "Senussi" is only known as a religious name.
Hostilities should be avoided at all costs.'
40 Memorandum of the French Embassy in London to the British FO, 29 July 1915, FO
371/2353, (TNA).

goaded them to invade Egypt even against the overt wishes of their leader, while the Italians forced the British into various actions designed to blockade and starve the Sanussi and propel them towards war. It would take a much longer chapter to trace exactly what prompted certain Sanussi regiments to march into Egypt in November of 1915, but amazingly after the hostilities started Ahmad al-Sharif wrote to Henry McMahon claiming that it was rogue pro-Turkish elements within his own camp which had crossed the border and he apologised personally for the ensuing conflict.[41] That Ahmad al-Sharif sent this letter and that he was not initially in control of the invasion force does not mean that he was not elated that his forces very quickly reached the vicinity of Marsa Matruh. Seen with a hundred years remove, it is impossible to know if these letters contain genuine sentiments or were merely attempts by Ahmad al-Sharif to deflect blame and prevent himself from suffering British retribution in the event of his forces' defeat. In some instances, it appears likely that Ahmad al-Sharif used his intimate relationship with the British to mislead them, such as when he assured a key go-between that the skirmishes at Sidi Barani, which started the war, betrayed no hostile intent on his part and were unlikely to lead to further fighting.[42]

Having read many warm letters between the two sides in flowing Arabic, some of which were written while the fighting was going on, as well as having studied the reports of the different internal factions in the Sanussi camp, I subscribe to the thesis the Sanussi attack on Egypt was 'a mistake' imposed by certain pro-Turkish military elements who were able to control the paystrings of the Sanussi army and hijack its religious legitimacy for their actions. Those warmongering elements grasped that, if they precipitated an attack and if the first engagement was vaguely successful, then Ahmad al-Sharif would have to throw the whole weight of the Sanussiyya behind the invasion.

The pro-British political elite of the Sanussiyya simply did not have the ability to rein in their own followers, especially because much of the Sanussi forces were a ragtag bunch of tribal militias only nominally commanded by their supposed political leadership and largely motivated by micro-issues rather than the global war.[43] The Ottoman and Bedouin warmongers may have also cleverly played into tribal feuds and the various border grievances

---

41 Situation in Cyrenaica: Italy and The Senussi. Engagements between Italians and Arabs at Sollum, FO 141/653/1, (TNA).

42 McGuirk, *The Sanusi's Little War*, pp 152–3.

43 The exception to this was the Sanussi's regular force, the Muhaafizia.

that long characterised tensions between the Awlad 'Ali on the Egyptian side of the border, and Barassa and 'Ubaidat on the Cyrenaican side. It is, therefore, unsurprising that the pro-British political elite of the Sanusiyya simply did not have the ability to rein in their own followers when such tensions were unleashed, just as they had difficulty preventing cross border raids and blood feuds in the period 1900–1911 even though the Order was trying to increase its sovereignty and decrease tribal violence in this still largely lawless sphere.[44]

During the attack many British Arabist officials refused to admit that their protégés had temporarily turned on them, so they blamed the attack exclusively on the Germans and Turks instead, wishing to consider the Sanussi as innocent but wayward actors who would soon return to the fold.[45]

Therefore, although the subsequent historiography refers to the war as the Anglo-Sanussi war, many of the participants considered it simply a front in the Anglo-Turkish confrontation happening in the Middle East. That many of the so-called Sanussi officers were actually Turkish, that many of the soldiers were Egyptian Bedouin or Egyptian Arab nationalists, and that the majority of their armaments and supplies came from Germany makes this buried narrative hard to refute.

Supporting the hypothesis that Britain and the Sanussiyya sought not to go to war with each other, the archival evidence points to many examples of deliberate minimisation of casualties.[46] The military details of conflict show that it was quite far removed from the form of total war that prevailed at both Kut in Iraq and on the Somme. In fact, the fighting during the First World War

---

44 Ellis, 'Between Empire and Nation'.

45 Recent scholarship by John Slight has criticised this view claiming that the British denied agency to local actors and conspiratorially saw a Germano-Turkish hand attempting to stir up a Pan-Islamic jihad behind local resistance movements across the Islamic world during WWI. Slight rightly points out that the bogeyman of a Pan-Islamic jihad was overplayed by British actors leading them to act out of fear and to attempt to co-opt Islamic movements like the Hashemites and the Sanussiyya to bolster the religious legitimacy of British actions. This point does not however invalidate the argument that the original British narrative of Turkish co-optation of the Sanussi officer core appears to hold up to further scrutiny. Slight, 'British Understandings of the Sanussiyya Sufi Order's Jihad against Egypt'.

46 Ibid., p 165. For example, there is the tale of a key British Arabist officer, Cecil Snow, who refused to fire on a Bedouin soldier cornered in a cave and chose instead to speak in Arabic with him in an attempt to convince him to surrender. Tragically, he ended up being shot at close range for his civility.

in Egypt's Western Desert had certain elements of the North African tradition of baroud (ceremonial war).[47]

This non-Clausewitzian dynamic reveals that the study of the First World War in Libya cannot only inform debates about how Cyrenaican identity came about, but also shed light on various buried aspects of the war as a global phenomenon. A particularly striking aspect of the First World War that is largely absent in the centenary scholarship on Gallipoli, the Somme, Marne, Kut, Gaza, etc., is the extent to which the First World War was actually a series of local conflicts stitched together and fundamentally altered[48] by an overarching global war. This dynamic was not new to the First World War. In the 18th century, the Seven Years' War in Europe and the French and Indian War in North America were simultaneously the same conflict and yet very different local conflicts stitched together by the global nature of imperial wars.

The local conflict between Italians and Sanussis from 1911 onwards could be seen as analogous to the conflict between the French and British in America in the middle of the 18th century – they both pre-existed the global wars that spurred them to take a new angle and boil over into new fronts, adapt new alliance systems, and to suck in new actors. In the case of Libya, the global conflict re-routed the pre-established conflict pattern when the Italians chose to join an alliance bloc against Turkey, providing Turkey with the opportunity to attempt to get back its provinces that she had formally lost to Italy in 1912 and maintain its empire from decay elsewhere by pinning Britain's troops down on this front. The Sanussiyya became pawns in this larger process which they tried to master to gain more power, armaments, sovereignty, and governance capabilities.

The final proof for seeing the conflict as a part of larger Anglo-Turkish/German war is the manner in which it was catalysed. A German submarine attacked British positions at the key border post of Sollum on 5 November 1915. In response, the British evacuated all of their military and governance positions west of Marsa Matruh.[49] It was this British decision to evacuate that

---

47 In the tradition of baroud, war is conducted like a form of ritualised theatre. Demonstrations of force and raiding parties send a message to respected adversaries without seeking to inflict maximal damage. Conversation with Dr Emile Joffe, February 2012.

48 As the Cyrenaican and Tripolitanian resistance to Italy was not fundamentally altered by the War, I have not considered it in this chapter (as explained in footnote 1) or in this larger point about the intersection of the War's local and global faces.

49 McGuirk, The Sanusi's Little War.

acted like a vacuum, sucking the Turco-Sanussi forces into Egypt. As such, when the invasion quickly reached as far as Marsa Matruh without encountering any resistance, the Sanussi did not seek to inflict many casualties or to cause damage to civilian installations. Similarly to the failed Turkish attack on the Nile earlier in the year, they intended to rouse Egyptian nationalists to rise up against their colonialist oppressors. Conversely, the British attempts to expel the invaders in December 1915/January 1916 sought to push their enemies' forces backward into Cyrenaica but not to destroy the Order or to uproot the traditional mechanisms through which support flowed from the Bedouin communities to the Sanussiyya. Rather, the British were acutely aware that only a functioning Sanussi Order could keep the peace on Egypt's western border,[50] and as such they sought to use the war to exert enough leverage to purge the pro-Turkish elements from the Order and replace them with more pliant pro-British ones.

As soon as the Sanussi attack was repulsed, Sanussi-ophilia again gripped the upper ranks of British officialdom in Cairo which pushed for the British to be the guarantors of a Sanussi buffer state between Italian Libya and British Egypt. To actualise this, the British drew upon their longstanding relationship with the nephew of the current head of the Order, Mohamed Idriss ibn al-Mahdi al-Sanussi, who was also the grandson of the founder of the Sanusiyya and hence had always exerted a claim as the Order's rightful ruler. Many of Idriss's Arab and British supporters felt, since before the War, that Ahmad al-Sharif had merely been his 'regent' and that now due to Ahmad's participation in the war with Egypt that he should now be deposed.[51]

In attempts to bolster his independent power base, Idriss al-Sanussi had long cultivated British support for his quest to attain the headship of the Order, therefore, he used the ambiguous position of the Order in the wake of their

50 Memorandum of the French Embassy in London to the British FO, 29 July 1915, FO 371/2353 PRO, (TNA); French embassy to FO, 29 July 1915, FO 371/2354, Chanler report, (TNA).
51 Senussi-Italian Relations 1913, WO 106/1532, (TNA). To illustrate the longevity of this idea, a British intelligence report dated 3 November 1913 stated that Ahmad al-Sharif had only been 'regent' for Idriss and now that Idriss had come of age he was angered to see Ahmad receiving the attention from foreign envoys and the Italians that he should have received. This suggests that when the British hosted Idriss in Cairo in 1914 they were likely aware that they were tacitly supporting him in a struggle with his uncle for control of the Order and that they could call upon him to promote British interests at a later date if they helped him to displace his uncle.

defeat to oust his uncle and sign post-conflict peace negotiations which concluded at Akrama in April 1917 and cemented his position as the Order's new head.[52] Fascinatingly, it was as a formal part of the Akrama agreement that Italy and Britain 'agreed to recognise' Idriss as head of the Order.[53]

The final Akrama treaty was a testament to the deep mutual ties forged between the British and Idriss. Geostrategically, the British wanted a client state which could buffer destabilisation in Libya from affecting Egypt's Western desert.[54] Emotionally, they wanted Cyrenaica to gradually progress towards an authentic 'native state' ruled by the 'noble' Sanussiyya. These and other British interests in Cyrenaica ended up guaranteeing that the Sanussi would remain the dominant indigenous political force in Libya for decades to come and that a strong Cyrenaican identity being patroned simultaneously by Idriss and the British would mature. Looking back at the developments that led to the Treaty of Akrama, we must appreciate how peculiar this alliance system was (*i.e.* rather than the British wishing the Italians to crush those Bedouin ruffians who had just invaded Egypt, British policy was predicated on strengthening their former enemies as a buffer against their supposed allies, the Italians). And from the Sanussi side, Idriss's non-extant memoir quoted by E.A.V de Candole (*op. cit.*), describes the agreement he signed at Akrama in 1917 as 'a final settlement with the British but that with the Italians it was only a provisional pact.' In other words, Idriss appears to have indicated that he viewed the pact as finally sealing his strategic decision to chart the future of his Order as part of an Anglo-Sanussi alliance!

In the wake of the First World War, the Italians were afraid that growing Sanussi strength would threaten their position in Cyrenaica and hence they sought to foster urban trading elites, while local British officers felt that propping up natural leaders and fostering Cyrenaican identity would lead to stability and tranquility on their western Egyptian border. As such, from the end of the First World War until the rise of Fascism in 1921, a Sanussi buffer state was constructed in non-coastal Cyrenaica and its functionaries were armed and trained by the British. After what E.E. Evans Pritchard dubs the period of the

---

52 McGuirk, *Sanusi's Little War;* Anderson 'The Tripoli Republic, 1918–1922'; Gazzini 'Jihad In Exile: Ahmad Al-Sharif Al-Sanusi 1918–1933'.

53 It is rather strange to today's sensibilities to think of Christian nations bargaining about the conditions under which they would recognise a Muslim leader as head of his own Sufi Order, but this episode is deeply revealing of the nature of Imperialism.

54 Boundary between Egypt and Tripoli. Turkish claim to Sollum: WO 106/1553, (TNA).

Accords (i.e. 1917–1921) in his magisterial 1949[55] overview of the emergence of Cyrenaican identity *The Sanusi of Cyrenaica*, Mussolini came to power in Rome and he deliberately chased Idriss out of Cyrenaica and renounced Akrama and its successor agreements.

Idriss chose to sit out his exile in Cairo where he deepened his ties to his British patrons. Despite the stillborn attempt to form a Sanussi client state with British backing during and immediately after the First World War, the indirect model implicitly moulded all British interactions with Libya over the next four decades. So when the British tanks of the 8th Army rolled across North Africa in the Second World War they quickly sought to re-implant a Sanussi native state in Cyrenaica which was not so dissimilar to that which they hoped would take root from 1917 onwards and hence were staunchly against the return of the Fascist policy of supporting urban elites or trans-regional institutions which would link Cyrenaica and Tripolitania. Similarly, after the Second World War the British pushed their American and French allies to cede to them a protectorate (trusteeship) over Cyrenaica, while they did not want to rule Tripolitania where they perceived that they had no natural allies and only minimal interests.[56] When a variation of this proposal, termed the Bevin-Sforza plan, failed at the UN in 1949, the British did not abandon their Cyrenaican-centric approach to Libya. They advocated a federalist model that would allow a Sanussi King from Cyrenaica (which had a third the inhabitants of Tripolitania) to rule over all of Libya.[57] Anglo-Sanussi collaboration made possible Cyrenaican dominance and identity formation during the British Military Administration (1942–51) and the United Kingdom of Libya (1951–69).

Throughout the years of the Sanussi monarchy, British interests like its al-Adham airbase or its oil investments remained rooted almost exclusively in Cyrenaica. It was against such Cyrencaican dominance and the perceived neo-colonial nature of the Sanussi monarchy that Qadhafi's coup was launched.

---

55 In 1949, Cyrenaica formally was granted autonomy while Tripolitania was still under a British Military Administration. Evans-Pritchard's most famous book was an apology for Cyrenaican independence and an explanation of how the history of the Sanussiyya had made Cyrenaica unique and had connected it to Britain.

56 Louis, 'Libya: The Creation of a Client State'; Bills, *The Libyan Arena*; Kelly, *Cold War in the Desert*.

57 Adrian Pelt, *Libyan Independence and the United Nations : A Case of Planned Decolonization* (Yale University Press, New Haven: 1970).

The Anglo-Sanussi relationship and resulting British preference for Cyrenaican rather than Libyan identity formation has a surprisingly long shadow. The turmoil in Libya post-2011 has its origins in the historical inability of Libya to form nationwide institutions and identity. The Cyrenaican narrative of victimisation asserts that first Qahdafi and then the General National Congress deprived Cyrenaicans of their natural position of privilege and semi-autonomy within Libya.[58]

Today remnants of these colonial and pre-modern institutions still promote Cyrenaican insularity, traditionalism, and privilege and as such animated aspects of the dynamics of resistance to Qadhafi.[59] Although it would be incorrect to refer to events in Libya in 2011 as 'The Great Cyrenaican Revolt' (because the anti-Qadhafi movement was a truly national one) it would be equally unwise to ignore the specifically Cyrenaican dimensions of the country's ongoing conflict. Grappling with the legacy of British informal empire in Cyrenaica is the first step to understanding what makes modern Libyan regionalism unique.[60] The anti-Qadhafi rebels chose the Sanussi banner (in its iteration as the Libyan flag of the Monarchy period) and Omar Mukhtar (the Sanussi Sheikh and general who fought against the Italians) as the emotive symbols of their revolution. In so doing, they not only connected the 2011 Libyan uprisings to Libya's history. They inadvertently highlighted that many elements in today's Libya, notably the Federalist movement, but also General Haftar and many of the anti-Islamist bloc wish to re-establish the legacy of Cyrenaican dominance over Libyan affairs – a situation they can only achieve via strengthening their position with the exact same external allies that promoted Cyrenaican dominance after the First and Second World Wars: Egypt and the West.[61]

---

58 Jason Pack and Haley Cook, 'The July 2012 Libyan Elections and the Origin of Post-Qadhafi Appeasement', in *Middle East Journal*, Vol. 69, No.2, (Spring 2015) pp 171–198 (28).
59 Jason Pack, 'Introduction: The Center and the Periphery', in Jason Pack (ed) *The 2011 Libyan Uprisings and the Struggle for the Post-Qadhafi Future* (Palgrave Macmillan, New York: 2013).
60 This is a core argument that will be put forward in Jason Pack, *Britain's Informal Empire in Libya? The Anglo-Sanussi Relationship, 1889–1969* (Hurst/OUP, London: forthcoming 2017).
61 For an overview of Libya's current political cleavages and an analysis of the religious, regional, and international dimensions of the conflict please consult, 'Libya: Situation Report', *Tony Blair Faith Foundation,* November 2014, http://tonyblairfaithfoundation.org/religion-geopolitics/country-profiles/libya/situation-report. (This report is frequently updated.)

3

British intelligence and Arab nationalism: the origins of the modern Middle East

Steven Wagner

During 1917–18, Sir Mark Sykes represented the cabinet's Middle Eastern policy, working with members of General Allenby's staff in Cairo, including his staff intelligence and the Arab Bureau, which handled political intelligence in the region. These intelligence officers were also responsible for handling negotiations with the Hashemite chief Sherif Husayn of Mecca in 1915. Sykes and these officers had to simultaneously plan victory and Britain's postwar interests. Few British officials recognised the inherent contradiction in their promises to Zionists and Arabs between 1917 and 1919. This chapter argues that Britain's lack of appreciation for the conflict inherent in its various commitments derived more from weak assessments of Arab politics than from malevolence toward its new junior partners. By comparing what British intelligence officers believed about the relationship between Arab nationalist societies and the Hashemites against the reality of that relationship, it is possible to understand Britain's contradictory policy commitments, which were made as British war aims evolved along with the conditions produced by the conflict.

Before and during the war, British policymakers did not fear Arab nationalism, but they did worry about how to contain other forces. Some of these fears became irrelevant after the war. British officer in charge of Middle East policy, Mark Sykes, wrote in 1917:

...if we have agreements of an ancient Imperialist tendency, which the nationalities dislike it will be most probable that the Turk and German will score heavily to keep suzerainty and the Baghdad-Bahn, and land us (Great Britain) in a bad peace position in the Middle East, lacking both control and future security... I want to see a permanent Anglo-French Entente allied to Jews, Arabs and Armenians which will render pan-Islamism innocuous and protect India and Africa from the Turco-German combine, which I believe may well survive the Hohenzollerns.[1]

This view referenced German and Ottoman pan-Islamic propaganda that sought to raise *Jihad*, or Islamic holy war, against Christian forces in the Middle East. Such attempts sought to consolidate Islamic unity within the Ottoman Empire and to obstruct British mobilisation in Egypt and India.[2] In 1917, Sykes's main aim was to defeat the enemy. In the minds of policymakers, this propaganda could remain a threat even after the war and, in fact, did until the mid-1920s. Fear of pan-Islam dominated British planning for the postwar Middle East.[3]

Since the Balfour Declaration in November 1917, which promised to promote the creation of a 'Jewish National Home' in Palestine through immigration and development, there remained little scepticism about the virtues of Zionism within intelligence and policymaking circles.[4] Only by August 1919, once Britain's hold over Palestine was all but legally secured, did officers begin to understand that Britain's Arab and Zionist policies were irreconcilable.[5]

Mark Sykes had envisioned a British-Arab-Zionist-Armenian alliance to contain Turkish, German and pan-Islamic forces. In 1919 British intelligence officers were charged with implementing such a programme. The Zionist and Arab policies were seen as logical means to counter a united Middle Eastern front against the British Empire. Yet these policies would not be simple to implement; not only did the Middle East of 1919 look drastically different from

---

1 Mark Sykes, Memorandum on the Asia-Minor Agreement, August 14, 1917, RG65/P/349/28. Israeli State Archives (ISA), Jerusalem.

2 Hasan Kayalı, *Arabs and Young Turks: Ottomanism, Arabism, and Islamism in the Ottoman Empire, 1908–1918* (University of California Press, Berkeley: 1997) pp 187–188.

3 Steven Wagner, *British Intelligence and Policy in the Palestine Mandate, 1919–1939* (DPhil, University of Oxford: 2014) pp 26–28.

4 Gertrude Bell was one prominent figure who doubted that Arab would ever accept Zionism.

5 Wagner, *British Intelligence and Policy in the Palestine Mandate, 1919–1939*, p 52.

that of 1917, but the threat of pan-Islam was difficult to discern from other conflicts emerging in Anatolia, Cilicia, and across the Arab Middle East. Complicating our understanding of these events, in 1919 Sykes inconveniently died of the Spanish flu. Neither he nor Lord Kitchener – both responsible for Britain's Middle Eastern policies during the war – lived to see the consequences of their commitments.

Kitchener and Sykes drastically changed the Middle East, yet it quickly became a world which they likely would not have recognised. Their understanding of Arab politics was especially limited by a few channels of information, and the biases of some officers. What they understood about the connection between the Hashemite family and Arab nationalist societies differed from the true relationship. Arab nationalist societies had spread throughout the Ottoman Empire before and during the war. Fearing pan-Islam, Britain saw nationalism as a source for partnership against the religious threat aroused by the Ottoman Empire and Germany. Crucially, intelligence officers did not see the overlap between these communities within the Arab secret societies.

In Syria and Egypt a secret society called *al-'Urwa al-Wuthqa*[6] followed the teachings of Jamal al-Din al-Afghani and Mohammad 'Abduh. In the late 19th century the pair produced a journal with the same name. After publication ceased, al-'Urwa al-Wuthqa continued to teach that the prestige of Islam could only be rescued by the rebirth of the Arab nation. The movement strove to reconcile Islam and the Arab nation with modernity. It was deeply resentful of British control over Egypt, and the Ottoman Empire's weakness in the face of western powers.[7] Pan-Islam, sometimes featuring Salafist undertones, grew in popularity in the Levant from the end of the 19th century through the First World War.

During the First World War, Germany, the Ottoman Empire, and Britain each attempted to mobilise Islam as a weapon. The Sultan called for Jihad with Germany's encouragement, while Britain attempted to undermine Ottoman influence with the prospect of an Arab caliphate. Many pan-Islamists such as 'Abduh's student, Rashid Rida, took to those promises. Others, such as Shakib

---

6 A nickname for Islam or its principles, meaning 'the most steadfast support'. Menachem Milson, "العُرْوَة الوُثْقَى," *Arabic-Hebrew Dictionary Based on the Ayalon-Shneier Dictionary* (Hebrew University of Jerusalem), last accessed 20 November 2013, arabdictionary.huji.ac.il.; Also see Qur'an 2:256 and 31:22.

7 Eliezer Tauber, *The Emergence of the Arab Movements* (F. Cass, London; Portland: 1992) pp 22–24.

Arslan, were steadfast in their support of the Sultan. The war divided pan-Islamic and national movements and stunted their development. They were then were rocked by various revolts, communal conflicts, and the war in Anatolia between 1918 and 1923. Kemal's abolition of the Caliphate in 1924 shattered Islamic unity. After the war, a marriage between pan-Islam and pan-Arab nationalism emerged. Arslan and Rida, divided over the question of loyalty to the Ottomans, now became partners in the fight against Christian imperialism. British policy ceased to care about pan-Islam. In the words of John Ferris, 'a new orthodoxy emerged' among British observers who by the 1930s, used the terms pan-Arab and pan-Islamic as almost interchangeable synonyms.[8]

This was unknowable to Kitchener, Sykes and British intelligence officers during the war. From their point of view, the division between pan-Islamists and the nationalists should be exploited to help defeat the Ottomans. Yet, in 1914, when British officials were first approached by the Arab societies, their emissaries were all prominent pan-Islamists and students of 'Abduh and therefore were viewed with deep suspicion.

Pan-Islam was later transformed under the leadership of Arslan, Rida, and others, who politicised that movement, and allied it to Arab nationalism. Before the war, 'Abduh varyingly taught, mentored, and collaborated with figures including Sheikh Kamil al-Qassab, Rashid Rida, and Shakib Arslan. Qassab was the first to make contact with British officers in October 1914 when the Damascus branch of *Jami'at al-Arabia al-Fatat,* or the Young Arab Society (henceforth Fatat) sent him to contact the British residency. Fatat was one of a number of Arab societies founded before the war. They did not demand independence for Arabs until after the war broke out. Britain made no commitments to Qassab, and certainly would not agree to any limitations to France's ambitions in Syria. He left Egypt empty-handed, was arrested by the Ottomans upon his return to Damascus and released without charge after nearly a month. The next year, Qassab was instrumental in pressuring Husayn into alliance with Britain.[9]

Rashid Rida followed a similar pattern. Since 1911, Rida, worked to achieve unity against the Committee of Union and Progress (CUP) amongst Arab chiefs in the peninsula, to little avail, and was founder and head of a Cairo-based

---

8 John Ferris, '"The Internationalism of Islam": The British Perception of a Muslim Menace, 1840–1951', *Intelligence and National Security* 24, no. 1 (2009) pp 62–64, 70–72.

9 Eliezer Tauber, *The Arab Movements in World War I* (Routledge, London; New York: 1993) pp 58–59.

Arab society and was a member of others. After the war broke out, he and his compatriots began to work towards Arab independence. Rida secured funding for their emissaries from the British, who were no admirers of Rida but wished to maintain contacts with Syrian secret societies. Rida sent emissaries to the gulf, who were arrested by the British in Basra in possession of subversive anti-Christian propaganda.[10] British officials were also approached by 'Aziz 'Ali al-Misri – a hero to Arab nationalists for his participation in the Senussi campaign against the Italians in Libya during 1911–13. He had co-founded secret societies of military officers, called al-'Ahd, or the covenant, and another earlier iteration called Qahtaniyya. Upon Misri's return to Istanbul in 1913 he founded al-'Ahd and was arrested soon after by the Ottomans. The British ambassador's intervention rescued him from the death sentence. In August 1914, Misri reported to the British that he was asked by Enver Pasha to form a joint Turkish-Arab action against Egypt, but that he rejected it. In August 1914 he asked for British support in founding an Arab empire under British control. He admitted that he was head of a secret society concentrated in Baghdad ('Ahd), which could raise forces amongst the tribes in the peninsula, Iraq, and Syria. He was rebuffed, his British handler believed this was too dangerous a scheme – especially since the Ottomans had not yet entered the war. Misri instructed al-'Ahd not to take any action until there was a guarantee against any new foreign occupation.[11]

Historians have not provided an explanation of Anglo-Arab relations which examines why Qassab, Rida, and Misri were rebuffed so early on. This is significant since, at the exact same time as the Ottomans entered the war and serious approaches by Fatat began, Lord Kitchener gave an overture to the Hashemite family. On 31 October 1914, days after the Ottoman Empire entered the First World War, Lord Kitchener, Minister for War, sent the following message to Sherif Abdullah, 'It may be that an Arab of true race will assume the Caliphate at Mecca or Medina, and so good may come, by the help of God, out of all the evil that is now occurring.'[12]

This might be one of the more important announcements affecting the Middle East during the war. The Foreign Office recognised the danger inherent in promoting an Arab Islamic authority in Mecca to rival the Sultan. It would

---

10 Ibid., p 18; Tauber, *The Emergence of the Arab Movements*, pp 281–282, 315–316.

11 Tauber, *The Emergence of the Arab Movements*, pp 219–230, 233–234.

12 *Memorandum.* Damascus consul. 14 March 1924, FO 684/2. F01.28, The National Archives, Kew, London (hereafter TNA).

divide the Muslim world and could threaten a future peace settlement. In April 1915, the Foreign Office cabled Henry McMahon, High Commissioner in Egypt, saying:

> His Majesty's Government consider that the question of Caliphate is one which must be decided by Mahommedans themselves, without interference of non-Mahommedan Powers. Should the former decide for an Arab Caliphate, that decision would therefore naturally be respected by His Majesty's Government, but the decision is one for Mahommedans to make.[13]

Sherif Husayn of Mecca had already garnered some popular support for an Arab Caliphate, which generally came from within the British sphere of influence in Egypt and Sudan. There had been numerous schemes brought to the attention of British officials in Egypt which envisioned alternative Arab caliphates. Certain ones led by Rashid Rida began before the First World War – possibly with the encouragement of British policy, which saw the Berlin-Baghdad railroad as a threat. As a concept, Arab independence originated as a source of defiance to the Ottoman government in view of its weaknesses.[14] British policymakers were attracted the notion of an Arab Caliphate, but were also deeply suspicious of any pan-Islamic iteration thereof. They preferred that an Arab Caliph be a spiritual, rather than a temporal head of Islam.

The Caliphate question remained part of British policy through 1917, although in a much more considered way than Kitchener's first approach. A memo by Arthur Hirtzel of the India Office's political department examined British interests in Arabia in 1917. He stated that the ultimate success of Britain's policy in the Middle East 'depends to a large extent on the transfer of the caliphate from Turkey to Arabia. This in turn depends on the possibility of making the ruler of the Hejaz sufficiently strong to be able to pose as an independent sovereign. This again depends on keeping the Christian powers at a sufficient distance.'[15] Hirtzel was arguing for the exclusion of Italy from Yemen, but it is significant that in 1917, Britain expected an Arab-Islamic empire to take shape.

---

13 Ibid.

14 Kayalı, *Arabs and Young Turks*, pp 181–182.

15 Sir Frederick Arthur Hirtzel. British interest in Arabia.20 January 1917, L/PS/18/B247, India Office Records (hereafter IOR), London.

The fact that this came to be part of British policy at all is astonishing given Britain's hostility to pan-Islam during 1914–15. British policymakers were never fully aware of the social and political connections between the Hashemites, Fatat, 'Ahd, and the pan-Islamists. This is because they did not understand, or chose to overlook, how deeply engrained religious notions of power were within the secret societies. Months prior, Fatat and 'Ahd leaders gathered to formulate this programme. Many of these leaders wanted 'Abdul 'Aziz ibn Sa'ud to be the standard-bearer for their movement. He was popular for his military victories during previous years and was seen as a potential 'Bismarck of Arabia' who could unite the Arabic speaking peoples. Ibn Sa'ud rebuffed emissaries from al-Fatat, likely because his own military situation vis-à-vis his rival, Ibn Rashid, remained delicate. Sherif Husayn was their next choice. According to Eliezer Tauber, 'His noble ancestry, his status as guardian of the holy places of Islam, and the distance of the Hijaz from the main Ottoman forces made him a suitable candidate to lead the planned revolt.'[16]

Faysal bin-Husayn went to Istanbul in March 1915 and stopped in Damascus to meet with Fatat along his way. Faysal told them of Kitchener's letter to his father in October 1914, and stressed that no revolt would be possible without European assistance. On his way back in May 1915, Faysal saw them again – this time ready to accept the possibility of organised revolt. Fatat issued him with the 'Damascus Protocol' – a programme for Arab independence under Hashemite leadership. The scheme provided for Britain's recognition of Arab independence along specific boundaries, the abolition of foreign Capitulations, the conclusion of a defensive alliance between Britain and the Arab state, and the granting of economic preference to Great Britain. Faysal handed the Damascus Protocol to his father and recommended that he agree to lead the revolt. Husayn entered negotiations with Britain, but the Syrian soldiers with membership in Fatat and 'Ahd were sent to the Gallipoli front with the Ottoman Arab divisions after their mutinous plans were discovered by the Ottoman secret service. This delayed the possibility for revolt, but left time for British authorities and Husayn to reach terms.[17]

Britain remained hesitant to enter an Anglo-Arab alliance until one of the aforementioned Arab officers at Gallipoli defected to the British. This was 1st Lieutenant Muhammad Sharif al-Faruqi – a junior member of 'Ahd. Faruqi told

16 Tauber, *The Arab Movements in World War I*, p 61.
17 Ibid., pp 63–65.

the British everything about his secret society – its membership and leaders, their enciphered communications, and their ambitions. India Office papers with records of Faruqi's debrief at the Arab Bureau in Cairo contain some additional insight to his role in changing British minds. Underlined in the text was the society's wish to 'establish an Arab Caliphate in Arabia, Syria and Mesopotamia.' Also, significantly, the Arab Bureau recorded,

> el Farugi states that a guarantee of independence of the Arabian peninsula would not satisfy them, but this together with the institution of an increasing measure of autonomous government, under British guidance and control, in Palestine and Mesopotamia would probably secure their friendship. Syria is of course included in their programme but they must realise that France has aspirations in this region, though el Farugi declares that a French occupation of Syria would be strenuously resisted by the Mohamedan population.[18]

A minute covering Faruqi's description of the pan-Arab movement explained why this news was promising for British policy. Faruqi's story fitted what was already known from other sources. He offered a new bargain. McMahon examined the text of Faruqi's interrogation concluding, 'Interesting, if only because it may be merely a bait for us, is the idea that the Arab "Empire" is to be "national" and not religious in "accordance with the spirit of this century" and again "although the new Empire we wish to establish is to be headed by a Khalifa, its basis will be national and not religious. It will be an Arab not a Moslem Empire.' Importantly, the minute concluded: 'This is in striking contrast with the fanatical Islamism of Rashid Riza's [Rida] memorandum.'[19] Rida, previously had demanded absolute independence and a Caliph with temporal power. Faruqi gave the impression that Fatat and 'Ahd had adopted a realist policy: 'We would sooner have a promise of half from England than the whole from Turkey & Germany. We will accept reasonable terms from England, but nothing short of our entire programme from any other power.' The India Office noted that McMahon's assurances of Arab independence went 'considerably beyond the necessities of the case' and that Edward Grey, foreign minister, did not think that McMahon's assurances

---

18 McMahon to Grey. 12 October 1915, L/PS/10/523, (IOR), London.
19 Hirtzel, Coversheet 4024 1915, Arabia Pan-Arab Movement Treatment of Mohammed Sherif el-Faruqi. 1 November 1915, L/PS/10/523, (IOR), London.

mattered much because he did not believe that the pan-Arab scheme would materialise.[20]

Britain could not enter into an agreement with Husayn without first dealing with the interests of its main ally in the war, France. Muslim resistance to the prospect of French occupation after the war was the main motivation for the subsequent Sykes-Picot negotiations, which divided the region into spheres of influence, but not borders. Faruqi's description of his organisation's scheme appeared remarkably compatible with the India Office's strategy, which never wanted to occupy the interior of the region – just key points on the coast. Until Faruqi's revelations, the India Office saw British occupation of the hinterland of Arabia, Syria or Mesopotamia as wasteful. Moreover, the creation of an Arab state in Iraq had the potential to become a menace to Indian and British imperial interests. India was suspicious of McMahon's promises to Husayn about an Arab state, but accepted them believing it would hasten an end to the war. British policymakers preferred to maintain a stronger hand in governance within any prospective Arab state.[21]

The India Office was dubious about occupying large territories but policymakers in Egypt and London both favoured the occupation of Palestine. After the Ottomans nearly destroyed the canal in 1915, the army, foreign office and a number of ministers all saw Palestine as a flank defense to the Suez Canal. Along with the army, they wished to prevent any future threat to this vital strategic asset. Kitchener himself had long perceived this need, and had backed surveys of Sinai and the Negev while based in Egypt in the years before the war. His maps were later used by the army and planning staff.[22]

Kitchener viewed a pro-British Arab kingdom in Arabia, Syria and Iraq as cognate to Afghanistan's relationship with India: 'uncontrolled and independent within, but carrying on its foreign relations through us, we should be giving a maximum of satisfaction and assuming a minimum of responsibility; but this plan is not feasible unless we hold Syria.'[23] Compounding the perceived need to occupy territory east of Egypt, the Sherif's son Abdullah met British officials

---

20 Ibid.

21 Hirtzel, British interest in Arabia, 20 January 1917, L/PS/18/B247, (IOR), London.; Fol 16. Viceroy to India Sec. ca. October 1915, L/PS/10/524, (IOR), London.

22 Yigal Sheffy, British Military Intelligence in the Palestine Campaign, 1914–1918 (Frank Cass, London: 1998) pp 21–22.

23 Elie Kedourie, In the Anglo-Arab Labyrinth: The McMahon-Husayn Correspondence and Its Interpretations, 1914–1939 (Frank Cass, London: 2000) p 33.

in Egypt in April 1915 saying that his father had asked him to approach Kitchener 'with a view to obtaining with [sic] the British Government an agreement
similar to that existing between the Amir of Afghanistan and the Government
of India, in order to maintain the status quo in the Arabian peninsula and to
do away with the danger of wanton Turkish aggression.'[24] The Hashemites had
been worried for a number of years that the Ottomans aimed to replace their
control over Hijaz.

In December 1915, the cabinet invited Mark Sykes to discuss Middle East
policy and his negotiations with France. Among other things, he recommended holding territory beyond the Sinai Peninsula, which Arthur Balfour
said was normally regarded as a stronghold of Suez. Moreover, he recommended a large scale invasion of Ottoman territory east of Suez, especially
since France would not agree to a landing at Alexandretta – which was meant
to signal widespread revolt.[25] By this time the cabinet was well-disposed to
the idea of occupying Palestine as a buffer state. Kitchener was war minister
and British policymakers had long been exposed to the prospect of a British
occupation from Suez to Haifa and the Judean desert.[26]

Bearing in mind Britain's desire to occupy southern Palestine and create an
Arab buffer state beyond, it is easy to understand how British officers warmly
received Faruqi's claims. He confirmed what they previously had been told by
figures such as al-Misri, Qassab, and Rida, while mitigating suspicions about
them. Faruqi told them what they wished to hear. He confirmed the existence
of Fatat and 'Ahd, described their connections to Sherif Husayn and their
desire for independence from the Ottomans, and emphasised their ability
to support Britain's war effort. Yet, Faruqi had exaggerated the strength of
his movement, especially its ability to harm the Ottomans. He also never
described in detail how the Damascus Protocol came into existence. There is
little evidence that Britain knew about the Damascus Protocol until negotiations between McMahon and Husayn were rather advanced. After Faruqi's
defection, the Sherif sent a messenger to Egypt to continue the negotiations
and report on the military situation in Hejaz. Cemal Pasha had hanged fifteen
leading members of the Arab movements in in Syria – a move which pushed

---

24 Ibid., p 7.
25 War Committee – evidence of Sykes on Arab Question, 16 December 1915, TNA CAB
24/1/51, (TNA).
26 One Egypt-based official's views on who should occupy the buffer state are telling:
Kedourie, In the Anglo-Arab Labyrinth, p 34.

Fatat and 'Ahd closer to the Hashemites as their main lifeline to Britain. The messenger reported that 'the Arabs in Syria were under a signed compact to follow [Faysal].'[27] Britain was no longer afraid of Rashid Rida's influence over Husayn. The India Office noticed the similarities in Rida and Husayn's demands after the latter first approach to McMahon in July 1915.[28] By autumn 1915 the danger of that was overshadowed by the partnership between the Arab movements in Syria and Husayn. Few officials considered how many members of the Arab movements subscribed to Rashid Rida's pan-Islamic ideals, even if they were confident that Husayn and his sons did not.

The Sherif was portrayed as a capable leader of a disciplined movement when, in fact, he was their second choice. It was never clear to British observers what drove the unity amongst the Arab movements, which were more hetero-geneous than British officials had realised. Most misleading of all, Faruqi told British officials that his movement saw the future Arab state as a secular one. British soldiers and diplomats alike believed this because they had long been searching for a way to neutralise the Ottoman pan-Islamic weapon. Now, it seemed that Arabs were promising to form a state – part of the British Empire – governed according to the modernising principles which had been learned from Europe over the prior decades, which particularly impressed British officials.

Most assumed that the limitation of demands by Faruqi, and subsequently Husayn, was driven by Cemal's suppression of the Arab movements and exe-cution of its leadership. Meanwhile, there were benefits to the proposed alli-ance: Ottoman authority would be limited by a transfer of national-religious authority to Hijaz and away from the Sultan. Simultaneously, British officials believed that the Sherif's spiritual authority would be tempered by his own views and those of the Orthodox schools of Islam in Egypt which had opposed Ottoman pan-Islamic propaganda. Most British officials in Egypt, such as Reginald Wingate, believed that even if there were one Arab claimant to the Caliphate, 'an Arab "pope"... will appeal to Moslems nowhere.' Besides, a partnership between Britain and pan-Arabism could possibly be 'the founda-tion of a really constructive scheme for the future.'[29] The Arab Bureau in Cairo strongly favoured the Anglo-Hashemite alliance: Husayn wanted to create a

---

27 McMahon to Viceroy, 22 October 1915, L/PS/10/524, IOR, London.
28 Note on communication from the Sherif of Mecca, ca. August, 1915, L/PS/18/B215, IOR, London.
29 Note on a British policy in the near east, 26 August 1915, FO 882.13/ ff 379–380. MIS/15/9A, (TNA).

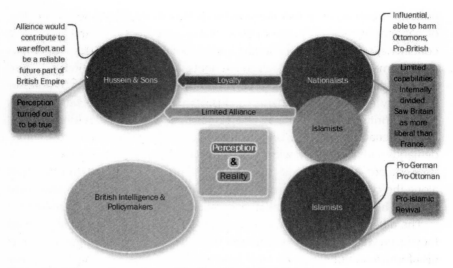

Figure 1: Intelligence Perception and Reality of Anglo-Arab Relations

pro-British buffer state in western Asia. Only the India Office saw the potential danger in a new pan-Islam under the Arab banner – but they were hushed by cabinet because the war needed this alliance.[30] Officers of the Arab Bureau investigated the truth of Faruqi's claims. Unsurprisingly, Husayn and various members of Fatat and 'Ahd confirmed what they long wished British officers to understand, and likewise, what those officers wished to hear.

Britain's support for an Arab revolt against the Ottomans aimed to create an Arab state which would fall within the British and French Empires as both an ally and junior partner. This vision was based on a skewed understanding of the relationships between the Hashemites, the Arab movements, and the pan-Islamists. After the war, Britain's policy for the region fell apart as the hetero-geneous Arab movements clashed amongst themselves, and with Britain and France over the issue of independence. In 1919 members of al-Fatat founded the *Istiqlal* (independence) party to expand its influence over other classes of society. In early 1920, the independence movement split into three. Kamel al-Qassab, who in 1914 risked much to approach Britain for an alliance, led a faction of dissenters who vehemently opposed British and French colonial

---

30 Minute by T.W.H. 9 November 1915; Minutes fol 34–35, reg no 3935:1915, L/PS/10/523, IOR, London.

policy. Qassab accused members of the Damascus administration of 'neglect of national interest'.[31] France's defeat of Faysal in 1920 was the result of a concatenation of misunderstandings. Received wisdom dictates that British policy aimed to divide the Arab movements when, in fact, it tried very hard to keep them together. Likewise, it is not entirely clear that France planned to occupy the Syrian hinterland, against its understanding with Britain and Faysal.[32] British officers believed that Britain's Arab policies would be realised largely because what they understood in 1915 about the Arab movements' demands had not evolved with the war. Then, they seemed to support an Arab state as a pro-British buffer state, agreeing to limited French and British control along the coasts. After the war, when Qassab helped to found *Istiqlal,* it was because he and other prominent leaders in fact held a maximalist policy.

The difference between the perception of British officers and the realities they faced was vast. This was caused by a mix of wishful thinking, some slight disinformation, but mainly by an overwhelming focus on winning the war. The Anglo-Arab alliance was correctly seen as an expedient towards a favourable outcome for Britain, whether the Ottomans sued for peace or were defeated. During 1914–15, Britain had to contend with the possibility of competing great powers such as Germany or Russia having dominant influence in the Middle East. Assessments from the Arab Bureau never anticipated that the Arab movements might revert to their original demands for absolute independence. That threat was masked by concern for pan-Islam. The ideology was more pervasive than could have been realized at the time, but its true threat to British interests was poorly grasped. Mark Sykes, in an analysis of modernisers and orthodox authorities in Islam, counted Mohammad 'Abduh among the apolitical Orthodox type in Cairo, despite his past association with pan-Islam and also despite the fact that his students included the pan-Islamists such as Rashid Rida and Shakib Arslan.[33] Sykes and other figures did not realise that their appreciation of the social and political connections within Islam and the Arab world was temporary, and conditioned by the circumstances of the war. The end of the war therefore radically challenged the basic assumptions of British policymakers and led to violent results.

---

31 James L Gelvin, *Divided Loyalties: Nationalism and Mass Politics in Syria at the Close of Empire* (Univ. of California Press, Berkeley: 1998) pp 59–62.

32 Wagner, 'British Intelligence and Policy in the Palestine Mandate, 1919–1939', p 54.

33 The text contains a number of other significant misapprehensions. TNA, FO 882/13. MIS/15/8. *Sykes to Callwell, DMO.* 2.8.1915. p.2.

4

The First World War and its legacy for women in Iraq

Noga Efrati

The notion that the First World War was a watershed in gender relations in European societies, has characterised contemporary narratives and, for a long time, also historiography. Women proved their 'patriotism and fitness for citizenship' and were rewarded with political and other rights.[1] A similar sentiment can be noted in post-First World War Iraq, if we stretch beyond the generally-accepted 1914–1918 timeline, as some suggest,[2] and include the 1920 revolt. Iraqi women's leaders portrayed the revolt against the British occupation as a defining moment for women not only manifesting women's

---

1 Birgitta Bader-Zaar, 'Controversy: War-related Changes in Gender Relations: The Issue of Women's Citizenship', in Ute Daniel, Peter Gatrell, Oliver Janz, Heather Jones, Jennifer Keene, Alan Kramer, and Bill Nasson (eds). *International Encyclopedia of the First World War* (Freie Universität Berlin, Berlin: 2014), accessed 30 January 2014. doi: 10.15463/ie1418.10036; Christa Hämmerle, Oswald Überegger, and Birgitta Bader-Zaar, 'Introduction: Women's and Gender History of the First World War – Topics, Concepts, Perspectives', in Christa Hämmerle, Oswald Überegger, and Birgitta Bader-Zaar (eds), *Gender and the First World War* (Palgrave Macmillan, Houndmills, Basingstoke, Hampshire: 2014), pp 10, 14 note 23.

2 Robert Gerwarth and Erez Manela suggested expanding the canvas on which the history of the Great War is written and see the fighting between 1914 and 1918 as part of a continuum of conflict that began with the Italian invasion of Libya in 1911 and did not end until the Lausanne Treaty of 1923, when a new order was in place not just in Europe and the Middle East but also in Asia and Africa. See Robert Gerwarth and Erez Manela (eds), *Empires at War: 1911–1923* (Oxford University Press, Oxford: 2014).

nationalist awareness but also demonstrating their willingness to make sacrifices for their country. It broke down barriers that had prevented women
from realising their capabilities and prompted the call for rights that were
their due.[3]

Indeed, Iraqi women participated in the revolt in both urban and rural areas.
In Baghdad, a women's committee was organised, headed by Na'ima Sultan
Hamuda, wife of Ahmad al-Shaikh Da'ud, who was among the Iraqi leaders
arrested during the revolt and thereafter exiled. The committee explained the
revolt's goals to women, encouraged their support, and collected donations of
cash and jewelry. Baghdadi women appealed to Oriental Secretary Gertrude
Bell regarding the fate of nationalist detainees and participated in mass funeral
processions, thereby transforming the funerals into nationalist demonstrations.
Dressed in black and veiled, they shouted nationalist slogans against British
imperialism. In the countryside, rural women accompanied fighting men to
battle and urged them on. They also carried equipment and provided supplies. There have been claims that women actually participated in combat,
but details of when and where were not provided. Women's contribution was
acknowledged in a letter from the leaders of the uprising.[4]

Recent scholarship, however, has not remained as euphoric. A more
nuanced view of war-related change concerning war's significance for
women's citizenship in Europe has evolved. Researchers point out that the
war did not result in full political rights, not to mention citizenship, in many
countries, including France, Italy, and even Britain.[5] This chapter will focus on
the legacy of the First World War for women in Iraq.

British forces occupying Iraq during the war faced the necessity of imposing
order over the vast rural countryside, preventing assistance to the Ottoman
armies, and securing supplies. Toward this end and with their understanding
of rural areas as tribal, the British sought to enhance the authority of shaikhs,

---

3 Sabiha al-Shaikh Da'ud, *Awwal al-Tariq Ila al-Nahda al-Niswiyya* fi al-'Iraq (al-Rabita,
Baghdad: 1958), pp 27–35; *al-Fikr al-Jadid*,10 March 1973, p 4.
4 For more about women's participation in the 1920 revolt see Da'ud, *Awwal al-Tariq*,
pp 27–35; Rufa'il Butti, 'Al-Mar'a al-'Iraqiyya al-Haditha', *al-Kitab* 4 (November, 1947), p 1877;
'Abd al-Rahman Sulaiman al-Darbandi, *Dirasat 'an al-Mar'a al-'Iraqiyya al-Mu'asira* (Dar
al-Basri, Baghdad: 1968), Vol 2, pp 250–251; 'Ali al-Khaqani, 'Sha'irat fi Thawrat al-'Ishrin', in
Muhammad 'Ali Kamal al-Din (ed), *Thawrat al-'Ishrin fi Dhikraha al-Khamsin*, (Dar al-Tadamun,
Najaf: 1971) pp 353–375.
5 Hämmerle, Überegger, and Bader-Zaar, Introduction, pp 10–11.

whom they saw as the tribes' natural leaders. Appointed shaikhs were given responsibility for maintaining order and, in return, they were given support, arms and title to lands over which they claimed possession. Another means to bolster the position of shaikhs was by prescribing their judicial authority over their tribes. Toward this end the British issued in February 1916, a Tribal Criminal and Civil Disputes Regulation (TCCDR). A few months before the end of the war, in July 1918 the regulation was revisited and reissued.[6]

The TCCDR was mandated by wartime conditions, but when the war was over the regulation remained. At the insistence of the mandate authorities, provision for a separate tribal jurisdiction was included in Iraq's constitution. In 1924 the Tribal Regulation became a state law and remained in force until the overthrow of the Hashemite monarchy in 1958.[7] The Regulation divided the citizens of Iraq into two groups with two different legal systems. The urban population was subject to civil and criminal courts and fell under the jurisdiction of the Baghdad Penal Code. But the rural population was subject to the Tribal Regulation which sanctioned and institutionalised customary practices.

Much has been written about the Tribal Regulation, the way it facilitated the cheap, indirect administration of Iraq's vast territories during the British occupation, how it reflected the British occupiers' perception of the social structure they found therein and how it provided a basis for loyalty to the civil administration and later to the Iraqi government.[8] But its implications for women, which stirred much controversy at the time, have received little scholarly attention. This chapter will elaborate on the harsh implications the regulation had for Iraqi women and, how it constructed them as non-citizens. It seeks to add to the re-evaluation of the First World War's significance for women's citizenship globally.

---

6 *Tribal Criminal and Civil Disputes Regulations* (The Times Press, Bombay: 1916), L/P&S 10/617, India Office Library, London (hereafter IO); 'Tribal Criminal and Civil Disputes Regulation (Revised)', in *Iraq Administration Reports: 1914–1932*, compiled by Robert L. Jarman, (Archive Editions, Slough, U.K.: 1992), Vol 8, pp 144–156 (hereafter *IAR*).

7 'The Tribal and Civil Disputes Regulations Amendment Law of 1924', in Iraq Ministry of Justice, *Compilation of Laws and Regulations Issued Between 1st January 1924 and 31st December 1925* (Government Press, Baghdad: 1926) p 63; Peter Sluglett, *Britain in Iraq 1914–1932* (Columbia University Press, New York: 2007) pp 169–172.

8 Sluglett, *Britain in Iraq 1914–1932*, pp 169–181; Samira Haj, *The Making of Iraq 1900–1963: Capital, Power, and Ideology* (State University of New York Press, Albany: 1997); Toby Dodge, *Inventing Iraq: The Failure of Nation Building and a History Denied* (Columbia University Press, New York: 2003) pp 83–100.

British occupation of Iraq brought with it an administration that was largely shaped by the British experience in India. Sir Henry Dobbs, at the time Revenue Commissioner, drew up the Tribal Regulation along the lines of the colonial code used on the Indian North-West Frontier. It was designed to arrange for the speedy settlement of tribesmen's disputes in accordance with tribal customs by a tribal *majlis* which would include mainly 'chiefs and shaikhs'. But, the system as a whole was supervised by, and subordinate to, the British administration and later to the Iraqi government.

The Regulation allowed 'tribesmen' to settle their disputes according to 'tribal custom', but it did not elaborate on the term *tribal custom* per se. British political officers, however, perceived 'tribal custom' as universal, age old, and unchanging.[9] Customs concerning women were well known and described as uncompromising and harsh. They found evidence for this callous treatment in numerous tenets: A woman who 'lapsed from the strict path of virtue', they reported, brought a stain to the family honour that could be washed away only by her blood; in the settlement of feuds, especially blood feuds, tribes required the guilty party, in addition to paying blood money, to hand over one or more women from his clan to the family of the victim for the purpose of marriage; a woman was compelled to marry her paternal cousin or to receive his consent to marry another man – and if overlooked, the cousin was justified in killing the woman or the man she ultimately married. Aberrations, when noted, were usually explained as exceptions to the rule or as deviation from tribal custom.[10]

Iraqi opposition to the regulation throughout the Hashemite period included the plight of women as an important justification. Iraqi officials and

---

9 Arnold T. Wilson, *Loyalties, Mesopotamia, 1914–1917: A Personal and Historical Record Vol 1* (Oxford University Press, London: 1936) p 69.

10 See, for example, 'Administration Report of Suq al-Shuyukh and Hammar District for the Year 1918', in *IAR*, Vol 2, p 363; 'Report on the Administration of Justice for the Year 1919', in *IAR* Vol 3, p 380; 'Monthly Report of Arbil District for the Month of October 1919', L/P&S11/168, IO; 'Monthly Report A.P.O. Basrah for the Month of December 1919', L/P&S 10/621, IO; 'Review of the Civil Administration of Mesopotamia for 1920', in *IAR* Vol 5 p 18; 'Annual Administration Report of the Mosul Division for the Year 1921', Foreign Office (hereafter FO) 371/7801/E10742, The National Archives, London, Kew (hereafter, TNA); E. S. Stevens, *By Tigris and Euphrates* (Hurst and Blackett, London: 1923), pp 275, 280–281; 'Report by His Majesty's Government in the United Kingdom of Great Britain and Northern Ireland to the Council of the League of Nations on the Administration of 'Iraq for the Year 1929', in *IAR* Vol 9, p 221.

intellectuals, Sunnis and Shi'is, men and women, protested the harsh implications the regulation had for rural women. Muhammad Fadil al-Jamali, a Shi'i
who in the 1930s held high positions in the Ministry of Education, argued in
his dissertation on Bedouin education, written at Columbia University Teachers' College where he studied between 1929 and 1932, that tribal women
were perceived as inferior beings and the possessions of men. He underscored
the use of women in dispute settlements stating that 'this means of atonement
for murder is certainly degrading to those women handed over to an enemy
tribe.' Ja'far Hamandi, the Shi'i director of legal affairs in the Ministry of the
Interior expressed his disapproval of practices that treated women as property
and criticised the *nahwa* (the right of men to prevent their female agnates'
marriage) as a vehicle for restricting personal liberty. In 1929, the Ministry
of the Interior instructed its officials to urge arbitrators in tribal councils to
use money rather than women to settle disputes, and steps were taken to
encourage the annulment of the *nahwa*. Hamandi claimed it was he who
convinced the ministry heads to issue the decree urging the settlement of
disputes monetarily and it was during his term as director of legal affairs, that
the government made agreements with several shaikhs and village leaders to
annul the *nahwa*.[11]

The renowned poet Ma'ruf al-Rusafi harshly attacked the Tribal regulation's recognition of 'barbaric' and 'pre-Islamic' customs. Guardians, he
protested, perceived their daughters as their property, selling women like
'sheep and cows' for the purpose of marriage. Guardians of married women
would force husbands to divorce their wives to obtain a higher *mahr*.[12] If the
women's husbands were absent, the guardians could give their wards in marriage again without bothering first to have them divorced, simply out of greed
for another *mahr*. Because women were perceived as property, men who
had many daughters thought themselves rich. Women, he protested, were
not only excluded from inheritance, but were also inheritable themselves; a
woman handed over in dispute settlement was disdained, humiliated, and put
to work like a slave. To demonstrate the role the TCCDR played in preserving
such practices, al-Rusafi described first-hand the proceedings of several cases

11 Mohammed Fadhel Jamali, *The New Iraq: Its Problem of Bedouin Education* (Bureau
of Publication, Teachers College, Columbia University, New York: 1934), pp 73–74, 144;
'Al-Nahwa' *Lughat al-'Arab*, 8 (1930), p 187. (No author was mentioned)
12 *Mahr* pl. *Muhur* – according to Islamic law, a sum of money or other property given by the
husband to the wife as an obligation of marriage.

brought before Iraqi administrative official to be tried under the regulation. In one, a man had attempted to seduce the sister of another man. The state official instructed the seducer to give his sister as a wife without *mahr* to the brother of the woman he tried to seduce. Al-Rusafi questioned this ruling, inquiring of the administrative officials what transgression the criminal's sister had committed that would justify her being handed over in this way for a crime perpetrated by her brother. The official admitted that a woman handed over in this manner enjoys no respect – indeed, she is disdained, humiliated, and put to work like a slave – but he stressed that 'tribal law' demanded such a verdict.[13]

Prominent women such as the poet Nazik al-Mala'ika and women's leaders Sabiha al-Shaikh Da'ud and Naziha al-Dulaimi protested against the legitimisation of honour murders. Nazik al-Mala'ika lamented in her poem 'Washing off Disgrace' the brutal murder of a young woman in the name of honour. The poem was seen as expressing a new generation's aversion to the archaic practices preserved in society.[14] However, her description of the murderer as he sat in a tavern boasting of his deeds and cleaning his dagger also bemoaned the fact that he could get away with it. Her criticism, subtle though it was, clearly conveyed the notion that women lived in fear and submissiveness because there was no law to protect them from their kin.[15] Da'ud and al-Dulaimi concurred that rural women were subjected to 'double servitude'- enslaved like rural men to the landlords and enslaved by their husbands as well. Rural women, both argued, were overworked, abused, and lost any personal freedom. Like beasts of burden, al-Dulaimi charged, rural women might, without recourse, bear the brunt of their husbands' anger, be beaten, or otherwise maltreated. They understood that opposition might have harsh consequences for they could be easily disposed of. Such an act was readily explained away under the pretext of 'washing away the shame', which was officially recognised as justification for murder.[16] The importance of such

---

13 Ma'ruf al-Rusafi, 'Al-Zu'ama fi al-'Iraq', in Sa'id al-Badri (ed), *Ara' al-Rusafi fi al-Siyasa wa-1 -Din wa-1 -Ijtima'*, 2nd ed. (al-Ma'arif, Baghdad: 1951) pp 9–15.
14 Khalid Kishtainy, 'Women in Art and Literature', in Doreen Ingrams, *The Awakened: Women in Iraq* (Third World Center, London: 1983) pp 149–150.
15 Nazik al-Mala'ika, *Diwan Nazik al-Mala'ika* (Dar al-'Awda, Beirut: 1986), Vol 2, pp 351–354. For an English translation see Ingrams, *The Awakened*, pp 150–151.
16 Naziha al-Dulaimi, *Al-Mar'a al-'Iraqiyya* (al-Rabita, Baghdad: [1950?]), pp 8–11; Da'ud, *Awwal al-Tariq*, pp 223–229.

critiques lies in their bringing to light the ramifications of the TCCDR. The regulation constructed women as tribal possessions and allowed men unbridled power over their lives.

British officials were not unaware of these aspects of the Tribal Regulation. Many depicted customs affecting women as 'barbaric' and their implementation through the Regulation as 'foreign to British judicial tradition' or 'a travesty of justice'.[17] Some political officers were reluctant to sanction the handing over of women in dispute settlements; others imposed punishments on perpetrators of honour murders.[18] One of these political officers Stuart Edwin Hedgcock documented the harsh treatment of women under customary law in his 1927 book *Haji Rikkan*", which he published with his wife.[19] Moreover, British legal experts and advisers in Iraq such as Edgar Bonham-Carter (who became senior judicial officer in Baghdad in 1917 and later served as judicial adviser in Mesopotamia from 1919 until 1921) and Edwin Drower (adviser to the Iraqi Ministry of Justice, from 1922 until 1946) favoured the transference of tribal criminal cases to the civil courts, which would allow punishment of 'crimes of honour' under the penal code. Such crimes, lamented Bonham-Carter, were regrettably common and would be difficult to eradicate.[20]

However, the Office of the Civil Commissioner cautioned against political officers' intervention, noting that such intrusion tends to undermine the force and the appeal of this method of settlement. Oriental Secretary Gertrude Bell advised that such interference was incompatible with the valued "local justice"

---

17 See, for example, 'Administration Report of the Amarah Division for the Year 1920–21', in *IAR* Vol 5, p 175; 'Review of the Civil Administration of Mesopotamia for 1920', in *IAR* Vol 5, p 18; 'The Court of Cassation, Annual Report for 1929', Baghdad High Commission File (hereafter, BHCF), Judicial Matters, 8/219, National Archives of India, New Delhi (hereafter, NAI); Stevens, *By Tigris and Euphrates*, p 275.

18 See James Saumarez Mann (ed), *An Administrator in the Making: James Saumarez Mann, 1893–1920* (Longmans, Green, London: 1921) pp 220–22; 'Administration Report for the Qurnah Area for the Year 1919', in *IAR* Vol 4, p 269.

19 Fulanain (pseudonym for Stuart Edwin Hedgcock and his wife Monica Grace Hedgcock), *Haji Rikkan: Marsh Arab* (Chatto & Windus, London: 1927).

20 Copy of Memorandum No.A.12/1571, Dated April 12, 1921, from the Judicial Adviser to the Adviser to the Ministry of Interior, Baghdad, CO 730/6, TNA; 'Report by His Britannic Majesty's Government to the Council of the League of Nations on the Administration of 'Iraq for the Year 1927', in *IAR* Vol 8, p 466; 'Report on the Administration of Justice for the Year 1919', in *IAR* Vol 3, p 380.

that promoted good conduct and order.[21] In 1923, when the Iraqi minister of justice, Naji al-Suwaidi, suggested a broad revision of the Regulation, including a section stipulating that offences affecting sexual morals and honour be punishable under the Penal Code, High Commissioner Dobbs objected – remarking that 'if there is any case in which tribal feeling is keen and tribal custom necessary to follow, it is the case of adultery and the like.'[22] In 1926, Dobbs threatened to invoke his powers under the Military Agreement should the Iraqi government attempt to 'emasculate' so effective a system of maintaining order in tribal areas.[23] Thus, British actions often seemed dissonant or contradictory.

A model suggested by Toby Dodge – which identified two competing British perceptions of how best to govern an alien society – at first glance seems to explain these conflicting positions. Those advocating non-intervention were those Dodge classified as adhering to romantic collectivism. Collectivists saw Iraq as premodern and tribal and thus endeavoured to rule the country on the basis of the tribal system with its tribal leaders and its distinct tribal law and customs. Their subscription to the notion of distinct 'tribal custom' was a major justification for deploying the regulation. Interference with practices affecting women challenged this notion and threatened to undermine an effective tool for controlling the countryside. On the other hand, those advocating ideas Dodge classifies as rational individualism, saw Iraq destined for modernisation and viewed the individual as the fundamental unit of society. They perceived the tribal system as in decay, were sensitive to the lot of individuals, men and women, under tribal law, and felt that the Regulation should be abolished and tribal law overruled.[24]

Yet it would be incorrect to conclude that overall British reticence to intervene in practices pertaining to rural women resulted only from romantic collectivism's dominance. In fact, those touting rational individualism revealed a tendency toward the marginalisation of women not unlike that of their colleagues. 'Saving brown women from brown men',[25] although a goal, was not

---

21 'Review of the Civil Administration of the Occupied Territories of Al 'Iraq, 1914–1918', in *IAR* Vol 1, p 57; 'Review of the Civil Administration of Mesopotamia for 1920', in *IAR* Vol 5, pp 17–18.

22 Proposed Amendments to the Tribal Disputes Law, from H. Dobbs to E. M. Drower,18 October 1923, Colonial Office (hereafter, CO) 730/103, TNA.

23 See correspondence between Henry Dobbs and Kinahan Cornwallis, dated 7 and 8 June 1926, CO 730/103, TNA.

24 Dodge, *Inventing Iraq*, especially pp 1–2, 83–100, 175–176.

25 Gayatry Chakravorty Spivak, 'Can the Subaltern Speak?', in Cary Nelson and Laurence Grossberg (eds), *Marxism and the Interpretation of Culture* (University of Illinois Press, Urbana: 1988) p 296.

high on their agenda. Higher priority was given to building a progressive legal system within a 'civilised government' and imposing order. Thus, for example, the main concern of those political officers who punished men who had murdered female relatives, was not the lot of women, but rather that a 'civilised government' could not condone such brutal acts of murder.[26] Bonham-Carter and Drower's support for abolishing the Regulation and transferring tribal murder cases to the civil courts reveals a similar set of priorities. To them, building a progressive legal system required a unified system, with the responsibility for punishment solely in the hands of the government. The elimination of 'tribal custom', however, was not an immediate concern. Both men suggested that the civil courts exercise the authority given to them by Article 41 of the Penal Code to punish tribal offenders according to tribal custom.[27]

The Hedgcocks' book was no exception. It indeed places great emphasis on the importance of the individual. Written in the form of tales told to the authors by Haji Rikkan, a marsh peddler and guide, women figures are given names and voices. The book touches repeatedly on themes of killing in the name of honour and the use of women as a means for settling disputes. Tragedies unfold, one after another: a father feels compelled to kill his beloved daughter for falling in love with a man from a tribe of lower status; a brother is taunted into murdering his sister; a girl fleeing with her cousin, whom she loves, from a forced marriage begs him to kill her when their escape fails; a grieving father laments the cruel fate of his daughter, who is to be handed over in a dispute settlement. The language the authors used in describing the women's plight is explicit. A woman handed over to a hostile tribe is torn from her parents and 'becomes the absolute chattel of the stranger to whom she is allotted. However bad her treatment – and it is not likely to be over-good – she cannot demand a divorce.'[28] However, in spite of their grim descriptions, implicit in the authors' narration is resignation to the fact that other considerations took precedence over women's well-being. Referring to the TCCDR as legislation that 'makes full allowance for the binding obligation on a tribesman

---

26 'Administration Report of the 'Amarah Division for the Year 1919', in *IAR*, Vol 4, p 9.

27 Copy of Memorandum No. A.12/1571, Dated 12 April 1921, from Judicial Adviser to the Adviser to the Ministry of Interior, Baghdad, CO 730/6, TNA; E. M. Drower to Sir Henry Dobbs, 21 October 1923, CO 730/103, TNA; 'Report by His Britannic Majesty's Government to the Council of the League of Nations on the Administration of 'Iraq for the Year 1927', in *IAR* Vol 8, p 466.

28 Fulanain, *Haji Rikkan*, pp 55, 56–57.

to take a life when his honour is at stake', the Hedgcocks implicitly sanctioned 'honour' murders. Although 'appalled' at the 'savage act' of a brother slaying his sister, the Hedgcocks accepted Rikkan's circular explanation: the woman must have been guilty, or she would not have been accused. Thus, ancient law required the murder to preserve tribal honour. Also, although disapproving of the handing over of women in dispute settlements, the Hedgcocks accepted the utility of the practice and recommended noninterference: 'To Western minds it seems intolerable that the custom of a money payment instead of payment of a woman, sometimes adopted among the tribes, should not be generally enforced. But the Arabs have learned by long experience that the old method of handing over women is by far the most effective for ensuring future amity between the tribes hitherto at feud. More surely than the payment of money, this inter-marriage brings about a lasting and real reconciliation.'[29]

Romantic collectivism and rational individualism, then, were not mutually exclusive British notions as far as practices affecting women were concerned. Those convinced of the validity of the tribal system tended to legitimise its laws and to moderate criticism that could undermine it. Those who put a premium on the building of a modern state allowed the utility of customary law in a society perceived as culturally different. That customs concerning women stirred so little British reaction followed from the marginalisation of women that was intrinsic to both perceptions and that was effected to facilitate the maintenance of law and order. This marginalisation was a major factor defining the nature of women's civil status in the emerging state.

The British official position during the Mandate period and after Iraq's re-occupation during the Second World War thwarted any attempt to interfere with the TCCDR or with customs affecting women by British administrators, Iraqi urban politicians, state officials, lawyers, nationalist journalists, and even tribal leaders. In 1933, tribal leaders were engaged in a process of drafting an amendment to the TCCDR and a detailed proposal was submitted to the king, just before he died. These same shaikhs or their relatives resubmitted an identical draft to the British ambassador in 1944.[30] The shaikhs' proposed law, the 'Tribal Code', set broader criteria for its application than did the TCCDR. In an effort to distance the state from tribal affairs, 'tribal magistrates' were to

---

29 Ibid., p 46, pp 55–56, 58.
30 Iraq Police, Abstract of Intelligence, No. 13, 28 March 1933, Air Ministry, Royal Air Force, Overseas Commands, Air 23/589, vol. XV, TNA; Tribal Code: Draft Law, February 1944, FO 624/38/493, TNA.

be put at the head of the tribal judicial system in place of state administrative officials. State officials would be prohibited not only from interfering in cases lying within the jurisdiction of tribal arbitrators, but also and in stark contrast to the regulation from arresting tribesmen involved in such cases.

Unlike the TCCDR, however, which left shaikhs and tribal arbitrators free to prescribe tribal custom, several chapters in this proposal delineated certain aspects of tribal law. Chapter VI, for example, contained several articles directly or indirectly dealing with customs affecting women. These articles challenged numerous British perceptions of tribal law pertaining to women. Whereas the British tended to assume that the killing of a woman for 'sexually inappropriate behaviour' was a foregone conclusion, the tribal leaders' proposal suggested otherwise. It stipulated that a woman 'compelled to commit adultery' was not considered guilty of an offence providing she reported it to her family within two days of the act. Thus, a woman who divulged to her family that she had been raped could save herself from death. The code also attempted to deter incidents of rape by meting out punishments to rapists. It also allowed marriage as an alternative following the seduction of a virgin. As for the handing over of women as part of a settlement in blood disputes, whereas the British assumed that tribes favoured this choice for subduing animosities, the proposal mentioned no such option. Under the title 'Murder and Blood Money', the proposal stated that 'blood-money in respect of a murdered person shall in general consist of 70 dinar'. A somewhat vague clause also restricted the *nahwa* (sanctioning it only in a case of a man marrying a woman 'of a condition unbecoming of his family').[31]

The British officials found the proposal presented to King Faysal 'too fantastic' to deserve further consideration, certainly not any legislative discussion. When it was resubmitted in the 1940s, official noted tribal leaders' efforts to limit state intervention in their affairs and commented that the proposed code left the government so little authority in tribal matters that even contemplating its acceptance was out of the question. The fact that the proposal exhibited a more moderate version of customary law and paved the way for legislation dealing with customs that were perceived as 'foreign to British judicial tradition' either escaped officials or was considered inconsequential. In fact, in 1944 one senior official, apparently C. C. Aston, political adviser to the Iraqi government, simply dismissed the chapter in which tribal leaders allowed legislation emphasising the monetary settlement of blood disputes, restricted

---

31 Tribal Code: Draft Law.

men's intervention in their female relative's marriage, set deterrents to acts that might lead to honour murders, and enabled the marriage of lovers who had eloped – saying merely that this section of the code was 'inconsistent with tribal practice'.[32]

Whether clauses concerning women in the 'Tribal Code' were a better reflection of the nature of customs prevalent in the Iraqi countryside or whether they were the result of a strategy serving the shaikhs' agenda is unclear. Willingness to modify customs criticised by the British, the king, and Iraqi urban intellectuals could serve shaikhs seeking to extend their influence and minimise state intervention in their affairs. It is also possible, however, that this relative leniency regarding women was in fact a reflection of the reality in the Iraqi countryside. There is evidence to indicate that customs prevalent in rural areas under the mandate and the monarchy were not static. What should be emphasised here, however, is British reaction. The British had been presented with a golden opportunity to deal through state law with customs concerning women that they perceived as 'foreign to British judicial tradition'. But they refused to do away with the TCCDR, which allowed them such firm control over the 'tribal system'. The TCCDR was seen as the proper tool of control, and 'tribal practices', including those detrimental to women, were a main justification for deploying it. Thus, in the 1930s, the 'Tribal Code', which was intended to replace the regulation, was summarily dismissed; in 1944, when tribal leaders resubmitted the proposal, the British again rejected it, commenting that 'the dear old regulation of Sir Henry Dobbs has survived all attack and continues to be the cornerstone of the administrative building [in Iraq].'[33]

In 1951 some amendments were introduced to the TCCDR, but despite strong opposition calling for its annulment, the regulation remained in force. In fact, British administrator and author Stephen Longrigg in 1953, described the Tribal Criminal and Civil Disputes Regulation as 'one of the most valuable legacies of the British regime [to Iraq].'[34] This legacy, however, constructed Iraqi women as tribal possessions, abandoned outside state jurisdiction, rather than citizens whose rights and liberties should be protected.

A century after the First World War the notion that it was a watershed in gender relations and a catalyst of change for women's citizenship status has

---

32 Ibid.

33 Ibid.

34 Stephen H. Longrigg, *Iraq, 1900 to 1950: A Political, Social, and Economic History* (Oxford University Press, London: 1953) p 171.

been revisited. Historians' early emphasis that the war can be viewed as a catalyst for women's legal rights insofar as it put women's suffrage on the political agenda holds true only for a limited number of countries in Europe.[35] The First World War, moreover, was a *world* war and further study on citizenship and the war outside the European continent is desirable. The case of Iraq supports that such research will result not only in a more nuanced global view on war-related change but also further erode the watershed thesis. Indeed, the First World War was a setback rather than a catalyst for Iraqi women's citizenship.

---

35 Hämmerle, Überegger, and Bader-Zaar, 'Introduction', p 10 and p 14 note 23.

5

From anti-imperial dissent to national consent: the First World War and the formation of a trans-sectarian national consciousness in Lebanon

Mark Farha

'There now is no Muslim, Christian, Druze and Jew amongst us. For the scaffolds were erected for all alike. And the famine claimed the lives of all equally. And the locusts descended on everybody. This war has melded us all together in its boiling pot [*saharatnā fī bawtiqatihā*], so that we now are Syrians, Lebanese and Palestinians without distinction of religion or denomination.'[1]

Khalīl Sa'āda taking stock in 1917

As is indicated in the above quote by Khalil Sa'ada (1857–1934), a trans-sectarian spirit of solidarity emanated out of the cauldron of the First World War. Not only did the crippling famine of 1915 claim both Christian and Muslim lives; periodic repression and press censorship had already alienated authors,

1 K. Sa'āda, 'Kitāb Maftūh 'ilā as-Sūriīn wa al-Lubnāniīn wa al-Filistīniīn', in *Silsilat al-'A'māl al-Majhūla* (Dar al Rayes, Beirut: 1987) p 140.
'This chapter was made possible by NPRP grant # 6 – 028 – 5 – 006 from the Qatar National Research Fund (a member of Qatar Foundation). The statements made herein are solely the responsibility of the author.'

editors and activists of all confessions during Hamidian and Young Turk rule. This is not to paint a picture of an idyllic trans-sectarian harmony or homogeneity. For the political orientation of the various dissident groups in the period 1876–1920 was fluid, and communal faultlines were evident in the ownership and political orientation of the major newspapers in Beirut and Damascus. Yet in the shadow of the horrific dislocation wrought by the First World War, and the lethal contagion of emerging national and religious chauvinisms, disillusionment had set in, as ethno-nationalistic separatisms won the day in the Balkans, Anatolia and Palestine. With Ottomanism discarded, and Turkism resented by Muslim and Christian Arab intellectuals alike, inter-confessional polarisations softened; a still inchoate mix of Arabism and Syrian and Lebanese nationalism emerged as the default solution. To be sure, a communal rationale may still have coloured the conception and embrace of a new political identity and entity (kiyān). This was particularly the case for Maronite Christians who – unlike the geographically more spread and urbanised Orthodox – feared the prospect of being subordinated to a larger, pan-Arab or Syrian state dominated by a Muslim majority. But as Khalil Saadeh indicates, the shared suffering spawned a new consciousness which was reflected in symbolic and concrete acts of unity spanning the sectarian divide. This chapter reviews this crystallisation of Muslim-Christian cooperation and political secularism which the cataclysm of the First World War helped to spawn.

Reflecting the political turmoil and rapid transformations of this era, the political orientation of the proliferating dissident groups in the period 1876–1920 was neither monolithic nor etched in stone.[2] At the dawn of the twentieth century, a whole plethora of Syrian and Lebanese opposition groups began raising the pitch of open agitation against the repressive policies which marked Hamīdian autocracy, Young Turk military rule after 1909, and, subsequently, the French Mandate after 1920. Vestiges from this traumatic, intrigue-laden period in late Ottoman history are still apparent in the contemporary Lebanese political system, such as the law governing the formation of political organisations and parties which was drafted in 1909 and remains in force until

---

2 There had been sporadic slogans for a full Arab istiqlāl in local papers as early as 1858, Consul Skene reported from Aleppo that 'the Muslim population of Northern Syria hoped for a separation from the Ottoman Empire and the formation of a new Arabian state under the Sharif of Mecca'. Moshe Ma'oz, Ottoman Reform in Syria and Palestine, 1840–1861: The Impact of the Tanzimat on Politics and Society (Clarendon Press, Oxford: 1968) p 246.

the current day.[3] Dubbed the 'Law of Midhat Pasha', this important piece of legislation explicitly prohibited the formation of secret organisations, betraying the importance of the latter at this historical juncture.

Indeed, the (clandestine) opposition movements which emerged in defiance of the Hamīdian regime often functioned as a forum for inter-ethnic and trans-religious cooperation in pursuit of a common goal of independence; plethoric as their number was, they were not all of the same political stripe. There were CUP cells in Beirut, Damascus and Istanbul which continued to support a quasi-secular Ottoman state in the form of a constitutional, parliamentary monarchy. Other factions were veering towards a Lebanese national agenda such as was the case with the Lebanese Union of 1909 founded by Antoine Jummayil, Dawūd Barakāt and Adīb Yūsuf, the 'Association of the Cedar of Lebanon' founded in 1910 under the leadership of (subsequent President) Bishāra al-Khūrī, 'ādil Arslān and Habīb Pasha Sa'd, or *Nahda Lubnān* founded by Nawm Mukarzil and Ibrāhīm Najjār. The secularism of some of these opposition groups, such as that of the 'Central Party of Syrian Unity',[4] was still not of a comprehensive kind. Another case in point is the *Jam'īyat al-'Arabīya al- Fatāt* which was founded in Paris in 1911 in opposition to the Young Turks' oppressive push at centralisation. Its stated goal was to 'detach itself from the worm-eaten Ottoman trunk.'[5] Though self-avowedly secular in

---

3 The Ministerial decision n0.60/93 in fact added an additional clause requiring all political parties to obtain the permission of the Cabinet before registering with the Ministry of the Interior. On August 8, 2005 this law was abrogated. Today there still is no specific law regulating the establishment of parties proper in Lebanon as the Ottoman Law of 1909 is a generic law for all non-governmental 'associations'.

4 The fourth article of the party (headed by Abd al Rahmān Shahbandir, Fāris Nimr, Yakub Sarruf, Rashīd Ridā, Mukhtar al-Sulh) called for civil laws and decentralisation in Syria 'with the exception of personal status laws which are to remain as they are'. 'Isām Khalīfa, 'A La Récherce D'une Politique Ou D'un Concept De Secularisation Dans Le Liban Multiconfessionnel (1858–1975)' (Doctoral Thesis, Sorbonne University, Paris: 1980) p 56. The same incomplete endorsement of secularism was apparent in the leading liberal journals of the time such as al-'Ahd and al-Jadīd. The Sharī'a courts were never put in question in this time, though leading liberal voices of the Sunni elite such as Salīm 'Alī Salīm, Riyād al-Sulh and 'Abdullāh al-Mashnūq did were calling for a separation of Islam and Arabism on the one hand and religion and state on the other.
See: Hasan Sa'b, *The Arab Federalists in the Ottoman Empire* (Djambatan, Amsterdam: 1958).
5 Sa'b, *The Arab Federalists in the Ottoman Empire*, 207. Membership did not exceed seventy from 1911–1918. It was only after 1918 when al-Fatāt became the chief beneficiary of its previous alliance with the Hashemites that larger groups of people tried to join, leading the

its political orientation, *Fatāt* would support the campaign of Sharīf Husyan and endorse numerous calls to *jihād* for pragmatic reasons. Most importantly, like most dissident groups, *al-Fatāt* was confined to a small membership and failed to make significant inroads.

It was Jamīl Ma'lūf's *'Sūrīyā al-Fatāt'* which spelled out perhaps the clearest platform of Muslim-Christian unity and political secularism at this time, calling for a total separation of religious and civil powers and a national unification of education across Syria. In his Cairene exile, Ma'lūf issued a plea for human rights across the Ottoman Empire in *La Turquie Novelle et Les Droits de L'Homme*. Confessing his continued fear of Hamīdian censorship, Ma'lūf obliquely mentions the 'painful crisis' in Lebanon, but preferred to defer a more detailed discussion of Lebanon's predicament 'to a later, more opportune date.'[6]

Yet another opposition group espousing a (pan-)Syrian agenda was the Syrian-Palestinian Congress.[7] Founded by Rashīd Ridā along with a host of other Syrian Sunni notables such as Shakib Arslān, Mūsā al-Husaynī and Ihsān al-Jabrī, it suffered from a lack of sectarian diversity,[8] in the same way the Christian-dominated counterpart organisations lacked significant Muslim participation.[9] However, after its schism in 1927 one branch of the party – the faction of Michel Lutfallah and 'Abd al-Rahmān Shahbandar – renounced the Islamic revivalism which marked the discourse of Rashīd Ridā and Shakīb Arslān and even veered towards an embracing a 'Greater Lebanon' as it had become a *fait accompli* over against the objection of (largely Muslim) Lebanese unionists after 1920.[10] Thus, the Party of Arab Independence – which counted such noted figures as 'Ādil Arslān, Riyād Sulh and Rashīd Ridā amongst its members – reiterated its plan to constitute an Arab, Damascus-based Emirate.

---

al-Fatāt vanguard to found the *Arab Independence Party* to absorb the new recruits after 1918. James Gelvin, *Divided Loyalties: Nationalism and Mass Politics in Syria at the Close of Empire* (University of California Press, Berkeley: 1998) p 65.

6 Jamīl Ma'alūf, *Turkiyā al-Jadīdah wa-ḥuqūq al-Insān* (Maṭba'at al-Manāẓir, Sao Paulo: 1908) p 25.

7 Stephen Hemsley Longrigg, *Syria and Lebanon under French Mandate* (Oxford University Press, London: 1958) p 143.

8 The notable Maronite exception was the co-President and financier of the Congress, the wealthy businessman Michel Lutfallāh.

9 Asher Kaufman, *Reviving Phoenicia: the Search for Identity in Lebanon* (I.B. Tauris, London: 2004) p 198.

10 Kaufman, *Reviving Phoenicia*, p 240.

With nationalism in the air, we find that the discourse of 'Phoenicianism'[11] took on more strident tones just as Islamist ideologies became more pronounced in wake of the First World War. Antonius notes that it is only after the advent of Young Turk despotism in 1909 that Arab nationalism got a decidedly Islamist imprint in such organisations as *al-Qahtānīya* of Amīn Quzma or *al-Hizb al-Lāmarkazīya al-Idārīya al-'Uthmānīya* founded by the Lebanese exile Iskandar 'Ammūn.[12] Secular notions of equality and national unity came to imbue the discourse of Islamism and Phoenicianism alike, particularly in light of the 1909 failure.

Thus, the *Alliance Libanaise* was founded in Cairo in 1909 by Yūsuf al-Sawda, who would subsequently assume a leading role as the head of the *Hizb al-Ittihād al-Lubnānī* – the first party to explicitly embrace the idea of an expanded *Grand Liban*[13] – and as one of the drafters and main sponsor of the precursor to the National Pact of 1943. Sawda's role in formulating the fundamental premises of an independent, inter-communal, geographically expanded Lebanese state proved pivotal. While Sawda described both Arabs and Turks as invading *ghuzāt,* and while he promoted Lebanon as the haven of the Christians (*'mau'il al-masīhīīn'*), his brand of Lebanese nationalism was explicit in its insistence on the inclusion Muslims as fellow Lebanese citizens.[14]

For most Muslims and a number of Christians, however, it was the Ottoman State and the (dashed) promise it held out of secular egalitarianism and common citizenry as propagated in 1908 which was to remain the political umbrella under which protection was sought from an encroaching West, at least up until the Young Turk July Revolution. In fact, Midhat Pasha, the

---

11 The first writer to speak of 'Phoenician Lebanon' was possibly Tannūs al-Shidyāq (1784–1861), though his was a pluralistic, religiously heterogeneous feudal confederacy as opposed to the ethnocentric Phoenicia propagated by some right-wing Christian factions during the 1975 Civil War. Subsequently, Phoenicianism figured prominently in the writings of Charles Qurm, Ferdinand Tayyān's *La Nationalité Maronite* and Jouplain's (aka Nujayam), *La Question du Liban*. See Iliya F. Harik, *Politics and Change in a Traditional Society: Lebanon, 1711–1845* (Princeton University Press, Princeton, New Jersey: 1968) p 146.

12 George Antonius, *The Arab Awakening: the Story of the Arab National Movement* (Hamish Hamilton, London: 1938) p 109.

13 Presided by Antūn al-Jummayil, a petition was sent to Istanbul in 1910 asking for direct, popular elections, the restitution of previously enjoyed privileges (*imtīyāzāt*) and the return of the Biqā' as Bishāra al-Khūrī notes in his memoirs. Bishāra al-Khūrī, *Hāqāiq Lubnānīya,* 3 vols. (Manshūrāt al-Harf, Beirut: 1961) p 81.

14 Yūsuf al-Sawda, *Fī Sabīl Lubnān* (Alexandria: Madrasat al-Farīr, 1919) p 10.

erstwhile Ottoman governor of Syria, had still equated 'the Lebanese' with the 'Maronite Christians', reflecting the common linguistic conflation of 'Lebanese' and 'Christian' at the turn of the century:

> As France was supporting the Lebanese, England found herself to support the Druze...all these influences produced the very worst effect on the country, for one party of the Christians cherish a dream of union with Lebanon, whilst...the Mussulmans can only marvel at the disorder.[15]

Half a century later, after Midhat's elimination, 'Abdul Ḥamīd's toppling in 1909, and in particular after the pro-Turkish, anti-Arab policies imposed by the new interior minister Talat Pasha after 1910, Christian and Muslim reformers alike began to harbour increasing resentment of what were considered discriminatory, acrimonious Young Turk policies at odds with the previously advertised slogans of liberty, egality, justice, unity and fraternity.[16] Whereas Sultan 'Abdul Ḥamīd had actively recruited (largely Sunni) Arab administrators, many an Arab graduate of Western and Ottoman law schools now saw his career hopes dashed by Turkish bias in appointment policies. This discrimination against Arabs first became apparent in the central administration as al-'Asaylī lamented as early as 1908.[17] After 1911, the ethnic and linguistic bias extended to the provincial administration as well when Talat Bey discharged most qā'imaqāms and mutaṣarrifs of Arab descent. 'Turkification' thus continued to block the career paths of an ascending Arab middle class. On the one hand, the post-Tanzimāt era enabled a segment of the local Arab elites to study in Istanbul's modern military schools (ḥarbīya mektebi) and other prestigious institutions, yet on the other hand this new Arab administrative and military elite could scarcely find adequate employment in both the central and provincial administration, particularly after 1911, so that both (Arab) 'ulamā' and former CUP members in Beirut and Damascus were 'lost' to nascent

---

15 Midhat Pasha in a letter to the Grand Vizier, Sa'īd Pasha. March 29, 1879. 'Alī 'Midhat Bey, *The Life of Midhat Bey: A Record of His Services, Political Reforms, Banishment and Judicial Murder* (J.Murray, London: 1903) p 181.

16 Kawākibī articulated what some deem the contours of an anti-Turkish Arab nationalism. 'Abd al-Raḥmān al-Kawākibi, *Tabā'i'u al-Istibdād wa Masārī'u al-Isti'bād*, Muhammad Jamāl Taḥḥān (ed) (al-Awā'il, Damascus: 2003).

17 Mahmoud Ḥaddād, 'The Rise of Arab Nationalism Reconsidered', *International Journal for Middle Eastern Studies* 2, no. 26 (May 1994) p 208.

Arab, Syrian and Lebanese nationalisms which often, though not invariably, displayed a secular orientation.[18] Even a *bona fide* pan-Islamist like Rashīd Riḍā would be forced to condemn 'Young Turks who discriminated against and undermined the Arabs and Syrians at a time when they are in dire need of cohesion and unity.'[19] Abdel-Ghani Arayssi's *al-Mufid* newspaper went even further in labeling the Turkification policies as downright 'anti-Islamic'.[20] Like many of his colleagues, Arayssi would be led to the gallows on 6 May 1916. His parting words manifest an ideological transformation from pan-Islamism to the embrace of a nascent Lebanese-Arab nationalism: 'The glory of the Arabs is coming. States are not formed save through the suffering of their heroes. And ours form the basis for Lebanese independence.'[21]

The public execution of Muslim and Christian dissidents was just the culmination of a number of policies imposed from 1914–1919 by the Young Turk triumvirate which fed a growing alienation. All schools instructing in French were ordered closed in Beirut, with the notable exception of the *Alliance Israelite* school.[22] Regional identities were further fomented by the Young Turks'

---

18 Nonetheless, Syrian Christians like Zaydan and Anṭūn were afraid of the ramifications of a potential Young Turk failure and thus remained firm advocates of Ottoman unity. When Atatürk finally established the secular Turkish republic, Kurd 'Alī (1876–1953) severely criticised the latter's reforms. See Nāzik Saba Yārid, *Secularism in the Arab World* (Saqi Books, London: 2002) pp 34, 159.

19 Riḍā adds that 'it is important not to vent our hostilities on the Turks in general so as not to weaken the Caliphate. Rather, we should focus our efforts on uniting the Arabs so as to create a new and powerful force that is equipped to defend themselves, to press for their independence if the Ottoman state is defeated and to safeguard their rights if the Ottoman state emerges victorious, as is the wish of every Muslim.' Yunan Labib Rizq, 'Looking Towards the Levant', *al Ahram Weekly*, (20 September 1999).

20 Eliezer Tauber, 'The Press in Syria in the Late Ottoman Period', *Die Welt des Islams*, Bd. 30, Nr.1/4 (1990), p 172.

21 Chamie, Vol. I, p 59.

22 Mas'ūd Dāhir, *Tārīkh Lubnān Al-Ijtimā'ī: 1914–1926*, (Dar an Nahar: Beirut, 1974) p 177. The CUP's ties to the nascent Zionist movement were a topic of controversy even within Young Turkish circles. See the accusation leveled by Serif Pasha against CUP members who were Freemasons and Zionists. Hanioğlu, *The Young Turks in Opposition*, p 19ff. It should be noted however that an irascible Cemal Pasha at the end of his reign cast all caution to the wind once his defeat was sealed and expelled 7000 Jews from Jaffa, causing an embarrassing rift in the otherwise solid and amicable Turkish-Zionist alliance. See Feroz Ahmad, 'The Special Relationship: The Committee of Union and Progress and the Ottoman Jewish Political Elite, 1908–1918', in Avigor Levy (ed) *Jews, Turks, Ottomans* (Syracuse University Press, Syracuse N.Y.: 2002).

enforcement of Turkish *in lieu* of Arabic in state courts and schools in 1909, a policy initially pursued by 'Abdul Hamīd II, but one which until then had hitherto never been implemented in the Levant.[23] While initially nominally committed to Ottoman pluralism, the Young Turks drive at Turkification is better conceived as a partial inheritance from 'Abdul Hamīd who – while increasing the number of Arabs in the central administration – first decreed Ottoman Turkish the official language of all state institutions at all levels.[24]

The resultant anti-CUP sentiments could forge alliances between (Arab) Muslims and Christians in pursuit of a common cause (while conversely collaborators with the 'Turkish tyranny' were equally found amongst opportunistic Christian war profiteers)[25]. In Beirut, opposition to the Young Turks culminated in 1913 with the formation of a short-lived 'Committee of Reform' composed of eighty-six members of all denominations who demanded a form

---

23 Kemal Karpat, *Studies on Ottoman Social and Political History*, (Brill, Leiden: 2002) p 13.
24 To be sure, Hamīd's *firmāns* never affected Syria since Midhat and Aḥmad Ḥamdī Pasha (1879–1885) had bowed to the demands of Syrian notables and reformers to retain Arabic as the language of administration. While Arab delegates and students gained access to the *Mulkiye* and *Yildiz* under 'Abdul Ḥamīd, the latter also turkified higher positions of local bureaucracies, again prefiguring the later CUP policies. Şükrü Hanioğlu has perceptively pointed out that 'although the [Ḥamīdian] state endeavored to Ottomanise its subjects, the symbols used to evoke a supranational culture were Turkish.' Şükrü Hanioğlu, 'Turkish Nationalism and the Young Turks: 1889–1908', in Fatma Müge Göçek (ed) *Social Constructions of Nationalism in the Middle East* (Albany, State University of New York Press: 2002) p 86; Ḥaddād, 'The Rise of Arab Nationalism Reconsidered', p 216.
25 Famous examples include the Sursocks and Bayhums who cornered the market in the grain trade. Opportunism was also evident in the Maronite poet Shiblī Mallāt's effusive laudations to the Young Turks during the First World War. He would *ex post facto* justify this slip of the pen as a survival tactic, claiming that he was forced to eulogise (*madaha mukrahan*). See *al-Mashriq*, August 1920, p 636. Mallāt, to be sure, had a double motivation to remain on good terms with Istanbul as the founder of a journal in 1906 (*al-Watan*) and as an occupant of numerous posts in the Ottoman administration of Mount Lebanon. Likewise, Shakīb Arslān could move from an ardent Ottomanist to a self-promoting Francophile under the Mandate. Journals such as *al-Mashriq* and *al-Jinān* would preface their first editions with showering grandiloquent praise to the 'Sultan of Sultans' and the 'Government of the Sunna'. See opening editorial, *al-Mashriq*, First Edition, 1898, p 2. Defying the orders of Istanbul could spell the end of a publication as Ahmad Fāris al-Shidiyāq discovered when his pathbreaking *al-Jawā'ib* which was forced to shut down in 1879 after it declined to publish an Ottoman statement against the Egyptian Khedeve. See 'Azmeh and Tarābulsī, Ahmad Fāris al-Shidiyāq: Su'lūk al-Nahda', in *al-Nāqid* no. 79 (January 1995) p 26.

of 'home rule' for the *sanjak* of Mount Lebanon.[26] These hopes were deflated with the execution in Beirut of fourteen dissident Christian and Muslim activists in what came to be known as 'Martyrs' Square' on 6 May 1916. The 'martyrs' had appealed to the French consul in Beirut – none other than later Foreign Minister Georges-Picot – for support in gaining independence. The incriminating letters were obtained by Cemal Pasha, putatively thanks to a tip from Philip Zalzal, a former *dragoman* translator for Georges-Picot who had kept the files hidden in the Beirut French consulate. On 6 May 1916, fourteen dissidents were hanged in Beirut and seven in Damascus. These were however not the only executions based on the Georges-Picot files. On 6 June, two Christians (the Khazin brothers) and two Muslims (the Mahmasani brothers) were sent to the gallows in Beirut. This sectarian equilibrium set a precedent until the present day in Lebanon, whereby it is all but impossible to sentence to death a member of one major sect without a counterpart from another sect.

The 1915 famine probably was the single most incisive tragedy to beset Lebanon. Inhabitants of southern Lebanon and northern Palestine suffered and perished from swarms of locusts, rampant inflation and the war-induced disruption of trade routes. Elisabeth Thompson has estimated that Mount Lebanon – suffocated by a punitive siege imposed by Cemal Pasha and a recalcitrant decision by Beirut's governor Azmi Bey to stop vital US Aid administered through the Red Cross[27] – may have lost approximately 18% of its population to conscription and famine in the First World War, an unusually high decimation which far outstripped the human toll of 5% in France and Germany in the war. Indicatively, the Turkish word for 'conscription' *serferbelik* came to be synonymous with "famine" in Levantine Arabic.[28] The victims

---

26 Nicholas Z. Ajay, 'Political Intrigue and Suppression in Lebanon during World War I', *International Journal of Middle Eastern Studies* 5 (1974) p 143. British and French intelligence gathering was at its height upon the eruption of WWI. The demarcation line of respective spheres of influence seems to have been Sidon, with the French controlling the northern coastline and the British the southern one. Under the aegis of Cemal Pasha, the commander of the 4th army, the Young Turks abrogated the *Reglement* of 1861 and eliminated the nascent Lebanese independence cells. Cemal Pasha would later act as a liaison between Mustafa Kemal and the Bolsheviks in Russia.

27 Umar Abu Nasr, *Al-Harb al-Uthma, 1914–1917,* vol. 17, (Bayrūt, al-Majmūʻah al-Tārīkhīyah al-Muṣawwarah: 1938) p 20.

28 See Elisabeth Thompson, *Colonial Citizens* (Columbia University Press, New York: 2000) p 38.

of the massive famine between 1914 and 1917 were geographically centred in northern Mount Lebanon and thus overwhelmingly Christians, yet beyond Turkish bias, the allied blockade which was designed to produce 'shortages in supply' and thus stir the Arabs to revolt, exacerbated matters. Only in November of 1919 did the allies effectively put an end to the calamity by importing tons of grain, rice and vegetables.[29]

Even if the largely (Maronite) Christian areas of northern Lebanon were hit hardest, the First World War famine also claimed several victims amongst the Sunni population of Beirut and the Shia population of Jabal 'Āmil.[30] In his history of Jabal 'Āmil during the war, Sulaymān Ḍāhir recounts that vital grain supplies from the Hawrān were being siphoned off to Beirut, with war profiteering running rampant, so that inhabitants of southern Lebanon and northern Palestine suffered famine as well. The economic blockade imposed by the Allies – and the manifold disruptions of trade – in 1915 also served to strain inter-communal relations between the erstwhile trading partners of the Shia of Jabal 'Amil and the Druze of the Ḥawrān.[31]

Despite its gravity, the famine never received any official recognition, in contrast to the execution of opposition figures on 6 May 1916 which was commemorated as Martyrs' Day.[32] Indicatively, the memory of the Beiruti

---

29 Joseph G. Shāmī, *Le Mémorial Du Liban: 1861–1943* (Beirut), vol. I, p 45. According to one contemporary witness, 'the discrimination program of the Turks was not based on religion but on politics. But then again, most of Mount Lebanon was Christian. Many Muslims fled to Syria.' Ḥalīm Ashqar cit. in Ajay, 'Political Intrigue and Suppression in Lebanon', p 152
30 For an earlier study of the famine and its regional political parameters, particularly the role of the Allied blockade of the Syrian coast see Linda Schatkowski, 'The Famine of 1915–18 in Greater Syria', in J. Spagnolo (ed), *Essays in Honor of Albert Hawrānī* (Ithaca Press, Reading, UK: 1992) pp 229–258.
31 Tamara Chalabi, *The Shi'is of Jabal 'Amil and the New Lebanon Community and Nation State, 1918–1943* (Palgrave Macmillan, New York: 2006) p 14. By contrast, a local Arab dispatch mentions that the Turkish authorities prevented Western aid shipments. *Al-Muqattam*, March 30 – April 1, 1916 as cited in Arnold Toynbee, *Turkey: A Past and A Future* (D.H. Doran, New York: 1917) p 33. Lastly, tales of Young Turk atrocities against the local population may also have been fed by an inherent European racism which came to the fore in this letter of a German school teacher to the *Reichstag* in which prophesised, with perhaps too much confidence, that 'that the Turks proper will never achieve anything in trade, industry, or science.' This attitude was internalised by Tekin Alp, who nonetheless believed in the potential improvement of character through education. See Toynbee, *Turkey: A Past and A Future*, p 45.
32 Moawwad attributes this official neglect to the large number of Christian victims which

martyrs was itself subject to the political dichotomy of the day: Until 1937, two martyrs' days were celebrated: one unionist, Syro-Lebanese commemoration on 6 March, and another, Mandate-sponsored official commemoration on 2 September. In 2007, the Lebanese government under then Prime Minister Siniora took the decision to abolish this holiday, erasing the memoralisation of one of the rare instances of trans-confessional solidarity in Lebanon's contentious history.

A final verdict on this calamity must still be withheld. Even Lebanese history books diverge along confessional lines in their interpretation of the famine.[33] Still, its crucial role in eroding the legitimacy of the Ottoman state and fomenting local identities seems indisputable. Suffice it to say that fresh memories of the horrors of the First World War left an indelible mark on the subsequent Christian and Muslim founding fathers of the Lebanese Republic, including Bishāra al-Khūrī and Riyād al-Sulh, members of the leading Shia families Zayn, Khalil and Ussayran (all of whom were arrested by the Turkish authorities), as well as the founder of the staunchly secular Syrian Nationalist Party, Antūn Sa'āda. A young and brash Sa'āda – still smarting under the death of his mother during the First World War – staunchly refused to carry the Ottoman flag during a reception held in Broumanna for Cemal Pasha and tore the Ottoman flag to shreds in intrepid defiance of the presence of the feared commander of the 4th Army.[34]

The Levantine legacy of the Young Turks – and the brutal reign of Cemal Pasha in particular – remains fraught with controversy.[35] Even in the estimate

does not lend the famie to act as an inter-communal connector. Yūsuf Mouawwad, 'Jamal Pasha en Une Version Libanaise : L'Usage Positif d'Une Légende Noire', in Olaf Farschid, Manfred Kropp, Stephane Daehne (eds), *The First World War as Remembered in the Countries of the Eastern Mediterranean* (Ergon Verlag, Beirut: 2006) p 440.

33 Reflecting the sectarian lens of history textbooks in Lebanese schools, some textbooks (such as the Evangelical Pine secondary school) still adopt the official Ottoman narrative of a British embargo as the sole reason for the famine while others (such as the Shia Yew school) hold a deliberate Ottoman policy culpable. Kamāl Abū Shadīd, 'The State of History Teaching in Private-Run Confessional Schools in Lebanon', *Mediterranean Journal of Educational Studies* 5, no. 2 (2000).

34 See Adil Bishāra, *Lebanon: Politics of Frustration – the Failed Coup of 1961* (Routledge, London: 2005) p 41.

35 See for instance Muhammad Jamāl Tahhān's fierce critique of Azīz al-'Azma's attempt to de-link secularism from Arab Nationalism and the later from Cemal Pasha's repressive policies in Lebanon and Syria. *Al-Ijtihād*, v01.54, Spring 2002, p 306. Tahhān – who ironically

of the German general Liman von Sanders – a key ally of the Young Turks – it was Cemal Pasha's brutal crackdown which dealt the final death blow to any Turkish-Levantine alliance and managed to alienate Muslims and Christians alike, precipitating the formation of joint, nationalist *fora* and a plethora of opposition movements of variegated communal identities. As Melanie Schulze Tanielian has underscored, the First World War was a 'political event that was both destructive *and* formative in the civilian realm.'[36]

One salient instance of Muslim-Christian solidarity was evident in the press when the editors of the Sunni-owned *Al-Ittihad al-Uthmani* published an editorial in the Christian-led paper *Lisan ul-Hal* conjointly with the Christian-run paper *al-Thabet* which published its editorial in *al-Ittihad al Uthmani.*[37] When the Reform Society of Beirut was dissolved by the Turkish authorities in 1913, Lebanese papers of all stripes joined in another coordinated symbolic protest by framing their front pages with a black border.[38] The spirit of solidarity even stretched to the highest clerical levels. Cemal Pasha, upon asking the Maronite Patriarch Huwayyik why the latter lobbied for the release of Druze (rather than merely Maronite) exiles as well, was astounded to hear the prelate respond that his was not just a Maronite, but a Lebanese cause.[39]

While the prior dichotomy of predominantly Christian, Lebanese nationalist-'separatists' and the largely Muslim Arab 'unionists' still obtained, it would be a mistake to conclude that the two poles shared no cause in common, or that individuals could and would not shift their allegiances in this time of flux.[40] After all, Syrian-Lebanese nationalisms were still in their infancy and

---

espouses an anti-secularist Islamist position – accuses al-'Aẓma of attempting to 'whitewash' the bloody episode of Young Turkish quasi-secularism in Lebanon and of using secularism to 'combat Islam.' Şükrü Hanioğlu has provided us with the most nuanced account of this controversial, blood-stained period. See Şükrü Hanioğlu, *The Young Turks in Opposition* (Oxford University Press, New York: 1995) and Hanioğlu 'Turkish Nationalism and the Young Turks 1889–1908.'

36 Melanie Schulze Tanielian, 'Feeding the City: The Beirut Municipality and Politics of Food During World War I', *IJMES* 46, no. 4 (November 2014) p 740.

37 Tauber, p 170.

38 Ibid.

39 Mu'awwad, Yūsuf. 'Jamal Pasha en Une Version Libanaise. L'Usage Positif d'Une Légende Noire', in Olaf Farschid, Manfred Kropp, Stephane Daehne (eds) *The First World War as Remembered in the Countries of the Eastern Mediterranean* (Beiruter Texte und Studien, Orient Institut der DMG Beirut: Ergon Verlag. 2006) p 435.

40 Kamāl Ṣalībī, *The Modern History of Lebanon* (Greenwood Press, Westport: 1965) p 159.

anything but coherent political ideologies with fixed boundaries as seen in Jubrān Khalīl Jubrān's embrace of hybridity in 1916:

> I am a Lebanese and proud of it. I am not an Ottoman and proud of that. I shall remain an Easterner – Easterner in my conduct. Syrian in my desires, Lebanese in my feelings. Regardless of how much I admire Western progress.[41]

Jubrān's colleague, the novelist Amīn al-Rihānī (1876–1940) confirmed that the categories of Syrian and Lebanese still were not cut and dried and that a secular Syrian identity for some superseded any Lebanese patriotism which Rihānī feared would carry confessional connotations:

> I am Syrian first, Lebanese second, and Maronite third. I am Syrian born in Lebanon, and respect the source of my Arabic language. I am a Syrian-Lebanese who believes in the separation of religion from politics, because I realize that the main obstacle to national unity is religious partisanship. The Lebanese idea, i.e., the national sectarian idea, is an old and impotent idea. If we go by it, it will be a devastating blow to us. It was the cause of our defeat and misery in the past, and will be, if it prevails, the reason for our misery in the future.What a narrow conception of Lebanon.[42]

Rihānī's steadfast secularism however was not always congruent with all strands of Syrian (or Arab) anti-colonialism. As late as 1920, the Turkish troops who came to aid the Syrian rebels in their *jihād* against France would carry a flag, Turkish on one side, and Arab on the other with the words 'believers are brothers' emblazoned on it.[43] Five years later, Sultān al-Atrash, the legendary leader of the Druze insurgency in the *hūrān*, grandly vowed to 'make no distinction in religion or sects, as our only aim is to obtain our legal rights which belong equally to the sons of Syria.'[44] The rebellion he led, however,

---

41 Jubrān Khalīl Jubrān, *al-Majmū'a al-Kāmila li-Mu'alifāt Jubrān Khalīl Jubrān*, vol. 4 (Dār Sādir, Beirut: 1997) p 208.

42 Amīn Rihānī, *Qalbu Lubnān*, (Dar al-Jil, Beirut: 1971) p 56.

43 'Abdul Karīm Rāfiq, 'Gesellschaft. Wirtschaft und Politische Macht in Syrien. 1918–1925' in Linda Schatkowski and Claus Scharf (eds), *Der Nahe Osten In Der Zwischenkriegszeit* (Franz Steiner, Stuttgart: 1989) p 479.

44 Ibid., pp 426, 469.

bore a heavy confessional-Islamist tint, as is seen in the charged 'holy-war' vocabulary which Aṭrash himself would invoke at its onset, even as he cited the French revolutionary ideals of liberty, egality and fraternity.[45] Sectarianism was, in other words, at once deployed and deplored, instrumentalised and inveighed against by both parties to the conflict. The French cited the raids of armed bands (*'iṣābāt*) against Christians in such regions as Idlib and Tripoli as a pretext for intervention, even as individual Christian clans participated in the fight against the French while a full third of Faysal's advisory cabinet (*majlis al-shūrā*) after 6 October 1918 was staffed by Christians. Two out of nine ministers of his second cabinet formed on 3 March 1920, also were Christian. Even as Faysal and his modernist cabinet repeatedly emphasised their intent not to discriminate in governance according to religious identity, there was no consistency in the secularism of the Sharifian regime which after all based much of its legitimacy on the claim of the 'Sultan of the Arabs and Caliph of the Muslims' to prophetic descent.[46] Moreover, as the French threat grew along with shipments of French armaments to minorities in Syria, the references to Islamic rhetoric proliferated along with sporadic sectarian attacks in northern Syria. Incidentally, aside from the onset of the French occupation, it was the ascendancy of Turkish secular nationalism and Mustafa Kemal's final abandonment of pan-Islamist goals which would seal the Syrian revolt's fate. With the conclusion of the French-Turkish pact in London on 11 March 1921, the rebellion was stripped of vital Turkish support before it was launched.

Lebanese nationalism developed out of this crucible of the First World, even if its contours – and geographic borders – still lacked clarity.[47] After all, secular strands had pervaded Ottomanism, Syrian and Arab nationalism alike, so that Lebanism, even if it could hark back to a long legacy of quasi-secularism and proto-nationalism in the Emirate and Mount Lebanon, was not a foregone conclusion.

---

45 Edmond Rabbāth, *La Formation Historique Du Liban Politique Et Constitutionelle* (Librairie Orientale, Beirut: 1973) p 363.

46 Fred Lawson, 'The Northern Syrian Revolts of 1919–1921 and the Sharifian Regime: Congruence or Conflict of Interests and Ideologies', in Thomas Phillip and Christoph Schumann (eds) *From the Syrian Land to the States of Syria and Lebanon* (Würzburg, 2004) p 270.

47 Ibrāhīm Bek al-Aswad *Dalīl Lubnān*, (Baabda: al-Maktaba al-Uthmaniyya, 1906), p 139 in which the borders of the 1926 Republic are prefigured.

Kais Firro notes that after 1920 a merging of (predominantly Muslim) Syri-anist and (largely Christian) Lebanese nationalisms occurred, with the latter often borrowing arguments for a secular nationalism from the former.[48] Some-times the two identities were fused in a single person. A perfect example is Shukri Ghānim who was at once member of Sawda's *Alliance Libanaise* in 1909, the founder of the *Comité Central de la Syrie* in 1917 and the *Comité Libanais de Paris* which had been established in 1912 (the Egyptian branch was tellingly called *Comité Libano-Syrien*). Clearly, Ghānim's foremost preoccupa-tion was to resist the unification of Damascus and Arabia which he deemed a 'violation of history'.[49] By 1919 Ghānim – along with the French – had begun to yield to the logic of communal division and edged towards the embrace of a Lebanese nationalism to counter the threat of greater Syrian-Islamic unity which he surmised was propelling the Arab Revolt and the Emir Faysal.[50]

Ghānim was part of one of two Lebanese Delegations in Versailles in 1919 lobbying for full independence. Commissioned by Decree number 80 of the administrative council of Mount Lebanon, an interconfessional delegation led by Dāūd 'Ammūn, called for an expansion of Mount Lebanon and a return to the natural borders of the Emirate, a popularly elected parliament and French assistance to hasten independence.[51] Since the great powers were still holding parallel negotiations with Faysal, they did not commit themselves to the proposed state as yet so that, after a second promulagation of the admin-istrative council on 20 May 1919, a second delegation headed by Patriarch Huwwayek was dispatched, returning to Lebanon with a written commitment to Lebanese independence signed by President Poincare and Prime Minister Clemenceau.

---

48 The Jesuit Professors at St. Joseph Pierre Martin and Henri Lammens played an important role in propagating the lore of a Syrian homeland. See Kais Firro, 'Lebanese Nationalism versus Arabism: From Būlus Nujaym to Michel Shīḥā', *Middle Eastern Studies* 40, no. 5 (September 2004) p 3.

49 Ibid., p 3.

50 Aziz al-Azmeh has stated that the Arab Revolt 'does not belong to the register of Arab nationalism...It was Arab only in the narrow, ethnological, pre-nationalist sense. It was an Islamist rebellion, undertaken not in the name of the Arabs, but of a Meccan Caliphate.' Aziz al-'Aẓma, 'Nationalism and the Arabs', in Derek Hopwood (ed), *Arab Nation, Arab Nationalism* (St. Martin's Press, New York: 2000) p 69.

51 The members were Maḥmūd Janbulāṭ, 'Abdullāh al-Khūrī, Ibrāhīm Abū Khāṭīr, Tāmir Ḥamāda, 'Abdul Ḥalīm Hajjār and Emile Iddih. Bāsim al-Jisr, *Mithāq 1943* (Dār an-Nahār, Beirut: 1978) pp 45–47.

'Ammūn had himself gone through a very similar transformation as Ghānim. Both had set out as ardent supporters of the 1908 Revolution which had revitalised pro-Ottoman secular liberals as Carole Ḥakīm has shown in a cogent *exposé* of the fluid political identities of this era.[52] A liberal, pluralistic Ottomanism, it was thought, might allow Mount Lebanon to escape the clutches of a parochial, 'clergy-ridden' system. Even the suspended December 23 1876 constitution however, in Article 11, still identified Islam as the religion of state. Just as had been the case in 1876, the administrative council of the *Mutaṣarrifīya* refused to send any delegates to the Ottoman parliament in 1908, so that other avenues had to be pursued.[53] For a brief moment, 'Ammūn even joined the C.U.P, accepting Faysal's invitation to serve as ambassador in Washington, only to be elected in 1920 to the head of the administrative council in which he defended Lebanese claims to autonomy against Damascus and the Zionists.[54] In effect, the unilateral proclamation of a 'United Syrian Kingdom' took the Lebanese Maronites aback. After learning of fifteen Muslim delegates who had joined the Syrian Congress on behalf of Lebanon, another delegation was dispatched to Paris in protest against Syrian claims to Lebanon, leading to a French reaffirmation of Clemenceau's pledge one year earlier to prefer Lebanese national autonomy.[55]

Eventually, Ottomanism had made way for pan-Syrianism and finally for Lebanism. This trajectory is reflected in Ghānim's involvement in the *Ligue Ottoman,* followed by his founding of the *Comité Central Syrien* in 1917 and, finally, upon the dissolution of the latter at the dawn of independence, the *Comité de Defense des Droits du Grand Liban* in 1920. In the shadow of the horrific dislocation of the First World War and the global contagion of national and religious chauvinisms, disillusionment had set in, with corporate, ethnonationalistic separatisms winning the day.

That having been said, contrary to pervasive thought, the nineteenth century champions of an independent Lebanon were not – in the main – advocates of

---

52 Carole Ḥakīm, 'Shifting Identities and Representations of the Nation Amongst the Maronite Secular Elite', in Thomas Phillip and Christoph Schumann (eds), *From the Syrian Land to the States of Syria and Lebanon* (Ergon Verlag, Würzburg: 2004).

53 Ibid., p 246. The concern was that membership in parliament might curtail Lebanese privileges.

54 By establishing a court of cessations independent of Damascus and by opposing the Zionist land claims in the south. Fawwāz Ṭarābulsī, Ṣilāt bi-lā Waṣl: Mīshāl Shīḥā *wa al-Idyūlūjīya al-Lubnānīya* (Riyāḍ al-Rayyes, Beirut: 1999) p 20.

55 Zayn N. Zayn, *The Struggle For Arab Independence* (Caravan, New York: 1960) p 133 and Appendix H.

a communal Christian country. One of the first advocates of the Grand Liban, Yūsuf as-Sawda, explicitly included the Lebanese Muslims and rejected both French and Syrian tutelage.[56] While the administrative council in its declaration of March 12, 1920 explicitly rejected the Syrian Congress proposal of a federal Syria with Lebanon, this did not mean that the threat of (French) colonialism was completely ignored. Rather, for the first time a policy of non-alignment was proclaimed: Lebanon was to enjoy complete autonomy and neither 'be the subject nor object of any war' (*'lā yuharib wa lā yuharab')*[57], a mantra which was to be reformulated as the central plank of the National Pact of 1943 wherein Lebanon was not to serve as 'a passage way nor staging ground' for foreign powers (*'la mamar wa la maqar')*[58].

Still, the question remained: what mode of secular modernity was within the margins of the possible for as unusually pluralistic a society such as Lebanon? And where ought the borders of the prospective state to be drawn? By the end of the Young Turk occupation in 1918, a general consensus had settled amongst a class of urban, largely Christian politicians on the 'natural' boundaries of the Republic (which were predicated on those of the Ma'nite and Shihabite Emirate).[59] It is often forgotten that these borders were first drawn in December 1918 by the Administrative Council under Ḥabīb Pasha Sa'd. Under the subsequent French Mandate, Article 1 of Decree 318 of August 1920 formally codified the geographic borders of the Grand Liban composed of the Cazas of Ba'albak, the Biqā', Rāshayā and Ḥāṣbayā and the Sanjaks of Beirut, Sidon and Tripoli. As the sole state in the region, May 23, 1926 Constitution cannot be reduced to a 'gift' to the Maronites as its detractors are wont to claim. The very boundaries of the new state (by adding Tripoli, Beirut, Sidon and the Bekaa) – ironically supported by Patriarch Huwayyak yet opposed

---

56 al-Sawda, *Fī Sabīl Lubnān*, 10ff. Sawda thus must be distinguished from the group of six Christian exiles who on 12 March 1913 had petitioned the French counsel in Beirut to occupy Syria in order to save the Christians of the Near East.

57 Decree of July 10, 1920 cit. in 'Abd al-Azīz Nawwār (ed), *Wathā'iq Asāsīya min Tārīkh Lubnān al-hadīth, 1517–1920* (Arab University Of Beirut, Beirut: 1974) pp 457–458. The eight signatories of this resolution included the brother of the Patriarch, S'adallah al-Ḥuwwayyik who was arrested by the French before he could reach Damascus to mediate with the Syrian leadership. Zayn, *The Struggle For Arab Independence*, p 150.

58 Basim al-Jisr, *Mithāq 1943*, (Dar al-Nahar, Beirut: 1978) pp 84, 114.

59 Būlus Jouplain (aka Nujayam) (in *La Question du Liban*, Paris 1908) had already suggested the enlargement of the 'Lebanese nation' within Syria in precisely this manner, even though Jabal 'Āmil was conspicuously left out.

by most Maronites – was bound to dilute Christian demographic dominance which had prevailed in the Petit Liban from 1860–1914.The overwhelming majority of war-scarred Christians had expressed their support for an independent Lebanese state during the King-Crane questionnaire in 1919, but the borders remained a contested issue as a small Lebanon was not deemed viable economically, and given that the Orthodox preferred a different set of boundaries which would have granted them, as opposed to the Maronites, the status of the largest Christian demography.[60]

In the end, Lebanon's constitution introduced a novelty: confirming prior decrees passed by the High Commission, the 1926 Constitution is the only one to explicitly delineate a nation's borders in the very first Article 1. This innovation came as a *fait accompli* retort to the Muslim (and occasional Christian) opposition to the new state. At the same time, the creation of the enlarged Republic in 1920 also signaled Lebanon's fuller – if still incomplete – adoption of French secularism.[61] In the decades to come, the political identity of the new state, however, would have to pass through a more arduous process of debate, argumentation and constant re-negotiation of the terms of the prospective social contract.

In navigating the course from this tempestuous sea of virulent nineteenth century communalisms and identities in flux to a more stable shore of nationhood, intellectuals and politicians oriented themselves according to past domestic and foreign lodestars. To the likes of Jamīl Ma'lūf, Yūsuf al-Sawda, Makram Zakour, Khalil Saadeh (and his son Antun), or Buṭrus al-Bustānī's son Salīm al-Bustānī, national sovereignty and secularism, it seemed, were the hallmarks of progress and the ineluctable destiny of the age. This conviction was further strengthened by a large Lebanese exile community in France, the Americas and Egypt who acted as vocal ambassadors of Republicanism. Khalid Saadeh's odyssey, leading him to flee Ottoman and French persecution from

---

60 The 1919 King-Crane commission revealed that all Lebanese Christians wanted independence (with or without a French Mandate). The Orthodox were the only Lebanese Christian community favoring a union with parts of Syria. given the high number of Orthodox in the 'Wadi Nasaara' region. *Thākirat al-Kanīsa*, Jūrj Mughāmis (ed) (Manshūrāt Jāmi'at Sayyidat al-Luwayza, Beirut: 2000) p 128.

61 See Mark Farha, 'Secularism in a Sectarian Society? The Divisive Drafting of the Lebanese Constitution of 1926', in Bali and Lerner (eds) *Constitution Writing, Religion and Democracy,* (Cambridge University Press, Cambridge: 2016); 'Stumbling Blocks to the Secularization of Personal Status Laws in the Lebanese Republic (1926–2013)', *Arab Law Quarterly* (29) 2015, pp 31–55.

Beirut to Cairo to Argentina and Brazil, is a case in point. For the two journals he founded in exile, al Majalla and al Jaridah, became sounding boards for the same ideas of emancipation and anti-sectarianism Beiruti papers such as Michel Zakour's al-Ma'arad promulgated simultaneously.[62] Case in point is Al-Ma'arad's publication of a picture of a Muslim and Christian member of the American University student union shaking hands in front of a flag emblazoned with a juxtaposed crescent and cross and the words "holy union". On the occasion of the prophet's birthday, Christian students presented the gift of a copy of the Quran to their Muslim colleagues.[63] Lebanon had come a long way since the communal fires and jihads of World War I.

Even as the opposition to secular nationalisms began to recede in wake of the trauma inflicted by the First World War, societal confessionalism – and the real and perceived threat of communal hegemonies – still was perceived as a stumbling block to any full political secularisation. But the latter was increasingly advertised as the aspired goal in political discourse. The First World War had spawned a trans-confessional solidarity which had grown on the seedbed of shared sorrow.

Politically, even a sentimentalist like Jibran Khalil Jibran admitted to being shaken out of his stupor by the horrific tragedies and uncharacteristally assumed an active role as secretary of the Syria-Mount Lebanon Relief Committee and, subsequently, the League of Liberation which called for emancipation from "Turkish rule" in a government based on full inter-sectarian equality.[64] Artistically, there was no more vivid expression of this spirit of unity born from searing experience than the original "Martyrs' sculpture" crafted by Yūsuf Huwayyik. This commemoration of a Muslim and Christian women poised in dignified, unifying mourning over the victims of World War I was defaced by vandal journalist Salīm Slīm in 1948, perhaps an omen of the subsequent inter-communal strife. The sublimely simple, limestone masterpiece was ultimately replaced on May 6, 1960 when President Camille Sham'ūn unveiled the melodramatic "Martyrs' Statue" cast in black bronze

---

62 K. Saadeh, Suriya min al Harb wa al Maja' ila Mu'tammar al Sulh, Badr el Hage (ed) (Saadeh Cultural Foundation, Beirut: 2014).

63 Al Ma'arad, (Beirut) March/April, 1922, p.11

64 Adel Bishara, 'A Syrian Rebel: Gibran Khalil Gibran', in The Origins of Syrian Nationhood: Histories, Pioneers and Identity, (New York: Routledge, 2011), p 148. Gibran's seminal poem 'Dead are my People' is one of his best, eloquently expressing the poet's anguish in exile, and the inadequacy of words to lessen the pain of his people.

by the Italian sculptor Mazzucati. Tellingly, Huwayyik's solemn original was left isolated and abandoned in the garden of the Sursuq museum, while the foreign ode to patriotic pathos has since occupied Martyrs' Square, riddled with the bullets of the 1975 Civil War.[65]

---

65 Upon being released from prison after a bare week of internment, Slīm said he had been irritated for a long time by the 'tears and resignation' of the 'ugly' statue, and proudly recounted how he eagerly chipped off the noses and eyes of the two ladies before being stopped and detained by the police. See Joseph G. Shāmī, Le Mémorial Du Liban, Vol.II, p 257; Lisān al-Ḥāāl, 9 September 1948. For the artist's own recollection, see Huwayyik, Yaqzat al-Hajar, A'māl Nahtīya (Dār al-Nahār, Beirut: 2004) p 47.

6

Historicising hunger: the famine in wartime Lebanon and Syria

Najwa al-Qattan

In October 1916, Nasib 'Arida, a Syrian immigrant and editor of the New York City magazine, *al-Funun*, bitterly lamented the apparent (at least to him) passivity of the 'people' in Lebanon and Syria in the face of their humiliation during the First World War. 'Arida expressed his outrage by denying such a people a place in historical memory; in fact, he denied them the right to be remembered at all. Nonetheless, he ends on a self-conscious note and ironically references his own stance as an immigrant and poet:

> Shroud them,
> Bury them,
> Lay them in coffins down the deep grave.
> Then leave at once without weeping,
> For they are dead and will not wake.
>
> Their honour trampled
> Their land plundered
> Some were hanged
> But no one thundered
>
> Why then shed torrential tears?
> A people without courage reaps only death as its reward
> Let history fold over the page

And from its book erase
This tale of weakness and disgrace.

Revenge, shame, fire
The horror has made us all so brave
But moved us only to narrate.[1]

We may disagree with 'Arida regarding the utter passivity he ascribes to the communities in the region and, although the standards with which he judges people's suffering worth the historical memory are telling (as I will discuss below), one thing is clear: he does not exaggerate the devastation that hit Ottoman Syria and Lebanon during the First World War. A perfect storm of mutually reinforcing catastrophes decimated the population – the scholarly consensus estimates that up to one-third of the civilian population perished in the war. Nature, including human nature, colluded with wartime conditions and led to countless deaths by famine and disease.[2]

What did Syrian and Lebanese civilians who experienced the First World War make of it? For the most part, the sheer physical toll of the war drove many to silence – some, forever. Indeed, those who wrote about the war often reference the silence (as well as the darkness) that descended upon the houses, streets, and neighbourhoods emptied of the living. The sounds that break the silence are ominous: an ill-begotten symphony of screaming and moaning children, incessantly tolling church bells, and creeping and crunching locusts. Numerous accounts describe a world near annihilation, not only of the bodies, but also of the minds and souls of men and women. According to one writer: 'People became superstitious about words that begin with the letter "J": al-jarad (locusts); al-ju' (hunger); al-jaysh (the army); Jamal Pasha; al-jur (oppression); al-jarab (scabies); jinayat (tribunal); even

---

1 Nasib 'Arida, in Mustafa Badawi, *Mukhtarat min al-shicr al-hadith* [Selections from Contemporary Poetry] (Dar al-Nahar li'l-Nashr, Beirut, Lebanon: 1969) pp 111–112. This poem offers an interesting contrast to Abu al-Qasim al-Shabbi's famous poem, 'If the People Will to Live', first published in the 1930s. All the translations in this article are the author's.
2 George Antonius, *The Arab Awakening: The Story of the National Arab Movement* (Kegan Paul International, London: 1938) p 241; L. Schatkowski Schilcher, 'The Famine of 1915–1918 in Greater Syria', in John P. Spagnolo (ed), *Problems of the Modern Middle East in Historical Perspective: Essays in Honour of Albert Hourani* (Oxford University Press, Oxford: 1992) p 231.

jardon (rat), although rats went hungry as well.'[3] Eye-witnesses often grapple for words in order to convey how hunger created a world of beggars and beasts, animals and cannibals. Rashid 'Assaf's *zajal*, 'Barley Bread' (*Khibz Sh'ir*) written during the war, describes a world in which people were reduced to eating and acting like donkeys: Today we eat barley bread/ Tomorrow we'll start braying / 'Let's have a barley riot'/ The donkeys will soon be saying.[4]

Such visceral responses are important and provide rich insight into the experience of the war and its emotive dimensions.[5] In this article, I focus on writers and poets' use of history in articulating their responses to the war's carnage. I ask: was the experience historicised by those who stood witness, and if so, what were their terms of reference? How did they map their experience in relation to the historical past and the imagined future of their (imagined) communities (diachronically), as well as to the broader global war (synchronically)? What can we learn about their notions of identity and community? People suffered. What 'People'? What was the identity of those communities of suffering? Ottoman, Arab, Syrian, Lebanese, Christian?

Over the course of the past century, Lebanese and Syrian writers have referenced the war in textbooks, historical analyses, memoirs, and literature (novels, poems, and *zajal* – vernacular poetry). It should come as no surprise that the responses were and continue to be diverse, the product of specific times, places, and historical circumstances. They tend to inform more about their authors' real or imagined importance, points of view and contexts, than about the events themselves, particularly when written long after the war. Many authors, particularly of memoirs, present their accounts as 'a lesson and a memory' (*"ibra wa dhikra'*), instrumentalising the past in the service of a wide array of agendas and ideologies. In particular, the events of the war have provided rich historical material for nationalist narratives that speak to

---

3 Ibrahim al-Aswad, *Tanwir al-azhan fi tarikh Lubnan* [Enlightening the Minds in the History of Lebanon] (Al-Qiddis Gorgious Publishing House, Beirut, Lebanon: 1925), Vol 3, p 56. This three volume publication includes 'all that there is to know about Lebanon: its history, geography, and who is who'. It is dedicated to the French governor, M. de Joufnel. It is both pro-French yet critical of French rule and a plea for independence.

4 Rashid cAssaf in Joseph Abi-Dahir, *Al-Zajal al-lubnani: Shucara' turafa'* [Lebanese *Zajal*: Entertaining Poets] (N.p., Lebanon: 1991) p 10.

5 See, Najwa al-Qattan, 'When Mothers Ate Their Children: Wartime Memory and the Language of Food in Syria and Lebanon', in *International Journal of Middle East Studies* 46 (November, 2014) pp 719–736.

the suffering of the population and the bravery of those who sacrificed their lives in the face of Ottoman and/or European aggression.

For example, in Ussama 'Itani's dystopic novel, *Memoirs of a Beiruti (Mudhakirrat Beiruti)*, published in 2000, the narrator is a Lebanese-Brazilian immigrant who returns to Beirut in the late twentieth century after a fifty year absence to find a city totally transformed. At the airport, the traveller is met by officials who speak English, French, Armenian, even Hebrew, but not Arabic. It turns out that Beirut had been totally emptied of its Sunni population – and of all Arabic food, to boot. In shock, the narrator takes refuge in the old family home where he stumbles upon his grandfather's unpublished memoirs.[6] It is this fictional memoir that provides the narrator with the key to understanding the past: sectarian 'sickness' that has blinded the Lebanese to the truth that they belong within the Arab fold. In the language of this fictional memoir, the writing serves as 'a lesson and a memory' rather transparently. The culprit here is the West whose destructive role in Arab history is everywhere on display, including its role in fanning the fires of sectarian war in Lebanon in 1860 and the destruction of the Ottoman Empire in the First World War.

Although 'Itani's historical narrative does not dwell too long on the events of the First World War or reference the suffering of the civilians, two specific events are the target of his scandalised historical sensibility and evidence of the West's relentless crusade: Sir Edmund Allenby's triumphant entry into Jerusalem in December 1917 and General Henri Gouraud's post-Maisalun arrival in Damascus in July 1920.

Historical accounts of Allenby's arrival in Jerusalem note both its 'subdued' and scripted execution, as well as the huge symbolism that it represented for the Ottomans and their European foes. As Eugene Rogan reveals, the historical import of the moment was intensely felt in London as it was in Istanbul, particularly in the wake of the fall of other historically significant Ottoman cities such as Mecca and Baghdad.[7] Nonetheless, rather than reference a renewed crusade, as in 'Itani's gloss, Allenby's proclamation acknowledged Jerusalem's importance to the three monotheist faiths, a proclamation that was also read

---

6 Ussama cItani, *Mudhakirrat Beiruti* [Memoirs of a Beiruti] (N.p., Beirut, Lebanon: 2000) p 20.

7 Eugene Rogan, *The Fall of the Ottomans* (Basic Books, New York: 2015) pp 351–352; see also, Leila Tarazi Fawaz, *A Land of Aching Hearts: The Middle East in the Great War* (Harvard University Press, Cambridge, Massachusetts, and London, England: 2014) p 77; Antonius, p 229.

aloud in Arabic, Hebrew, French, and several other languages. None of this prevents 'Itani, however, from asserting that Allenby's proclamation included a pointed and clear reference to the Crusades. In a similar spirit, 'Itani gives historical credibility to the rumored tale about a visit that Gouraud made to Saladin's mausoleum in Damascus after ousting Faisal's Arab government in the summer of 1920: on that occasion, the General supposedly had said: 'Saladin, we are here. This is a new crusade.'[8]

In a different and decidedly anti-Ottoman spin on Saladin's symbolic import, Qadri Qal'aji's history, *The Generation of Sacrifice: The Story of the Arab Revolt and the Awakening of the Arabs* (Jil al-fida': Qissat al-thawra al-'arabiyya wa-nahdat al-'Arab), published in 1967, references the following wartime incident: that on the occasion of Wilhelm II's gift of a lantern to adorn Saladin's mausoleum, Cemal Pasha held a celebration at the Umayyad Mosque attended by foreign and local dignitaries, including Abdul-Rahman Shahbandar, a well-known Syrian nationalist. According to Qal'aji, Shahbandar was in the middle of a speech in which he praised Saladin for his fairness and compassion, even in the treatment of his enemies, when Cemal Pasha took to the stand, and ignoring the scripted order of the speakers, pointed out that Saladin was by no means the only kind of leader worth the historical memory: Sultan Salim, Cemal had noted, was a great leader even though he terrorised his brothers, family, and officials because he suspected them of conspiracy against the Muslim kingdom.[9]

Qal'aji's account is interesting not only on account of its spin on Wilhelm II's visit to Jerusalem and Damascus where he declared his utmost happiness at visiting the place where the great leader Saladin once taught even his enemies how to be heroes.[10] His history of Ottoman wartime policies in Syria and Iraq and of the Arab Revolt foregrounds Turkish nationalism and holds its Turanian strain responsible for almost every horror that befell the Arabs. He argues that the Turks were determined to use the cover of war in order to

---

8 'Itani, *Mudhakirrat Beiruti,* pp 47, 52. On the rumours pertaining to this incident, see Elizabeth Thompson, *Colonial Citizens: Republican Rights, Paternal Privilege, and Gender in French Syria and Lebanon* (Columbia University Press, New York: 2000) p 69.

9 Qadri Qalcaji, *Jil al-fida': Qissat al-thawra al-carabiyya wa-nahdat al-cArab* (Dar al-Kitab al-cArabi, Amman, Jordan: 1967), p 175. This incident is not mentioned in Abdul-Rahman Al-Shahbandar, *Mudhakirrat wa khitab,* (ed), Kamil al-Khatib (Ministry of Culture, Damascus, Syria: 1993).

10 Muhammad Kurd cAli, *Khitat al-Sham* (Beirut, Lebanon: 1983) Vol 3, p 131.

silence and terrorise all non-Turkish voices, Arab and Armenian, Muslim and Christian alike and used exile, starvation, drowning, and outright massacres to achieve their aims.[11]

Anis Frayha's 1979 memoir, *Before I Forget (Qabla an ansa)*, offers a much more attenuated eye-witness account of the war. Frayha's expressed intention is to elucidate the experiences of Lebanese peasants during the 'starvation war' which he differentiates from 'the dirty war we are living through today in Lebanon.'[12] Frayha's account, like other authors', is decidedly coloured by the present, yet neither the passage of time nor the Lebanese civil war prevent him from conveying with a mixture of directness and humor a glimpse of what people thought about the West and Cemal Pasha during the war. Recounting the day he first saw Cemal Pasha, he writes: 'We went to Shaghur Hammana to see the man whose name generated fear and terror. Soon enough he arrived, riding in a procession. He had a black beard and was wearing a black hat. He was short. As soon as he dismounted, our gang leader said: "Children, let us leave. We thought the pasha was a pasha; it turns out that he is just a man; in fact, half of a man".'[13]

Frayha remarks that, when news of the war was first heard in his village and before anyone knew what hunger, disease, and death the war would bring to Lebanon, some people rooted for Russia for 'without her we would not have a bell in al-Sayyida Church', some people said, while others thought 'a plague on both their houses.' But once the starvation and suffering started, people rarely talked about the war, for they had neither the time nor the energy to indulge in thinking about such things. Indeed, 'at the end of the war, nobody seemed to realise that Russia had quit the War in 1917, that it had experienced a Socialist Revolution – socialism – nobody had heard that word before.'[14]

Qal'aji, 'Itani, and Frayha's accounts, published decades apart long after the end of the war, are but three examples of a much larger twentieth century literature on the war; but they offer interesting variations on the themes that pervade it: nationalism, sectarianism, and the role of the West.

Fully aware that the events of the the First World War have served as rich foraging grounds for nationalist and sectarian narratives and myths in which the West invariably plays a significant role, I focus in the rest of this chapter

---

11 Ibid., pp 154–184.

12 Anis Frayha, *Qabla an ansa* (Dar al-Nahar, Beirut, Lebanon: 1979) pp 49–50.

13 Ibid., pp 56–57.

14 Frayha, pp 50, 53.

on sources written between 1916 and 1919. The sources comprise historical and personal accounts as well poetry and *zajal*. This is not to say that these sources are numerous or transparent, but they have filters of their own, or as Salim Tamari has observed of wartime memoirs: 'they are less filtered.'[15]

The material written on the war as it was taking place is not extensive. As Frayha notes, for civilians, the war was hardly about fronts and battles far away from home; rather the war came to be understood and experienced as famine. And if few people had the time or the energy to reflect on far away battles, not many more had the wherewithal to document their daily lives.

In analysing authors' historical understandings of the war and the question of the identity of the communities that suffered, I shall look at three inter-related sites of tension: first: the tension between the global war and local events as imagined locally; second, the tension between the urge to forget and the need to construct historically meaningful memory; third, the tension between the obliteration of communal differences and the obliteration of collective identity.

Mikhail Nu'aima's poem, 'Brother', written in New York in 1917, from the beginning sets the Lebanese experience of the war against that of the West. Rather than memorialise the dead and celebrate victory, he calls upon his Syrian brothers abroad to 'Instead, like me, kneel silently / And in reverence / To weep over our dead.' Indeed, as the poet imagined it, whereas at the end of the war, surviving Western soldiers would return triumphantly to the land of the living, in Lebanon:

Hunger has left us no friend to love / Other than the ghosts of our dead.
Brother, who are we? Without a home or clan or neighbor
Humiliated day and night
The world cares not for us as it never cared for our dead
Grab a shovel and follow me
So we may bury our living.[16]

---

15 Salim Tamari, *Year of the Locusts: A Soldier's Diary and the Erasure of Palestine's Ottoman Past* (University of California Press, Berkeley, California: 2011) p 86.

16 Mikhail Nucaima, in *Hams al-jufun* (Sadir al-Rihani Publishers, Beirut, Lebanon: 1943) pp 95–97. As a point of interesting fact, the author felt obligated as an emigrant to the US to join the fighting in Europe in 1918. He survived the war and returned to Lebanon in 1932. See also, Hussein Muhammad al-Dabbagh, 'Mikhail Naimy: some aspects of his thought as revealed in his writings' (Ph.D. thesis, Durham University: 1968).

Nu'aima's tone of mourning stands in stark contrast to the anger expressed in 'Arida's poem quoted at the beginning of this article. Yet neither attempts to instrumentalise the suffering; indeed it is the absence of a connection of the suffering to any meaningful action that troubles both poets. 'Arida refuses to bestow nationalist sanctity to the communal suffering on account of the disgrace and humiliation that defined it. Such suffering communities have not earned their place in historical memory; they never were a people. Nu'aima, like the rest of the authors discussed in this chapter, is very much aware of the global dimensions of this war as well as the differences that distinguish the local experience: the death of hundreds of thousands of civilians through famine and disease.

For example, in the Preface to his eyewitness account (and textbook), *The Greatest War in History* (*A'zam harb fi al-tarikh*) (1918), Jirjis al-Maqdisi describes the war as 'a global fire', the arrival of which in Lebanon he superbly documents. He opens his account on a picture-perfect day in the summer of 1914 when he sat 'imagining a good future for Syria and Lebanon.' From his vantage point in the village of Suq al-Gharb, surrounded by the beauty of the place, he felt no connection to the war. Writing of sentiments that are remarkable for their resemblance to Frayha's record of half a century later, he confesses that: 'We read about the fighting in Europe as if it were a story, and sometimes we even thought "a plague on both their houses", unaware that when western states are bent on destroying each other that they will bring down the rest of the world along with them.'[17] True to his word, Maqdisi's account begins with an overview of the European political and military history of the war, but the focus is on the local events: 'When the war came, to our country,' Maqdisi writes, 'it took away everything.'[18]

Similarly, the wartime poetry of Beshara al-Khoury (nicknamed, 'al-Akhtal al-Saghir'), one of Lebanon's foremost poets, vacillates between the obliteration of social life locally and a broader historical view of the events of the war. In his long and meandering poem, *1914*, his starting point is a section called 'We in Lebanon' (*Nahnu fi Lubnan*), in which he notes: 'All that can be seen are beggars and the desperate / People dispersed by hunger, they eat grass / Death written on their faces.' The poet then widens his scope to critically consider European politics in 'The Great Powers', making sure to dwell on the

---

17 Jirjis al-Khuri al-Maqdisi, *Aczam harb fi al-tarikh* (al-Matbaca al-cIlmiyya, Beirut, Lebanon: 1918) pp 3–7, 8–9, 26, 30.
18 Ibid., p 69.

new technologies and the carnage they have wrought to the theater of war in 'The Arts of War' and 'The Horrors of War.' Like Maqdisi, he registers the global nature of the war and like him he strikes a pessimistic note regarding western civilisation and industry, wishing in 'The Conference of Inanimate Things' to return to the stone-age. Sandwiched between, he repeatedly returns to Lebanon. Despite his refrain: 'I cannot write enough about such horrors', he documents the suffering graphically, and concludes with a message in 'To the Age': 'You give birth in order to kill, were it that women would stop bearing children.'[19] Like Maqdisi, Beshara al-Khoury is very much aware that the carnage at home was connected to larger events, equally destructive in other places. His ironic juxtaposition of 'people eating grass' in the age of technological breakthrough, notwithstanding, he nonetheless laments and mourns all deaths and addresses himself to a humanity whose very future is under threat everywhere, whether from the fire or the famine of war.

Writing from the distancing perch of an American exile as already mentioned, 'Arida and Nu'aima's poems express anxiety regarding the historical meaning of the Syrian and Lebanese wartime experience and the extent to which it is worth the historical registry. This is not the case in Milhem Hawi's zajal, written in Lebanon during the war. Entitled '1917', the work echoes the descriptions of suffering mentioned already, leaving no doubt as to the catastrophic nature of the wartime period and the extent to which it leveled differences among people: 'Hardship is widespread, the rich, the poor, the ahali, are all in danger.' He, too, notes the humiliation of a 'people used to giving; now they beg for food.' Acknowledging 'death, hunger, poverty and scarcity all over the world', he, nonetheless, insists that 'the people of the East have tasted especially dire desolation.' The poem ends with 'O people of the East, you have been betrayed by history.'[20] Voicing outrage on behalf of people reduced to begging and on the verge of extinction, Hawi, unlike 'Arida and Nu'aima, directs his anger at history itself, denying it moral meaning, if not all meaning.

In contrast, another zajal, entitled 'Safarbarlik', composed in Lebanon in 1916 by Yusuf al-Birri, registers deep anxiety that Lebanon's ordeal will be

---

19 Beshara Abdullah al-Khoury, Shicr al-Akhtal al-Saghir: Beshara Abdullah al-Khoury [The Poetry of Beshara Abdullah al-Khoury] (Dar al-Kitab al-cArabi, Beirut, Lebanon: 1972) pp 342–356.

20 Milhem Hawi, in George Salim Shehadeh, Kitab al-harb al-kabir [A Long History of the War] (N.p., New York: 1917). Safarbarlik is the name that given to the war in Lebanese and Syrian memory.

forgotten by history. Al-Birri's act of writing is expressly a refusal to be erased as per 'Arida's wishes:

> Oh messenger, spread this missive among mankind,
> Tell them to repeat it until the end of time:
> Of events no one has recorded, their history untold.
> Its author intent on writing till it's known around the world.

As if in echo to Nu'aima's invitation to a mass burial, al-Birri describes a society rapidly approaching extinction:

> Death is intent on all of us
> Scores of funerals every day.
> The dead are worthless, buried like beasts,
> Most are dead, the rest will follow suit.
> In a few months' time, Lebanon's death will be complete.

Like 'Arida, he expresses moral outrage at the extent to which people's humanity was compromised and talks of

> Desperate villages where starvation kills young and old,
> Where children roam the streets like prey,
> With even good people in pursuit.[21]

As horrified as he is at the reduction of people to animals and cannibals, he does not stand in judgment of their actions. Unlike 'Arida who invites his listeners to forget, al-Birri's poem is an attempt to rescue the memory even as or because most people are being buried, their collective future at risk. Yet 'Arida's too, it must be noted, is an act of remembering, for as Cormac O'Grada has remarked: 'the rhetoric of fatalism is silence.'[22]

The inability of the poets and eyewitnesses, such as Hawi and al-Birri, to conjure a future for those who suffer is the case in a long poem titled, 'Victim and Sacrifice' (Dahhiyya wa-tadhiya), written in 1918 by Yusuf Shalhoub.

---

21 Yusuf al-Birri, in Antoine Butrus al-Khuweiri, Tarikh al-zajal al-Lubnani (Dar al-Abjadiyya, Sarba, Lebanon: 2011) p 195.
22 Cormac O' Grada, Black '47 and Beyond: the Great Irish Famine in History, Economy, and Memory (Princeton University Press, Princeton, N.J.: 1999).

Shalhoub's *zajal* does not look forward to the future; instead he describes an impending end; the sense of doom is evident for the dangers he mentions include not only public starvation, but communal and familial breakdown in which mothers feed on their children and men eat while their wives and children die. The only sound is 'I am hungry.' At the same time, Shalhoub extends the wartime suffering back in time. In a section of the poem called 'Ghul al-maja'a' (The Demon of Starvation), he references the year 1916 as follows:

In year 12 of Turkey's old war, hunger destroyed the people
The red winds arrived and humiliation, hunger, fear
And it was dangerous.[23]

Shalhoub's extended time-line of the war at once dissociates the experience of the civilians from 'Turkey's' war and sets the local suffering at a different historical plane from an imperial politics that plays to a different tune. Civilians died not because this war was their war. They died under the radar of imperial politics and were carelessly consigned to the dust-bin of history.

Shalhoub's eulogy for a people undergoing physical and historical obliteration certainly echoes the views of the authors already discussed. Yet in tension with the pessimism generated by anxieties about possible historical erasure are several authors' commentaries on how the suffering leveled differences and almost obliterated sectarian and class distinctions.

Antun Yamin's eye-witness account, *Lebanon during the War: Memory of the Events and Injustices in Lebanon during the World War* (Lubnan fi al-harb: Aw, Dhikrat al-hawadith w'al-mazalim fi Lubnan fi al-harb al-'umumiyya), published in 1919 is divided into two volumes. In the first, he focuses mainly on the abuses of the Ottoman army and the atrocities of Cemal Pasha. Yamin likens the 'Turks' to locusts and wolves and argues that the army's attack on our 'honour and land' (al-'ard w'al-ard) and Cemal's imprisonments, exiling, and hangings attest to the 'Turk's hatred of the Arab race' (al-'unsur al-carabi).[24]

---

23 Yusuf Shalhoub, in Khalil Ahmad Khalil, *Al-Shicr al-shacbi al-Lubnani: Dirasat wa-mukhtarat* [Lebanese Popular Poetry: Studies and Selections] (N. P., Beirut, Lebanon: n.d.) p 262.

24 Antun Yamin, *Lubnan fi-1 -harb: Dhikrat al-hawadith wa-1 -mazalim fi Lubnan fi-1 -harb*

Yamin's account develops several juxtapositions. While noting the Turkish/ Arab dimension of local events, he does suggest at several points that the target of Turkish wrath was Lebanon. In one instance, he quotes a Turkish official as saying, in response to complaints regarding high food prices: 'Let Lebanon and Beirut die for the sake of keeping alive the army that fights.' At the same time, he stresses that Turkish abuses were blind to all social distinctions: the young and old; the sick and the healthy; Christians and Muslims.[25]

In the second volume, Yamin shifts gears. On the one hand, while still blaming the Ottomans for much of what happened in Lebanon, he directs his searing anger at the Lebanese elites who profiteered from the war, at several points naming names with fury. 'The Sursuqs, Trads, Asfars, Bayhums, Ghandours, and George Thabit – sold out to the Turks, profiteered, and feasted while the majority starved and begged for food left over from dogs.'[26] On the other hand, Yamin devotes much of the second volume to a detailed description of the suffering that he was witnessing. He draws harrowing images of women, old men, and children eating garbage and grass. The refrain he returns to is: 'this is how the people of Lebanon perished' and 'this is how a people died.'[27] In so doing, he reminds us that it was the profiteers of war as much as politics that 'let Lebanon and Beirut die' with total disregard as to age, gender, and religion.

In a similar manner, Maqdisi's narrative of the war 'in our country' returns over and over again to two points of tension: first, that as the war wore on, people forgot their differences; and second, that they also forgot much else: their will to fight; indeed, their very identity as humans. Interestingly, he references the hangings and the Arab Revolt, but devotes no more than a single page to them and makes no connections between them and the suffering of the civilians. In other words, his account unmoors the suffering from historical time and refuses to instrumentalise it in the service of nationalism. Regarding the disappearance of food in Lebanon, he poignantly asks 'Who, I wonder, would do this?' Although he blames the government's mismanagement, he

---

al-cumumiyya, 1914–1918 (al-Matbaca al-Adabiyya, Beirut, Lebanon: 1919) Vol I, pp 21–27, 60. Also see, 'Introduction' where the author asks that 'the living remember us, victims to Turkish abuse, to the rich who pilfered, and to disease....for our suffering is new, comparable only to the suffering inflicted by Nero.' Vol I, p 7.

25 Ibid., Vol I, pp 141, 91–92.

26 Ibid., Vol II, Preface, pp 14–18, 52–53.

27 Ibid., pp 7–8.

also points the finger at local merchants and officials: 'They are the killers, no doubt about it.'[28]

Two years into the war, according to Maqdisi, we were witnessing 'a calamity unequaled in Syria's history.' His description of the suffering is highly emotive: he speaks of the fear that drove the Muslims to leave Beirut and the Christians to flee to it; of the rumours and panic following the arrival of Armenian refugees, 'for people were worried that the same would happen to them'; and of the moral exhaustion and the disappearance of compassion, even among the kind-hearted. Interestingly, his account is also, in his own words, 'free of sectarian bias' and he stresses at different points in his story that the enormity of the suffering was such that that it erased class distinctions by reducing all but the few to a state of desperate poverty. Indeed, the shared suffering 'united Muslims and Christians together.' Once the war had ended, however, they went back to their differences. [29]

Finally, more than anything Maqdisi finds it difficult to understand people's response, or more accurately, the lack thereof. He writes: 'There is no doubt that death, however it comes, is frightening. But I believe that the worst way to die is by starvation. Those who die at war die with dignity, but those who die of hunger die humiliated.' And then he adds that 'it is noteworthy that the hungry in Syria and Lebanon died of hunger without trying to get at the food that was available, as if hunger made them quiescent and too weak to fight. There was nobody to lead the people on a food riot or revolution…such things need preparation and Syrians don't plan well.'[30]

The last work I examine is by the Lebanese writer Buturs Khuweiri: *Travels in Syria during the World War, 1916: Dangers, Horrors, and Wonders* (Al-Rihla al-Suriyya fi al-harb al-'umumiyya, 1916: Akhtar wa-ahwal wa a'ajib). Published in 1921, this is a book driven by the urge to document events that the author finds too horrifying to believe and to ensure that no one forgets what happened. Khuweiri's descriptions of the civilian carnage are visceral (and of biblical proportions), but also concrete and precisely localised: in Junieh, Byblos, the Cedars, Damascus, Ma'lula, and numerous towns and villages where he stops, he sees 'walking skeletons and other sights I long to forget.'[31]

---

28 Maqdisi, pp 65–66.

29 Ibid., pp 28, 66, 69–70, 72, 97.

30 Ibid., 70.

31 Buturs Khuweiri, 'Al-Rihla al-Suriyya fi-1 -harb al-cumumiyya', in Yusuf Tuma al-Bustani (ed) *1916: Akhtar wa-ahwal wa- acajib* (N.p., Cairo, Egypt: 1921), pp 26, 34.

But it is difficult to forget his tales of death by starvation and cannibalism, particularly when he provides the names of many of the victims (and how young so many of them were when they died).

Most interesting about this account, however, is that the author's journey appears to be both real and intellectual: the object behind the journey was espionage on behalf of France. The author's mission, according to him, was to assess Turkish military conditions in Syria and to prepare the way to liberate Lebanon once the battle of Verdun was won.[32] Early on while still in Lebanon, he is convinced that the Turkish government is determined to 'exterminate' the Lebanese (although he also gives ample weight to the locusts). Once in Damascus, however, he reports on a rather strange exchange with an unnamed Syrian man who argues that the state (Cemal Pasha and the Unionists) did not only want to purify the country of all its Christians, massacring the Armenians and starving the Lebanese, but also Syrians; indeed all Arabs, Muslim and Christian. 'From that point', he declares,'I was convinced that the Turks were determined to exterminate all but their own kind.'[33]

Few would challenge the profound impact of the war on the politics, economy, and society of Lebanon and Syria. Over the course of the century since the end of the war, Lebanese and Syrian poets, novelists, memoirists, and historians, have produced an extensive body of literature on the war. In focusing on sources produced during or shortly after the war, I offer a glimpse at war as it was experienced and imagined by Syrians and Lebanese who lived it and witnessed firsthand the deprivations that would become the raw materials of historical and nationalist memory. Though not extensive, the material suggests the following conclusions.

First, although the famine was the result of a variety of causes: natural, social, and political, many of which are acknowledged by the authors themselves, there is universal agreement that this famine was different in that it was primarily caused by an Ottoman policy that deliberately targeted civilians, a policy whose consequences were gravely exacerbated by corruption and profiteering. At the same time, the material validates Linda Schilcher's observation that, whereas the Ottomans were held responsible for the famine, the role of the Entente blockade of the Eastern Mediterranean has been forgotten. Her study underscores the profound impact of the blockade – which lasted

---

32 Ibid., pp 4–5.
33 Ibid., pp 34–36, 49, 80.

until 1919 – on the availability of food in the region, in light of the simultaneous ravages of the locusts and unusually cold winters.[34]

How to explain this (at least partly) mis-directed blame? As the rich scholarship on famines has taught us, famines both as events and as memories
are about politics and power. To be starved is to be subject to 'execution by
hunger.'[35] As a consequence, the identity of the purported instigators is not
only essential, but is also intrinsically bound to the imagined identity of the
victims. Hence, blaming the 'Turks' and the rich may be explained by reference to the dashed expectations or moral economy of Lebanese and Syrian
citizens by their government and local elites; at the same time, it also speaks
of the centrality of the local experiential dimensions of the war.

The centennial of the First World War has occasioned a plethora of conferences and memorialising in many parts of the globe. In Middle Eastern studies,
there has been a density of scholarly publications and conferences on the
war.[36] Equally exciting has been the interest in cross-regional and comparative analysis of social and cultural aspects of the war experience, an interest
that has led to a call for the integration of the war histories of 'peripheral'
areas and regions into the general history of the First World War. The truth is
that for those who were there, what they experienced was as central to their
lives as it was catastrophic. 'The war was like a global fire', wrote Maqdisi, 'it
burned the clothes of some and the skins of others. Some were burned; others
were incinerated, depending on their proximity to the fire. Every person in the
world has the right to ask: "What effect did the war have on my country, my
town, my family and myself."'[37] Maqdisi reminds us that the Great War in Syria
and Lebanon – the only Great War – was the war at home, the civilians' war.

Who were the civilians? The sources are unanimous in pointing the blame
at the 'Turks' (also Ottomans and Unionists, or just Cemal Pasha). At the same
time, they speak of an erasure of (almost) all differences among 'the people' –
the target of these policies. The 'communities of suffering' so constructed are
highly indicative of a fluid identity at that time in Syria as well as in Lebanon.
This should no longer surprise: Carol Hakim's study of Lebanese nationalism

---

34 Schilcher, p 232. A good example of this bias is Antonius, *Arab Awakening*, pp 189–242.

35 Miron Dolot, *Execution by Hunger: The Hidden Holocaust* (W. W. Norton Company, New
York: 1985).

36 In addition to the studies by Rogan and Fawaz see, for example, *International Journal of
Middle East Studies* 46 (November, 2014) and *Jerusalem Quarterly* 56 (Winter/Spring 2014).

37 Maqdisi, p 69.

argues that the crystallisation of what she calls 'Lebaneseness' took place only after the end of the war and the imposition of the French mandate in 1920.[38]

Second, as positive as the erasure of differences among the people may appear, the erasure is at other times so extreme, that there is no identity, memory, or history attached to that period. The sources vacillate between an imagined community in which all (but class differences) are erased and an imagined (absent) community of beggars, beasts, and victims to be erased from history. Such accounts also vacillate between the need to forget and the urge to remember. This is to say that it is not only the extreme of the suffering that drives forgetfulness; it is also the (historically) humiliating victimisation and the lack of glory. Those who experienced the war were already articulating their ambivalence about its historical significance, about how their story fits in the larger global context of the war as well as what this will mean in the future. Whether they invite us to remember the suffering or to forget the humiliation, they share discursive assumptions regarding national glory and historical memory.

Finally, historians, most recently and cogently Salim Tamari, have argued that the suffering experienced by civilians during the four years of the war managed to erase 400 years of Ottoman legacy in the Arab East.[39] This is true. Yet a closer look at this erasure indicates that the war itself was ruptured from historical memory on account of the trauma that it caused. As Arab subjects of the Ottoman Empire, civilians were per force not only removed from the military campaigns – even as those impacted their lives – they were also starving provincial citizens in an empire fighting a losing war. In other words, the war years interrupted the narrative flow of history and challenged memory. I have tried to capture this rupture in time.

---

38 Carol Hakim, *The Origins of the Lebanese National Idea: 1840–1920* (University of California Press, Berkeley, CA: 2013).

39 Tamari, *Year of the Locusts*, p 5.

7

The patriarch, the amir and the patriots: civilisation and self-determination at the Paris Peace Conference

Andrew Arsan

It has long been a notion held dear by historians that the modern Middle East was born on the negotiation table at Paris, the Frankenstein-like offspring of the feverish horse-trading and double-dealing of British and French diplomats and statesmen. As David Fromkin put it in his oft-cited account of these negotiations, the familiar geopolitical outlines of the region 'emerged from decisions made by the Allies during and after the First World War'. The 'countries and frontiers' of the region, Fromkin argues, following a familiar motif, were artificial conceits 'fabricated in Europe' in ignorance of local conditions, and imposed upon the peoples of the region with little consideration for their wishes and concerns.[1] Reprising this refrain, Kais Firro has insisted that 'the colonialist eye that drew the borders of the new Arab states of the Middle East following the First World War had little regard for the socio-economic and

---

1 David Fromkin, *A Peace to End All Peace: The Fall of the Ottoman Empire and the Creation of the Modern Middle East*, 2nd ed. (Phoenix, London: 2000) pp 15, 17. For further renditions of this narrative, see Elie Kedourie, *In the Anglo-Arab Labyrinth: The McMahon-Husayn Correspondence and its Interpretations, 1914–1939* (Cambridge University Press, Cambridge: 1976); Jonathan Schneer, *The Balfour Declaration: The Origins of the Arab-Israeli Conflict* (Bloomsbury, London: 2010).

cultural realities pre-existing on the ground'.[2] In this reading, the views and aspirations of the literati and notables of the Arabic-speaking Eastern Mediter-ranean mattered little to Sykes and Picot, T.E. Lawrence and Robert de Caix, Lloyd George and Clemenceau. And, accordingly, they must matter little to the latter-day historian, whose mission is to trace the tortuous process by which the Middle East came to be, in order better to understand the baleful consequences of these five years of irreconcilable commitments, of letters and appeals and memoranda and treaties. After all, for all the rhetorical force of the language of self-determination popularised by Woodrow Wilson and his American acolytes, British and French politicians and policy-makers tended still to treat the Middle East as but one piece of a larger imperial puzzle, allowing broader strategic priorities and domestic pressures to dictate their policy in the region.[3] What good, then, is it knowing what people thought or wanted in Damascus, Jerusalem, Beirut or Ba'bda, the capital of the autono-mous Ottoman district of Mount Lebanon, if 'Europeans and Americans were the only ones seated around the table when the decisions were made'?[4] And what good is it considering, as this chapter does, the particular claims made by the Lebanese and Hijazi delegations that appeared before the Peace Con-ference, and the political languages in which they are couched – lexicons, such as those of stadial thought, and democratic or ethnic nationalism, that

---

2 Kais Firro, *Inventing Lebanon: Nationalism and the State under the Mandate* (I.B. Tauris, London: 2003) p 9.

3 On British policy, see Roger Adelson, *London and the Invention of the Middle East: Money, Power and War, 1902–1922* (Yale University Press, New Haven: 1995); Toby Dodge, *Inventing Iraq: The Failure of Nation-Building and a History Denied* (Hurst, London: 2003); Elizabeth Monroe, *Britain's Moment in the Middle East, 1914–1971* (Chatto & Windus, London: 1981); Peter Sluglett, *Britain in Iraq: Contriving King and Country* (I.B. Tauris, London: 2007); James Renton, *The Zionist Masquerade: The Birth of the Anglo-Zionist Alliance, 1914–1918* (Palgrave, Basingstoke: 2007); James Renton, 'Changing Languages of Empire and the Orient: Britain and the Invention of the Middle East, 1917–1918', *Historical Journal* 50 (2007): pp 645–67; Bruce Westrate, *The Arab Bureau: British Policy in the Middle East, 1916–1920* (Pennsylvania State Press, University Park: 1992). On the French, see Christopher Andrew and Sydney Kanya-Forstner, *France Overseas: The Great War and the Climax of French Imperial Expansion* (Thames and Hudson, London: 1981); Gérard Khoury, *La France et l'Orient moderne: naissance du Liban moderne* (Armand Colin, Paris: 1993); William Shorrock, *French Imperialism in the Middle East: The Failure of Policy in Syria and Lebanon* (University of Wisconsin Press, Madison: 1972).

4 Fromkin, *Peace*, p 17.

long predated the 'Wilsonian moment' and cannot be reduced to its extra-European resonances and echoes?

Unsurprisingly, historians of Versailles have tended by and large to pay little attention to the Hijazi and, especially, Lebanese delegations that presented their claims before the Supreme Council on 6 and 15 February 1919. All too often, these scholars echo contemporaries like Robert Lansing, who saw Amir Faysal – who, though he attended the Conference as an emissary of the Kingdom of the Hijaz, claimed to speak in the name of the 'Arabs of Asia' – as an exotic envoy of Arabia, whose 'manner of address and ... voice seemed to breathe the perfume of frankincense and to suggest the presence of richly colored divans'.[5] With his gravitas and poise, Faysal provides not just relief from the grandstanding bluster of a Venizelos or the plodding ponderousness of a Dmowski, but also a reminder of the tragic outcome of a conference that ignored the Arabs' aspirations and hopes to parcel out their lands between the imperial powers. As for the two Lebanese delegations to the conference – the first a group of public men headed by the lawyer Dawwud 'Ammun, the second a group of prelates led by the Maronite Patriarch Ilias Huwayyik, who arrived in France in August of that year to persuade the French of the merits of Lebanon's claim to self-determination and national existence – they receive scarcely a mention. Margaret MacMillan is typical both in her hasty dismissal of these emissaries, and in her tendency to regard them as mere puppets of French interests. Dispensing with them briskly, and not without a touch of irony, she notes only that they were 'brought in' by 'the French' to provide a counterweight to the Hashemite claims supported by the British.[6] In similar fashion, others have reduced the Lebanese delegation's role to that of a diplomatic option, another card in the Quai d'Orsay's pack alongside the Lebanese committees of Paris and Cairo and the Comité Central Syrien of the émigré political entrepreneurs Shukri Ghanim and Georges Samna.[7]

This chapter, however, starts from the contrary premise that the political visions of the Lebanese and Hijazi delegations and the bodies they claimed to represent, the Administrative Council of Mount Lebanon and the Syrian General Congress sitting in Damascus, must be taken seriously if we are to

---

5 Alan Sharp, *The Versailles Settlement: Peacemaking in Paris, 1919* (Macmillan, Basingstoke: 1991) p 179.

6 Margaret MacMillan, *Peacemakers: The Paris Peace Conference of 1919 and its Attempt to End War* (John Murray, London: 2001) pp 402–3.

7 Andrew and Kanya-Forstner, *France Overseas* pp 177–79.

fully understand the Peace Conference and its Middle Eastern afterlives.[8] 'In 1919', MacMillan has written, 'Paris was the capital of the world', becoming for the space of six months 'the world's government, its court of appeal and parliament, the focus of its fears and hopes'.[9] Arthur Balfour may well not have been wrong when he noted that 'at this Conference all important business is transacted in the intervals of other business' – 'everything … happening', as Paul Cambon put it, 'behind the scenes' of official goings-on, in the private conclaves of European and American diplomatists.[10] Nevertheless, we would possess an impoverished sense of the conference's proceedings and its place in the world were we to focus only on the words and actions of its European and American participants. Just as scholars have, in recent years, gone about constructing a global history of the First World War, so too must we attempt to lay the foundations of a global history of the Conference.[11]

Indeed, both Faysal and his Iraqi and Syrian acolytes and the Lebanese delegations deserve better than to be treated as distracting sideshows from the serious business of the day, marionettes moving to the rhythms dictated by their French and British puppeteers or laggard provincials reacting to political developments at the centre and captivated by the gleaming promise of the new-fangled doctrine of Wilsonian self-determination.[12] As MacMillan herself

---

8 On the administrative or consultative council of Mount Lebanon, see Engin Akarlı, *The Long Peace: Ottoman Lebanon, 1861–1920* (University of California Press, Berkeley: 1993). On the Congress, established by Faysal to represent the wishes of the Syrian people, but which soon developed an agenda of its own, see James Gelvin, *Divided Loyalties: Nationalism and Mass Politics in Syria at the Close of Empire* (University of California Press, Berkeley: 1998); and Elizabeth F. Thompson, 'Rashid Rida and the 1920 Syrian-Arab Constitution: How the French Mandate Undermined Islamic Liberalism', in Cyrus Schayegh and Andrew Arsan (eds) *The Routledge Handbook of the History of the Middle East Mandates* (Routledge, London: 2015) pp 244–65.

9 MacMillan, *Peacemakers*, p 1.

10 Sharp, *Versailles*, p 19.

11 On the First World War, see Heike Liebau, Katrin Bromber, Katharina Lange, Dyala Hamzah and Ravi Ajuha, (eds), *The World in World Wars: Experiences, Perceptions and Perspectives from Africa and Asia* (Brill, Leiden: 2010); and Hew Strachan, *The First World War*, vol. 1, *To Arms* (Oxford University Press, Oxford: 2001). On the Peace Conference, see Erez Manela, *The Wilsonian Moment: Self-Determination and the International Origins of Anticolonial Nationalism* (Oxford University Press, Oxford: 2007); and Adam Tooze, *The Deluge: The Great War, America, and the Remaking of the Global Order, 1916–1931* (Penguin, London: 2015) which, though it takes a global perspective, skirts around the Middle East.

12 Manela, *Wilsonian Moment*.

has counselled, '[t]here were two realities in the world of 1919 ... one ... in Paris and the other ... on the ground, where people were making their own decisions and fighting their own battles'.[13] This was as true of Mount Lebanon and Damascus as it was of Anatolia, where a rump Ottoman army under Mustafa Kemal rallied against Allied offensives, or Beijing, where crowds of students gathered on 4 May 1919 to protest their government's apparent capitulation to the forces of imperialism gathered at Versailles. As historians of the Middle East have made clear, eddies of debate swirled through the Arabic-speaking Eastern Mediterranean in the years between 1918 and 1920 as the canopy of Ottoman sovereignty was folded away and the region's inhabitants drew up the plans of new political edifices in which to live.[14] Emissaries of the world outside the Hall of Mirrors, the Hijazi and Lebanese delegations were not hesitant mummers, looking to the prompts of Lawrence and Georges-Picot for guidance. To be sure, their words were, to an extent, chosen and fitted out for their Parisian audiences. Utterances do not float in thin air, detached from context; they address and seek to affect particular interlocutors. But these delegates' pronouncements also carried the traces of the maelstrom of political discussion, of claims, counter-claims and arguments whirling in the Eastern Mediterranean, just as the declarations and stances of political actors in the region itself were shaped by news of the proceedings in Paris. What's more, these two delegations spoke to, and against, one another, each seeking to contradict and negate the claims of the other. As Mikhail Bakhtin argued, 'any concrete utterance is a link in the chain of speech communication of a given sphere'; responding to its predecessors, which it 'refutes, affirms, supplements and relies upon', it is also filled with expectation of a desired response.[15]

Far from so much chaff blown away on the winds of great power opportunism, the words of the Lebanese and Hijazi delegations can reveal a great deal about the way in which the Arabic-speaking public men and literati of the

---

13 MacMillan, *Peacemakers*, p 6.
14 Gelvin, *Divided Loyalties*; Carol Hakim, *The Origins of the Lebanese National Idea, 1840–1920* (University of California Press, Berkeley: 2013); Philip S. Khoury, *Urban Notables and Arab Nationalism, The Politics of Damascus, 1860–1920* (Cambridge University Press, Cambridge: 1983); Eliezer Tauber, *The Arab Movements in World War I* (Frank Cass, London: 1993); Keith Watenpaugh, *Being Modern in the Middle East: Revolution, Nationalism, Colonialism, and the Arab Middle Class* (Princeton University Press, Princeton: 2006).
15 Mikhail Bakhtin, *Speech Genres and Other Late Writings*, trans. Vern W. McGee (University of Texas Press, Austin: 1986) pp 94–5, 91.

early-twentieth century Eastern Mediterranean understood their relationship to international society. And, what's more, the language in which their claims were couched matters as much as the precise content of their demands. That they did not get their wishes – in the case of the Lebanese envoys, a greater Lebanon attached to France only by ties of technical assistance and collaboration, and in that of the Hijazi delegation, an Arab Kingdom in Syria, centred on Damascus and including Mount Lebanon and Palestine – in no way diminishes the importance of their words to the historian of early twentieth-century Eastern Mediterranean international political thought.

Accordingly, this chapter will reconstruct the rhetorical strategies these delegates deployed to buttress their demands for independence, focusing in particular on their uses of the language of stadial evolution. As Cemil Aydın has argued, both the Lebanese and Hijazi delegations questioned the 'imperial power structures of the world order', querying their subjection to mandatory rule, even as they asked for the 'fulfilment of the promises of ... civilisation' and universal modernity. But, unlike the Ottoman pan-Islamists and Japanese pan-Asianists on whom Aydın concentrates, they did not so much seek to construct 'alternative' visions of 'global order' as strive to contest and reform the workings of international society from within.[16] Even as they rejected the application of the Mandates to the Eastern Mediterranean, claiming full independence for their own nations, they embraced the rhetoric of civilisation that underpinned mandatory reasoning.[17]

Historiographical assessments of the effects of the First World War on non-European perceptions of the West have largely fallen into two camps. On the one hand are those who, like Michael Adas, argue that this cataclysmic conflict allowed the mask of civilisation to slip from the face of the West; revealing the 'appalling flaws' that lay beneath, it showed 'what the colonizers

---

16 Cemil Aydın, *The Politics of Anti-Westernism in Asia: Visions of World Order in Pan-Islamic and Pan-Asian Thought* (Columbia University Press, New York: 2007) pp 8–9.

17 On the Mandates system, see Susan Pedersen, *The Guardians: The League of Nations and the Crisis of Empire* (Oxford University Press, Oxford: 2015); and Mark Mazower, *No Enchanted Palace: The End of Empire and the Ideological Origins of the United Nations* (Princeton University Press, Princeton: 2009). On the engagement of Middle Eastern populations under mandatory rule with the terms of the Mandates, see Natasha Wheatley, 'The Mandate System as a Style of Reasoning: International Jurisdiction and the Parceling of Imperial Sovereignty in Petitions from Palestine', in *Routledge Handbook*, pp 106–22; and Wheatley, 'Mandatory Interpretation: Legal Hermeneutics and the New International Order in Arab and Jewish Petitions to the League of Nations', *Past & Present* 227 (2015): pp 205–48.

had trumpeted as unprecedented virtues to be fatal vices', and precipitated the loosening of the 'psychological bondage of the colonized elite' to notions of European technological and cultural superiority.[18] On the other stand those who, like Erez Manela, see the years after the armistice as ones of blithe hope and bitter disappointment, of enchantment and disenchantment, for the 'colonized, marginalized and stateless peoples of the world' in whom Wilson found an 'unintended but eager audience' for his pronouncements on self-determination. Their 'imaginations' 'captured' by his apparent 'promise of a new world order', they came to see the American president as 'both an icon of their aspirations and a potential champion of their cause' and 'adopted [his] rhetoric of self-determination and the equality of nations'. They were soon disabused, however, of any illusions, as the details of the peace began to filter out, revealing that their hopes of an 'immediate and radical transformation of their status in international society' were ill-founded. This revelation heralded the end of the 'Wilsonian moment'.[19] Falling out of love with the American president as quickly as they had succumbed to his rhetorical charms, they angrily turned to protest and revolt, like wronged lovers shredding their partners' clothes. But as attractive as the stark analytical clarity of these narratives might be, they are not without their problems. While accounts that treat the 'Wilsonian moment' of late 1918 and early 1919 as the point of origin of ideas of self-determination tend to overlook the tangled genealogies of these notions, both in Europe and the world beyond, in the preceding decades, the First World War cannot be seen as drawing a blood-red line under mythical notions of Western superiority.[20] For non-Western political actors continued to strive for affirmation of their civilisational status, and the full integration into the international system this would entail, as they had done since the mid-nineteenth century.[21]

---

18 Michael Adas, 'Contested Hegemony: The Great War and the Afro-Asian Assault on the Civilizing Mission Ideology', *Journal of World History* 15 (2004) pp 63, 52.

19 Manela, *Wilsonian Moment*, pp 4–5, 7.

20 See Eugenio Biagini and C.A. Bayly (eds), *Giuseppe Mazzini and the Globalisation of Democratic Nationalism, 1830–1920* (Oxford University Press, Oxford: 2008); Borislav Chernev, 'The Brest-Litovsk Moment: Self-Determination Discourse in Eastern Europe before Wilsonianism', *Diplomacy & Statecraft* 22 (2011): pp 369–87; Derek Heater, *National Self-Determination: Woodrow Wilson and his Legacy* (MacMillan, Basingstoke: 1994); and Arno J. Mayer, *Lenin vs. Wilson: Political Origins of the New Diplomacy, 1917–1918* (World Publication Company, Cleveland: 1964).

21 See Gerrit W. Gong, *The Standard of Civilization in International Society* (Clarendon Press,

Strikingly, neither the Memorandum of 1 January 1919 presented to the Peace Conference in Faysal's name, nor the Lebanese Declaration of 13 February 1919 spoke of self-determination as such. Rather, both called for the recognition of their respective claims to 'independence'. The Hijazi delegation thus asked for the 'Arabic-speaking peoples of Asia, from the line Alexandretta-Diarbekir southward to the Indian Ocean, be recognized as independent sovereign peoples, under the guarantee of the League of Nations'. The Lebanese deposition, meanwhile, argued that the administrative 'autonomy' of Lebanon, 'consecrated' in the wake of the sectarian massacres of 1860 by the 'treaty of 1861–1864', which the European concert undertook to guarantee and uphold, now amounted to a de facto independence 'as a consequence of the collapse of the Sublime Porte'. While Faysal emphasised the linguistic and ethnic homogeneity of the territories he sought to claim as his own, insisting that they were 'inhabited by "Arabs" – by which we mean people of closely related Semitic stocks, all speaking the one language, Arabic', the Lebanese delegation framed its argument in political terms. Its members, they insisted, held their 'mandate from the great administrative Council of Mount-Lebanon, our national Parliament, elected on a democratic basis by the votes of the entire Lebanese nation'. The two delegations thus deployed the differing claims of ethnic and democratic nationalism to press home their claims. If, for Faysal, the Arabs were 'eventually' to be united 'into one nation' because they were 'one potential people' possessing an intrinsic 'unity' and 'jealous of their language and liberty', the Lebanese delegation saw in 'the national government and elected Parliament' of the Mountain the essential components of statehood.

Such claims were not born of the moment and the striking apparition on the scene of Wilson. Rather they drew upon the registers of political community and reform elaborated by the public men and literati of the Arabic-speaking Eastern Mediterranean in a series of campaigns directed at the late Ottoman

---

Oxford: 1984). On the Ottoman empire, see Selim Deringil, *The Well-Protected Domains: Ideology and the Legitimation of Power in the Ottoman Empire, 1876–1909* (I.B. Tauris, London: 1998); Thomas Naff, 'The Ottoman Empire and the European States System', in Hedley Bull and Adam Watson (eds), *The Expansion of International Society* (Clarendon Press, Oxford: 1984) pp 143–69. On China, see Gerrit W. Gong, 'China's Entry into International Society', in *Expansion*, pp 171–83; Xu Guoqi, *China and the Great War: China's Pursuit of a New National Identity and Internationalization* (Cambridge University Press, Cambridge: 2005).

state in the years before 1914. To cite but one example, the organisers of the 'first Arab congress', held in Paris in 1913 to call for the devolution of administrative powers to the Arab provinces of the Ottoman empire, had launched an 'appeal to the sons of the Arab nation' which called upon all Arabic speakers to unite against the centralising policies adopted by the ruling Committee of Union and Progress in Istanbul.[22] For its part, the 1912 campaign for reform of the organic statute of Mount Lebanon, in which 'Ammun had played such a crucial part, rested on the claim that Lebanon had enjoyed 'full administrative autonomy in its internal affairs' since time immemorial – a privilege that had been reaffirmed by the settlements of 1861 and 1864, even as they transformed an 'absolute principality into a parliamentary government'.[23] These were arguments, once part of the panoply of imperial reform, which could easily be brought out of the closet, dusted down and fitted out again for the purposes of independence.

It is not that the Lebanese and Hijazi memoranda neglected Wilson's words entirely. The former thus insisted that the grafting of the coastal cities of Beirut, Tripoli and Sidon, and the fertile plain of the Biqa' valley – a longstanding demand of the irredentist public men of Mount Lebanon – would represent 'an act of justice and reparation, while conforming to the principle of the liberty of peoples'.[24] The latter, too, insisted that its demands were in fitting with 'the general principles accepted by the Allies when the United States joined them' – and went so far as to include in an appendix an extract from Wilson's Mount Vernon speech of 4 July 1918, in which he had castigated the forces of 'exterior influence and mastery', to remind the Council that they should 'attach more importance to the bodies and souls of the Arabic-speaking peoples than to their own material interests'.[25] But far from underpinning their claims to independence, these appeals to Wilsonian principles represented only one relatively small part of a broader rhetorical arsenal. Indeed,

---

22 'Da'wa ila 'Abna' al-Umma al-'Arabiyya', in *al-Mu'tamar al-'Arabi al-Awwal* (Matb'at al-Busfur, Cairo: 1913) *p* 9.

23 Al-Ittihad al-Lubnani, *al-Mas'ala al-Lubnaniyya* (Matb'at al-Ma'arif, Cairo: 1913), pp 3–4.

24 'Déclarations de la Délégation officielle du Mont Liban', in Antoine Hokayem and Marie Claude Bittar (eds) *L'Empire ottoman, les Arabes et les grandes puissances, 1914–1920* (Presses Universitaires du Liban, Beirut: 1981) p 107.

25 *Address of President Wilson Delivered at Mount Vernon July 4, 1918* (United States Government Printing Office, Washington, D.C.: 1918) p 4; 'Territorial Claims of the Government of the Hejaz', in *L'Empire ottoman*, p 105.

they were – if anything – strategic interpolations, grace notes woven into the score of the memoranda to prick up American ears. If the case for Lebanese or Syrian independence was to be made, it was not on the basis of the Fourteen Points alone. As we have seen, appeals to the precedents of both international and municipal law and arguments grounded in the commonplace terms of ethnic and civic nationalism, as well as invocations of contributions made and 'sacrifices' incurred during the war and appeals to the hierarchical logic of civilisational thought mattered as much, if not more, as citation of Wilsonian principles.[26] It is to the last of these, the register of stadial evolution, that this chapter now turns.

This language ran through many of the memoranda, petitions of desiderata and pamphlets put together by Arabic-speaking literati in 1919. It is apparent, for instance, in the appeal the Syrian General Congress forwarded in August 1919 to the King-Crane Commission, the American body sent to investigate the political wishes and desires of the peoples of the Eastern Mediterranean.[27] After calling for 'complete political independence for the Syrian land ... without any protection whatsoever' – *bidun himaya wa la wisaya* – and establishing that 'the government of this country' should be 'monarchical, civil, and parliamentary', the Congress sought to justify these desiderata by an appeal to civilisational reasoning. For, it went on, 'the Arabs resident in the Syrian land are a people whose level of progress is no lower' than that of 'the Bulgarian or Serb people, or Greece and Romania' – and, accordingly, the people of Syria deserved not abasement to the 'ranks of [the] intermediate peoples' the League of Nations sought to place under 'mandatory' rule, but recognition of their just demands by the international community. In calling for treatment comparable to that accorded the states of South-Eastern Europe, the Congress signalled at once a sophisticated understanding of the stadial underpinnings of early twentieth-century international thought, and a

---

26 'Déclarations', p 107.

27 On the King-Crane Commission, see Harry N. Howard, *The King-Crane Commission: An American Inquiry in the Middle East* (Khayats, Beirut: 1963); Andrew Patrick, 'Reading the King-Crane Commission of 1919: Discourses of Race, Modernity, and Self-Determination in Competing American Visions of the Post-Ottoman Middle East' (PhD diss., University of Manchester, 2011); Leonard V. Smith, 'Wilsonian Sovereignty in the Middle East: The King-Crane Commission Report of 1919', in Douglas Howland and Ann Luise White (eds), *The State of Sovereignty: Territories, Laws, Populations* (University of Indiana Press, Bloomington: 2009) pp 56–74.

tacit acceptance of its terms. Thus, it did not reject out of hand the Mandates system sketched out in Article 22 of the League's Covenant so much as reject its application to Syria. Should the country receive any foreign aid, this should be limited to a level of 'technical and economic assistance', which should in no way affect its 'full independence'. After all, any 'thought of conquest or colonialism' had been dispensed with once and for all by Wilson's declarations on America's entry into the war.[28] Wilsonian principles, it is clear, had their place in such a rhetorical scheme. But they played second fiddle to a broader argument rooted in nineteenth-century civilisational thought and diplomatic practice.

Others too made use of such comparative moves to underpin their claims to self-determination. This was the tactic adopted, for instance, by Khayrallah T. Khayrallah, the socialist, freethinker, and Lebanese patriot, in his November 1919 open letter to Sir Eric Drummond, the League's first Secretary-General. 'There was', he wrote, 'one consideration' more important than all others in considering the future of the 'liberated Arab regions of the Ottoman empire'. For this land was the 'cradle of humanity, and civilised humanity could not fail to respect its origins without showing ingratitude'. To be sure, the 'skies had since darkened' on the Middle East: 'Babylon, Nineveh and Palmyra' had fallen into 'ruins', and 'Byblos, Tyre and Sidon' reduced to the status of 'villages', while Damascus and Baghdad were 'pale shadows of the cities of the caliphs'. Nevertheless, there could be no denying that it was in these 'memorable regions' that were 'born the great philosophical and religious ideas that now constitute the universal patrimony' of mankind. And, what's more, from this 'decrepitude' there now was rising a 'new soul, and this anguished soul has come to ask the civilised world the right to live'. How could the states grouped together in the League refuse this request when 'the modern era [had] witnessed great resurrections' like those of Athens, which 'has retaken its spot in the sun of liberty' and Rome, which witnessed again the 'solemnities of the Capitol'? Like Italy and Greece, the peoples of 'Iraq, Syria and Lebanon', the 'direct heirs of [the] civilisations' of these 'antique land[s]' asked only to be accorded the 'honour' of creating 'a new life and a new civilisation' on their own soil.[29] To turn away their request for self-determination and

28 'Nas al-Qarar aldhi Wajahuh al-Mu'tamar al-Suri ila Lajna al-Istifta' al-Amirkiyya', in L'Empire ottoman, pp 26–7.
29 K.T. Khairallah, Le Problème du Levant. Les régions arabes libérées. Syrie – Irak – Liban. Lettre ouverte à la Société des Nations (Ernest Leroux, Paris: 1919) pp 10–11.

statehood, Khayrallah intimated, would not only be churlish; it would also represent a break with diplomatic precedent, hitherto sympathetic to such claims.

The language of civilisation, however, was more than just a potent means of claiming international acceptance. It also served as a rhetorical foil to the demands of others, and a means of parsing between different parts of the Eastern Mediterranean. Even Amir Faysal, often taken to have been the advocate of a unitary Arab nationalism, sought to distinguish between and classify the various components of 'Arab Asia'. To be sure, the Memorandum presented in the Amir's name in February 1919 made it clear that 'the aim of the Arab nationalist movements ... is to unite the Arabs eventually into one nation' – the consummation of a natural process, for a 'race [that] has for 600 years resisted Turkish attempts' to break down its ethnic homogeneity. The latest proof of this inner strength and resilience was to be found in the Arab revolt, in which 'Syrians, Mesopotamians, and Arabians' had fought side by side under the banner of the 'Sherif of Mecca'. The 'ideal of Arab unity', then, could not but 'triumph'. This seems, on the face of it, an unambiguous statement of the 'principle' of ethnic nationhood.[30]

And yet one should not lose sight of the gradualism that ran through the Memorandum. Unity was the 'ultimate' aim of the Arab movement and the Hashemite family at its head, not its immediate objective. Indeed, 'no attempt' should be 'made now to force it, by imposing an artificial political unity on the whole'. There could be no doubt that 'the development of railways, telegraphs and air-roads' had greatly facilitated 'the unity of the Arabs in Asia', helping to overcome the tyranny of distance which in 'old days' had hampered the circulation of 'common ideas'. But despite such welcome developments, 'the various provinces of Arab Asia' remained too 'different economically and socially' to 'constrain them into one frame of government'. Syria, 'an agricultural and industrial area thickly peopled with sedentary classes, is sufficiently advanced politically to manage her own internal affairs'. Thus, while 'foreign technical advice and help will be a most valuable factor in our national growth', no 'part of the freedom we have just won for ourselves by force of arms' could be given up to secure such assistance. 'Jezireh and Irak', on the other hand, 'are two huge provinces, made up three civilised towns, divided by large wastes thinly peopled by semi-nomadic tribes'. Accordingly, though the 'government' should be 'Arab', it should follow the

---

30 'Mémorandum de l'émir Feysal à la Conférence de la Paix', in L'Empire ottoman, p 102.

'selective rather than the elective principle ... until time makes the broader basis possible'. What's more, Arab rule 'will have to be buttressed by the men and material resources of a great power' if Mesopotamia was to fulfil the potential the world expected of it. As for the Hijaz, this was 'mainly a tribal area, and the government will remain, as in the past, suited to patriarchal conditions'. It should therefore 'retain ... complete independence' under the stewardship of the Hashemite dynasty, which 'appreciate[d]' its conditions 'better than Europe'.[31]

It is clear, then, that far from rejecting out of hand the civilisational hierarchies of Euro-American international thought in the name of self-determination, the Hijazi memorandum sought to adapt these to its own ends. Rather than expressing disdain for the technological advances of the West, dismissing them as only so many frivolous distractions from the matters of the person and the spirit, this text sang a paean to the beneficent effects of modernity, which collapsed distance and facilitated the integration of the Arab people. Indeed, it called for more – not less – 'technical' and 'material' assistance from the world. In this respect, this text was at odds with the contemporaneous writings of South Asian thinkers like Rabindranath Tagore and Mohandas Gandhi, who expressed a growing wariness of the trappings of modern life, and argued that the time for Eastern emulation of Western ways was revolute in the wake of the Great War, which had revealed the monstrous capacities of European-made machines for mass destruction.[32] Moreover, the Memorandum used the very same stadial schema that underpinned the Mandates system to array the different component parts of 'Arab Asia' according to their mode of government and the conditions of life of their populations – the 'tribal' regions of the Hijaz sitting firmly at the bottom of the pile, while 'semi-nomadic' Iraq occupied the second place, and sedentary Syria the apex of this rough hierarchy.[33] All this represented, though, a canny attempt to reconcile Britain's commitments and interests with the Hashemites' own desires and objectives. Thus, the Memorandum's insistence on the homogeneous ethnic make-up of western Asia represented a rejection of the equivocation of Sir Henry McMahon's letter to Husayn of 24 October 1915, which had argued that the 'districts of Mersina and Alexandretta and portions of Syria lying to the west of the districts of Damascus, Homs, Hama and Aleppo cannot be

---

31 Ibid., p 103.
32 Adas, 'Contested Hegemony'.
33 'Mémorandum', p 103.

said to be purely Arab, and should be excluded' from any future independent entity – and reserved for French use. But, in acknowledging the specific social circumstances of Iraq, it implicitly accepted the British demand for 'special administrative arrangements' there – and the undeniable facts on the ground of British military occupation.[34] And while its insistence that the Hijaz was unready for foreign assistance might appear to run contrary to Article 22's insistence that those territories particularly remote 'from the centres of civilisation' should not just be placed under mandate rule, but 'administered under the laws of the Mandatory as integral portions of its territory', this could also be seen as an attempt to exploit the language of informal rule, with its stress upon the need to protect certain populations from contact with European civilisation, in order the better to maintain them in a pristine state of tradition.[35] The Hijazi memorandum, one could argue, did not so much blithely accept the precepts of stadial thought as fit this vision of the world to its own ends, deploying it strategically in its attempts to wrest concessions from the Peace Conference.

Much the same can be said of the pleas presented to the Peace Conference by the supporters of Lebanese independence. The first Lebanese delegation thus relied on this language in the Memorandum it presented to the Council of Ten in February 1919. 'Lebanon', it declared, 'would consent to participate in an integral Syria, while keeping its distinct personality, only if the latter were to benefit from the same French collaboration'. Without the guarantees this would provide, Lebanon 'preferred the precariousness of its isolated situation' to the dangers of 'being dragged in the wake of a country which lacked governmental traditions and was less evolved than it was'. This might be regarded as a strategic use of the language of stadial evolution, at a time when the Lebanese delegation remained determined to secure French 'finances' and 'technicians' to assist in the construction of its new state, and unwilling to break entirely with the schemes of the Comité Central Syrien of Shukri Ghanim, which sought the incorporation of an autonomous Mount Lebanon into a federal Syrian polity.[36] Uncertain of France's intentions, and

---

34 'Letter from Sir Henry McMahon to Sharif Hussein, 24 October 1915',
http://www.balfourproject.org/translation-of-a-letter-from-mcmahon-to-husayn-october-24–1915/, last accessed 7 July 2015.
35 'The Covenant of the League of Nations', http://avalon.law.yale.edu/20th_century/leagcov.asp#art22, last accessed 24 July 2015.
36 'Déclarations', pp 108–9.

eager to secure the support of a seemingly powerful patron in the shape of Ghanim, 'Ammun and his colleagues sought to hedge their bets, deploying the language of evolution to make clear the intrinsic distinction between Lebanon and Syria even as they opened the door to a potential political relationship between the two states.

By the autumn of 1919, when the second Lebanese delegation, led by the Maronite patriarch Ilias Huwayyik, presented its memorandum to the Peace Conference, the breach had been made. For one, Ghanim and his views had lost all credibility in the Allies' eyes in the wake of his calamitous appearance before the Council of Ten on 13 February, a week after Faysal and two days before 'Ammun. Though officials at the Quai d'Orsay had hoped Ghanim would 'make a great impact on the Americans'[37], the U.S. delegation was particularly sensitive to the Faysal's charge that Ghanim, for all his claims to speak as the plenipotentiary of the Syrian people, represented only 'certain Syrian committees established abroad', which 'represented but an infinitesimal part of the [Syrian] population'.[38] It was comforted in this belief by the testimony of Howard Bliss, the American missionary president of the Syrian Protestant College in Beirut, who appeared immediately before Ghanim. Related by marriage to Wilson's close advisor Cleveland Dodge – his daughter, Mary, and Dodge's son Bayard, had married in 1914 in Beirut – Bliss was adamant that 'the people of Syria' had not yet had the opportunity 'to express in a perfectly untrammelled way their political wishes and aspirations'. The implication was clear. Ghanim, financially reliant on a French state hungry for territory in the Middle East, was not the man to give a clear and frank account of the desires of his countrymen. As Ghanim rose to speak, the American delegation's Near Eastern advisor, William Linn Westermann, handed Wilson a note pointing out that Ghanim had not returned to Syria, the land on whose behalf he claimed to speak, for some thirty years. But if Bliss had loaded the gun, Ghanim willingly fired it himself. Speaking for some two and a half hours with his habitual pomposity, he drove Wilson to leave his chair to pace impatiently around the room and stare out of the window, and Clemenceau 'savagely' to demand an explanation from his foreign minister, Stephen Pichon.[39] After this showing, Ghanim was an embarrassing liability not just for the Quai d'Orsay, which had long relied on his pen, but also for Lebanese public men like Dawwud

---

37 Andrew and Kanya-Forstner, *France Overseas*, p 187.

38 Khoury, *La France*, p 181.

39 Andrew and Kanya-Forstner, *France Overseas*, pp 187–8.

'Ammun, with whom he had collaborated in the years before the First World War on campaigns to reform the organic law of Mount Lebanon.[40]

For another, the despatch of the King-Crane Commission to the Eastern Mediterranean, and growing anxiety about the intentions of the Arab government established in Damascus, pushed the Administrative Council of Mount Lebanon to declare, on 20 May 1919, the 'political and administrative independence of Lebanon in its historical and geographical borders'.[41] The Rubicon had been crossed; accommodation was no longer possible with the Arab Kingdom. The language of the memorandum presented in the name of Patriarch Huwayyik to the Peace Conference reflected this. 'The independence of Lebanon', this document argued, 'is not simply a de facto independence born of the collapse of Ottoman power; it is also, and especially, a complete independence from any Arab State that might be formed in Syria'. After all, it was clear that 'nothing united these two countries, neither their past, nor their aspirations and intellectual and political evolution'. 'While European education and culture are, with the exception of the great cities, not widespread in Syria where the nomadic element forms an important part of the population, ... there is not a small town or village in Lebanon which does not have a school.' Lebanon, then, was without any doubt the 'principal site of western culture in the East'. The 'degree of culture' it had attained represented 'one of its most incontestable claims to independence'.[42]

But this claim was not simply a riposte to the efforts of Faysal to fold Mount Lebanon and its adjoining territories into the Arab Kingdom. It also implicitly ran counter to the language of Article 22 of the Covenant of the League of Nations, which lay the foundations of the mandates system. This article affirmed that the 'tutelage of such peoples' which 'as a consequence of the late war have ceased to be under the sovereignty of the States which formerly governed them and which are inhabited by peoples not yet able to stand by themselves under the strenuous conditions of the modern world should be entrusted to advanced nations', who could watch over their wards 'until

---

40 On these campaigns, see Hakim, *Origins*, ch. 7; John Spagnolo, *France and Ottoman Lebanon, 1861–1914* (Ithaca Press, London: 1977) chs. 10–11.
41 'Nas al-Qarar Raqm 561 aldhi Atakhadhuh Majlis Idarat Jabal Lubnan fi 20/05/1919', in *L'Empire ottoman*, p 29.
42 'Mémoire de la délégation libanaise à la Conférence de la Paix', in *L'Empire ottoman*, pp 198–200.

such time as they are able to stand alone'.[43] But Lebanon, the Memorandum insisted, was not simply the residue left when the essence of Ottoman sovereignty was burned away. Far from an newly-acquired house which stood empty, waiting to be furnished with the accoutrements of independent life, it had long possessed all the necessary requisites. For not only could it demonstrate impressive cultural attainments, evidence of which gave the lie to the notion it required a tutor to bring it up to speed in the ways of the world. What's more, to this could be added an exceptional level of 'autonomy' from its Arab and Turkish overlords, an 'autonomy' which amounted at times to 'complete independence' and whose founding 'principle' – the separate existence of a Lebanon distinct from the 'neighbouring districts' – the Sublime Porte had continued to uphold even in the depths of the war, as it suppressed the capitulations, committed massacres and starved the Lebanese. This was a precedent the Powers could not ignore.

Indeed, the Memorandum returned in its final pages to the vexed question of the Mandate. If, as Article 22 of the Covenant insisted, 'the wishes' of the 'communities' to be placed under this rule 'must be a principal consideration in the selection of the Mandatory', then the choice of the Lebanese was clear: 'SENTIMENT, AFFINITY ... CULTURE [and] HISTORICAL CONSIDERATIONS' all dictated that France should acquire this right. But while the Memorandum's authors acknowledged – somewhat reluctantly, despite their professions to the contrary – that 'the help and assistance of a great western power' may well be of use 'in the political and economic crisis through which the world is passing', they were far from acquiescing eagerly in the temporary suspension of Lebanon's independence a Mandate would represent. On the contrary, they could not resist querying the very premise of Article 22:

> The present conjuncture and the desire to facilitate the Peace Conference's task, already so laborious, make it a duty for the Lebanese delegation to avoid raising the question of whether Article 22 ... applies to Lebanon, a country which has long been independent, and whose independence, though restrained in form, was confirmed in principle by the règlement organique of 1860–1861.

Even as they professed not to ask the question, then, they provided the answer. Their stance was clear. The 'aim' of the mandates system was 'to

---

43 'Covenant', last accessed 24 July 2015.

hasten the accession to national sovereignty of the peoples to which it was applied'. But Lebanon, 'placed for sixty years under an international mandate' – a reference to the *règlement*, which, because it was guaranteed by the Concert of Powers, was regarded by many Lebanese as a form of international government – 'and having long since completed its political education, deserves today to be a sovereign State'[44] For all that they sought to hedge their reservations in the circuitous niceties and legal circumlocutions of diplomatic prose, the Lebanese delegation's members could not disguise their profound reservations at the post-war order emerging from the negotiations at Versailles. Such doubts give the lie to the notion that these men were mere puppets, subservient clients rolled out onto the international stage to confirm France's claims to control of Syria.

From the think-tank wonks of the Beltway to the propagandists of ISIS, contemporaries seem bent on insisting that the states of the modern Middle East have their origins in the febrile imaginations and cartographic draughtsmanship of European adventurers, diplomats and statesmen, from Sir Mark Sykes and François Georges-Picot to Robert de Caix and Winston Churchill[45] Indeed, few stories seem to sum up these figures' blithe disregard for local sentiments and deep-seated ethno-religious differences better than that of 'Churchill's hiccough'. It would be foolish to deny that there is no truth to such claims. What's more, this would be to disregard the work of generations of scholars who have patiently reconstructed the protracted, and sometimes acrimonious, Anglo-French negotiations that gave rise to the Treaty of San Remo, which gave final shape to the territorial settlement of the Arabic-speaking Eastern Mediterranean. And yet, such narratives tend all too often to gloss over the words of the Hijazi and Lebanese delegations to the Peace Conference. Treating their members as moral archetypes, they draw facile contrasts between Faysal's noble resistance to the imperialist ambitions of the European powers, and the Lebanese delegates' supine collaboration in pursuit of their own irredentist pipedreams. This chapter has sought to correct this oversight and to amend these crude characterisations by homing in on the language in which the Lebanese and Hijazi delegations dressed up their demands for independent statehood. Both parties, it has argued, made strategic use of

---

44 'Mémoire', pp 204–5.
45 For a sharp dissection of such narratives, see Sara Pursley, '"Lines Drawn on an Empty Map": Iraq's Borders and the Legend of the Artificial State', http://www.jadaliyya.com/pages/index/21759/lines-drawn-on-an-empty-map_iraq's-borders-and-the, last accessed 26 July 2015.

the language of stadial evolution and civilisational hierarchies, deploying it to press home their own claims, to denigrate those of their rivals and, increasingly, to contest the terms of the post-war settlement and the application of Article 22 of the League of Nations Covenant to Lebanon and Syria. They did not, however, turn their backs entirely on the new global order built upon the language of civilisation – an order at whose centre lay the Mandates system, that artefact of late imperial stadial thought. But nor did they accept its terms unreservedly. Turning this language in upon itself, they used it to argue for full sovereign statehood without any foreign suzerainty. In the end, both delegations may have shared more than they wished to acknowledge

8

A thoroughly modern Caliphate: could legitimate governance for the Middle East in the aftermath of the First World War have been found by looking within?

Louise Pyne-Jones

The First World War marked a momentous turning point for Middle Eastern questions of power and authority. The notion of democracy, as it is understood by current definitions, was only just developing. The newest growth was a regional awakening to nationalism, symptomatic of its ever-expanding international reach. At that time nationalism took on new forms, adopting elements of the nation-states it passed through. In the Arab world, a similar pattern emerged in other nations that were moving away from the reaches of colonialism. However, in this region there was one key factor that stood to oppose the imported European vision of nationalism[1] – the long held wish for a Caliphate *khilafah*[2]. Emerging from and resisting centuries of Ottoman rule, Arabs in the region found not only a newly defined identity and unity in nationalism, but also called into question their definition of what a legitimate Caliphate should be, in contrast with the Ottoman version under which they

---

1 C.Ernest Dawn, 'The Amir of Mecca Al-Husayn Ibn-'Ali and the Origin of the Arab Revolt', in *Proceedings of the American Philosophical Society* 104 (1960) p 11.

2 Transliterations as per IJMES style.

had been subjects for centuries. The notion of an Islamic state was therefore strong under the Ottoman Empire, however the Ottomans 'dispensed altogether with Khalafah as the framework of government. In effect, the classical paradigm was rendered irrelevant by the seeming contradiction between substance (state) and form (government).'[3] There were many characters that played a significant role in this transition; one key figure was the Sherif Al-Husayn Ibn-'Ali of Mecca, whose intermediary and diplomatic role went some way in spearheading various derivative movements of these juxtaposed ideas of tradition and modernity.

This chapter aims to address some of the means by which a form of governance or authority can claim legitimacy. Enemo suggests that legitimacy comes through self-determination. She states, 'For a government to be regarded as legitimate it must receive the "consent" of the population of the relevant states that are entitled to institute a government for themselves and delimit the power exercisable by their government. The legitimisation of a government depends on the "will" of the members of the relevant population. A people are entitled to thus, whether by popular elections or a hereditary succession, or by other such means, to indicate the system of governance which they desire and the identity of the personnel administering such a system.'[4] She suggests that any form of selecting rulers and administration is necessary for a legitimate government. It is the people's possession of choice that constitutes real legitimacy. Defining terms etymologically would similarly lead to the conclusion that is undeniably what a democracy should be. The primary concern of the legitimate modern state lies in the freedom of choice. As such a dictatorship in which the citizens of a state had no right to determine their governance, would therefore not be considered legitimate. For those states that were developing within an era of crumbling empires, self-determination could have also been crucial for independence.

Following the theme of self-determination, Wilfred Scawen Blunt also suggests that self-determination, or at least acceptance of internal responsibility of the actors within a state may be a preferred mode of governance. On the future of Islam in 1882 he stated, '..in all great movements of human intellect,

3 Tareq Y. Ismael and Jacqueline S. Ismael, *Government and Politics in Islam* (Frances Pinter, London: 1985) p 25.
4 Ifeoma Enemo, 'Self-determination as a Fundamental Basis of Governance', in Edward, K. Quashigah and Obiora Okafor, O.C (eds), *Legitimate Governance in Africa: International and Domestic Legal Perspectives* (Kluwer Law International, The Hague: 1999) p 404.

the force of progression or decay should be looked for mainly from within, not from without..'[5] Any issues with governance should be organised internally, within the structure, culture or politics of the state itself as opposed to externally. His reference to progression and decay echo the theme of modernisation that was apparent during and following the First World War, and that he most probably felt very strongly at the time of his writing.

One of the most relevant forms of self-determination was the French policy of 'association'. In the earlier part of the Third Republic, the French still used assimilationist tools such as education and the assumed illustriousness of the French language to acquire some form of legitimate rule amongst subjects of the empire. Although, the movement away from traditional to more modern forms of authority, as well as the French move towards secularity (laicite) meant that these polices soon became too stark a contrast to the rising modernity.[6] As such, 'association' became the new policy thought up to give the natives in French colonies the opportunity to govern themselves to an extent, with the direction or advice of the French imperial administration, but with a native leader or 'chief' at the helm. The British also had a similar, but less official and somewhat more successful[7] policy in their colonies during the same period.

Weber's types of legitimate domination[8] summarise not only three key models of governance, but also illustrate perfectly the transition from the traditional to the modern. The three types of authority: traditional, charismatic and rational-legal are perfect tools for a clear and linear analysis of governance in the Middle East at this time. Traditional authority is defined as, 'patriarchal rule over others without question.'[9] It is handed down through history and is given legitimacy by its customs and traditions. As such the familial or tribal rule of the Hijaz had been such a type of rule for a significant part of its history. A move away from this could have been another part of the persistent

---

5 Wilfred Scawen Blunt, The Future of Islam, (ed) Riad Nourallah (Routledge Curzon, London: 2002) p 154.

6 Raymond Betts, Assimilation and Association in French Colonial Theory, 1890–1914 (Columbia University Press, New York: 1961) pp 1–224.

7 Michael Crowder, 'Indirect Rule: French and British style', in Africa: Journal of the International African Institute 34 (1964) p 197.

8 Max Weber, Economy and Society: an outline of interpretative sociology (Bedminster Press, New York: 1968) p 212.

9 Ibid., p 227.

international shift towards modernity, or perhaps a natural change with its effects being found primarily internally. Weber's charismatic authority can be seen in many leaders of the current era. The charismatic form of authority is given legitimacy by the leader's apparent mystical powers and revelations. Finally, in Weber's model is rational-legal authority, which is possibly the model that is most analogous with today's Western democracy, leaders are elected, and it is their status that allows them to rule their populations. The fact that these leaders are elected in turn affirms their legitimacy, and it is the population having an influence over that decision by way of choice that makes the population more willing to accept them as leader. Rational-legal author-ity is pivotal to contemporary society as it is based on rationalisation, and is widely considered the ideal form of authority. Therefore, the era of modernity that was progressing rapidly leading up to and in the aftermath of the First World War could be interpreted as a move from more traditional authority towards rational-legal authority.

Foucault's ideas also shed some light on the idea of governance. His lecture series at the College de France are particularly insightful on this subject. In his 'Lectures at the College de France' series he suggests that it is success or failure of governance that will 'replace the division between legitimacy and illegitimacy.'[10] 'In other words, governments can be mistaken…what makes it a bad government, is not that the prince is wicked, but that he is ignorant.'[11] In these lectures Foucault enters his familiar knowledge/power paradigm while considering political economy as the rationality, which allows a government to self-regulate, and therefore legitimate itself in this way.

Foucault's work has also detailed the 'paradox of the shepherd – the sac-rifice of one for all, and all for one.'[12] In line with this notion of 'pastoral', Bordieu also suggests that the group favours 'subordination of the *I* to the *us*, or the sacrificing of individual interest to the general interest.' [13] In other words it is always easier to follow the rules. Bordieu also defines legitimacy as needing some level of ethicality. He states that, 'groups always reward

---

10 Michel Foucault, *The Birth of Biopolitics: Lectures at the College de France 1978–1979* (Picador, New York: 2008) p 16.

11 Ibid. p 17.

12 Michel Foucault, *Security, Territory and Population: Lectures at the College de France 1977–78.* (Picador, New York: 2009) p 129.

13 Pierre Bordieu, *Practical Reason: On the Theory of Action* (Polity Press, Cambridge: 1998) p 142.

conduct that conforms universally (in reality, or at least in intention) to virtue.'
[14] Therefore the notion of the leader's authority is seen as supreme, because the population trust in the legitimacy of their leader because he is virtuous. Again, as stated earlier this form of governance has been recorded in some of Husayn's actions and policies.

The historiography of Husayn Ibn 'Ali al- Hashimi of Mecca is somewhat mixed, some note him as a strong leader, who, 'enjoyed a certain degree of legitimacy as Amir of Mecca.'[15] An account from an English officer in Mecca in describes Husayn with admiration:

> The present Shareef, Sayyid Hussain, is a very popular man. From what I could see he fully deserves the estimation in which he is he is held.[16]

His part in the equivocal negotiations with McMahon is sometimes criticised. Husayn faced a multitude of challenges in maintaining the ideal of a virtuous, just ruler. He struggled between striving to be an upright religious leader for his community, a true Sharif (in itself meaning 'noble'), whilst working under the authority of the Ottoman Empire, which he believed to not be carrying forward the ultimate and appropriate version of a Caliphate. Once the Sharifate became his in 1924, 'Husayn declared himself Caliph. The issue of an Arabian and/or Sharifan Caliphate had been floating about since at least the fifteenth century. Husayn may, therefore, have harboured such a notion throughout his adult life.'[17] This substantiates the notion of the Sharifan Caliphate being a form of self-determined governance, which could have been popularly accepted with successful implementation. The outcome of Husayn's rule, however, was that it did not get the opportunity to recognise such a long-term success.

The role of 'Sharif' was taken very seriously by the rulers of Arabia. In his significant 14th century text the Muqaddimah, Ibn Khaldun states that the 'restraining influence, hence his power, derived from the "great respect and veneration" he enjoyed among the people. This would suggest that the

---

14 Ibid., p 142.

15 Joshua Teitelbaum, *The Rise and Fall of the Hashemite Kingdom of Arabia.* (Hurst and Company, London: 2001) p 4.

16 A.J.B Wavell, *A Modern Pilgrim in Mecca* (Constable and Company Ltd., London: 1918) p 210.

17 Teitelbaum, *The Rise and Fall,* p 42.

shaykh possesses authority because his conduct is deemed legitimate in the light of some ideology or system of values.'[18] Honour and nobility were key elements of this type of rule and these values were instilled in leaders at a young age. In order to avoid corruption, 'members of the ruling elite were to be systematically trained from early youth in military and administrative skills and, at the same time were to be profoundly imbued with a pervasive ethos intimately linked to the legitimacy of the state they served. They were to be cut off from the temptations of kin and wealth, which otherwise distract men from the performance of their political duty.'[19] If we acknowledge Husayn's possible upbringing in this manner, his intentions in the correspondence with McMahon could be reinterpreted. Reconsidering the correspondence with further understanding of the Sharif's background could shed more light on his actions and requests toward the British, and similarly on his responses to them. The overall tone in the correspondence is greatly misunderstood by each side. Husayn often refers to a coldness in the tone of McMahon's words. One instance of which McMahon makes a swift and diplomatic apology:

> I regret that you should have received from my last letter the impression
> that I regarded the question of limits and boundaries with coldness and
> hesitation."[20]

It is quite clear to see how the miscommunications could have arrived. Any promises made, Husayn may have believed were in confidence and trust, as per tribal chiefdom rule, a man's word was binding and honourable.

Using the Weber model Sharif Husayn's initial style of authority could then be categorised as 'traditional'. This type of leadership is also echoed in Foucault who outlines a pastoral power model. Pastoral for Foucault represents

---

18 Steven, C. Caton, 'Anthropological Theories of Tribe and State Formation in the Middle East: Ideology and the Semiotics of Power', in Philip.S Khoury, and Joseph Kostiner (eds), *Tribes and State Formation in the Middle East*, (University of California Press, Los Angeles: 1990) p 87.

19 Ernest Gellner, 'Tribalism and the State in the Middle East', in *Tribes and State Formation in the Middle East*, p 114.

20 Curzon of Kedleston. *Letter from Sir H McMahon, His Majesty's High Commisioner, Cairo, to the Sherif of Mecca, dated October 25 1915.* Copy of letter from Lord Curzon to Lord Cornwallis, covering copies of correspondence between the Sherif of Mecca and Sir H. McMahon for communication to H.H Emir Feisal. CAB/24/89/41. The National Archives, Kew.

the 'theme of the king, god, or chief as a shepherd *(berger)* of men, who are like his flock.'[21] Parallel to the importance of morality upheld in the rule of the *Sharif*, Foucault's 'pastoral power is entirely defined by its beneficence; its only raison d'etre is to do good.'[22] Described in this text predominantly as a Judeao-Christian concern, it can be also be seen echoed in the rule and 'systematic training,'[23] of the Sharif.

The question of morality and its significance to legitimacy is an important one in the context of Arabia at that time. As mentioned earlier, it was key in legitimising tribal forms of authority. 'One vital characteristic of chiefdoms, therefore is the status and role of their chiefs...for a tribal leader to become a chief, he must first combine a certain "moral authority" over his fellow tribesmen with the ability to deliver a "continuous flow of goods and services to his other followers", to retain his wider leadership.'[24]

Weber also said that 'the legitimacy of the political leader lay in his conformity to 'moral standard' or 'operative ideals' of society'[25] Applying Weber's types of authority, Husayn could have exemplified the traditional leader in that he was 'honourable' and 'had virtue'[26] Although he characterised the more traditional form of authority his encouragement of nationalism, in spite of his intentions there, outlined a move towards the modern 'rational-legal' form of governance, which as explained previously has been categorised as modern. Ibn Saud's takeover of the Hijaz in 1925 completed a circle in types of governance for the region as he moved it firmly once again to a traditional form of governance, where it has remained until this day.

Nationalism may not have had its most prolific foothold in the Middle East. It is considered that the ideas of modern versus traditional were quite markedly polarised and this may have hindered the success of nationalism in the region. Piscatori interprets this polarity as lying within the Islamic schools of thought as two opposing views on nation-states. He compares the nation-state as a fact of life, in which 'national pluralism is a fact of life which cannot be

---

21 Foucault, *Security*, p 123.
22 Foucault, *Security*, p 126.
23 Gellner, *Tribalism*, p 114.
24 *Tribes and State Formation in the Middle East*, p 8.
25 David Beetham, *Max Weber and the Theory of Modern Politics* (Polity Press, Cambridge: 1992) p 115.
26 Weber, *Economy*, p 227.

ignored'[27] versus the nation-state as natural 'more unfortunate fact of life…a natural institution and to be expected in the order of things.'[28]

Contrastingly, however, the concept of a core nation-state in the Arabian peninsula was also considered of particular importance as the Ottoman Empire was coming to an end. Viewed with enormous hope and a point of reference for future Arab states, the Hashemite Kingdom of the Hijaz was the first independent state to emerge from the Ottoman Empire[29]. Primarily the potential incompatibility and cause for future failure, lay with the notion of the nation-state, which was essentially a more distant concept to the Arab world in general 'a novelty to Arab-Islamic history. In the first place, it is based on the concept of internal sovereignty. A basic component of this internal sovereignty is the idea of citizenship, which presupposes transforming tribal and, in general, prenational ties into a national identity and loyalty. Second, the modern nation-state is based on the concept of external sovereignty, which refers to the mutual recognition of boundaries by a set of states that form a systematic framework of interaction, a concept that has no counterpart in Arab-Islamic history.'[30] The concept was therefore not a part of the Islamic intellectual tradition. In the Hijaz specifically the most important reason for a lack of nationalism was the 'strength of religious identity among the people and the elites of the Hijaz.'[31] Oschenwald outlines the irony of the revolt starting in the Hijaz which was not nationalistic and whose leader was 'a very late recruit to the cause of Arab nationalism.'[32]

Nationalism worked in some part that it unified Arabs, and helped to give them a stronger sense of identity, which could be used as a force to rebel against the Empires. During a time of war nationalism helped equally to seal a sense of patriotism, and of course encourage conscriptions.[33]

If legitimacy in the overall context of the Middle East equalled self-determined governance in the aftermath of the First World War, the traditional

---

27 James Piscatori, *Islam in a World of Nation-States* (Cambridge University Press, Cambridge: 1986) pp 82–83.

28 Piscatori, *Islam in a World of Nation-States*, pp 82–83.

29 Teitelbaum, *The Rise and Fall*, p 3.

30 Tibi, 'The Simultaneity', p 127.

31 William Oschenwald, 'Ironic origins: Arab nationalism in the Hijaz, 1882–1914', in Rashid Khalidi, Lisa Anderson, Muhammad Muslih, and Reeva S. Simon (eds), *The Origins of Arab Nationalism* (Columbia University Press, New York: 1991) p 190.

32 Oschenwald, 'Ironic Origins', p 199.

33 Aylward Shorter, *African Recruits and Missionary Conscripts: The White Fathers and the Great War (1914–1922)* (Missionaries of Africa, London: 2007).

tribal authority could then be put forward as a legitimate form of governance. Subsequently, as mentioned at the beginning of this chapter this would also require resonance and popularity with the population in order to constitute a truly legitimate form of governance. Firstly, the re-examining of what defines tribal governance would be beneficial for a just analysis to be made. Historical perceptions of tribe can be somewhat homogenous, as Tapper criticises in his text. He says, 'The nature of indigenous concepts of tribe, whether explicit ideologies or implicit practical notions, has too often been obscured by the apparent desire of investigators (anthropologists, historians, and administrators) to establish a consistent and stable terminology for political groups.'[34] He concludes that this singular view of tribes is incorrect as there are a variety of types of authority within any individual tribe. 'Some tribes are renowned for their independent spirit and democratic institutions; elsewhere the stereotype is of strong centralised confederacies under powerful and aristocratic chiefs.'[35] Therefore, a critical analysis would need to take place to re-examine the term, which goes beyond the scope of this work.

Secondly, other indicators for noting the satisfaction of a populace with their ruler need to be noted. The extent to which there is dissent or protest about their rule could be an indicator. Ethnographic data analysed in Caton's text[36] demonstrated that inequality was not contested by the tribesmen. 'Although real economic and political inequalities exist, it is not clear from the ethnographic data that the relationship of the elites to their tribal followers can said to be "exploitative."'[37] In a case study of the Kababish people Caton argues, 'that though economic inequality exists, it would be wrong to suppose that the tribes people feel "oppressed" by their tribal elite.'[38] Herein it could be argued that tribal inequality did not cause extensive division within the communities. The associationist policy employed by the French empire is an example of to allow people to be ruled by a tribal leader without feeling as oppressed as by an imported ruler.[39] The relationship can quite clearly be made therefore

---

34 Richard Tapper, 'Anthropologists, Historians, and Tribes people on Tribe and State Formation in the Middle East', in Philip.S Khoury and Joseph Kostiner (eds), *Tribes and State Formation in the Middle East*, (University of California Press, Los Angeles: 1990) p 55.

35 Tapper, 'Anthropologists, Historians', p 55.

36 Caton, *'Anthropological Theories'*, pp 83–84.

37 Ibid., p 84.

38 Ibid.

39 Betts, *Association*, p 156.

between the success of governance that allows greater self-determination and it creating greater legitimacy. In order to further this analysis, this framework needs to be directly applied to the events of the time.

Achieving a clear definition of an Islamic state may be beneficial for the considerations of this chapter, primarily because the term in its Islamic context is somewhat paradoxical. In Islamic teachings a 'state', in the modern sense, herein defined as the nation-state, did not exist as a concept at that time. Not in the sense that borders could be drawn and territory defined. The notion of a Muslim *ummah* was stronger for Sharif Husayn and the people of Arabia, than the notion of statehood.[40] At the start of the First World War, Muslim community would have been a stronger force than an Arab identity, particularly in this region. As the centre of the Islamic faith, 'the Hijaz was socially fragmented and ethnically mixed.' [41]diminishing nationalist notions, and increasing religious ties in its society.

However, the international, borderless Muslim *ummah* were coming into contact with nationalism. This was much more significant in countries of the Levant that were experiencing a more direct contact with European ideas and peoples.[42] In the Islamic tradition there was, and always had been, an identifiable interest in the shift between traditional and modern. Those who travelled were also educated, as directly commanded in the Quran, which encourages the Muslim to educate himself and use the gift of rational thought.[43] Gellner notes, '..the Muslim world is pervaded by a reverence for the high-culture variant of Islam – egalitarian, scripturalist, puritan and nomocratic. This ethos seems to have a life and authority of its own, not visibly dependent on any institutional incarnation. In normal conditions this ideal is implemented, at most, in a relatively small part of Muslim society by the urban scholars and by their socially well-placed clientele. The ideal presupposes literacy and an ethic of abiding by rules rather than of personal loyalty.'[44] Gellner's notion of this element of a Middle Eastern 'quasi-state'[45] suggests that the Islamic ideal, although upheld by the elites, actually echoed the western modern traditions

---

40 Elie Kedourie, *In the Anglo-Arab Labyrinth: The McMahon-Husayn Correspondence and its Interpretations 1914–1939.* (Cambridge University Press, Cambridge: 1976).

41 Alangari, *Struggle*, p 44.

42 Dawn, *'The Origins of Arab Nationalism'*, p 1.

43 'Read. Read in the name of thy Lord who created;' Quran (96:1–5).

44 Gellner, 'Tribalism', p 113.

45 Ibid. p 109.

that were emerging in the aftermath of the war. The Islamic ideals of literacy and reason equating intellectual and spiritual strength reverberated much more closely with western enlightenment ideals than is widely imagined. This reconsideration of Islamic thought as rational and modern. Ismael and Ismael consider Classic Islamic Thought as a progressive intellectual movement, 'Islam has usually been perceived as a 'traditional' force, resisting progressive change. This image has contributed to the failure to recognise the significance of Islamic solutions to the issues of social and political development.'[46] This analysis is key to developing a legitimate self-determined form of governance.

If a rational legal state requires a legal system and rational choice, then the structures of Al-Shura and Shari'a could in part apply these two concepts. Al-Shura is a form of democracy, coming from the Quran that states that Muslims must make decisions on their governance in consultation with others. Within Al-Shura there is an element of accountability. If legitimacy equates to ethicality could this create legitimacy. As mentioned earlier, this is illustrated well by Bordieu, who considers 'virtue' to play an important role in legitimating governance. Sharia is considered God's law, which due to its very nature is considered the ultimate authority. The rational/legal mode of authority, which as mentioned earlier is the considered the ideal form of modern authority, could therefore be compatible with Al-Shura or Islamic democracy where authority is decided in consultation, and democratically with elections. Ultimately, as Gellner suggests: '...the question of legitimacy is said to be a function of the provisions of the law, and is therefore context-dependent.'[47] Therefore, legitimacy is context dependent and would possibly best suit the laws native to that same context.

Legitimacy, in the modern sense, is often associated with rationality. Moving into the modern era following the First World War, rational-legal authority granted the populations of an increasing number of world-states some form of agency. Additionally, it provided the administration with legal guidelines within which to better govern. If as suggested by Weber, legitimacy must come from the population's belief in the system that governs it, then that belief renders that same system legitimate. As a result of that legitimacy, the population would then follow the lead of that same system. Others have also claimed that 'the legitimacy of the political leader lay in his conformity to

---

46 Ismael and Ismael, *Government*, p 3.
47 Enemo, 'Self-determination', p 405.

'moral standard' or 'operative ideals' of society'.[48] As discussed in this paper, these two characteristics could be found in Arabia before the First World War, and are equally representative of Islamic principles. Therefore, it could be concluded that a Caliphate could have worked well as a rational-legal, modern, and legitimate form of governance in Arabia. However, this ideal was not achieved in the long-term in Arabia, nor in other states in the Middle East in the aftermath of the First World War.

The irony is, as Oschenwald describes[49], that nationalism started in the state of the Middle East that had the least natural propensity for it. Despite Arabia and Husayn playing a considerable role in the establishing a sentiment of nationalism, it was later to be in Syria, Lebanon, Iraq and Palestine in the cross hairs of the British and French mandates, where the strongest Arab national identity was shaped.

48 Beetham, *Weber*, p 115.
49 Oschenwald, *Ironic Origins*, p 199.

9

From the Archduke to the Caliph: the Islamist evolution that led to 'The Islamic State'

Aaron Y. Zelin

On the first night of Ramadan in 2014, Abu Muhammad al-Adnani, the spokes-man for the Islamic State of Iraq and al-Sham (ISIS), announced a step that he described as 'a dream that lives in the depths of every Muslim believer': the re-establishment of the Caliphate. 'It is a hope that flutters in the heart of every mujahid [one who does jihad] muwahhid [monotheist],' he continued. 'It is the caliphate. It is the caliphate – the abandoned obligation of the era...We clarify to the Muslims that with this declaration of the caliphate, it is incumbent upon all Muslims to pledge allegiance to the caliph [Abu Bakr al-Baghdadi].'[1]

The announcement of the Caliphate's creation on the first day of Ramadan, which is the holiest month of the year for Muslims, was no doubt meant to invoke the religious significance of the event. But the Gregorian date has sig-nificance as well: The 29 June announcement came one day after the 100th anniversary of the assassination of Archduke Franz Ferdinand of Austria and his wife, Sophie, Duchess of Hohenberg, which marked the beginning of the First World War. While many historians point to Ataturk's abolition of the caliphate on 3 March 1924 as the end of the last line of Caliphs, Islamic State followers see this as just the logical conclusion of a process that started a decade earlier with the First World War, which led to the partition of the

---

1 Abu Muhammad al-Adnani, 'This Is the Promise Of God', al-Furqan Media, 29 June 2014.

Middle Eastern states – a narrative that resonates for many in the region. Therefore, the 29 June 2014 announcement has been framed as an end to a century-long calamity, and as marking the return of dignity and honour to the Islamic umma.

The Islamic State argues that it is the heir of past Caliphates, especially the original Rashidun Caliphate (632–661). The Islamic State also claims that it has been able to achieve what no other Islamist movement, such as the Muslim Brotherhood or al-Qaeda, has been able to do in the past century: fill the void left by the abolition of the caliphate and create a Muslim renaissance. It could now also argue that – unlike the past failed attempts to resurrect the Caliphate by the Khilafat Movement in British India and the stillborn Sharifian Caliphate in what is today Saudi Arabia – the Islamic State was actually able to deliver a success for Muslims, and provide them with hope and strength once more.

To better understand how we got to this point, it is important to look back at how some Muslims reacted to the abolition of the Caliphate. To do this, I will look at the intellectual history that evolved out of this that has led to the Islamic State and the re-emergence of its so-called 'Caliphate.' There are two main elements that contributed to the creation of the ideology and movement of jihadism: the socio-revolutionary Muslim Brotherhood-style Islamism of Sayyid Qutb and doctrinal/legalistic Salafism. Understanding their evolutions will help illustrate how jihadism came to be and how it differentiates itself. Each movement tried to answer how to revitalise Islam in society and return it to the glory of the idealised Caliphate years.

Although the contemporary use of the term *Islamism* did not come into vogue until the 1970s, the trend itself began to make a mark organisationally in the late 1920s with the creation of the Egyptian Muslim Brotherhood (also called the *Ikhwan* for short).[2] Put simply, according to Peter Mandaville, Islamism is an ideology and political project that 'forms of political theory and practice that have as their goal the establishment of the Islamic political order in the sense of a state whose governmental principles, institutions, and legal system derive directly from the shari'a.'[3] It has also been described by Guilain Denoeux as 'a form of instrumentalization of Islam by individuals, groups, and organizations that pursue political objectives ... provides

2 Martin Kramer, 'Coming to Terms: Fundamentalists or Islamists?', in *Middle East Quarterly*, Spring 2003, pp 65–77.
3 Peter Mandaville, *Global Political Islam* (Routledge, London, New York: 2007) p 57.

political responses to today's societal challenges by imagining a future, the foundations for which rest on reappropriated, reinvented concepts borrowed from Islamic tradition.'[4]

Part of this transformation was a result of encouraged or forced reforms especially on legal and judicial matters in countries that came under the influence of Western European nations as well as colonial or mandatory rule. Not only did it change the relationship between ruler and the *ulama* (religious scholars), but also how the structure of the 'state' was set up. Prior to the introduction of Westphalian nation-state model, the relation between the ruler and *ulama* was more informal. Making matters more complicated, new Islamist players did not conceive of their vision through the lens of the classical Islamic state, but rather envisioning their program through the modern nation-state. With the formalisation of the state came the codification of law. The codification of the shari'a specifically changed everything:

> The transformation of the shari'a – from a body of doctrines and principles
> to be discovered by the human efforts of scholars to a set of rules that
> could be looked up in a code – effected a corresponding transformation
> in the social meaning of the role of the scholars as keepers of the law.
> In the classical era, a person asking the question 'where is the law?' in
> the Islamic world could be answered only by an interlocutor's pointing
> to the scholars and saying 'the shari'a is with them.' After the *Mecelle*
> [Turkish civil code that codified the shari'a], the same question could
> be answered by pointing to the code itself – not to those empowered to
> apply it. Codification therefore sounded the death knell for the role of the
> scholars as keepers of the law … The other reason codification deprived
> the scholarly class of its role was that when the lawmaking body usurped
> the scholars' final authority over the law, it shifted the locus of ultimate
> legal authority. What had remained for centuries in the hands of quasi-
> independent class of scholars now passed into the ambit of the state.[5]

As a result, the *ulama* became co-opted by the state and ruler and therefore lacked the same type of independence it previously had. This led to a loss of

---

4 Guilian Denoeux, 'The Forgotten Swamp: Navigating Political Islam', in *Middle East Policy*, Vol 9, No 2, (2002).

5 Noah Feldman, *The Fall and the Rise of the Islamic State* (Princeton University Press, Princeton: 2008) p 63.

legitimacy, which the *ulama* still struggles with today in a number of locations. This taking away of the *ulama*'s status and power created a vacuum, which would be filled not by those that had studied religion as a form of occupation, but by laymen. Since the founder of the *Ikhwan*, Hasan al-Banna, articulated his ideological project, Islamist actors have continually critiqued the *ulama* as palace scholars or lackeys that have let the *umma* (worldwide Islamic community) down.

According to Richard Mitchell, al-Banna and the *Ikhwan* had two main problems with the Egyptian *ulama* at al-Azhar, the most respected Sunni place of high education. First, 'the leading voice of Muslims in the world had failed in its assigned role of spokesperson for a living and dynamic Islam' and second, 'that it had not been vigorous enough in its resistance to encroachment on the Islamic preserve by foreign ideas and values.'[6] Therefore, 'the failure of the al-Azhar was that "it graduated religious literates, not ... spiritual guides".' The 'al-Azhar *ulama* are thus seen as inefficient teachers of an irrelevant doctrine.' Moreover, 'having failed to understand their positive mission the *ulama* failed in their negative one -the "defense of Islam".'[7]

As a consequence of this, Nelly Lahoud argues that within the vacuum that the *ulama* created by being co-opted by the state, Islamists that lacked the training and background in classical Islamic doctrine misused it for their own political aims. The Islamists decontextualised the original meaning and purpose and applied it to the current circumstance even if that is not its appropriate use:

> One critical consequence of the politicization of the religious sphere has been the emergence of a political space that allows contenders without classical religious training to challenge, on the basis of Islamic teachings, not just the political establishment but also religious establishment itself. These contenders have assumed ownership of the classical Islamic corpus either as groups (as in the case of Islamists) or as individuals (as in the case of jihadis), giving the classical texts a life of their own and applying them to a modern reality that may not have been intended by the ancients when they wrote their treatises ... For example, what might have been written to advance a purely theological and theoretical

---

6 Richard P. Mitchell, *The Society of the Muslim Brothers* (Oxford University Press, Oxford: 1993) pp 212–213.
7 Ibid.

exercise may be used by some today as a doctrine that has practical application.[8]

Over time, this new lay-led grassroots social movement that first began in Egypt and would later expand elsewhere in the Arab world started becoming real political players on the ground. This created a threat to those in power and in Egypt there would be a major crackdown on the *Ikhwan* in the 1950s and 1960s that led to the radicalisation of its ideology.

The man that would transform Islamism into an even more radical ideology was another Egyptian Sayyid Qutb. In response to the harsh torture that Qutb endured in Egyptian prisons, he created a shift away from al-Banna's program that focused more on building up the *Ikhwan* organisationally and socially within society as well as throwing off the yoke of colonial rule to then try and institute an Islamic State.[9] Rather, Qutb created an intellectual argument so potent that it gave credence to the notion that Egyptian leaders, along with other Arab or Muslim leaders who were not following 'true' shari'a and breaking God's *hakimiyya* (sovereignty), were in fact not truly Muslims but were living in a state of *jahiliyya* (pre-Islamic ignorance).[10] Qutb popularised various ideas and terms that would help establish the ideological framework for overthrowing Muslim regimes to also then implement an Islamic State, which in the past had been taboo since members of the *ulama* were afraid of *fitna* (discord) in society as seen by the civil wars following the death of the Muslim Prophet Muhammad.

According to William McCants and Jarret Brachman, '[Qutb's] narrow definition of true Muslim identity and broad denunciations of existing Muslim societies helped determine the *takfiri* or excommunicative tendencies of subsequent jihadis, who are thus sometimes known interchangeably as Qutbis and as takfiris.'[11] Moreover, Qutb inspired a new generation of individuals that

---

8 Nelly Lahoud, *The Jihadis' Path to Self-Destruction* (Columbia University Press, New York: 2010) pp 105–106.

9 Brynjar Lia, *The Society of the Muslim Brothers in Egypt: The Rise Of an Islamic Mass Movement 1928–1942* (Ithaca Press, Reading, UK: 2006).

10 Sayed Khatab, *The Political Thought of Sayyid Qutb: The Theory of Jahiliyyah* (Routledge, London: 2006); Sayed Khatab, *The Power of Sovereignty: The Political and Ideological Philosophy of Sayyid Qutb* (Routledge, London: 2006).

11 William McCants & Jarret Brachman, 'The Militant Ideology Atlas', Combating Terrorism Center at West Point, November 2006, p 346.

were proto-jihadis in the late 1960s through early 1980s, including his own cell organised in prison; Salih Siriyyah's al-Gama'at al-Shabab Muhammad that led to a failed coup d'état against the Egyptian state on 18 April 1974; Shukri Mustafa's Gama'at al-Muslimin, which was destroyed after a botched kidnapping of former minister of *awqaf* (religious endowments) Muhammad al-Dhahabi on 3 July 1977; and Shaykh 'Umar 'Abd al-Rahman's al-Gama'at al-Islamiyyah and Muhammad 'Abd al-Salam Farrag's Tanzim al-Gihad, who were responsible for the assassination of Egypt's president Anwar al-Sadat on 6 October 1981.[12] All believed these actions would be first steps to a new Islamic State.

Farrag, who was founder of Tanzim al-Jihad, although inspired by the thoughts of Qutb was critical of his programme and provided the first contemporary legitimisation of what we know as jihadism today. Fawaz Gerges notes that Farag's seminal work *al-Gihad al-Farida al-Gha'iba* (Jihad: The Neglected Duty) was the operational manual for jihadis in the 1980s and first half of the 1990s.[13] In it, he promotes the singularity of jihad in Islam and that one should not have spiritual training ahead of time, which was his main issue with Qutb. As he saw it, jihad was a 'neglected duty', so it was necessary to rebel against the 'near enemy' (the Egyptian regime of President al-Sadat in his case). Once this was accomplished, it was one's obligation to create an Islamic state.[14]

While the notion of jihad-first may be taken for granted today it helped propel individuals into the contemporary phenomenon of global jihadism in Afghanistan in the 1980s, which departed from Farag's push for local jihad. Before we get to this, it is important to review Salafism, which combined with the socio-revolutionary ways of the 1960s Ikhwani movement are the key ingredients of what became the ideology of al-Qaeda and the Islamic State.

There are many contours, interpretations, and evolutions within Salafism as a theo-ideological construct and project. The term itself is derived from the Arabic word *al-salaf al-salih*, which is religiously in reference to the pious predecessors: primarily, the first three generations of Muslims. There is much

---

12 For more on Qutb's legacy see: Aaron Y. Zelin, 'al-Farīḍa al-Ghā'iba and al-Sadat's Assassination, a 30 Year Retrospective', *International Journal for Arab Studies*, Vol 3, No 2, (July 2012).

13 Fawaz Gerges, *The Far Enemy: Why Jihad Went Global*, 2nd ed. (Cambridge University Press, Cambridge: 2009) pp 9–10.

14 Muhammad 'Abd al-Salam Farag, *al-Jihad al-Farida al-Gha'iba*.

reverence for the *salaf*, even among non-'Salafi' Muslims. As Sayed Khatab highlights, 'Muslims are overwhelmingly agreed that the salaf are better in their application of Islam then are the *khalaf*" (the successors, which is where the term Caliph is derived, those that succeed Muhammad's believed prophecy).[15] Those that believe in Salafism 'try to emulate *al-salaf al-salih* as closely and in as many spheres of life as possible and construct their beliefs, their behavior and their reading of the sources of Islam to further that goal.'[16] Therefore, 'its emphasis is on doctrinal purity and not politics', in contrast to the Muslim Brotherhood, as Bernard Haykel elucidates.[17]

Further, Haykel explains the backbone of what the intellectual aspects of Salafism is:

Salafism can be understood by looking at three constitutive elements of the movement: theology, which is encapsulated by the concept of *tawhid* [pure monotheism]; law, which is centered on the question of *ijtihad* [independent reason] and whether one should adhere to the teachings of a particular school of law; and politics, which is determined by the particular *manhaj* [methodology] or way Salafis choose to engage in the world. On matters of theology the movement's members appear to be in unanimous agreement on the creedal tenets that define Salafism. On questions of legal theory and practice, the consensus frays somewhat, though most Salafis are of the view that *ijtihad* is a requirement, and that *taqlid* should be avoided, even by the unschooled Muslim. The divisions within the movement are most prominent as is to be expected perhaps, on how to make Salafi teachings pertinent to political life and questions of power.

These differences have led scholars such as Quintan Wiktorowicz to categorise Salafism into three key trends quietists, politicos, and jihadis. According to Wiktorowicz, quietists, are non-violent and primarily focus on *da'wa* (propagation of Islam) and spiritual purification; politicos, attempt to implement

15 Sayed Khatab, *Understanding Islamic Fundamentalism* (American University in Cairo Press, New York: 2011) p 14.
16 Joas Wagemakers, *A Quietist Jihadi: The Ideology and Influence of Abu Muhammad al-Maqdisi* (Cambridge University Press, New York: 2012) p 3.
17 Bernard Haykel, 'On the Nature of Salafi Thought and Action', in Roel Meijer (ed), *Global Salafism: Islam's New Religious Movement* (Columbia University Press, New York: 2009) p 14.

the Salafi *aqida* (creed) to political life, and jihadis, call for violent warfare to upend society to institute its brand of Islam.[18] While other academics such as Thomas Hegghammer have disputed the relevance of these differences when trying to understand the political aspirations and goals of Islamists in general and Salafis more specifically, for the sake of argument, it provides one way of categorising different trends within Salafism.[19] That said, there is the exception of Shaykh Abu Muhammad al-Maqdisi, the most important living jihadi theorist, and whom Joas Wagemakers describes as a hybrid of the quietist and jihadi trends.[20]

Much of the intellectual underpinnings of Salafism comes from the 14th century jurist Taqi al-Din Ibn Taymiyyah and the 18th century ideologue Muhammad Ibn 'Abd al-Wahhab. Their ideas were further sharpened by 20th century Salafi scholars such as Muhammad Nasir al-Din al-Albani, Muhammad Ibn al-Uthaymin, and 'Abd al-'Aziz Ibn Baz. The most relevant religious leader to our discussion is Maqdisi, who used the ideas of Salafism to turn them first against the Saudi state in the 1980s, a Salafi theocracy, that Maqdisi believes is not living up to or upholding true Islam as interpreted by past Salafi scholars. Therefore, similar to Qutb, but within a Salafi construct, Maqdisi believes it is necessary to conduct jihad against the *murtad* (apostate) Saudi regime. Accordingly, Wagemakers tells us that Maqdisi "mostly treats jihad as a tool to oppose *kufr* [disbelief] and *shirk* [polytheism] in order to advance the cause of Islam embodied in *tawhid*, and therefore does not limit jihad to just fighting, but also sees da'wa as a form of struggle ('jihad of the tongue') through which this goal can be achieved."[21]

Before getting deeper into the discussion of contemporary jihadism/global jihad, it is important to explain the Islamic concept of jihad to show how current ideologues are in line with the original conception as well as places where they have innovated or stretched their understanding of the concept.

In its raw form, the Arabic root for the term jihad *j-h-d* means striving or to struggle. Therefore, etymologically jihad does not mean holy war; rather,

---

18 Quintan Wiktorowicz, 'Anatomy of the Salafi Movement', in *Studies in Conflict & Terrorism*, Vol 29, Issue 3 (August 2006) p 208.

19 Thomas Hegghammer, 'Jihadi Salafis or Revolutionaries? On Religion and Politics in the Study of Militant Islamism', in Roel Meijer (ed), *Global Salafism: Islam's New Religious Movement* (Columbia University Press, New York: 2009) pp 248–251, 257–264.

20 Wagemakers, *A Quietist Jihadi: The Ideology and Influence of Abu Muhammad al-Maqdisi.*

21 Ibid., p 58.

if one were to translate the term holy war into Arabic, it would be *al-harb al-muqaddas*.[22] That being said, as Michael Bonner notes:

> When followed by the modifying phrase *fi sabil Allah*, 'in the path of God,' or when-as often-this phrase is absent but assume to be in force, jihad has a specific sense of fighting for the sake of God. In addition, several other Arabic words are closely related to jihad in meaning and usage. These include *ribat*, which denotes pious activity, often related to warfare, and in many contexts seems to constitute a defensive counterpart to a more activist, offensive jihad ... *Ghazw, ghazwa,* and *ghaza'* have to do with raiding. *Qital*, or 'fighting,' at times conveys something similar to jihad/ribat, at times not. *Harb* means 'war' or 'fighting,' usually in a more neutral sense, carrying less ideological weight than the other terms.[23]

Further, Bonner explains that jihad is in reference to a legal doctrine within Islam that is contained in *shari'a* manuals by Islamic scholars. Within these manuals include a 'book of jihad.'[24] Moreover, according to the Encyclopedia of the Qur'an, there are only ten verses connecting the term *jihad* and warfare or fighting (*qital*), while the other verses are in reference to: (1) 'combat against one's own desires and weaknesses'; (2) 'perseverance in observing religious law'; (3) 'seeking religious knowledge'; (4) 'observance of the *sunnah*'; and (5) 'obedience to God and summoning people to worship him.' As has been described in the exegetical literature and *hadith* (sayings and actions of Muhammad), there are two forms of *jihad*: *jihad bi-1 -nafs* (struggle or striving of the self) and *jihad bi- 1-sayf* (striving through fighting).[25] Moreover, as famously cited in the *hadith* literature, after fighting in a battle, Muhammad

---

22 Jihad and the Islamic Law of War (The Royal Aal Al-Bayt Institute for Islamic Thought, Amman, Jordan: 2007), p 1.

23 Michael Bonner, *Jihad in Islamic History: Doctrines and Practice* (Princeton University Press, Princeton: 2006) pp 2–3.

24 Ibid; More specifically, the book of jihad usually discusses: 'law governing the conduct war, which covers treatment of non-belligerents, division of spoils among the victors, and such matters. Declaration and cessation of hostilities are discussed, raising the question of what constitutes proper authority. A Book of Jihad will also include discussion of how the jihad derives from the Quran and the Sunna, or in other words, how the jihad has been commanded by God.'

25 Ella Landau-Tasseron, 'Jihad', in Jane Dammen McAuliffe (ed), *Encyclopedia of the Qur'an*, Vol. 3 (Brill, Leiden, The Netherlands: 2001) p 37.

stated: 'We have returned from the lesser (asghar) jihad (battle) to the greater (akbar) jihad (jihad of the soul).'[26]

While this might be the case, and some scholars such as Muhammad Abdel Haleem have argued that jihad was mainly a defensive measure within a Qur'anic framework. Historically, however, 'there is no denying that the classical legal literature as a whole recognised offensive as well as defensive warfare. There is no denying that Islamic states, such as the caliphate of the Umayyads and 'Abbasids and the Ottoman empire, regularly sent raiding expeditions into non-Muslim territory, in addition to large-scale expeditions of conquest that they undertook from time to time.'[27] This is important because both Qutb and Farag believed in the idea of offensive jihad. Later jihadis such as the godfather of the contemporary jihadi movement, 'Abd Allah 'Azzam, believed that it was more in line with orthodox Islam to justify jihad within a defensive framework.

While 'Azzam, a Palestinian who received his doctorate from al-Azhar University (the preeminent Sunni Islamic school), was interested in framing his arguments about the necessity of jihad in Afghanistan in the 1980s, he did stretch things a little. In 'Azzam's book al-Dafa'a 'an Ard al-Muslimin (Defense of Muslim Lands), he explains the differences and obligations that go with fighting an offensive or defensive jihad. According to 'Azzam, an offensive jihad is fought only in the context of an Islamic state when one is fighting in the kufr's territory. Therefore, the jihad is fard al-kifayah (a collective obligation) meaning not all Muslims need to fight. More importantly, for 'Azzam, was the defensive jihad, which was to "expel the kafir [infidels] from our [Muslim] land," and it is fard 'ayn (individual obligation).[28] 'Azzam's main departure from the orthodox understanding of fard 'ayn, is that in the past it was an individual obligation for those within the territory that had been attacked or occupied to fight jihad against the enemy, whereas 'Azzam argued that it was a duty impinged on all Muslims anywhere to come and help out their fellow

---

26 David Dakake, 'The Myth of a Militant Islam', in Joseph E.B. Lumbard (ed), Islam, Fundamentalism, and the Betrayal of Tradition: Essays by Western Muslim Scholars (World Wisdom, Bloomington, IN: 2004) p 3.

27 Muhammad Abdel Haleem, Understanding the Qur'an: Themes and Style (IB Tauris, London, UK & New York, NY: 1999) pp 60–62; Bonner, Jihad in Islamic History: Doctrines and Practice, p 160.

28 'Abd Allah 'Azzam, Defense of Muslim Lands, (Maktaba Dar- us-Salam, Kingdom of Saudi Arabia: 1993) pp 14–15.

Muslims in need. As a result, this created what became the contemporary phenomenon of Muslim foreign fighting.[29]

Before getting into more granular detail on the contemporary phenomenon of (global) jihadism, it's important to highlight how 'Azzam's message diverted from what became the modus operandi of figures like Usama bin Ladin and his organisation al-Qaeda (and all of the later branches, affiliates, fellow travellers, and rivals). There are key yet subtle differences, which Hegghammer coined: namely, classical jihadism versus global jihadism. According to Hegghammer, classical jihadism, though different, is closer to the orthodox Islamic understanding of jihad than the more radical global jihadism, which is often conflated with classical jihadism. Classical jihadism was first put forth by 'Azzam, who argued: 'non-Muslim infringement of Muslim territory demanded the immediate military involvement of all able Muslim men in defense of the said territory wherever its location.'[30] On the other hand, bin Ladin created the doctrine of global jihadism in the mid-1990s. Hegghammer explains that 'while 'Azzam advocated guerrilla warfare within defined conflict zones against enemies in uniform, bin Ladin called for indiscriminate mass-casualty out-of-area attacks.'[31] Therefore, recruiting individuals to participate in the jihads in Afghanistan in the 1980s and Bosnia and Chechnya in the 1990s would be considered classical jihadism (and did not directly relate to the United States), while al-Qaeda's attacks on Western targets in a variety of locations is global jihadism.[32] Each were hoped to be different ways of bringing about the return of an Islamic State.

In many ways, the anti-Soviet Afghan jihad of the 1980s that brought Muslims together from all over the world – to fight with the Afghan 'mujahidin' against the invading and occupying Soviet Union – helped fuse the more socio-revolutionary aspects within the movements inspired by Qutb in the previous decade with the more doctrinal/legalistic theology of Salafism.

---

29 For more on this phenomenon, see: Thomas Hegghammer, 'The Rise of Muslim Foreign Fighters: Islam and the Globalization of Jihad', *International Security*, Vol 35, No 3 (Winter 2010/11) pp 53–94.

30 Thomas Hegghammer, *Jihad in Saudi Arabia: Violence and Pan-Islamism since 1979* (Cambridge University Press, Cambridge, UK: 2010) p 7.

31 Ibid.

32 It is possible with the growth and evolution of the Islamic State from al-Qaeda that we might be seeing a third type of contemporary jihadism that in a way combines those two, along with the idea of state building, or as the Islamic State prefers to call it: the Caliphate project.

Both Lahoud and Lav pinpoint key departures between Ikhwani Islamism and jihadism as well as purist-Salafism with jihadi-Salafism. Lahoud tells us that a key difference in the former is the more mainstream Islamists are based on a communal emphasis while jihadism is more about the individual. As a consequence of this individualistic way, it is more difficult to control the jihad then, which has led in some cases to backlashes against them such as in Algeria, Iraq, and Somalia, among others:

> In contrast to the communal orientation of Islamism, jihadism is premised on an individualist basis and has completely rejected the nation-state and its secular political processes, focusing solely on jihad as the only path towards bring about an Islamic state/Caliphate that would unite all Muslims worldwide. The jihadis' unbounded zeal for jihad has led them to de-emphasize religious education in the interest of pure activism … Unlike al-Banna's organized conception of jihad, the individual nature of this new jihad purposefully lacked any regulatory mechanisms to organize or police jihad.[33]

Lav emphasises how there are two creedal issues that separate the more mainstream 'purist' Salafi school with the newer 'jihadi' school:

> The extent to which they do or do not adhere exclusively to neo-Hanbali [one of the four Sunni Muslim schools. Much of Salafi doctrine derives from the Hanbali school] doctrine of faith, and the extent to which they view it as applicable to the issue of governance … Thus the period of the emergence of the salafi jihadi school was marked both by a struggle against the quietists to prove that the issue of *hakimiyyah* was a legitimate salafi one, and also by an internal struggle within the radical camp to arrive at a correct reformulation of the issue.[34]

These two points and the mixing of them together in Afghanistan, led to what many describe today as jihadism, salafi-jihadism, or global jihadism. As Lav further highlights, it "shows it to be a total ideology that subsumes all these variations under a global, even cosmic, battle between faith and unbelief."[35]

---

33 Lahoud, *The Jihadis' Path to Self-Destruction*, pp 118; 121.
34 Daniel Lav, *Radical Islam and the Revival of Medieval Theology* (Cambridge University Press, New York: 2012) pp 122, 128.
35 Ibid., p 201.

According to Khatab, in 1988, Sayyid Imam al-Sharif (aka 'Dr. Fadl' and 'Abd al-Qadir Bin 'Abd al-'Aziz), the leader of Egyptian Islamic Jihad, first coined the term 'jihadism': 'he labeled items as the "Milestones of Jihad", and stated that 'we might call these milestones the "creed of jihadism" ['aqidat al-jihadiyya].'"[36] The use of the term did not appear in the academic literature related to the subject until ten years later, though.[37]

While broadly speaking the ideology has been consolidated over the years, there have been key disputes and differences related to doctrinal purity and military strategy within the global jihadi community. Abu Mus'ab al-Suri, a Syrian who was involved in jihadism from the early 1980s until his arrest in Pakistan in 2005, is believed to currently still being jailed in Syria. According to his biographer, Brynjar Lia, Suri was 'a dissident, a critic, and an intellectual in an ideological current in which one would expect to find obedience rather than dissent.'[38] Suri sought to utilise lessons learned from failures in past jihads and integrate it with Maoist and Marxist guerrilla tactics to further the jihadist movement. This is a departure from most purist clerics whom only relied on past Islamic precedents instead of using what is perceived to be polluted outside ideas.

This led Suri into disputes with the Palestinian jihadi ideologue Abu Qatada al-Filistini in London in the 1990s over the Algerian jihad and issues related to takfir. Suri also took issue with al-Qaeda, criticising the 9/11 attacks because he believed that Afghanistan, which was being governed by the Taliban, was crucial to the global Islamic resistance: 'The outcome [of the 9/11 attacks] as I see it, was to put a catastrophic end to the jihadi current. The jihadis entered the tribulations of the current maelstrom which swallowed most of its cadres over the subsequent three years.'[39] Though his ideas about a more decentralised jihad would become more popular over the years with Western jihadis especially and advocated by Americans Adam Gadahn, head of al-Qaeda's media wing al-Sahab, and Anwar al-Awlaqi, former head of external operations for al-Qaeda in the Arabian Peninsula before he was droned.

A more relevant fissure to current discussions is related to Maqdisi's critiques of Abu Mus'ab al-Zarqawi. Until recently, many analysts viewed jihadism only

---

36 Khatab, *Understanding Islamic Fundamentalism*, p 145.

37 Hegghammer, "Jihadi Salafis or Revolutionaries? On Religion and Politics in the Study of Militant Islamism", pp 251–252.

38 Brynjar Lia, *Architect of Global Jihad: The Life of al-Qa'ida Strategist Abu Mus'ab al-Suri* (Oxford University Press, Oxford: 2009) p 3.

39 Ibid., p 314.

through the prism of al Qaeda, which misses the influence of independent jihadi religious scholars. Since the excesses of Zarqawi and al-Qaeda in the Land of Two Rivers last decade, Minbar al-Tawhid wa-1 -Jihad (the Pulpit of Monotheism and Jihad), a library of jihadi primary source material founded by Maqdisi who is currently advocating the cause in Jordan, has attempted to steer the jihadi community to a more 'pure' jihad. To do this, Maqdisi established a shari'a committee of like-minded scholars in 2009 for Minbar that provide *fatawa* (religious jurisprudential rulings) answering questions along a range of topics from the mundane to political to jihad.[40]

One of the main critiques Maqdisi presents, and hopes to create a course correction within the jihadi movement, is his differentiation between the idea of *qital al-nikayya* (fighting to hurt or damage the enemy) and *qital al-tamkin* (fighting to consolidate one's power), which he expounds upon in his book *Waqafat ma' Thamrat al-Jihad* (Stances on the Fruit of Jihad) in 2004.[41]

Maqdisi argues the former provides only short-term tactical victories that in many cases do not amount to much in the long-term. Whereas, the latter provides a framework for consolidating an Islamic state. In this way, Maqdisi highlights the importance of planning, organisation, education, as well as *da'wa* (calling individuals to Islam) activities. As Wagemakers has noted, the creation of the Minbar *shari'* committee was to forward these views to 'protect' the jihad and to better advance the pursuit of a true Islamic state based on the sanctity of the *tawhid* of God. Many groups in the post-Arab uprising era have followed this way, especially the Ansar al-Sharia phenomenon in Tunisia and Libya.[42]

More recently, there have also been debates between al-Qaeda (and its official branch in Syria Jabhat al-Nusrah) and the Islamic State over *manhaj*. The Islamic State and Jabhat al-Nusrah have acted differently on the ground in Syria. For The Islamic State, which believes it truly is an Islamic state, all residents of territory it takes over fall under the group's sovereign will and must abide by its interpretations of God's law. In this model, no competition or power sharing can be acceptable. It is true that The Islamic State added

---

40 Joas Wagemakers, 'Protecting Jihad: The Sharia Council of the Minbar al-Tawhid wa-1 -Jihad', in *Middle East Policy*, Vol 18, Issue 2, (Summer 2011) pp 148–162.
41 Wagemakers, *A Quietist Jihadi: The Ideology and Influence of Abu Muhammad al-Maqdisi*, p 84.
42 Aaron Y. Zelin, 'Maqdisi's Disciples in Libya and Tunisia', *Foreign Policy's Middle East Channel*, November 14, 2012.

a 'hearts and minds' component to its governing strategy, but it has kept its narrower interpretations of *shari'a* pertaining to social or criminal issues. In contrast, Jabhat al-Nusrah viewed itself as one among many groups (primarily other Islamist allies) that must work together not only to fight against the Assad regime, but also to govern liberated spaces. It takes the long view that it cannot force its ideas on individuals and therefore must pursue a more gradualist approach, based on the lessons of past failed attempts at jihadi governance in Iraq last decade, as well as Somalia, Yemen, and Mali. The key is to socialise and normalise its ideas over time so that eventually the group can legitimately implement its more narrow interpretations of *shari'a*.[43]

For now, though, The Islamic State is more popular within the global jihadi milieu because it has tapped into the issue of identity, empowerment, and territorial victory bringing us back to the division of Sykes-Picot and the abolition of the Caliphate. In the view of The Islamic State, all other forms of Islamism have failed including Ikhwani reformism, the local jihadism of Qutb's disciples, and al Qaeda's global jihad. The Islamic State is changing the reality on the ground, which has appeal amongst some young Muslims that feel they are finally overturning the era of Western colonialism and providing agency once more to the region. This is why, the same day as the 'Caliphate' announcement, The Islamic State also released a video symbolically destroying the Sykes-Picot borders by using a bulldozer against a berm on the Iraqi-Syrian border on 29 June.[44] Not only a rebuke to al-Qaeda, which tried to force The Islamic State to only stay in Iraq, which Baghdadi rebuffed since he does not follow the Sykes-Picot borders, only the sovereignty of God, but also the deal itself that happened nearly a century ago.[45] This video was to highlight that the unthinkable could be reversed and that the Muslim *umma* was once again awake. Indeed, for The Islamic State, a new era began.

---

43 For more on the fight between the Islamic State and al-Qa'idah/Jabhat al-Nusrah see: Aaron Y. Zelin, 'The War Between ISIS and al-Qaeda for Supremacy of the Global Jihadist Movement', *Washington Institute for Near East Policy*, Research Notes Number 20, June 2014.
44 The Islamic State of Iraq and al-Sham, 'The End of Sykes-Picot', al-Hayat Media Center, 29 June 2014.
45 Dr. Ayman al-Zawahiri, 'Untitled Statement', in *al-Fajr Media*, 23 May 2013; Abu Bakr al-Hussayni al-Baghdadi, 'Remaining in Iraq and al-Sham', *al-Furqan Media*, 15 June 2013.

10

Some reflections on whether the Mandates were a slow burning fuse for toxic sectarianism in Arab countries

John McHugo

This chapter[1] asks a question. To what extent, if at all, is sectarianism in Arab countries attributable to the Anglo-French partition of the predominantly Arabic speaking provinces of the Ottoman Empire? Was that partition, which took the form of giving League of Nations Mandates to Britain and France over largely Arabic speaking territories in which the majority of the population was Muslim, a fuse which lit the fires of the sectarianism which has subsequently spread across the Arab world?

Three factors link sectarianism directly to the Mandates. The first is the incorporation of the Balfour Declaration into the Palestine Mandate and the ensuing drive to establish a Jewish 'national home' in the form of a predominantly Jewish state on Palestinian soil. This opened a new divide between

---

1 This paper was delivered at the Gingko conference in London in December 2014. Because of time constraints when speaking at the conference, I was unable to deliver the opening sections of the paper on the international law background to the Mandates. In preparing the paper for publication, I would like to thank those participants at the conference who offered constructive criticism from the floor, especially Jason Pack who pointed out that in the text as delivered I had overlooked the significance of the Ottoman *millet* system as part of the essential background to my topic. I would also like to thank Jemima Bland for her insightful comments on my initial draft.

Arabic speaking Jews on the one hand and Arabic speaking Muslims and Christians on the other.

The second is the project, which was encouraged by France as the mandatory power, to establish a Maronite dominated state in Lebanon and to 'protect' and privilege Christians generally at the expense of Muslims.

The third is the natural sense of solidarity among Muslims which provided one of the strands of opposition to the governments of the Mandates – and to the concept of the Mandates themselves. This sometimes excluded non-Muslims or identified them with the mandatory power, thereby fuelling sectarian tendencies.

This chapter begins with some initial words about the concepts of self-determination of peoples and the Mandates. It will then be convenient to touch on the creation of Greater Lebanon and the partition of Palestine, since these flowed directly from the establishment of the Mandate system. The paper will then turn to the attempt to establish a secular, Arab nationalist state in Greater Syria at the end of the First World War. France, with Britain's support, waved a piece of paper called a Mandate to ensure that this attempt did not succeed. Yet, if that state had been allowed to survive and thrive, it is reasonable to hypothesise that it would have hindered the rise of sectarianism. The chapter will then conclude by noting three other important factors behind the much later growth of sectarianism in the territories once covered by the Mandates that cannot be attributed to the Mandates themselves.

The peace conferences at the end of the First World War viewed the world in terms of nations and states, not religions, denominations and sects. In the eyes of the victors, the most important territorial question to be decided was how to incorporate a large land mass which stretched from the Baltic to the Balkans into the system of nation states. This massive area was suddenly free from imperial rule by Austria-Hungary, Russia and Germany. Completely new states came into being: Poland, Czechoslovakia, Lithuania, Latvia and Estonia. At the same time, Romania doubled in size while the new Yugoslavia was in some respects almost unrecognisable from the old Serbia.

The main principle used to redraw the map was the self-determination of peoples. This idea can be traced back to the American Declaration of Independence and the French Revolution[2], and was invoked at various points in the nineteenth century. At the end of the First World War it became, in

2 Cassese, *Self-Determination of Peoples: A Legal Reappraisal* (Cambridge University Press, Cambridge: 1995) p 11

the words of Antonio Cassese, 'the animating *political* ideal which encapsulated the new post-war order.'[3] Its main proponents were Lenin and Woodrow
Wilson, although they advocated the principle in different contexts and Lenin
need not be considered here. Wilson argued that peoples were no longer to
be 'bartered about from sovereignty to sovereignty as if they were mere chat-
tels and pawns in a game'.[4] He saw self-determination as the guiding principle
to be adopted in the post-war division of the Habsburg and Ottoman empires.
Yet, as Robert Lansing, his own Secretary of State, pointed out as early as
December 1918, there was a vagueness to Wilson's concept: 'When the President talks of "self-determination", what unit has he in mind? Does he mean a
race, a territorial area, or a community?'[5]

The concept sometimes clashed with the interests of the victors, including the USA itself. It was not a binding doctrine in international law, and
the victors had no qualms about disregarding it when this suited them.[6] No
provision on self-determination was included in the Covenant of the League
of Nations, and plebiscites to establish the wishes of the populations of specified areas were only rarely contained in the peace treaties executed with the
defeated powers. The principle of self-determination would have to wait until
the 1960s and later before it would become a legal rule, and then only in
strictly defined parameters: chiefly with regard to colonial territories but also
in respect of peoples subject to military occupation.[7] As self-determination
finally emerged as a concept in international law, it was linked to the principle of territorial integrity, and would be deemed to apply to the people of the
political unit which was to be decolonised as a whole. It could not be used
to confer a right of secession on a minority or as an argument for the partition
of a territory between different ethnic or religious groups on decolonisation.[8]

---

3 Ibid, p 4. Emphasis in the original.

4 Ibid, p 20 where his speech of 11 February 1918 is quoted.

5 Ibid, p 22.

6 Ibid, pp 24–7. Thus, the Austrian delegation argued that a plebiscite should be conducted
to establish the wishes of the population in the predominantly German speaking area of South
Tyrol/Alto Adige which was transferred from Austria to Italy, but the request was refused. See
p 24, note 40.

7 Ibid, p 90. The 1970 UN Declaration on Friendly Relations finally 'spelled out' the principle
and made it clear that '"alien subjugation, domination and exploitation" may exist outside a
colonial system'.

8 See Ibid., p 112, where the author writes that (as of 1995) 'the principle of territorial integrity
was, and still is, considered sacred'. However, he subsequently qualifies this on p 119 by

Reverting to Robert Lansing's words, to this day there has been no successful attempt to define 'people' in international law[9]. In the negotiations at the
end of the First World War, provisions to protect 'racial, religious or linguistic
minorities'[10] were inserted in some of the peace treaties which established
the new nation states. (The word "racial" generally carried the meaning that
"ethnic" carries today.) Religious affiliation could be a major marker of ethnicity, and the two were sometimes treated as synonyms or merged and confused
in the negotiations at the peace conferences. This was particularly the case
with regard to discussions about the Jewish populations in eastern European
territories such as Poland and Romania, in respect of which references to 'the
Jewish race and faith'[11] occur, implying that 'race' (or ethnicity) and 'faith'
were, at least in this case, considered to be practically synonymous.

Much of the thinking that went into drafting the new settlement for eastern
and central Europe can also be detected in the wording of the three Mandates
which provided the new territorial framework for the predominantly Arabic
speaking former Ottoman territories (and the predominantly Kurdish areas
included in northern Iraq). The difference was the imposition of the mandatory

---

raising the possibility that it could be argued that secession might be warranted 'when the
central authorities of a sovereign State persistently refuse to grant participatory rights to a
religious or racial group, grossly and systematically trample on their fundamental rights,
and deny the possibility of reaching a peaceful settlement within the framework of the State
structure.' Developments such as the secession of South Sudan and Russia's annexation of
Crimea may suggest that territorial integrity is not quite as sacred today as it was in 1995,
but it remains an immensely strong principle. James Crawford, in *The Creation of States in
International Law* (2nd edition, Oxford University Press, Oxford: 2006) is of the view that 'the
definition of a "people" at large, outside the context of "generally accepted political units" has
proved fraught with difficulty' (p 125). Cassese points out (p 121) that there has been no state
practice since the 1970 UN Declaration on Friendly Relations regarding secession by religious
groups. This surely remains the case today.

9 As Crawford puts it in *The Rights of Peoples* (Oxford University Press, Oxford, 1988) pp
168–9: 'There is no reason to suppose that what constitutes a "people" for the purposes of
one right necessarily satisfies the requirements of another. In other words, the definition of
'people' could well be – indeed having regard to the breadth of the claims to peoples' rights,
is likely to be – context-dependent.' See also note 7 above.

10 Treaty between the Principal Allied and Associated Powers and Poland, 28 June, 1919, Art.
9. See H. W. V. Temperley, *A History of the Peace Conference of Paris* (Henry Frowde and
Hodder and Stoughton, London: 1921) Volume V, p 135. See also Volume IV, pp 137–8 for
identical obligations assumed by Czechoslovakia, Greece, Romania and Yugoslavia.

11 See e.g. Ibid, Vol 5, p 122.

as a kind of 'great trustee'[12] which was intended to supervise the people of the mandated territory in their progress to independence. The basis on which the Mandates were established was the self-determination of peoples, and the preparation of the territory's people for independence was a 'sacred trust of civilisation'.[13] France was granted a Mandate over Syria and Lebanon, while Britain acquired two separate Mandates: Iraq and Palestine (which included what is now Jordan).

But was self-determination intended to apply to the people of each mandated territory as a whole, or was it intended that ethnic or religious groups were to be able to secede? The former was surely the case. The diversity of each territory was implicitly recognised, and discrimination between its inhabitants on grounds of 'race, religion or language'[14] was prohibited. The French Mandate included a reference to the eventual independence of Lebanon as a state separate from Syria.[15] Save for this single exception, the texts of the Mandates suggest that the three new political units were expected to achieve independence as individual sovereign states.[16]

Yet these Mandates had no legitimacy in the eyes of the majority of the inhabitants of the territories included in them. The only systematic attempt to ascertain the wishes of the population was contained in the report of the King-Crane Commission which was deliberately ignored. Nevertheless, the truth

---

12 The expression was used by Faysal in his speech to the Paris peace conference. For the text, see Hurewitz, *Diplomacy in the Near and Middle East: A Documentary Record, 1914–56* (D. Van Nostrand Co, New York: 1956) pp 38–9. His speech was delivered in Arabic and translated into English for the delegates by T.E Lawrence. The English expression is thus presumably attributable to Lawrence.

13 Article 22 of the Covenant of the League of Nations.

14 See the Palestine Mandate, Article 15, the Mandate over Syria and the Lebanon, Article 8, and the Anglo-Iraqi treaty (containing the Iraq Mandate), Article 3.

15 Article 1 of the Mandate envisages that the mandatory shall 'enact measures to facilitate the progressive development of Syria and the Lebanon as independent states'.

16 Note Temperley, Vol VI, p 521, who writes that in respect of the three Mandates 'it is clear that the exercise of powers by the mandatory are to be regarded as purely temporary, and that the role of the mandatory is to provide such protection, advice and assistance as will enable the three countries of Mesopotamia, Syria, and Palestine to become independent States Members of the League [of Nations]'. As mentioned above, the exception was the French Mandate which envisaged a single mandatory government for Syria and Lebanon, but stated at the outset in Article 1 that the mandatory shall 'enact measures to facilitate the progressive development of Syria and Lebanon as independent states'.

was known. H. W. V. Temperley, the official British historian of the peace conferences, recorded that Syrian opinion 'became more and more opposed to any division of [Greater Syria]'[17] in the aftermath of the war. This was scarcely surprising. As well as flying in the face of the principle of self-determination, the partition into the three Mandates created international boundaries where none had existed. This brought baleful consequences such as tariff barriers and other hindrances to trade and economic development, the separation of major centres such as Aleppo and Damascus from much of their natural hinterlands, and the disruption of communal ties.

The boundaries which Britain and France drew for the three Mandates would be inherited on independence. There were no provisions in the Palestine or Iraq mandates to suggest that anything other than a unitary state would be envisaged. The texts of the Mandates carry no hint of future partitions along sectarian or ethnic lines. The analysis above of the principle of self-determination is consistent with this. Yet the mandatories would impose further divisions of their own accord. The most important would be caused by two projects which the people of Greater Syria could only ever have seen as sectarian. The first was the French *fiat* in August 1920 which established a Maronite dominated 'Greater Lebanon'; the second was the dismemberment of Palestine in order to create a Jewish state in 1947–9.[18] Neither project would have succeeded if the Mandates had not been imposed.

The French created a Greater Lebanon right at the start of their Mandate over Syria and Lebanon. The predominantly Maronite sanjak on Mount

---

17 Ibid, Vol. VI, p 143. This volume of the history was published in 1924, but in the passage concerned Temperley was writing about events in December 1918.

18 Other notable divisions were the hiving off of Transjordan from the Palestine Mandate in September 1922 and the French cession of the Sanjak of Alexandretta to Turkey in 1939 in flagrant breach of Article 4 of the Mandate over Syria and the Lebanon. There was no sectarian factor in either of these dispositions of territory and therefore they are not considered here. Article 25 of the Palestine mandate gave the mandatory the discretion to make arrangements appropriate for existing local conditions in respect of the administration of the territories east of the Jordan, but did not suggest that those territories might be constituted as a separate state. On the partition of Palestine in 1947–8 and the creation of Israel, see Crawford, *The Creation of States in International Law*, pp 421- 434; Victor Kattan, *From Co-existence to Conquest; International Law and the Origins of the Arab-Israeli Conflict, 1891–1949* (Pluto Press, London: 2009) p 156. Half-hearted French attempts to separate predominantly Druze, Alawi and other areas from the rump of Syria on a sectarian basis were unsuccessful and were eventually abandoned.

Lebanon had been established after the war and massacres of 1860 as a separate province but was too small (and too poor) to be reconstituted as an independent state. The French therefore expanded it by adding the mixed city of
Beirut and the districts of Tripoli, Ba'lbek, Tyre and Sidon in August 1920, only
one month after the battle of Maisaloun and their conquest of Syria. This was
against the wishes of the largely Muslim inhabitants of those districts, most of
whom would have preferred to remain part of Syria. The expanded Lebanon's
constitution was based on confessionalism: a system that institutionalised and
perpetuated sectarianism.[19]

The express purpose of the Palestine Mandate was to establish a 'Jewish
national home' in Palestine, but without prejudicing the rights of the indigenous population. At the time, many Europeans spoke unthinkingly of 'the
Jewish race', and we need no reminding of the dark chapters of European
history to which such language was part of the background. To the extent that
the conception that Jews were a racial group penetrated the Arab world, it was
entirely as a result of European influence[20].

Zionism deepened the gap between Arabic speaking Jews and their Muslim
and Christian neighbours. Even before the Mandates had begun, the Zionist
Commission (which later became the Jewish Agency) was working among
Jews in Palestine and the wider Greater Syria to attempt to persuade them to
support the Zionist movement when they gave testimony to the King-Crane
Commission in 1919.[21] Arabic speakers considered Jews to belong to a religion – in the same way that Muslims and Christians consider themselves to

---

19 Philip Khoury, *Syria and the French Mandate* (Princeton University Press, Princeton: 1987)
pp 57–8.
20 This is the view of Bernard Lewis. See *Semites and anti-Semites* (Phoenix Grant, London:
1986/1997) pp 131–4. European style anti-Semitism has now spread widely in Arab countries,
the best known example probably being the Hamas Charter. (For a treatment of this, see
Ashcar, *The Arabs and the Holocaust* (Saqi, London: 2010), pp 237–40). It should not be
overlooked that this has parallels in anti-Arab racism in Israel and the West. Thus, in January
1968, the Israeli foreign minister, Abba Eban, objected to annexing areas of territory occupied
in the 1967 war if this would substantially increase the Arab population of Israel. His grounds
were that there was a limit to how much arsenic the human body could absorb. See Avi Raz,
The Bride and the Dowry (Yale University Press, New Haven and London: 2012) p 268.
21 A. Patrick, *The Zionist Commission and the Jewish Communities of Greater Syria in 1919*
(Jerusalem Quarterly, 56 & 57) p 115. The author writes: 'having been essentially asked to
choose between their neighbours and their co-religionists, [the Arabic-speaking Jews of
Greater Syria] largely chose the latter.'

belong to a religion – rather than a 'race'.[22] It is therefore hard to see how the privileging of Jews under the Palestine Mandate in order to establish the 'national home' could ever do otherwise than lead to specifically sectarian tensions and resentment from the indigenous Muslim and Christian population, many of whom were eventually dispossessed (frequently through what we would now call ethnic cleansing) by the militias that became the Israeli army.[23]

The decision by the victorious powers to impose the Mandates put an end to the attempt to establish a secular, Arab nationalist state in Greater Syria. The Amir Faysal's ill-fated kingdom never achieved more than a tenuous hold on the territories east of the coastal mountains and the Jordan, and he was unable to consolidate it as a functioning state without the active support of the Allied Powers. The Allies frustrated his attempt to develop Syrian military forces which would have given him genuine bargaining power like that possessed by Mustafa Kemal in contemporary Turkey. Yet, as James Gelvin has suggested, 'with adequate resources and time, it might have been possible for the Arab government and its allies among the nationalist elites gradually to enlist the support of the remainder of the population'.[24] Forced into compromise positions, from which Syrian opinion then compelled him to back-track, he and his government lost the popular legitimacy to which they aspired. When the

---

22 Lewis, p 131.

23 Approximately half the Palestinian Arabs who were expelled or fled from the area that became the state of Israel within the 1949 cease-fire lines had already been turned into refugees by the time the state of Israel was proclaimed on 15 May 1948. For a succinct and measured treatment of the fate of the Palestinians in 1947–9, see Rashid Khalidi, 'The Palestinians and 1948: The Underlying Causes of Failure', in Rogan and Shlaim (eds) *The War for Palestine: Rewriting the History of 1948* (Cambridge University Press, Cambridge: 2001) pp 12–36, especially p 13. See also Rashid Khalidi, *The Iron Cage* (Oneworld Publications, Oxford: 2006) p 126 where the author writes, 'It was of course vitally important for [the planners of the establishment of the state of Israel] that Zionist and later Israeli forces first overcome Palestinian resistance and then clear as much as possible of the country as they could of its Palestinian population ... Most importantly, they understood the well-established demographic calculus of Palestine, which meant that without such ethnic cleansing, the new state would have had nearly as many Arabs as Jews (the expanded territory eventually incorporated into Israel after the 1949 armistice agreements would have had many more Arabs).'

24 Gelvin, *Divided Loyalties: Nationalism and Mass Politics in Syria at the Close of Empire* (University of California Press, Berkeley and Los Angeles: 1998) p 136.

French finally invaded in July 1920, they had no difficulty defeating the small Syrian army and occupying the country.

Faysal's words given in a speech delivered in Aleppo on 11 November 1918 deserve to be more widely known today:

'The Arabs were Arabs before Moses, and Jesus and Muhammad. All religions demand that [their adherents] follow what is right and enjoin brotherhood on earth. And anyone who sows discord between Muslim, Christian and Jew is not an Arab.'[25]

On another occasion, he told an audience in the same city that 'if we are divided into parties and sects, [the civilised world] will despise us, because they regard all religions as equal and do not distinguish between peoples.'[26]

His government made donations to Christian and Jewish religious leaders and associations, as well as to mosques, Muslim notables and nationalist groups.[27] The secularism he advocated was paralleled by his recognition of the diversity of the Arab countries. He knew that unification of the Arabic speaking lands could only be achieved through a federal structure or confederation.[28]

Yet appeals to traditional values such as Islam and Arab honour carried a much greater resonance with the mass of the population, and existed alongside the rhetoric of modern, European-style nationalism.[29] As the French prepared to invade, there were calls for jihad to repel them, and an eminent shaykh, Muhammad al-Sharif al-Ya'qubi, even led a contingent of his religious students against the French at the battle of Maisaloun.[30] In the great rebellion against the French in 1925, religious rhetoric, such as calls to jihad, was also much in evidence. Yet such religious resonances must not obscure the fact that the struggle against the French was a nationalist struggle.

---

25 Quoted in Ali A. Allawi, *Faisal I of Iraq* (Yale University Press, New Haven and London: 2014) p 167.

26 Gelvin, p 183. See ibid., pp 181–185 for the secularism espoused by Faysal, the Arab government and the westernised intellectuals.

27 Ibid., p 29

28 Allawi, p 168.

29 Gelvin, p 187, writes (with reference to the period after the visit of the King Crane Commission), 'the use of Islamic symbols was hardly atavistic. Islamic symbols did not dislodge nationalist symbols from popular texts; rather, in most texts the two sets of symbols were fully conjoined.'

30 Ibid., p 116.

Today many streets in Syrian towns and cities are named after the Syrians who fell in 1925. Those who died in battle are described as martyrs whatever their faith, while the concept of jihad is secularised, at least partially, when it is used to refer to the struggle for independence. The French were unprepared for the way in which Druze, many Sunni Muslims, Shi'i Muslims and some Christians made common cause as they rose up in different parts of the mandated territory in the hope of driving the occupiers into the sea.

The banner behind which they united was Syrian independence and reunification, as well as the end of foreign rule. Muslim religious rhetoric and symbols were employed to further this struggle, but nationalism, not religion, was the cause for which the rebels were striving. Pride in Islam and the history of the unification of the Arabs by the Prophet and his followers, as well as the great Arab conquests which ultimately created the Arab world of today, are inseparable from Arab identity. It was therefore only natural that the warrior rhetoric that is an integral element of the Qur'an infused this nationalism, and that this rhetoric would be pressed into service by nationalist ideologues.

This rhetoric did not appeal only to Muslims. There were cases of non-Muslim nationalists in Arab countries who used Qur'anic rhetoric to get their message across to the masses in a way we would now consider to be Islamist. One early example from the dawn of nationalist sentiment in the Middle East is all too frequently overlooked. This is the Jewish activist, playwright and satirist James Sanua, who used Islamist rhetoric in the Egypt of the 1870s and 80s against the governments of the khedives Ismail and Tawfiq, the British occupiers, and the foreign communities who gathered so much of Egypt's commerce and finance into their hands.[31] There were cases, too, during the French mandate. The Christian journalist Yusuf al-'Issa called in 1923 for the birthday of the Prophet to be made a national holiday so as to unite the entire Arabic speaking nation.[32] But the greatest example is perhaps no other than Michel Aflaq, whose famous Ba'thist slogan 'one Arab nation with an eternal message' is redolent of Qur'anic language.

These examples are evidence of an Arab nationalism that encompassed Christians and Jews as well as Muslims. Yet the creation of the Mandates and rule by non-Muslim powers would tempt some Muslims down an alternative path which we might call religious separatism.

---

31 For Sanua, see Eliane Ettmueller, *The Construct of Egypt's National Self in James Sanua's Early Satire and Caricature* (Klaus Schwarz Verlag, Berlin: 2012).
32 Benjamin White, *The Emergence of Minorities in the Middle East* (Edinburgh University Press, Edinburgh: 2011/2) p 52.

A sense of religious community, reflected in shared values, customs and loyalties, was to be found among Muslims across all provinces of the Ottoman empire as it faded away after the First World War. The new, aggressively secular and nationalist Turkish republic would consider being a Sunni Muslim an essential part of Turkish identity. There were cases of Arabic speaking Sunni Muslims who remained loyal to the Ottoman state until its army was forced to retreat from their land, and who may only subsequently have become passionate Arab nationalists.[33]

Yet Islam was a natural focus for identity in its own right, and not purely as part of a developing Turkish or Arab national identity. It was observed at the time that some Syrian Muslims would have preferred rule by the new nationalist Turkey, rather than France. [34] Until Arab nationalism became firmly embedded in Aleppo, largely as a result of the Ibrahim Hananu revolt, many Muslims in the city were unsure whether their preference (if they had been given the opportunity to choose) would have been to be part of the new Turkey or the French mandate of Syria.[35] Some policies of Mandate governments had the effect of forcing Sunni Muslims back into their religious identities and were intended to divide them from other groups. In Syria, the French division of the country by parcelling it out into a patchwork quilt of small entities, intended to need permanent French support, disadvantaged the Sunni majority. Not only did the Mandate threaten the power of the traditional Sunni elites but, as has been mentioned, many found themselves in the new Christian dominated Lebanon against their wishes.

The same applied to a lesser extent in the *Région Alaouite36* and possibly the autonomous Druze area around Suwayda. Sunnis included in these areas by the stroke of a pen wielded by a French administrator had every right to feel aggrieved. The intention behind establishing these entities was explicitly to privilege other groups over Sunnis.

The French also stoked sectarianism during the great revolt by recruiting militias composed largely of Christian Armenian refugees who frequently

---

33 An intriguing case is Yasin al-Hashemi. Although he was a supporter of the nationalist secret society al-Fatat, he remained in Ottoman service until the cease-fire and distrusted the Arab Revolt, the Hashemites and Britain. Nevertheless, he became president of the Arab government's war council. See Gelvin, pp 88–89.

34 Temperley, Vol. VI, p156.

35 Khoury, pp 104–5; Gelvin, p 83, 129.

36 Balanche, *La région alaouite et le pouvoir syrien* (Karthala, Paris: 2006), p 34.

terrorised Muslim and Druze villages.[37] Attacks on the Mandate authorities sometimes included Christian villages among their targets.[38] There were obvious parallels in Palestine, where Islamic sentiment and rhetoric – exemplified, perhaps, by Shaykh Izz ai-Din Qassam who was killed fighting the British in 1935 and the leadership of the Mufti of Jerusalem – played a role in the resistance to the mandate.

When the Ottoman Sultan-Caliph entered the First World War as an ally of Germany and called for Jihad against Britain, France and Russia, the response from Sunni Muslims outside his dominions was minimal. Religious solidarity between Sunni Muslims was not sufficient to deter the Sharif Husayn of Mecca from leading an Arab revolt against the Ottomans from June 1916 onwards. Yet one significant fact seems often to be airbrushed from history. The Shi'is of Iraq rallied to the Sunni flag of the Sultan-Caliph once British forces landed at Basra and began to march up the Euphrates valley.

The Iraqi Shi'i mujtahids, led by Grand Ayatullah Kadhim al-Yazdi, saw the British invasion as a threat to Islam itself. They therefore put aside religious differences with the Ottomans. Interestingly, they did not receive support from ethnically Persian mujtahids in the shrine cities of Karbala and Najaf. However, the native Arabic-speaking Iraqi mujtahids helped assemble a vast tribal army which joined the Ottoman army as auxiliaries at the battle of Shu'ayba in April 1915.[39]

When Iraq was under British occupation once the fighting had ended, there was support among many Shi'is as well as Sunnis for rule by a Sunni prince from the family of the Sharif Husayn of Mecca[40], while joint meetings were held in Sunni and Shi'i mosques in 1920 to denounce the British Mandate.[41] Gertrude Bell noted that the Arab nationalists had, from her point of view, 'adopted a difficult line in itself to combat, the union between Shi'ah and Sunni, the unity of Islam.'[42]

In 1923, a Turkish invasion to recover Mosul – or even the whole of Iraq – seemed a real possibility. Shi'i divines nailed a fatwa to the entrance of the

---

37 Provence, *The Great Syrian Revolt and the Rise of Arab Nationalism* (University of Texas Press, Austin: 2005) pp 130–1, 137.

38 As early as February 1920 (i.e. before the mandate had begun), the Alawi chieftain Salih al-Ali attacked Christian villages while raiding the French depot in Tartus. There were also instances of attacks on Christian villages during the 1925 revolt. See e.g. Provence, pp 61–2.

39 Allawi, p 341.

40 Ibid., p 348.

41 Ibid., p 356.

42 Ibid., p 357.

shrine at Kadhimain, where the seventh and ninth Imams of Twelver Shi'ism are buried. It forbade armed action to repel an invasion, even though the Turkish army would have been Sunni.[43] Faysal was perceived to have betrayed the unity of Islam: the cause for which Shi'i tribesmen had fought at Shu'ayba. That July, the appeal was repeated by exiled Iraqi ayatullahs in Iran. Their call was for the Caliph in Istanbul to deliver Iraq 'from the foreigners…and from Faisal and his father who came to dominate the Muslims by fighting in the ranks of the Allies and by disuniting the Muslims under the cloak of Arab nationalism in disobedience to the laws of God.'[44]

It should not be inferred from these events that there were no problems between Sunnis and Shi'is in Iraq as the Ottoman era ended. No Shi'i had a prospect of a bureaucratic or military career in the Ottoman state.[45] In the words of one scholar, the Shi'is had been 'inhabitants of the Ottoman state, but they scarcely engaged with it'.[46] Yet examining these events does show that, with time, the divide between Sunnis and Shi'is might have been bridged.

Three roots of the toxic sectarianism which has subsequently afflicted Arab countries are thus clearly traceable to the Mandates: the fact that Muslim solidarity proved to be an effective weapon to unite Muslims against the Mandate governments, something that could only risk sidelining or alienating non-Muslims; the manner in which the French favoured and privileged Christians and other religious minorities in a way likely to stoke resentment; and the gulf which the British Mandate of Palestine and the ideology of Zionism opened between Jews, including Arabic speaking Jews, and Arabs who were Muslims or Christians. Yet identifying these three roots leads to another question: what other factors were there which gave rise to sectarianism but which cannot be attributed to the Mandates? Three can be readily identified.

The first is the fact that, throughout the history of the Ottoman Empire, religion had been the strongest marker of identity for its subjects. Attempts to build an Ottoman patriotism and the abolition of the different status of Muslims, Christians and Jews in the public sphere[47] by the Tanzimat reforms had brought

---

43 Ibid., p 417.

44 Ibid., p 425.

45 Ibid., p 343.

46 Charles Tripp, *A History of Iraq* (Cambridge University Press, Cambridge, 3rd edition: 2007) p 12.

47 Nevertheless, Muslims, Christians and Jews retained their own law of personal status – something that remains the case to this day in all the successor states to the Mandates.

secularism to the Empire. However, the fissures between the different communities remained. The Mandates would drive wedges into those fissures.

The second is often overlooked. This is the role that patronage has played in the politics of so many Arab countries. Patronage may be a universal feature of human society which can never be done away with entirely. Yet over the century since 1914 it has proved a major problem for Arab societies trying to modernise. Once it was the patronage dispensed by the notable classes. Later, it became the patronage of politicians and army officers building up their own networks of supporters. This was followed by revolutionary regimes, such as the Ba'thist regimes of Syria and Iraq, which used patronage as the way to secure their position.

That is why the elite of Iraq from the days of the Ottomans right down to Saddam Hussein was predominantly Sunni, and why the Republican Guard was recruited from the Sunni tribes of the north west. This was the politics of patronage, not of sectarianism.[48] However, it is scarcely surprising if it led to religious solidarity among the excluded Shi'is and encouraged them to adopt religion based politics. Nor is it so surprising that when a fragile parliamentary democracy was set up after the US-led invasion, Prime Minister Nouri al-Maliki should have reversed this process and used the politics of patronage among the Shi'i majority to bolster his position. This fatefully opened the door to Da'ish, the so-called 'Islamic state'.

There is a similarity here with what happened in Syria where members of the once lowly and despised Alawi sect-class rose to take control of the country: first Salah Jadid, and then Hafez al-Assad. (It might be noted that the fact that men who were Alawis could become the rulers of the country is proof of the extent of secularism in Syria).

Many Alawis were placed in positions of power by Hafez al Assad, and they came to dominate the security apparatus. But this was not sectarianism: it was another very traditional manifestation of patronage.[49] Nevertheless, it is

---

48 For the role of patronage in Iraqi politics, see Tripp, *passim*. As Tripp puts it on p 318, when discussing the rule of Saddam Hussein: 'although not a communal regime in any sense, the vast majority of the inner circle came from distinct groups within the Sunni Arab population, perpetuating thereby the grip which men from these communities had had on the levers of the state since its foundation.'

49 For full treatment of this, see Hanna Batatu, *Syria's Peasantry, the Descendants of its Lesser Rural Notables, and their Politics* (Princeton University Press, Princeton: 1999); Nikolaos van Dam, *The Struggle for Power in Syria: Politics and Society under Asad and the Ba'th Party* (I.

scarcely surprising if it also led to the flourishing of politics based on religion in many opposition circles, once democracy in Syria was well and truly in the deep freeze.

It might also be suggested that, in a similar way, the creation of Israel and the privileging of Jews in their 'national home', in a way that excluded Muslims and Christians, led to the considerable success of religion based politics among dispossessed Palestinians. This can be exemplified by the growth of Hamas from the time of the First Intifada in 1987 onwards.

The final root is well known but should still be emphasised: the sectarian politics of Wahhabism from Saudi Arabia coupled with *takfir* based ideology stemming from the thought of figures such as the Egyptian Syed Qutb.

These ideologies with their hate speech against non-Muslims and the heterodox led directly to al-Qaeda and then to Da'ish. The Mandates made a normal path to nationhood very difficult for the Arabic speaking peoples of the Fertile Crescent. Ultimately, this made them much more vulnerable to the sectarian conflicts that risk tearing them apart.

B. Tauris, London: 2011).

11

Oil, state and society in Iran in the aftermath of the First World War

Kaveh Ehsani

The First World War and its aftermath (beginning with the Soviet Revolution of 1917) were watersheds that revolutionised not only the military organisation of warfare, but also major spheres of public life across much of the world. Among those relations that began to be questioned and altered were the nature of the government and its relation to society, the perceptions and attitudes of ordinary people as well as elites toward politics and political participation, and the re-organisation of the corporate, financial, and industrial structures of capitalism and its modes of regulation. Oil played an important role in these changes, initially as fuel for the new mechanised war machine, and soon after by increasingly replacing coal as the main source of energy and raw material in the emerging Fordist political economy that transformed the management and scale of the consumer, transportation, chemical, and industrial sectors.

In the Middle East, a company owned by the British speculator William Knox D'Arcy first discovered oil in commercial quantities in 1908 in Iran's southwest province of Khuzestan. In the wake of the First World War, the British government purchased a majority share of D'Arcy's company, which was subsequently renamed the Anglo Persian Oil Company (APOC). By the end of the First World War the British government and APOC had imposed a 'veiled protectorate in Southwest Persia'[1], and their operations had effectively

---

1 Ronald Ferrier, *History of the British Petroleum Company*, vol. 1 (Cambridge University

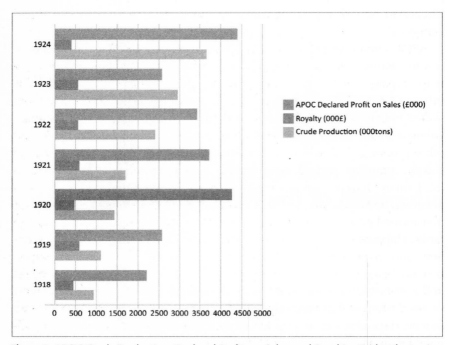

Figure 1: APOC Crude Production, Declared Profits on Sales, and Royalties Paid to the Iranian Government (1918–1925)

Source: R.W. Ferrier, *The History of the British Petroleum; The Developing Years 1901–1932* (Cambridge University Press, London: 1982), pp 234, 370, 474.

transformed the existing local society and geography[2]. As G. N. Curzon acknowledged, petroleum had become an unthinkably important strategic resource, helping 'the allies to float to victory on a sea of oil'[3], with the

---

Press, Cambridge, UK: 1982) p 116; Marian (Kent) Jack, 'The Purchase of the British Government's Shares in the British Petroleum Company 1912–1914', *Past and Present*, no. 39 (April 1968): pp 139–68.

2 Kaveh Ehsani, 'The Social History of Labor in the Iranian Oil Industry: The Built Environment and the Making of the Working Class (1908–1941)' (PhD Dissertation, Leiden University, 2014).

3 *Times*, 22 November 1918.

Khuzestan oil industry acting as a key supplier to the British military and economy[4].

APOC's main oilfields were in Masjed Soleyman, located in the mountainous territories of the powerful pastoral and nomadic Bakhthiari tribes (see map on pages 16–17). At a time when petroleum technology was still in its infancy, APOC built a 150 km pipeline using local labour recruits and more skilled Indian workers to link the oil fields of Masjed Soleyman to Abadan, where a major refinery was erected to process and export the crude and other products, primarily to the wartime British military machine. Abadan was an island on the confluence of the Karun and Shatt al-Arab rivers, on the Iranian-Ottoman border, and located within the territory of Arab tribes governed by Sheykh Khaz'al. By the end of the war the entire area had been transformed into an industrial and mining landscape of smokestacks, storage tanks, shipping docks, and crisscrossed with narrow gauge railways, pipelines and roads. The war and rapid industrialisation had altered the region beyond recognition, dotting it with fortified enclaves for European employees and administrators, surrounded by sprawling settlements of hovels and tents where the tens of thousands of migrants and desperate refugees from the war, famine, dispossession, and epidemics sought to eke out a living under appalling conditions in the shadow of the oil complex.

This chapter will discuss the impact and consequences on Iran of the First World War, and the role played by the oil complex in the lasting transformations that were brought about at the local, national, and regional levels.

Iran's fate in the First World War was shaped in a large part by a legacy dating from the mid 19th century – that of being a weak state trapped amidst far more powerful imperial neighbours. Britain, Russia and the Ottomans saw Iran as an arena for neutralising each other, and for the ruthless pursuit of their own interests by exerting relentless pressure to control her foreign policy, trade, and economy. When the War broke out, the neighbouring powers continued this trend by readily ignoring Iran's declared neutrality, and turning the impoverished country into a proxy warzone, with dire consequences for the general population.

---

4 Abadan's output had increased tenfold to nine hundred thousand tons annually. But in the wake of the Russian Revolution and forecasting post war global expansion, the Company planned to increase production to 1.2 million ton annually and expand ports, jetties, storage facilities, and pipelines. For supply of petroleum products from Abadan to the British military, 1914–1920, see Ferrier, *History of the British Petroleum Company*, p 289.

Iran had lost major territorial claims in its last wars with Russia (1828) and Britain (1857), and thereafter was at the mercy of their far superior military might. The financial crisis of the late 19th century further exacerbated the Qajar state's chronic vulnerability. Iran's currency, the Qran, was based on silver, which was severely devalued following the global depression of the 1890s. The subsequent inflation and financial crisis forced the Qajar Court to resort to foreign loans, mainly from Russia and Britain, which began to use credit as an effective instrument of furthering their influence on the feeble Persian state[5]. Fearing the crushing debt dependence, the long ruling Nasser al-Din Shah resorted to selling lucrative concessions over major segments of the country's trade and resources to foreign prospectors as a desperate means of finding quick sources of income. The move backfired spectacularly. The remarkable monopoly concessions granted to British nationals, first in 1872 to Julius Reuter over mining, industry, and trade, and then in 1890 to G. Talbot over all tobacco production and trade, created a major backlash among Russians, as well as outraged Iranian merchants, clergy, and ordinary people. The Shah had to withdraw the concessions and pay hefty compensation, which only increased the court's dire financial situation. The 1901 D'Arcy oil agreement granted by Mozaffar al-Din Shah was the last of these notorious concessions, whose consequences were to alter and reshape the future of Iran and the entire region.

After the 1857 uprisings in India Britain had become concerned with threats to the security of its valuable colony, and began to consider the Persian Gulf as the gateway to India, and Iran (as well as Afghanistan) as her buffer states.[6] But at the turn of the new century, this strategy began to be re-evaluated in reaction to a number of major global and regional social and geopolitical shifts. On the one hand, the emergence of the United States and Germany as competitive rivals that could challenge Britain's military, financial, and industrial might had become a major strategic concern. On the other hand, the rise of mass politics had introduced a new element in political calculations, both at home and abroad. In the region, Germany had begun a rapprochement with

5 Peter Avery and S. Simmonds, 'Persia on a Cross of Silver: 1880–1890', in *Middle Eastern Studies* 10 (1974) pp 259–86.

6 David McLean, *Britain and Her Buffer State: The Collapse of the Persian Empire, 1890–1914* (Royal Historical Society, London: 1979); George Nathaniel Curzon Curzon, *The Place of India in the Empire: Being an Address Delivered before the Philosophical Institute of Edinburgh* (J.Murray, London: 1909).

the Ottomans, investing in its railroads and helping her military modernisation. Russia, on the other hand, had experienced a shocking defeat by Japan, and a popular revolution in 1905 that tarnished the image of the Tsarist power, and made a direct impression on the tens of thousands of Iranian migrant oil workers in the Caucasus.[7] The following year the Constitutional Revolution broke out in Iran (1906–1909), and plunged the country in a protracted struggle to establish a parliament (Majlis) and the rule of law against Qajar absolutism.

Amidst these upheavals Britain's policy shifted dramatically, from treating Iran as a buffer state against Russia, into forging an alliance with Russia over the 1907 Anglo-Russian Convention that divided Iran into mutual spheres of influence, and turned her into a bastion against the potential German alliance with the Ottomans.[8] This strategic shift roughly coincided with the discovery of oil in Khuzestan in 1908, and the beginning of the establishment of the oil industry there by APOC. Thereafter, the protection of Khuzestan's oil facilities became an added priority in setting Britain's policy toward Iran.

The 1907 Anglo Russian Convention had significant and far-reaching consequences. While Britain's buffer state policy in Iran had required a unified country under the control of a weak and dependent central government, the new policy of dividing the country into a southern protectorate of Britain, a Russian sphere of influence in the north, and a 'neutral' zone in the middle under the token control of Tehran, effectively spelled the fragmentation of the country and the loss of the nominal sovereignty of the central government. In Tehran the new arrangements outraged Constitutionalists, who had considered parliamentary Britain as a potential supporter of their cause, and planted within the Iranian political culture a deep and lasting mistrust of British intents, and an exaggerated view of its duplicity and conspiratorial ability to corrupt political figures to manipulate its desired outcomes at the expense of Iranian

---

7 Touraj Atabaki, 'Disgruntled Guests: Iranian Subalterns on the Margins of the Tsarist Empire', in Touraj Atabaki (ed), *The State and the Subaltern* (I.B. Tauris, London: 2007), pp 31–52.

8 John Marlowe, *The Persian Gulf in the Twentieth Century* (Frederick A. Praeger, New York: 1962) pp 38–40; Nikki Keddie and Mehrdad Amanat, 'Iran under the Late Qajars', in *Cambridge History of Iran, From Nadir Shah to the Islamic Republic*, vol. 7 (Cambridge University Press, Cambridge: 1991) pp 174–213; Joel Beinin, *Workers and Peasants in the Modern Middle East* (Cambridge University Press, Cambridge: 2001).

national interests.[9] As a result, British policies began to be viewed by the majority of Iranian nationalists as harmful to national interests, and none more so than Britain's actions in its sphere of influence in the south, and especially in the expanding oil operations in Khuzestan. On the other hand, many local magnates and tribal leaders in southern Iran saw this development as an opportunity to enrich themselves, and to forge an alliance with Britain against the future encroachment of the central government on their autonomy.

Following the discovery of oil in 1908, APOC and the government of Britain signed a series of bilateral agreements with the southern magnates, without the consent of the Iranian central government. Tehran objected that this was a violation of both its sovereignty as well as of the terms of the 1901 concession, which had been granted to a private individual (D'Arcy) and not to a foreign government. The fact that both APOC and British government representatives were joint parties to negotiations and had co-signed the agreements with powerful and virtually autonomous tribal leaders became a major bone of contention with the Iranian government, and undermined APOC's later claims that it was not an extension of the British state.

The first bilateral agreements were signed with the Bakhtiyari Khans to lease the oilfields of Masjed Soleyman, to recruit labour gangs and armed guards to work on building the oil wells, pipelines, and roads, and to protect their operations against threats from rival tribesmen and saboteurs. In Abadan, Ahvaz and Mohammareh APOC and British representatives, led by Percy Cox and Arnold Wilson, struck similar agreements with Sheikh Khaz'al to lease land for building the refinery, shipping ports, a company town, and for obtaining his protection.[10]

These agreements had far reaching repercussions. They created a relatively stable enclave for APOC to lay the foundations of one of the largest oil complexes in the world, in a very rugged and difficult setting, which was soon to become a war zone. At the same time, these arrangements undermined the existing social and political fabric of the local pastoral and agrarian society.

---

9 Ahmad Kasravi, *Tarikh-E Mashrouteh Iran* (Amir Kabir, Tehran: 1951); Ervand Abrahamian, *Iran Between Two Revolutions* (Princeton University Press, Princeton: 1982); Keddie and Amanat, 'Iran under the Late Qajars'; Janet Afary, *The Iranian Constitutional Revolution, 1906–1911: Grassroots Democracy, Social Democracy and the Origins of Feminism* (Columbia University Press, New York: 1996); Marlowe, *The Persian Gulf in the Twentieth Century*, p 32; William J Olson, *Anglo-Iranian Relations during World War I* (Frank Cass, London: 1984) p 18.
10 Ehsani, 'Social History of Labor in the Iranian Oil Industry', pp 126–130.

The bilateral pacts with APOC and the British government benefited the local elites of Bakhtiyari Khans and Arab Sheikhs at the expense of ordinary tribesmen and peasants, many of whom lost their customary rights to pasture and agrarian land without adequate compensation, and thus were forced to join the industrial reserve army of wage labour for the oil industry. The bitterness against their dispossession by APOC, in collusion with their own leaders, eventually led to the gradual unraveling of the social cohesion and political ties that held together the tribal and pastoralist societies, and paved the way for their eventual defeat in the 1920s by the newly reorganised national army led by Reza Khan.[11]

On the other hand, the central government and nationalist elites began to see the southern tribes and their leaders as little more than British pawns. They resented the brazen disregard of government sovereignty and authority over the southern provinces, and feared that the Bakhtiyari and Arab tribal leaders were plotting with Britain for the territorial separation of the south, similar to what had occurred with Kuwait's separation from Ottoman Mesopotamia.[12]

At the outbreak of the First World War, Iran had become the proxy battlefield of a Great Game played by its more powerful neighbours. The Constitutional Revolution had released great aspirations for constitutional rule among the fledgling bourgeoisie, lay intelligentsia, progressive clerics, and ordinary people. However, the political momentum had come to a stop as a result of the protracted conflict with reactionary forces led by Mohammad Ali Shah, and the country's division into spheres of Russian and British influence. On the eve of the war, the state was effectively bankrupt and heavily indebted to Russian and Britain. It had no effective authority beyond the borders of the capital, and was in no position to command respect for its decision to stay out of the war.

Iran declared its neutrality at the outbreak of the First World War, but its neighbours summarily ignored its decision. Although the scale of the direct military conflict in Iran did not reach the carnage of the battlefields of Anatolia or Mesopotamia, nonetheless most of its territory was either directly occupied or turned into a proxy theatre of war for rival Russian, British, Ottoman, and German armies and saboteurs. The effects were ruinous as warfare, chronic insecurity, famine, epidemics, runaway inflation, and rising poverty decimated

---

11 Ibid.; Stephanie Cronin, *Tribal Politics in Iran: Rural Conflict and the New State 1921–41* (Routledge, London: 2007).

12 Svat Souchek, 'Arabistan or Khuzistan?', in *Iranian Studies* 17, no. 2–3 (1984) pp 195–214.

the urban and rural populations.[13] The Russian army had occupied the northern provinces even before the war had begun, the Ottomans invaded the
west, and the British troops landed in Mohammareh and Basra to defend the
Abadan refinery and start the occupation of Iraq. To protect the security of
their interests, especially the oil installations, the British also set up the South
Persia Rifles (SPR), composed of Iranian recruits, Indian cavalry and British
officers, all under the command of Percy Sykes.[14]

Under these circumstances the nominal authority of the Qajar central government began to unravel. A new monarch, Ahmad Shah Qajar, had been
installed on the throne in 1914, but he was a minor with no authority or power.
A majority of the Majlis deputies and the cabinet objected to the country's
occupation, and fled from the capital and advancing Russian troops to attempt
to set up a provisional government in exile in Kermanshah. As all semblance
of state authority began to disintegrate, desperate bread riots broke out in
many cities; marauding armies confiscated food and draft animals; warlordism
became a blight on settled populations of towns and villages; and brigandage
and raids disrupted trade, transport, and agriculture. During the war staple
food prices increased well beyond the means of ordinary people, with wheat
prices rising sevenfold, barley fourfold, legumes eightfold, rice sixfold, fodder
tenfold, and sugar by 54 percent.[15] The apparatus of tax collection, such as it

---

13 Mohammad Tamadon, *Oza'e Iran dar Jang Jahani-e Avval* (Tamadon, Tehran: 1971); Afshin
Parto, 'Khizesh-e Fars dar Jang-e Jahani-ye Avval', *'Ettela'at-e Siasi-Eqtesadi*, no. 135/136
(January 1999) pp 70–87; Morteza Dehqan Nejad and Zarifeh Kazemi, 'Avamel-e Moaser Dar
Feqdan-e Tose'eh Rah-Haye Tejari Fars az Aghaz-e Jang-e Jahani-e Avval ta Payan'e Jang-e
Jahani-ye Dovvom', *Tarikh-e Ravabet-e Khareji* 12, no. 46 (2010) pp 27–52; L. C. Dunsterville,
The Adventures of Dunsterforce (Naval and Military Press, London: 2009) pp 102–117; Maj
M. H. Donohoe, *With The Persian Expedition* (Naval and Military Press, London: 2009)
pp 113–131; C. J. Edmonds, *East and West of Zagros: Travel, War and Politics in Persia and Iraq
1913–1921*, Yann Richard (ed) (Brill, Leiden: 2010); Mohammad Gholi Majd, *The Great Famine
and Genocide in Persia, 1917–1919* (University Press of America, Lanham, Md.: 2003).
14 Malek al-Sho'ara Bahar, *Tarikh-e Mokhtasar-e Ahzab-e Siasi-ye Iran (History of Iran's
Political Parties)*, vol. 1 (Jibi, Tehran: 1978) p 47; Florida Safiri, *Polis-e Jonoub-e Iran-SPR (South
Persia Rifles)* (Nashr-e Tarikh-e Iran, Tehran: 1985); Percy Sykes, 'South Persia and the Great
War', *The Geographical Journal* 58, no. 2 (1921) pp 101–18; Christopher Sykes, *Wassmuss, 'the
German Lawrence'* (Longmans, New York: 1936).
15 Soheila Torabi, 'Negahi be Vaz'iyat-e Arzagh dar Iran dar Salha-ye Jang-e Jahani-e Avval
(A Look at the State of Food Provision in Iran during the WWI Years)', *Ganjineh Asnad*, no. 3/4
(1991) p 26.

was, had broken down and the empty treasury was unable to pay troops to collect arrears or to ensure the safety of tax assessors and collectors.[16] Exacerbating matters, APOC refused to pay oil royalties to the treasury, objecting to the government's inability to protect pipelines against sabotage by German agents. Popular protests, riots, and labour struggles during this period were often mobilised to defend the remaining moral economy by objecting to food hoarding, bread adulteration, and unpaid wages.[17]

The situation reached a calamitous scale with the widespread famine of 1917–1918. The famine was caused in part by a severe drought that began in 1916 and lasted for the next three years, and led to the collapse of grain production and animal husbandry in a number of major food producing regions. Food hoarding, adulteration, and speculation by unscrupulous merchants made matters worse, but generally went unpunished in the absence of effective political authority.[18] However, it was above all the chaotic military and political conditions that undermined any effective counter measures, and turned the drought into a major famine that decimated the population. Although surplus food was available in some regions that had not been as badly affected by drought, the near total breakdown of the distribution and transportation networks prevented supplies from reaching the badly affected areas. The British and Russian armies, as well as the Oil Company enforcers in Khuzestan, regularly requisitioned mules and camels, the main means for transportation[19], leaving the country's underdeveloped transportation network in serious disarray. Furthermore, the recurring forced requisitioning of foodstuffs by occupying armies turned the famine into a calamity: in November 1915, when the total granary of the southeast province of Sistan was sold to the British army, the price of wheat skyrocketed, but there was little to be

---

16 Ibid., p 28; Arthur C Millspaugh, *The American Task in Persia* (Century Co., New York: 1925); Morgan Shuster, *The Strangling of Persia* (Century Co., New York: 1920).

17 Touraj Atabaki and Kaveh Ehsani, 'Shifting Governmentality in the Shadow of Labor Activism: Revisiting the Roots and Impact of the 1929 Abadan Oil Workers' Strike', in *Middle East Studies Association* (Annual conference, New Orleans, 2013).

18 Iran National Archives (hereafter INA), INA240–3920; 293–3828; 240–1493; 240–6246; 240–5161. For further analysis of these events see Touraj Atabaki and Kaveh Ehsani, 'Oil and Beyond: Expanding British Imperial Aspirations, Emerging Oil Capitalism, and the Challenge of Social Questions in the First World War', in Helmut Bley and Anorthe Kremers (eds), *The World During the First World War* (Essen: Klarte Verlag, 2014) pp 261–90.

19 British Petroleum Archive (hereafter BP), BP141294, January 1938; Laurence Lockhart, *Unpublished Record of the Anglo-Iranian Oil Company, volume I: 1901–1918*, p 268.

found in the market at any price.[20] In the northeast province of Khorasan, Russian troops blockaded all roads and prohibited any transfer or exchange of grain except to supply their own army.[21] These measures disrupted the distribution of foodstuff and other goods throughout the country to the extent that during the war, the cost of transport in many parts of Iran exceeded the price of scarce grains.[22]

The Iranian government tried to impose a universal ban against all exports of grain and livestock, but its decree was simply ignored, and the military confiscations by the occupying foreign armies of food, grain, livestock, mules, and camels continued unabated.[23] From the Khuzestan port of Mohammareh alone, throughout the years of famine, every month an estimated 1,000 tons of wheat and 15,000 head of sheep were exported to Basra to supply the British troops in Mesopotamia.[24] The South Persia Rifles (SPR) also played a major role in exacerbating the food crisis, by drawing up long-term contracts for the bulk purchase of foodstuff with large landlords in Fars, Kerman, and other southern provinces.[25]

By 1917–1918 the continual warfare and widespread famine were causing an incessant movement of vast numbers of refugees, and destitute people fleeing hunger and insecurity, and searching for work and survival.[26] The chaotic conditions paved the way for the lethal spread of pandemics and contagious diseases. Cholera, plague, and typhus spread with frightening speed and claimed staggering fatalities. In 1915 new cases of cholera were reported in the war torn province of Azerbaijan.[27] By the following year the disease had spread widely across the northern provinces[28], and had begun to reach the south. Typhoid, too, spread in many parts of the country and caused so much

---

20 The Archives of Documents and Diplomatic History, Iran Ministry of Foreign Affairs. GH-133–58–4-91, GH-1333–58–4-68.

21 INA293–003828.

22 INA 240–18279.

23 Ibid.

24 Ibid.

25 Amir Afkhami, 'Compromised Constitutions: The Iranian Experience with the 1918 Influenza Pandemic', *Bulletin of the History of Medicine* 77 (2003) p 372–373.

26 For an eyewitness account of the famine and epidemic spreading over Iran during the First World war see: Qahreman Mirza Salour, *Rouznameh Khaterat 'Ayn al-Saltaneh*, volume 7 (Asatir, Tehran: 1999) pp 5275–5277.

27 INA 360 -1569.

28 Archive of the Iranian Ministry of Foreign Affairs. GH-1334–25–1-305.

death that according to an eyewitness, 'the high mortality in Tehran was not due to famine, but rather because of Typhoid and Typhus'.[29]

In the Iranian historical memory, the carnage of the First World War is associated as much with famine and epidemics as it is with casualties of combat. Amir Afkhami, who has studied the devastating impact of the 1918–1920 influenza pandemic in Iran observes that, 'ironically, Iran a neutral power in the war, lost as many citizens to war-related catastrophes as belligerent countries lost in the trenches'![30] He estimates that between 900 thousand to 2.4 million people, or between 10–22 percent of the overall population, perished as a result of food shortages, famine, and disease caused by the war related devastations and the political breakdown.[31] There were no official or systematic means of keeping records of mortality or births at the time; death records only began to be kept in 1922, when the Tehran municipality demanded that body washers in cemeteries record deaths and their causes.[32] But there are harrowing accounts by foreign diplomats, travellers, and military officers of the hardships suffered by the general population, including some cases of cannibalism.[33] Forbes-Leith, an officer on expedition in western Iran recalled the famine in the west of the country:

> The country was in a terrible state and the peasantry was in the last stages
> of starvation. Every time I was forced to stop my car, I was surrounded
> by hundreds of near-skeletons who screamed and fought for such scraps
> as I was able to spare. In a single day's journey of fifty-six miles between
> the towns of Kirind and Kermanshah, I counted twenty-seven corpses by
> the roadside, most of them those of women and children, and the general
> condition of life amongst the peasants was so frightful that I was ashamed
> to eat my simple rations in their presence[34]

---

29 Abdollah Mostowfi, *Sharh Zendegi Man*, volume 2 (Zavvar, Tehran: 1964) p 513.

30 Afkhami, 'Compromised Constitutions: The Iranian Experience with the 1918 Influenza Pandemic', p 371.

31 Ibid., pp 383–384.

32 A.R. Neligan, 'Public Health in Persia; 1914–24. Part 1', *The Lancet* 207, no. 5351 (March 20, 1926) p 636.

33 Report from the US Legation in Tehran, 1 November 1918, US National Archive 891.00/1072; Majid Foroutan, *Oza' Siyasi va Ejtemai-e Hamedan dar Jang Jahangi Avval* (Ketabdar, Tehran: 2011); L.C. Dunsterville, *The Adventures of Dunsterforce* (Naval and Military Press, London: 2009).

34 F. A. C. Forbes-Leith, *Checkmate; Fighting Tradition in Central Persia,* (Arno Press, New York: 1973) p 20.

The Iranian government attempted to organise the distribution of grains and sometimes of cooked meals in major cities, but these measures were short lived as limited supplies soon ran out.[35] As famine spread bread riots broke out in major cities and desperate crowds began to loot bakeries, food stores, and grain depots. Guilds and nascent trade unions tried to organise demonstrations and pressure the government to increase food rations, standardise the price of bread, and regulate the quality, the supply, and the sales of foodstuff. Nevertheless, under the circumstances, neither the national government nor the international powers were in a position to do much to alleviate these crises, and the devastations caused by famine and contagious diseases lasted throughout the war and for some years after.[36]

From the onset, APOC faced a number of monumental logistic and socio political difficulties in building a major industrial and mining complex during war time in remote, rugged, and undeveloped Khuzestan. Nearly all the material for the industry and for accommodating the personnel had to be imported. More significantly, APOC faced the chronic challenges of political insecurity, labour shortages, and managing increasingly difficult relations with the local populations and the central government of Iran.[37] Below, I will discuss several of the main challenges facing the oil operations in wartime Khuzestan, and their long term and wider repercussions once the conflict had ended.

APOC's operations in Khuzestan became a source of constant friction with local populations and tribesmen, who resented the Oil Company's continual encroachment on their territories in what they soon realised amounted to their effective dispossession. The oil works kept expanding throughout the years of war and famine. They attracted a growing flood of desperate migrants and refugees who continued to pour into the sprawling work camps of Masjed Soleyman and Abadan, turning them into major towns. Masjed Soleyman was transformed into a mining town, clustered around oil wells and pumping stations; Abadan became a port and a major industrial city that surrounded and served the refinery. From the onset, both towns were intended to be

---

35 Willem M. Floor, 'The Creation of the Food Administration in Iran', *Iranian Studies* 16, no. 3/4 (July 1, 1983) pp 199–227.

36 Atabaki and Ehsani, 'Oil and Beyond'.

37 Ferrier, *History of the British Petroleum Company*; Laurence Lockhart, 'The Record of the Anglo-Iranian Oil Company, Ltd.' (Anglo Iranian Oil Company (AIOC), London: 1938); L.P. Elwell-Sutton, *Persian Oil: A Study in Power Politics* (Lawrence and Wishart, London: 1955); Ehsani, 'Social History of Labor in the Iranian Oil Industry'.

'partitioned cities'[38], where APOC, with the help of Sheykh Khaz'al and the Bakhtyari Khans, imposed strict spatial segregation between the oil installations, European living quarters, and various segments of the population. But these settlements rapidly expanded beyond control. Their mounting problems became the cause of continuous urban unrest, and posed major challenges for the Oil Company and government authorities through the following decades.

We can only rely on speculative estimates of the population in Khuzestan during the first three decades of the 20th century to get a sense of the scale of the rising demographic problems caused by the war and the advent of the oil industry. It is important to note that prior to the First World War, there had been no permanent settlements in Masjed Soleyman and only a few scattered villages in Abadan, and neither place had any urban infrastructure to begin with. Masjed Soleyman was a seasonal mountain pasture for migrating Bakhtiyari nomads, and the scattered villages in Abadan had some date groves and sheep to sustain small agrarian communities. Thus, the local economy of neither place was capable of feeding, accommodating, or sustaining the rising flood of destitute refugees and migrants who began to pour into these areas (see table 2).

APOC was a commercial company, and had no interest to engage in costly social projects to alleviate the worsening local conditions. The Iranian central government had virtually no direct presence in Khuzestan, except for a handful of Kargozar (executives), who had practically no financial and institutional resources at their disposal. Initially, the Company relied on its alliance with the local tribal Khans and Sheikhs to mediate relations with the local population, and to repress any signs of protest or resistance to its operations. At several points British troops and warships from India were deployed to bolster security, and gradually the Company set up its own police force, and hired tribal security guards to impose its own rule of law.[39] However, the challenge of dealing with local social conditions could not be ignored indefinitely, and by the mid 1920s APOC was forced to accept, with great reluctance, the

38 Peter Marcuse, '"Dual City": A Muddy Metaphor for a Quartered City', *International Journal of Urban and Regional Research* 13, no. 4 (1989) pp 697–708; Kaveh Ehsani, 'Social Engineering and the Contradictions of Modernization in Khuzestan's Company Towns: A Look at Abadan and Masjed-Soleyman', *International Review of Social History* 48, no. 3 (2003) pp 361–99.
39 Arnold T Wilson, *SW Persia; A Political Officer's Diary 1907–1914* (Oxford University Press, London: 1941).

	1880s-1900 (Opening of Karum to commercial navigation)	1910s (Constitutional Revolution, Establishment of Oil Industry, WWI)	1920s (Consolidation of New Central Government, Apoc Reorganization, Demise of Local Autonomy)
Khuzestan	180	N/A	140
Abadan	14 (in scattered villages)	24	40-60
Masjed Soleyman	Seasonal	1-5	> 6 - 17
Ahvaz	0.3-1.0	4	10
Mohammareh/ Khorramshahr	3.0-6.0	10-16	

Table 2: Estimated Population of Khuzestan and Selected Cities (in 000s)[40]

responsibility of implementing a growing number of urban and development policies to alleviate the worsening social conditions.

Early on, these measures were limited to digging ditches to drain sewage into the river, installing a number of communal drinking water taps, and drawing boundaries to maintain a strict spatial segregation between

40 Author's estimates compiled from the following sources; Ludwig W. Adamec, *Historical Gazetteer of Iran*, vol. 3- Abadan (Akademische Drucku. Verlagsanstalt, Graz: 1976), p 5; Mostafa Ansari, 'The History of Khuzistan, 1878–1925: A Study in Provincial Autonomy and Change' (PhD Dissertation, University of Chicago, 1974); James Bamberg, *History of the British Petroleum Company*, vol. 2, 3 vols. (Cambridge University Press, Cambridge, UK: 1994); Ferrier, *History of the British Petroleum Company*, 1:276; Charles Issawi, *The Economic History of Iran, 1800–1914* (University of Chicago Press, Chicago: 1971); John Gordon Lorimer, *Gazetteer of the Persian Gulf, Oman and Central Arabia*, 6 vols. (Archive Editions, Gerrards Cross, Buckinghamshire, Eng.: 1986); Neligan, 'Public Health in Persia, Part 1'; Ian Seccombe and Richard Lawless, *Work Camps and Company Towns: Settlement Patterns in the Gulf Oil Industry*, vol. 36, Occasional Papers (University of Durham, Durham: 1987) p 32; Richard Lawless and Ian Seccombe, 'Impact of Oil Industry on Urbanization in the Persian Gulf Region', in Hooshang Amirahmadi and Salah el Shakhs (eds), *Urban Development in the Muslim World* (Center for Urban Policy Research, New Brunswick: 1993) pp 191–194; Shahbaz Shahnavaz, *Britain and the Opening of South-West Persia 1880–1914* (Routledge Curzon, London: 2005).

Europeans, Indians, and indigenous workers and populations. The Company also built a hospital and some dispensaries intended to serve its employees and their families. These facilities also treated local people not employed by the Company, albeit in separate wards. However, these limited measures proved woefully inadequate: as Company operations grew exponentially, so did the scale of the human tragedy caused by war and displacement. As soon as the war ended, APOC began to complain to the central government that it was responsible to provide relevant measures to deal with critical issues that ranged from sanitation and public health, to the acute housing shortage, the adequate provision of food and drinking water, public education, municipal planning, and so on. The central government refused to take responsibility. For one thing, it was in no financial or institutional position to undertake any of these tasks. For another, it insisted that the dramatic growth of Abadan and Masjed Soleyman were a consequence of the operations of the Oil Company, and the human crises besetting the province had been caused by a war that had been imposed on Iran by its imperial neighbors. The haggling continued, but gradually, and with great reluctance, APOC had to begin to implement a growing number of these social and municipal measures in order to limit the crisis.

Security concerns were another area of permanent concern for the Oil Company. During the war, the danger of sabotage or invasion by the central powers remained a major concern. In 1915 disgruntled Arab tribes with the help of German operatives sabotaged a number of pipelines. APOC used the opportunity to suspend royalty payments to the hapless central government for failing to live up to its obligation to provide security.[41] This measure became a major bone of contention that further poisoned the Company's relations with the Iranian government, and was only resolved, temporarily, during the bitter 1933 renegotiations of the Concession.[42] Meanwhile, the occupation of Mesopotamia by the British military alleviated the immediate dangers of hostile military incursions, allowing Khuzestan to remain relatively calm for the remainder of the war. However, following the Soviet Revolution, the fear of labour radicalisation became a new concern, and the Company began to

---

41 Pierre Oberling, *The Qashqai Nomads of Fars* (Mouton, Hague: 1974); Sykes, *Wassmuss, 'the German Lawrence'*; Ferrier, *History of the British Petroleum Company*, 1:359.

42 Ehsani, 'Social History of Labor in the Iranian Oil Industry'; Katayoun Shafiee, 'A Petro-Formula and Its World: Calculating Profits, Labour and Production in the Assembling of Anglo-Iranian Oil', *Economy & Society* 41, no. 4 (2012) pp 1–30.

YEAR	IRANIANS	INDIANS	EUROPEANS	OTHERS	TOTAL
1914	2,744	1,074	64	395	4,277
1915	2,203	979	80	187	3,449
1916	2,335	1,366	120	104	3,925
1917	n.d.	n.d.	n.d.	n.d.	n.d.
1918	n.d.	n.d.	n.d.	n.d.	n.d.
1919	3,979	2,641	117	47	6,784
1920	8,447	3,616	244	35	12,342
1921	9,009	4,709	271	51	14,040

Table 3: APOC Employees in Khuzestan, 1914–1921

Source: Ferrier, *The History of the British Petroleum*, pp 276, 401

establish a harsh and intrusive surveillance system to stem any indication of political agitation or labour protests.

Labour shortages of various kinds were the other systemic problem facing the Company. APOC employed thousands of workers for its expanding operations, but both the quantity and the quality of its employees remained a major strategic concern throughout the war and after. The scale of the work was staggering in all its technical, physical, and logistic aspects, and the demand for workers and technical staff of all kind was insatiable. However, appalling living and working conditions, harsh labour and management practices, inadequate pay, the remoteness of the region, and the fear of military and physical insecurity made labour recruitment, especially of more skilled personnel from India or Europe, a difficult challenge.

From the onset labour relations were beset with pitfalls and difficulties. The early phases of exploration and the construction and maintenance of wells, pumping stations, access roads, pipelines, machine shops, jetties, storage tanks, refinery installations, shelters, service and administrative facilities, hospitals, etc. required thousands of workers of varying skills. The competing demands of the British army in Mesopotamia were equally insatiable, and it paid better wages and higher prices for scarce food, livestock, and pack animals than the Oil Company. Nor was APOC very successful in attracting more skilled Indian workers, or European and British employees. Living and working conditions in Khuzestan were dreadful, even for the Europeans who lived in much better accommodations. The climate was extremely harsh, reaching above 50°C in the summer and below freezing in winter, with little shade or adequate shelter. Work hours were long, regularly above twelve hours a day, all week. Food and clean drinking water were scarce, and there were no social or leisure amenities to alleviate the monotony and isolation. Unskilled Iranian casual workers were mostly drawn from Bakhtiyari clans and Arab tribes, and were organised in work gangs. Most were still attached to their pastoral and agrarian lives, and readily decamped during the harvest or migration seasons. There were many violent clashes with British and Canadian overseers over the mistreatment and abuse of workers, or when accidents happened in the dangerous work environment. APOC found itself in a constant struggle with the British army, the Government of India (who monitored the emigrant Indian workers), and indigenous Iranian laborers, to attract and retain a sufficient, adequate, and docile workforce to operate its expanding operations during the war years.[43]

Iranian society continued to be embroiled in strife and crises well after the end of the First World War in 1918. British troops were the last foreign soldiers to finally evacuate Iranian soil three years later, but the country's internal situation, as well as that of its neighbors, in the Caucasus, Turkey, and Iraq, remained highly unstable. As is always the case, it was ordinary people who continued to bear the great brunt of the continuing dislocations and violence. In this concluding section we will look at the fallout of the First World War in Iran from the perspective of a number of major actors involved there.

In the wake of the First World War, for the first time, Britain appeared as the master of the situation in the Middle East. Its major rivals – the German, Ottoman, and Russian empires – had collapsed, thus eliminating the long maintained anxiety about defending the Indian empire from hostile encroachments. Its military dominated the region, with half a million troops occupying much of the Near East and protecting strategic interests, such as the oil installations of Khuzestan.[44] In Iran, the Qajar state was in a position of near total dependency on the good graces of His Majesty's Government, with an effectively bankrupt

43 Ehsani, 'Social History of Labor in the Iranian Oil Industry'; Touraj Atabaki, 'From 'Amaleh (Labor) to Kargar (Worker): Recruitment, Work Discipline and Making of the Working Class in the Persian/Iranian Oil Industry', International Labor and Working Class History 84 (Fall 2013) pp 159–75.
44 Roger Adelson, London and the Invention of the Middle East: Money, Power, and War, 1902–1922 (Yale University Press, New Haven: 1995) p 171.

treasury and a threadbare and outdated bureaucracy.[45] The apparatus of tax collection had broken down and the Royal Court was heavily in debt to Britain and Russia to foot its basic daily expenses, let alone to invest in any meaningful economic development or relief efforts for the impoverished population.[46] The small, fragmented, and ill trained military forces were being paid from loans from the country's only (British owned) Imperial Bank.[47]

For all practical purposes, southern Iran stayed under direct British rule, with the marauding South Persia Rifles deployed to combat German and Ottoman incursions and to subdue local resistance and brigandage.[48] In Khuzestan, APOC had consolidated its operations and was planning major expansions, relying for protection on British troops in Mesopotamia as well as its local alliances with the virtually autonomous tribal chieftains.[49] In northern Iran the situation was even more precarious. Successive British expeditionary forces had been deployed against rising Soviet influence, but none had fared well. Meanwhile, across the country, a number of provincial movements demanding regional autonomy had broken out to challenge the nominal authority of the government in Tehran.

In this political vacuum, the British diplomatic machine was being conducted, for the first time, by a set of career politicians who specialized in the so-called 'Eastern question'. With the influential George Nathaniel Curzon at

---

45 Millspaugh, *The American Task in Persia*; Mosharrafod-dowleh Hassan Khan Naficy, 'L'Impot et la Vie Economique et Sociale en Perse' (PhD Dissertation, Universite de Paris, 1924); Majid Yektayi, *Tarikh-e Daraayi-e Iran (History of Iranian Finances)*, 2nd ed. (Parviz Publishers, Tehran: 1961); Hossein Khan Moshar-Ghadimi, 'Les Finances Publiques de la Perse' (PhD Dissertation, Universite de Paris, 1922); Shuster, *The Strangling of Persia*.

46 Moustafa Fateh, *The Economic Position of Persia* (P.S.King and Son, London: 1926), pp 66–68; Hassan Mojdehi, 'Arthur C. Millsapugh's Two Missions to Iran and their Impact on American Iranian Relations' (PhD Dissertation, Ball State University: 1975) pp 44–45; Naficy, 'L'Impot et la Vie Economique et Sociale en Perse', pp 54–55.

47 Geoffrey Jones, *Banking and Empire in Iran: Volume 1: The History of the British Bank of the Middle East*, vol. 1 (Cambridge University Press, Cambridge: 1986); Stephanie Cronin, *The Army and the Creation of the Pahlavi State in Iran, 1910–1926* (I.B.Tauris, London: 1997); Bahar, *Tarikh-e Mokhtasar-e Ahzab-e Siasi-ye Iran (History of Iran's Political Parties)*, 1:46–47.

48 The SPA was finally disbanded in 1921. Sykes, 'South Persia and the Great War'; Cronin, *The Army and the Creation of the Pahlavi State in Iran, 1910–1926*; Monireh Razi, *Polis-e Jonoub-e Iran (South Persia Rifles)* (Markaz-e Asnad-e Enqelab-e Eslami, Tehran: 2002); Safiri, *Polis-e Jonoub-e Iran- SPR (South Persia Rifles)*.

49 Ferrier, *History of the British Petroleum Company*, 1:274–311.

the helm of the Foreign Office (FO), consecutive coalition governments were content to leave strategic decisions to a man who saw the priority of British policy in Iran as the revival of the old buffer state policy, now directed against the Soviet menace, as well as American attempts to gain a foothold in the region.[50] Curzon's proposed 1919 Anglo Persian Accord was effectively meant to turn Iran into a British protectorate.[51] Such an outcome would have accomplished the long held desire of securing the western approaches to India[52], and as good as guaranteed the continued monopoly of British control over the oil resources of Iran and the Persian Gulf area. Under these circumstances, the post First World War era ought to have been the golden years of unchallenged British hegemony in Iran. Ironically, this proved not to be the case, and by mid 1920s the whole edifice had altered beyond recognition.

For one thing, the severely weakened British economy was no longer in a position to maintain a costly expansionist policy. Coping with this weakness led to internal discord within the sprawling foreign policy establishment, and undermined the pursuit of unified imperial policies.[53] The eruption of nationalism and mass politics in the region proved difficult to handle for Victorian politicians who had spent years dismissing the motives of the despised 'Persians', Arabs, and Turks alike. Against Curzon's expectations, the Iranian Majlis voted against the 1919 Accord, and in 1921 the Cossack Brigade of the Iranian Army carried out a coup d'état that brought the military strongman Reza Khan to power, possibly with the consent of General Ironside, the senior British commander in Iran.

As Minister of War and Prime Minister, Reza Khan proceeded to establish a unified national army, and ruthlessly began to confront and subjugate the regional autonomy movements. When the army moved against Sheikh

50 On evaluating Curzon's role on Middle East policymaking, see Adelson, *London and the Middle East*; Sabahi, *British Policy in Persia*; Bose, *A Hundred Horizons: The Indian Ocean in the Age of Global Empire*; Christopher N. B. Ross, 'Lord Curzon and E. G. Brown Confront the "Persian Question"', in *The Historical Journal* 52, no. 2 (May 15, 2009) pp 385–411; Homa Katouzian, *State and Society in Iran* (IB Tauris, London: 2000).

51 Mojdehi, 'Arthur C. Millsapugh's Two Missions to Iran and their Impact on American Iranian Relations', pp 38–41.

52 Curzon, *The Place of India in the Empire*.

53 Charles S. Maier, *Recasting Bourgeois Europe: Stabilization in France, Germany and Italy in the Decade after World War I* (Princeton University Press, Princeton: 2011); Roger Adelson, *London and the Invention of the Middle East: Money, Power, and War, 1902–1922* (Yale University Press, New Haven: 1995).

Khaz'al in 1924, a shocked APOC and British government tried to dissuade Reza Khan and to broker a peace, but without success. The British government and APOC reluctantly withdrew their patronage of their local *protégés*, and left the tribal magnates to face their fate. Thereafter, APOC began to rely on the Iranian police and army for protection. The independent political and military power of southern tribal leaders never recovered from this blow, and the army and central government bureaucracy proceeded to establish their sovereignty over local society in ever more intrusive ways.

However, the Oil Company continued to maintain firm control within the exclusive oil enclaves of Masjid Soleyman, Abadan, and other newly discovered oil fields, by turning these areas into fortified company towns. The Company's expanding operations and the fallout from the war had resulted in major social disruptions and had led to huge concentrations of desperate populations in these oil enclaves, which now faced pressing social and urban crises that urgently needed to be addressed. Deadly epidemics affected everyone regardless of race or nationality, while the appalling housing and living conditions, as well as repeated forced evictions by the Company to claim areas for the refinery and other facilities, time and again led to urban unrests that disrupted oil operations. In addition to the oil workers and their families, the poor living conditions affected the entire urban population of shopkeepers, casual and precarious workers, unemployed migrants, landlords, prostitutes, tribesmen, bureaucrats, and other disgruntled local inhabitants, who bolstered the ranks of malcontents and protesters. While outright mass labour protests were relatively rare in Khuzestan's oil towns, new forms of collective urban politics began to emerge in the interwar years in response to the constant frictions between the fast growing heterogeneous local populations, the central government, and the Oil Company. For the latter the eruptions of urban discontent were a serious concern, as Khuzestan had gained an awful reputation as a place to work and to live, which discouraged the much-needed recruitment of more skilled workers and technical staff from India and Europe[54].

APOC responded to this new paradigm by adopting a carrot and stick approach. It maintained order by establishing an extensive network of surveillance and security forces against the threats of political agitators, labour discontent, and urban unrest. However, the Company also reluctantly began to establish a difficult and often contentious collaboration with the weak and nascent state bureaucracy in order to fill the vacuum left by the deposed

---

54 Ehsani, 'Social History of Labor in the Iranian Oil Industry'.

local magnates. This collaboration included a number of measures, such as the establishment of municipalities, the slow but vital construction of some urgently needed urban infrastructure such as sewerage and drinking water outlets, and a number of other public and social services to alleviate the crises of housing, food provision, and public health.[55]

However, these measures remained far too limited compared to the scale of the problems facing the populations of Abadan and Masjed Soleyman. Nevertheless, the very adoption of these limited social policies by a private oil company and the fledgling Iranian bureaucracy indicated a paradigm shift in the post war era. The First World War had spelled the end of the old laissez-faire liberalism. Globally, the post war era was marked by paradoxical socio-economic challenges. On the one hand there were the widespread social and economic problems of mass poverty and unemployment that plagued nearly every participant country in the conflict. On the other hand, politically, the early post war era was marked by the egalitarian promises of the Soviet Revolution, of universal franchise in countries such as Britain, of the millions of war veterans and working people feeling entitled to expect a better life, and of nationalist movements demanding self-determination and independence. In Iran, the nationalists supporting the authoritarian modernisations of Reza Khan were captivated by the promise of a strong state that would regain the country's independence, and improve the general state of the population.

In Iran, during its early years of operations (1908–1921), APOC had acted as a rapacious mining operation, intent on extracting as much profit and crude oil as possible. As circumstances began to change after 1921, the Company had to acknowledge the need to modify this predatory approach, in order to mend relations with the central government and to mollify local discontent. The labour strikes of 1920 and 1922, mainly led by the more skilled Indian workers, had highlighted rising labour discontent, and contributed to the Company's continued difficulties recruiting more skilled personnel from India and Europe. Various lethal epidemics, cholera, the influenza pandemic, plague, etc. had struck the region, highlighting the dangers of the near complete lack of adequate urban infrastructure. Famine continued to pose a significant danger to the destitute population that had congregated in oil towns.

Meanwhile, the Company's relations with the local populations in Khuzestan began to further deteriorate, especially once the tribal elites who had mediated these relations to the benefit of the Company were removed by the

---

55 Ibid.

central government and replaced by bureaucrats and military officers. There was a constant fear of the politicisation of workers, either by communist agitators, or in sympathy with anti-colonial uprisings in neighbouring Iraq (1920), and rising nationalist sympathies in India. The unexpected incursion of the Iranian army in Khuzestan in 1924 to remove Sheikh Khaz'al and to take direct control of the province had curtailed the near total sway of the Company over the management of provincial affairs. With the British government also forced to reconfigure its strategy toward Iran, the Oil Company likewise had to find a new modus operandi to continue successfully to expand its operations.

In summary, the First World War left a deep mark in Iran. It caused enormous suffering on ordinary people, and brought with it political chaos and economic ruin. The discovery of oil and the establishment of an oil industry of global significance changed the strategic role of Iran. But the oil industry also revolutionised social and political relations in southern Iran. It undermined the traditional ties between tribal leaders and the central government as well their own rank and file tribesmen. These processes led to the large-scale dislocations of destitute populations, and the exponential growth of newly established oil towns in Khuzestan. The fallout from these events led to an upsurge of Iranian nationalism, and support for the authoritarian military strongman Reza Khan, who proceeded to use the newly established national army to uproot all his local rivals, and to establish the administrative institutions of a centralising state. Britain and the Anglo Persian Oil Company reluctantly came to accommodate the new political situation. It was only by the middle of 1920s that the revolutionary shockwaves of the First World War had finally come to settle down in Iran. A radically altered society and polity had emerged from the ruins of the First World War, and oil was an integral component of this post war order.

12

The new Arab intellectuals of the post-First World War period: the case of Taha Husayn

Bruno Ronfard

Ardıç, in a study on Islam and secularisation, remarks that 'much of the literature on religion and secularism involves the idea of a fundamental conflict between politics and religion as the basic assumption'[1]. Following this logic, Islam and modernity are conceived as incompatible. The aim of this study is to contribute to the literature on 'alternative' or 'multiple modernities'[2] by explaining some differences between the modernisation of the Middle East and the model that evolved in Western Europe. It is to understand the modernity in the Middle East as a process of

> ongoing reconstructions of multiple institutional and ideological patterns carried forward by specific social actors in close connection with social, political, and intellectual activists, and also by social movements pursuing

---

1 Nurullah Ardıç, *Islam and the Politics of Secularism: The Caliphate and Middle Eastern Modernization in the Early 20th Century* (Routledge, London, New York: 2012) p 11.

2 Shmuel Noah Eisenstadt, 'Multiple Modernities', *Daedalus* 129 (2000) p 1. For Eisenstadt, different societies develop different types of modernity. We refer to Ardıç (2012) for a critical review of the different paradigms on secularisation theory and the Middle East (or Islam).

different programs of modernity, holding very different views on what makes societies modern.[3]

Therefore, we choose to focus on some particularities of Egypt's modernisation in the context of the Middle East after the First World War – a period of transformation, involving social, economic and political changes coloured by ideological struggles, a period also of intellectual effervescence and constitution and reconstitution of cultural programs – through the *figure* of Taha Husayn.

The First World War had multiple consequences for Egypt. The country became a British Protectorate in December 1914. By the end of the war, social and economic conditions fueled the protest of Egyptians, from the peasants to civil servants to intellectuals. Egyptian nationalism was no longer a movement supported by the *élite* alone. Crowds took to the streets of Cairo when the British arrested and deported Sa'ad Zaghlul who wanted to send a delegation (*Wafd*) to the Paris Peace Conference, evoking Wilson's twelfth point: 'Nationalities which are now under Turkish rule should be assured ... an absolutely unmolested opportunity of autonomous development'. In this context, our question is the following: Why did liberal Egyptian intellectuals lose their influence between the two World Wars when winds of change seemed to blow in their favour?

During the post-First World War period, the intellectual scene underwent a profound change in the Arab world and particularly in Egypt. The traditional roles of shaykhs were openly challenged by competition from new sources of knowledge and new forums like journals available to those who wanted to speak on the needs of the state and society. Men of letters left their traditional ivory tower in order to intervene in political, social, cultural and even religious debates. Intellectuals were questioning the religious, state, educational and cultural institutions shaping political and national identity. They were echoed in the opinion of the public eager for fundamental transformations.

For most of the intellectuals of the First World War generation, the core principle for the reshaping of society was nationalism.

> Nationalism (..) served the misrecognised interests of a new social
> category, composed of individuals who possessed types of cultural

---

3 Shmuel Noah Eisenstadt, *Comparative Civilizations and Multiple Modernities* (Boston, Leiden: 2003) p 532.

capital that were new in Egypt, thanks to the introduction of a new kind of educational system. Cultural producers who emerged from this group used nationalism (..) to convert their cultural capital into symbolic capital.[4]

After the First World War, the nationalist movement was turning indeed from a rural revolt into an urban (mostly in Cairo) activism. The number of the educated was increasing and, especially, the number of students was growing dramatically during this period. University enrollments multiplied three times between 1925 and 1940.[5] 'The activists were drawn largely [from the students and] from the 53,000 or so people who had been identified as professionals in 1937, the vast majority of them school teachers'.[6] During that time, by the late thirties, fifteen years of parliamentary democracy had not solved the social problems of injustice and poverty. And, nationalistic groups recruited also among workers or employees in a time of demonstrations and political activism.

Intellectuals of this generation were often polemists, critics and indeed *columnists*, which means writers being in tune with their contemporaries, their discontent with the political situation and their desire for changes. Then the works of intellectuals 'appeared as the chronicle of a world in tremendous turmoil, dictated by events and written by authors in the process of shaping their craft and in the process of being shaped by them'.[7] The importance of publishing periodicals, which originated in the nineteenth century, stimulated public debate. Hundreds of newspapers and journals were founded between 1860 and 1920 and the number of copies was increasing ten times or more before and after the First World War.[8] It was creating as well opportunities

---

4 Benjamin Geer, *The Priesthood of Nationalism in Egypt: Duty, Authority, Autonomy* (PhD Thesis, School of Oriental and African Studies, University of London, 2011), p 34, last accessed 5 January 2015, http://eprints.soas.ac.uk/13185/. In his thesis, Geer adapts Pierre Bourdieu's concept of habitus to the context of the Egyptian Nationalism.

5 Jean-Jacques Waardenburg, *Les universités dans le monde arabe* (Mouton, Paris: 1966) pp 78–80.

6 Roger Owen, *State Power and Politics in the Making of the Modern Middle East* (Routledge, London, New York: 2004) p 15.

7 Dyala Hamzah, *L'intérêt général (maslaha 'amma) ou le triomphe de l'opinion : Fondation délibératoire (et esquisses délibératives) dans les écrits du publiciste syro-égyptien Muhammad Rašīd Ridā (1865–1935)*, (PhD Thesis, Freie Universität, Berlin and EHESS, Paris, 2008) p 12.

8 Ami Ayalon, *The Press in the Arab Middle East: A History* (Oxford University Press, New York-Oxford: 1995) pp 148–149.

for polemicists to express their talent and their will to seek change. Taha Husayn and others, like al-'Aqqad, Haykal or al-Hakim (even Rashid Rida[9]), were not scrupulous experts with high academic standards. Their importance was in their open-mindedness and their courage: 'They accustomed an entire generation to thinking along new lines.'[10] They were intellectuals and gave themselves the mission to change the society in transforming the culture and the politics. And they were seeking the wide support of the masses. Besides writing their articles and pamphlets, they stood up for their nationalist beliefs. They were both writers and activists. That is why, for example, Ahmad Lutfi al-Sayid was involved in the struggle for Parliament rights along with the Liberal Constitutionalist Party as well as Taha Husayn who was writing in *al-Siyāsa*, the mouthpiece for this party, headed by Haykal in the beginning of the 1920s. The polemics against the Wafdist government were intense and *al-Siyāsa* was banned two times on January 1924. Taha Husayn was questioned but did not say a word.

Taha Husayn was part of this generation which saw European power and heritage as a challenge. This generation tried to respond by changing society in different ways. The debates first focused on adapting Islam, changing laws and political institutions, and later raised questions about language, culture, religion and personal and social identities. And the desire for change was urgent. 'The Nation was becoming aware of itself', as Taha Husayn later wrote.[11] The challenge was quite a paradox. On the one hand, nationalism meant *egyptianising* the society and the economy but, on the other hand, for intellectuals it meant creating a new society with liberal and democratic values, close to the European model.

Out of the traditional rivalry between Conservatives, Reformists and Modernists, out of the traditional East/West opposition, one of the most important public debates concerned the place of religion. As we will analyse it in the second part of this paper, religious institutions still had a large influence in the

---

9 Dyala Hamzah deconstructed Rida's figure. She wrote about the editor of al-Manār : 'When read as a 'alim, producing a theoretical work, in the framework of a time-honoured methodology, Rida is bound to appear incoherent, non-systematic, inconsistent. 'Umar Ryad, 'A Printed Muslim "Lighthouse", in *Cairo al-Manār's Early Years, Religious Aspiration and Reception (1898–1903)'*, Arabica 56 (2009) p 30.

10 Pierre Cachia, *Preface to An Egyptian Childhood, by Taha Husayn* (The American University in Cairo Press, Cairo: 1932/1997) p 4.

11 Taha Husayn, 'Destins de la Littérature Arabe', *La Revue du Caire* 157, (1953) p 17.

society. More importantly, religion had and has always played a fundamental role in the definition of Arab identity.

It is not our purpose to initiate a methodological debate about reform and revolution or reformists and secularists or *faṣl* (rupture) and *waṣl* (continuity/ persistence). We shall at least mention that the two parts – Islamic tradition and openness to modern criticism – which al-Afrani or 'Abduh had tried to hold together, were questioned in new ways. For example, some took a position against western ideas to move closer to a kind of Muslim fundamentalism. Others accepted Islam as a body of principles together with secular and liberal norms to regulate the society. Some wanted to subordinate nationalism to religion, others attempted the opposite. Taha Husayn belonged to the latter group, but he had a special place because of his personal journey from al-Azhar to the Egyptian University. He wanted to take a new look at Islamic tradition to share new lessons and a new way of thinking with his contemporaries and he wanted to help Egypt be part of the dialogue with Western Europe. He was, indeed, 'the writer who has given the final statement of the system of ideas which underlay social thought and political action in the Arab countries for three generations'.[12]

Taha Husayn was one of the most important intellectuals of the post-First World War period and he was at the crossroads of several traditions which are sometimes in contradiction. Blind at the age of four, the result of faulty treatment by a barber, he went from the small quranic school to al-Azhar, from the conservatism and repetition of tradition to the discovery of literature with al-Marsafi, one of 'Abduh's protégés, from the new Egyptian University to the French Sorbonne, from the dark world of al-Ma'arri, his subject dissertation at the Egyptian University[13], to the 'philosophie sociale d'Ibn Khaldoun', his subject at the Sorbonne. In brief, the young blind boy went from the traditional circles of al-Azhar, which gave him an enormous knowledge of religious texts, to the modern western practices of critics like Ahmad Lutfi al-Sayid and the Egyptian University professors and finally to the teachings of Durkheim who was his professor at the Sorbonne. His public career began in 1919, an explosive time. After meeting Sa'ad Zaghlul who was on his way to plead Egypt's case in Paris, Taha Husayn went back to Egypt with his French

---

12 Albert Hourani, *Arabic Thought in the Liberal Age, 1798–1939* (Cambridge University Press, Cambridge, New York: 1983) p 326.
13 It was indeed the first Egyptian doctorate thesis. He applied Western framework of criticism to analyze the work of the blind poet Al-Ma'arri.

wife. He had spent three years in France. Throughout the 1920s and 1930s, he was somehow leader of the Modernists and part of a number of gifted liberal writers. 'All masters of Arabic style, with a European education (English or French as the case might be) solidly grounded in a traditional culture, they were primarily men of letters. Their ideas were expounded for the most part in magazine articles, or by implication in novels and plays'[14] And the most important writings of Taha Husayn were produced between the two World Wars. In a very few years, he published ten books: collections of his columns and articles, novels, an autobiography which became a reference work, studies of Islamic history, and translations and studies of Western literature.

The place of religion was central in these years. In the 1920s some reformers, like Rashid Rida, focused on the cultural threats to Islam posed by European thought and powers. For Taha Husayn civil authority should be separated from religious authority. For him, al-Azhar should teach 'the religion of freedom, science and knowledge'; and it should stop teaching the 'old idea of religious nationalism'. So, he applied the philosophical methods of Descartes to pre-Islamic poetry in a book published in 1926. He wrote nothing against Islam, but critiquing pre-Islamic poetry seemed to be the first step before applying this method to the entire tradition and that was the main issue for al-Azhar. In a way, this example shows how vigorous the intellectual life was. Economic and political issues were much more important than a book written by an intellectual and bought by hundreds of readers at best. Anyway, the book was withdrawn. Taha Husayn had to leave Egypt for several months; six years later, he was dismissed from his position as dean at Cairo University. This subversive book was an indelible mark on its author, even if he published a softer version later on. For some of his compatriots, he was the man through whom opportunity comes.

Later, Taha Husayn tried to read or explain the story of the beginning of Islam in new way, 'in ways which would appeal to the modern Egyptian consciousness'.[15] For example, 'Uthman was becoming the modern symbol of human weakness (and the first Caliphs are described as establishing a reign of social justice): all positions difficult for his contemporaries to accept. He was not the only one to make this shift to Islamic subjects. Haykal and al-Hakim did the same. It was a way for the intellectuals to reach a wider public and to be closer to traditional Egypt, to prove also that their purpose in separating

---

14 Hourani, *Arabic Thought in the Liberal Age*, p 325.
15 Ibid., p 334.

religious and political affairs was never a fight against religion itself, but against conservatism. It shows a shift and the end of the liberal times. The society was changing and some liberal writers took a more positive interest in religion. Religion was no longer synonymous with lifeless tradition even if they still argued for the importance of science and reason against ignorance. This in turn revealed a 'very real anxiety in the face of the other'.[16] represented in their life by the religious subject/authority.

The Arabic language was as important as religion in the 1920s. Back to his book on pre-Islamic history, the issue here is not to decide if he was right or wrong – he was partially wrong indeed – but the interesting point is that the public debate was on linguistic and literary criticism issues. More interesting, during this difficult time, Taha Husayn wrote, in nine days, the first part of his autobiography which is a major piece of world literature and almost the first attempt of this kind in Arabic in modern times. In *al-Ayyam*, he remembers his childhood, the days at the quranic school with an ignorant and arrogant teacher called 'Our Master'. Even more, the life in the villages seems a mix of superstition, prejudices against modern science and medicine and ignorance propagated by popular religious figures. This first part of the autobiography ends up with the tragic death of his sister and later his brother, and his departure for Cairo and al-Azhar. This piece seems to be the expression of a catharsis. While dictating *Al-Ayyam*, Taha Husayn is abroad, in the heart of a social and personal crisis. And in this book, he is telling the story of a young man – using the third-person – going from his village to Cairo, from traditional Islam to a critical point of view about it, from childhood to autonomy, from his introvert childhood memories to the quest for identity, from a self-centered society to the world where everybody is one among others, from remembering the past to the future (Indeed, the very last pages of the book are a letter to his young daughter). In brief, this book did not represent only an inner and personal quest of an enlightenment writer who wages many intellectual public battles, but also a shift of an ideological framework of the whole country. In this book, Taha Husayn is Egypt. At least, he describes the future he wished for Egypt.

Writing these two pieces on pre-Islamic poetry and his autobiography almost at the same time, he emphasised the revival of the language at this

16 Christina Philips, 'The Other in Modern Arabic Literature: A Critic of Postcolonial Theory', in Geoffrey Nash, Kathleen Kerr-Koch and Sarah E. Hackett (eds), *Postcolonialism and Islam* (Routledge, London, New York: 2014) p 127.

time of reshaping the nation. He was known as the Dean of Arabic literature. Taha Husayn had a great sense of observation and analysis and a unique style: slightly repetitive, sometimes mannered with long sentences but poetic, delicate and energetic, classical and modern at the same time. Moreover his first dictation produced the final version of a text. He never revised any pages and never asked for a paragraph to be read back to him.

His idea was also to make it possible to receive an education in Arabic and to provide access to all important texts of world literature. For example, he translated Aristotle's *The Constitution of the Athenians* in the early 1920s during the debate on an Egyptian constitution. He was also urging Egypt to discover other cultures than the European ones and wrote critiques of non-European writers. Against the position of most of the ulemas, he wanted to legitimise novels as a new type of cultural production. Among other pieces, he wrote *Adib* (the writer), a reversed mirror of his autobiography. Adib was, like him, a student in France during the First World War, but his intellectual journey was a tragic one. Too far from his own world and too close to the other (the Western world), he went insane when the world fell apart. This novel is a deep reflection on the concepts of self and the other.

His book *Mustaqbal al-Thaqafah fi Misr* (The Future of Culture in Egypt) shed light on the public role of Taha Husayn. It was written following the signing of the Anglo-Egyptian treaty in 1936 in London which 'restored to Egypt a large measure of both her internal et external independence'[17] and it is one of the manifestos of Arabic modernity. In this context, he wants to present a new goal for the age of independence. This goal is a vast and detailed program of reform. The main purpose is again identity as it was twenty years earlier about the Arabic language, identity through language, traditions and modernity. The book begins with a historical part about Egyptian roots and finishes with an encouragement to intellectuals about the necessity for cooperation with Arab countries. In between, the author develops his concrete ideas for educational reform. For Taha Husayn, culture, knowledge and language are the basis of civilisation and independence. Against al-Azhar, he claims that the teaching of the Arabic language should not be monopolised by one institution. Taha Husayn did not want to leave the Arabic language in the hands of the men of religion:

'I urge the State to (...) encourage competent scholars to change the
language and related sciences so as to put them in tune with modern

---

17 Taha Husayn, *The Future of Culture in Egypt* (Octagon Books, New York: 1944/1975) p vii.

life and thought. I warn those who are resisting reform that we face the
dreadful prospect of classical Arabic becoming, whether we want it or
not, a religious language and the sole possession of the men of religion'.[18]

Among the different reasons, he mentioned that Arabic is also the language
of Coptic Egyptians: 'the Arabic language is not the language of Muslims only,
but the language of all who speak it, however much they differ in faith.'[19] For
Taha Husayn, the Arabic language is at first the classical one and, for him,
the masses should be able to understand the classical Arabic. The colloquial
might 'disappear' into it.

A single sentence summarises the main idea of the book in his poetic style:

'Egyptian culture may be clearly combined the ancient Egyptian artistic
component, the Arab-Islamic legacy, and the borrowings from the best
of modern European life. These elements are strongly antithetical to each
other. As they clash, the un-Egyptian qualities are rejected and a purified
blend emerges which is then transmitted from father to son and from
teacher to pupil.'[20]

With this sentence, he wants to convince not 'the hypocrites, liars, and
troublemakers', but 'the decent men who are honestly afraid that our religion
will be contaminated by the evils they hear are latent in the European way
of life which I have been advocating.'[21] Again religion is the starting point
of a public debate, about education. For Taha Husayn, in search of a newly
thought out modern identity, the Arab heritage has to be revitalised. It is like
gardens long-neglected but vivid and it is better than the well-ordered ones.

In brief, the aim of this paper has been to analyse how the intellectuals
tried – and maybe succeeded only partially – to change their society and the
world. A symptomatic anecdote involving Suzanne, Taha Husayn's wife, is
quite significant about this generation. Suzanne Taha Husayn explains in her
memoirs the following situation. In the beginning of the 1930s, when Taha
Husayn was deprived of state employment in the University and felt alone in
a deep crisis, he received a letter from a close friend, the French orientalist,

---

18 Ibid., p 86.
19 Ibid., p 139.
20 Ibid., p 153.
21 Ibid., p 17.

Louis Massignon. He invited Husayn to come to the United States in order to retain an academic position. Suzanne Taha Husayn wrote: 'He considered this proposal for three days and said: 'Massignon's letter awoke me. I am a revoked professor and a scholar who no longer has the right to work. My duty is not to play politics, but to write books. In America, I would be a foreigner; I would look at the country's life and not participate in it. I would have a limited duty'.'[22] The keyword here is duty. As Pierre Cachia wrote in the introduction of The Days, Taha Husayn's autobiography: 'Sustaining him through this tempestuous career was the belief – perhaps naïve but firmly held, and shared by many of his contemporaries – in the duty and the power of the intellectual to reshape his society by fearless assertion of the truth as he sees it.'[23]

With his vast culture, his talent in polemics, his verve in using the Arabic language, his wish to create an Arab self-awareness in modern times, Taha Husayn was one of the best sons of this generation. Polemicist and master of literary language with a wide culture, he wanted to turn himself into an intellectual with a transformative social mission, a promoter of modernisation of society. In 1949, thirteen years after independence, he expresses disappointment in al-Mu'adhdhabun fi al-Ard: 'This country which was made for freedom is still enslaved.'[24]

His criticism of the social and economic system is, however, sketchy, and nowhere does he show a detailed knowledge of social problems outside those of education. He wrote in the same book: 'Egypt is ailing (...) Egyptians may adopt a new life similar to the one they knew in the aftermath of the First World War, based on unity, cooperation and the eradication of the distances between the strong and the weak, between the rich and the poor, between the healthy and the ailing.'[25]

This generation wanted to change the society, not with a revolution but with a revitalisation of a great cultural heritage. And, in the end, many questions of this time concerning representative government vs. autocracy, secularisation (not at first as a conflict between politics and religion, but as a new way of places and relations between them – because the world today seems

---

22 Suzanne Taha Husayn, Avec toi: De la France à l'Égypte: « un extraordinaire amour » Suzanne et Taha Hussein (1915–1973) (Le Cerf, Paris: 2011) p 122.
23 Cachia, Preface, p 5.
24 Taha Husayn, The Sufferers, (transl) Mona al-Zayyat (American University in Cairo Press, Cairo: 1993) p 152.
25 Ibid., p 153.

secularised and religious), and social questions, such as poverty, were not addressed. This generation tried to create a true Egyptian-Arab identity, but failed to create an alternative to promote their new ideas and to change the society. One hundred years later, in the relations between the Western world and Arab countries, the desire for change is still urgent.

Taha Husayn describes the man of letters 'like a mirror receiving images without knowing how it receives them.'[26] This theme is a recurrent one in the texts of the writer. It is associated with identity, self-questioning and remembering. In search of identity through 'multiple modernities' in confrontation with the vivid Arabic heritage: this sentence could be an abstract of this period in Egypt as well as a résumé of the life of Taha Husayn.

---

26 Taha Husayn, *Hadith al-Arbi'a*, (Dar al-Kitab al-Lubnani, Beyrouth: 1974) p 246.

13

A tale of two nationalists: parallelisms in the writings of Ziya Gökalp and Michel Aflaq

Michael Erdman

The first stirrings of Arab political nationalism are widely recognised to have occurred during the latter years of the Ottoman Empire.[1] Missionary schools and international trade had opened up the Middle East to the ideas of Romantic Europe, and the creation of nation-states by the European Great Powers was rapidly laying waste to Ottoman sovereignty, if not suzerainty, over the Balkans. Despite this, the vast majority of Arabs in the Middle East would have to wait two or three decades after the collapse of the Ottoman Empire in 1918 to achieve full-fledged independence. The establishment of British and French Mandates in the intermediary period thwarted desires for self-determination, and despite the fact that Arab nationalists expressed no nostalgia for the Ottoman period, the brunt of their anger and vitriol was reserved for Paris, Rome and London.[2] This hierarchy of oppression and resistance is a core strand of the Ba'thist ideology.

---

1 See Philip S. Khoury, 'Continuity and Change in Syrian Political Life: The Nineteenth and Twentieth Centuries', in *American Historical Review* 5, p 1384; Mohammed El-Attrache, 'The Political Philosophy of Michel Aflaq and The Ba'ath Party in Syria' (PhD dissertation, The University of Oklahoma, 1973) p 23.
2 Shibli Al-Aysami, *Hizb al-Ba'ath al-'Arabiy al-Ishtiraki: (1) MarHala Al-Arba'inat At-Ta'asissiya 1940–1949* (Dar at-Tali'a Lit-Tiba'a wa an-Nashr, Beirut: 1975) p 11.

226 THE FIRST WORLD WAR AND ITS AFTERMATH

Ba'thism was closely linked to praetorian régimes and militarism after the 1966 coup in Syria, and the 1968 coup in Iraq. At its origin, however, the movement was an intellectual one, and indeed one of its founders, Michel Aflaq, was persecuted by military figures in the early days of Syrian independence.[3] Such ironic twists of history can be observed in other radical régimes, including other administrations that, through the course of the 20th century, have become closely identified with military forces. In particular, Ottoman and Turkish parallels to the ideology of Ba'thism should not be sought in Young Turk military circles, or the eventual emergence of a markedly militarist Turkish Republic in 1923, but rather in the philosophical underpinnings of the Young Turk era. More specifically, commonalities are evident in the pre-Republican writings of Ziya Gökalp, one of the Young Turk period's influential ideologues and sociologists. Despite being men of two very different eras, the similarities between Ziya Gökalp and Michel Aflaq are striking. Both men were members of minorities (Gökalp was of Kurdish ancestry[4]; Aflaq, an Orthodox Christian[5]) who espoused the identity of the majority (Turkishness[6]; Islam[7]) in order to further their primary aim, nationalism. More importantly, both men were thinkers and intellectuals in historical periods dominated by military figures. Both of their ideologies, therefore, seek to provide that which military government could not: a philosophical and normative basis for the unification of the disparate camps supporting the disruptive forces sweeping their respective nations.

It is not possible to talk of a direct legacy or influence of Ziya Gökalp on Michel Aflaq. To do so would require definitive proof of an impact of the former on the latter, through Aflaq's studies and reading habits. Rather, what can be distilled from a careful reading of both Gökalp's and Aflaq's works is a striking parallelism in the manner in which both men adapted specific currents of contemporary thought to their particular historical situations. These parallelisms are most evident in the following three categories:

---

3 Michel Sab', *Sa'adat wa 'Aflaq fii al-Fikr as-Siyasi al-Orthothuksiy* (Manshurat Afaq Jami'iya, Beirut: 2005) p 263.
4 Uriel Heyd, *The Foundations of Turkish Nationalism: The Life and Teachings of Ziya Gökalp* (Luzac and Company Ltd., London: 1950) p 21.
5 Raymond Hinnebusch, *Authoritarian Power and State Formation in Ba'thist Syria* (Westview Press, Boulder, CO: 1990), p 87.
6 Ziya Gökalp, *Turkish Nationalism and Western Civilization*, (transl.) Niyazi Berkes (George Allan and Unwin Ltd., London: 1959) p 44.
7 Hinnebusch, *Authoritarian Power and State Formation in Ba'thist Syria*, p 89.

1 Solidarism, in name or in spirit, as a basis for economic development;
2 The role of Islam as a spiritual and moral force rather than a source of legislative or administrative guidance;
3 The subordination of individual will to the will of the nation.

Before analysing the role of solidarism in the works of both Gökalp and Aflaq, I will begin with brief biographies of the two men, in order to explore the influences and experiences that led them to their chosen creeds.

Ziya Gökalp was born Mehmet Ziya in Diyarbakır, contemporary southeastern Turkey, in 1876.[8] His upbringing was thoroughly provincial: Gökalp only left his hometown for Istanbul at the age of 20, in 1896. By his own admission, he was not a diligent student, despite his love of both mathematics and literature. It was his father who steered the young Ziya towards an interest in Namık Kemal, one of the earliest proponents of national consciousness among the Muslim peoples of the Ottoman Empire.[9] Shortly before leaving for Istanbul, Gökalp had an epiphany that brought an end to several years of depression and psychological agony over the path to Truth; rather than positive science or theology, it was 'nationality and liberty' that would show him the righteous path.[10] It is possible that some of these ideas might have been the product of his friendship with opponents of Abdül Hamid II's régime, exiled to Diyarbakır while Gökalp was still living in the city. Among them was Abdullah Cevdet, one of the founders of what would become the Committee of Union and Progress (CUP). Cevdet introduced him to French sociology, which would come to influence profoundly Gökalp's writings and perception of Turkish society.[11] Gökalp's ideas about modern science, religion, liberalism and the national spirit were further shaped by charismatic individuals he met in Istanbul.[12] One such source of inspiration was a fellow inmate at Taşkışla Prison, where he served ten months of his one year sentence for political activities against the régime in 1897–98.[13]

After completing his sentence, the young Gökalp was exiled back to Diyarbakır, where he stayed for the next ten years, devoting much of his

---

8 Heyd, *The Foundations of Turkish Nationalism: The Life and Teachings of Ziya Gökalp*, p 19.
9 Gökalp, *Turkish Nationalism and Western Civilization*, pp 35–36.
10 Ibid., p 39.
11 Heyd, *The Foundations of Turkish Nationalism: The Life and Teachings of Ziya Gökalp*, p 24.
12 Gökalp, *Turkish Nationalism and Western Civilization*, pp 39–40.
13 Heyd, *The Foundations of Turkish Nationalism*, p 28.

time to studies of Western philosophy and political science. In 1909, after Sultan Abdül Hamid II was deposed, he was invited to attend the CUP Congress in Salonica, where he was elected a member of the Central Council. He was greatly influenced by the intellectual climate of the city, where he remained until its cession to Greece in 1912. Its majority non-Muslim population exhibited a propensity for the liberal and nationalist ideas that were sweeping across the Empire.[14] It was here that he took the name Gökalp, and it was also during his time in Salonica that his linguistic, social and political views coalesced around what would later be called Turkism.[15] In 1912, he moved to Istanbul, where he was engaged in writing articles, lecturing at Istanbul University and advising the Young Turk government on social reform and education.[16] In 1919, he was arrested and tried for war crimes, resulting in his exile by the British to Malta in 1920.[17] He was allowed to return to Turkey in 1921, but did not resume public activities until 1922, when he was recalled to Ankara to lead the Committee for Writing and Translation. He became an ardent supporter of Müstafa Kemal (Atatürk) and was elected to Parliament as a representative for Diyarbakır in 1923. This allowed him to participate in the Parliamentary Education Committee, continuing his influence over Turkish youth. Ziya Gökalp died in Ankara in 1924 and was granted a state funeral.[18]

Such an honourable end was not afforded to the founder of the Ba'th Party. Michel Aflaq was born in Damascus in 1912, the son of a middling grain merchant. He was educated at a Greek Orthodox school in the city and left for France at the age of 17 to continue his education at the Sorbonne.[19] He returned to Syria in 1932 and began cooperating with the Syrian Communists in 1934, but became disillusioned after their support for the Syrian-French Treaty of 1936 and suspended his work with them indefinitely.[20] Aflaq worked as a high school teacher in Damascus until 1940, when he was fired for his

---

14 Taha Parla, *The Social and Political Thought of Ziya Gökalp: 1876–1924* (Brill, Leiden: 1985) p 13.

15 Heyd, *The Foundations of Turkish Nationalism*, pp 32–33.

16 Ibid., pp 35–36.

17 Parla, *The Social and Political Thought of Ziya Gökalp*, p 14.

18 Heyd, *The Foundations of Turkish Nationalism*, pp 38–39.

19 Gordon H. Torrey, 'The Ba'th: Ideology and Practice', in *Middle East Journal* 23, 4 (Autumn 1969) pp 445–446.

20 Nabil M. Kaylani, 'The Rise of the Syrian Ba'th, 1940–1958: Political Success, Party Failure', in *International Journal of Middle East Studies* 3, 1 (January 1972) p 4.

political activities. In the late 1950s, he claimed that during this period he had come to realise the inadequacies of a universalist approach to Arab problems, and embarked on a path tailored to the peculiarities of the Arab nation.[21] His political activities continued in private until 1943, when he launched the Arab Resurrection Socialist Party (حزب البعث العربي الاشتراكي).[22] By various accounts, he was an articulate and charismatic man, albeit one who remained above quotidian issues of party policy and administration.[23]Although he held the position of Minister of Education in a national unity government in 1949,[24] he spent most of his time from 1943 until 1952 as the *éminence grise* and Secretary-General of the Party, contributing to its ideological development.[25]

In 1952, a year after Adib Al-Shishakli seized power in a coup d'état, Aflaq was arrested, but managed to escape abroad in January 1953. Later on that year, he was amnestied by Al-Shishakli and returned to Damascus.[26] Aflaq again went into brief exile in Beirut in 1960, two years after the merger of Syria and Egypt into the United Arab Republic (UAR).The UAR was ended officially in March 1963 by a coup carried out by Ba'thist officers not allied to Aflaq's wing of the Party.[27] After the coup, Aflaq became embroiled in ideological and practical disputes with left wing members of the Syrian and Iraqi Ba'th parties; his influence gradually waned in the face of increased military intervention into the Party's internal politics.[28] In February 1966, General Salah took power in a coup d'état and Aflaq went into hiding, officially branded a traitor and ejected from the party.[29] Such was the new régime's dislike for Aflaq that it officially proclaimed Zaki Al-Arsuzi, rather than Aflaq, the founder of the Ba'th Party.[30] In 1968, Aflaq fled to Iraq, which was under Ba'thist military control,[31] and remained in Baghdad until his death in 1989.[32]

---

21 Ibid., p 448.
22 El-Attrache, 'Political Philosophy', p 30.
23 Torrey, 'The Ba'th: Ideology and Practice', p 446; El-Attrache, 'Political Philosophy', p 32.
24 Hinnebusch, *Authoritarian Power and State Formation in Ba'thist Syria*, p 93.
25 El-Attrache, 'Political Philosophy', p 31.
26 Torrey, 'The Ba'th: Ideology and Practice', p 455.
27 Ibid., pp 456–459.
28 P. M., 'Siria', in *Oriente Moderno* 44, 3/4 (March-April 1964), p 201.
29 Robert W. Olson, 'The Ba'th in Syria 1947–1979: An Interpretative Historical Essay (Part Two)', *Oriente Moderno* 59, 6 (June 1979) p 453.
30 Kaylani, 'The Rise of the Syrian Ba'th, 1940–1958: Political Success, Party Failure', p 3.
31 Olson, 'The Ba'th in Syria 1947–1979: An Interpretative Historical Essay (Part Two)', p 471.
32 Amatzia Baram, 'Broken Promises', in *The Wilson Quarterly* 27, 2 (Spring 2003) p 45.

With these aspects of Gökalp and Aflaq's lives in mind, I will now proceed to an exploration of their intellectual legacies. As economics and economic development were among the most pressing motivations for the transformation of both the Ottoman Empire and Post-Mandate Syria, it is with the theory of solidarism that I shall begin this examination.

Solidarism as an economic philosophy emerged from Western Europe – particularly France – in the late 19th century. It sought to counter the liberal economic model, in which personal interest and the invisible hand determined the development of a given economy, with a managed or directed system. In this system, private enterprise was not to be outlawed, but rather the State would take an actively interventionist role in the most important sectors of the economy. The State would interact with individual economic units by means of corporations, which grouped both workers and managers in specific industries. In this way, individuals' concerns and interests would be represented before the State through corporate structures, and the State would be better able to implement policies and plans in the interest of the nation via a reduced number of interlocutors, namely the corporations.[33]

Gökalp, who was a student of Durkheimian sociology and broader French sociological and philosophical trends, was in turn influenced by the solidarist strain of thought.[34] He understood solidarist social organisations to be more attuned to the Turkish-Islamic culture with which the late Ottoman Empire was imbued than other theoretical structures.[35] As such, the adoption of solidarist policies would not be inappropriate for the cultural sphere within which Gökalp operated, as opposed to the liberal proclivities of the Tanzimat reformers whom he often criticised.[36] In the opinion of Gökalp, the essential nature of traditional Turkish culture made a third way between unfettered capitalism and Communism ideal for the Turks. As a people who loved both individual liberty and equality, the Turks would develop along European lines and retain their traditional culture only through solidarism. This is because Gökalp's solidarism recognised the validity of private property only 'insofar as it correspond[ed] to social solidarity.'[37] He called for profits in excess of

---

33 Taha Parla, *Ziya Gökalp, Kemalizm ve Türkiye'de Korporatizm* (Deniz Yayınları, İstanbul: 2009) p 111.

34 Ibid., p 127.

35 Ibid., p 77.

36 Ibid., p 74.

37 Ziya Gökalp, *Türkçülüğün esasları* (Toker Yayımevi, İstanbul: 1995) p 180.

those necessary for the creators of surplus value to maintain themselves to be collected by society and reinvested in the expansion of productive capacity.[38]

Solidarism, according to Gökalp, was about more than just state-managed private enterprise. It was also an answer to the relative retardation of Turks with respect to their non-Turkish compatriots in the economic sphere. Prior to the First World War, non-Muslim citizens and residents of the Ottoman Empire were disproportionately more involved in industry and commerce than Muslim Ottoman subjects.[39] Rather than interrogate the unbalanced development of human capital in the Ottoman Empire of the 18th and 19th centuries, Gökalp sought the cause of this phenomenon through comparison of the Turks with the advanced economies of his era. The reason for Europe's economic development was the emergence of concentrated urban centres in which groups became specialised and individuals recognised their own unique agency.[40] This change broke traditional social structures and spurred the desire among European urbanites to surpass the economic, social and educational achievements of their forefathers.[41] Turks, however, had failed to adopt productive professions throughout their history, and thus had been gradually sidelined from the development of capitalist structures within the Empire. Solidarism, thus, was a means of accelerating the development of such social structures. It would allow for the government to intervene and correct such preferences amongst the Turks through relationships between the state and citizens reorganised along corporate lines.[42]

Although Michel Aflaq espoused Socialism as one of the titular elements of the Ba'thist program, he refused to adopt Marxist economic thought wholesale.[43] As John Devlin has pointed out, the economic philosophy that Aflaq embraced was much more concerned with social justice than the socialisation of the factors of production. The aim of the Ba'thists was to make the distribution of goods and productive resources in Arab society more equitable.[44] Indeed, in 1950, the delegates to the First Ba'thist Congress called for

38 Ibid.

39 İbrahim Türk, *Türk Toplumunda Sosyal Sınıflar* (Öncü Kitabevi, Istanbul: 1970) p 49.

40 Gökalp, *Turkish Nationalism and Western Civilization*, p 274.

41 Ibid., p 275.

42 Ibid., p 73.

43 Michel 'Aflaq, *Mukhtarat min Aqwal mu'assis al-Ba'th* (Al-Mu'assisat al-'Arabiyya lid-Dirasat wa-an-Nashr, Beirut: 1975) p 45.

44 John F. Devlin, *The Ba'th Party: A History from its Origins to 1966* (Hoover Institution Press, Stanford, CA: 1976) p 33.

the Syrian constitution to recognize an *upper limit* to private property, not an outright ban.[45] Again, Aflaq's concern was with the use of control over natural resources and productive capacity to exploit Arab citizens. The role of the state, in this sense, was the management of large-scale endeavours and initiatives in the national interest, in order to ensure that their exploitation would benefit the nation as a whole, rather than individuals or foreigners.[46] Similarly, the ownership of factories and their administration was to be shared between workers and management. While this might appear to be a simple social democratic compromise between the various classes, it is in fact a hallmark of Aflaq's general preference for solidarist constructs: in return for worker participation in factory management, the state would also undertake to limit wages according to the profits of the firm.[47] In other words, workers would not control all factors of production and their revenue streams, and capitalists would not have free reign to exploit labour. Instead, the state would organise broadly productive activities, treating workers and managers together as economic blocks, rather than opposing forces.

Other parallelisms with Gökalp's economic thought are evident in Aflaq's calls for the Arabisation of the national economy. The existence of a compra-dor class – a group of local intermediaries who represented colonial interests in the Levant[48] – during the Ottoman and Mandate periods meant that the simple transfer of ownership from foreigners to Arabs would not be suffi-cient for the realisation of the Ba'thist economic program.[49] Indeed, despite Aflaq's refusal to endorse the class struggle as a central component of Ba'thist doctrine,[50] the Ba'thists nevertheless called for the destruction of the feudal class responsible for the perpetuation of social injustice.[51] The feudal class may very well have been supported by the Mandate powers, but they were distinctly local in their composition.[52] It is perhaps for this reason that Aflaq called for the nationalisation (تأميم) – as in extending the control of the state

45 *Al-Ba'th... Wa NiDal at-Tabaqat Al-'Amila* (Dar at-Tabaqat, Beirut: 1974) p 52.

46 Ibid., p 32.

47 Ibid., p 33.

48 Türk, *Türk Toplumunda Sosyal Sınıflar*, p 49.

49 Kassim Sallam, *Le Ba'th et la Patrie Arabe* (Éditions du Monde Arabe, Paris: 1982) p 308.

50 Devlin, *The Ba'th Party: A History from its Origins to 1966*, p 34.

51 Raymond Hinnebusch, *Syria: Revolution from Above* (Routledge, London: 2001) p 30.

52 Al-Aysami, *Hizb al-Ba'th al-'Arabiy al-Ishtiraki: (1) MarHala Al-Arba'inat At-Ta'asissiya 1940–1949*, p 12.

over – rather than the Arabisation (بيرعت) of nationally vital industries.[53] Much as in Gökalp's writings, it was the state and not the people, whether in aggregate or as enlightened classes, that was to take responsibility for national economic development and social justice.[54]

Thus, the solidarism that was so overtly propounded by Ziya Gökalp was shared to a certain extent, albeit tacitly, by Michel Aflaq. Private property was to be limited, not banned, and the state was to assume a key role in directing national economic development via collectives of workers and managers, without socialising the factors of production. For Aflaq, the economic struggle was as important as the national liberation struggle. Unlike the European nations, who had the benefit of centuries of slow social and economic change prior to the emergence of the nationalist creed, the Arabs would be forced to undergo both revolutions at once.[55] This sentiment closely resembles that of Gökalp, who several decades earlier had called on his Turkish brethren to follow the European social, political and economic changes if they wished to keep pace with the West. These common approaches to the adaption of contemporary ideas to local circumstances were not limited to economic concepts, but touched upon social constructs as well. Indeed, this pattern was applied to the most sacred of components of both Syrian and Ottoman societies: Islam.

Ziya Gökalp's most active period of writing coincided with the period known as the Young Turk era: the decade following the 1908 Constitutional Revolution, which brought partisans of the Committee of Union and Progress to power in the Ottoman Empire. As the Young Turks were known, correctly or incorrectly, for their secularist views, it should be no surprise that Gökalp's view of Islam was far from a traditional one.[56] Rather than rallying around the Faith as an answer to the Empire's ills, he called for religion to be restricted to a specific section of daily life within the Empire. In particular, religion, for Gökalp, was to provide both a basis for moral and ethical conduct in the Empire as well as a connection to the *umma*, the community of believers within and beyond the Imperial borders. In doing so, Islam was to be present in the moral and ethical realm only, providing little or no hindrance to the adoption of European sciences and technology so vital to economic

---

53 'Aflaq, *Mukhtarat min Aqwal mu'assis al-Ba'th*, p 39.
54 Hinnebusch, *Syria: Revolution from Above*, p 30.
55 Sallam, *Le Ba'th et la Patrie Arabe*, p 327.
56 Erik Jan Zürcher, *Turkey: A Modern History* (I. B. Tauris, London: 2012) p 96.

development.[57] This was, in part, a compromise intended to provide the Ottoman Empire with access to the new concert of nations, while preserving the basis for internal cohesion and unity. If civilisation (in the sense of technology and science) could be divorced from culture (meaning religion, morals and ethics) then there would be no reason to fear that the adoption of European technology would sound the death knell for the essence of the Ottoman Empire.[58]

In contrast to Gökalp, Aflaq's ideological position vis-à-vis Islam was much more complicated. As an Orthodox Christian, he could have hardly espoused Islam as a basis for the Arab nation's political, economic and educational revival without embarking first upon some sort of religious conversion. More than just personal concerns impeded Aflaq's adoption of such as a stance, however. He recognised that there were two camps among Arab intellectuals in the 1940s: progressives and traditionalists.[59] Given his rejection of feudal and traditional economic structures, Aflaq could not have allied himself in cultural, political and social spheres with the very cadres whose power he sought to reduce or destroy in economic relations. On the other hand, the adoption of Western-style secularism would bring Ba'thism uncomfortably close to those Arabs whom he had denounced as collaborators with the French Mandatory régime.[60] As a compromise, Aflaq would appropriate those aspects of tradition and the past that he deemed most suitable for the political, economic and social renaissance (بعث) he aimed to lead in the Arab world, without deferring to traditional authorities.[61]

Much like Gökalp, Aflaq saw in the past the basis for social cohesion and unity of the nation. It was the past that 'the character and personality of the Arab nation was formed.'[62] No aspect of the past encapsulated this character and personality the way that Islam did. Indeed, Aflaq recast the battles of the early history of Islam as a theatre in which a proto-national consciousness developed among Arab tribes.[63] His exposition of these events is thus a profanation of the faith that seeks to allow for the nation to assume pride of

---

57 Gökalp, *Turkish Nationalism and Western Civilization*, p 76.

58 Parla, *Ziya Gökalp, Kemalizm ve Türkiye'de Korporatizm*, p 72.

59 Michel 'Aflaq, *Fi sabil al-ba'ath* (Dar At-Tali'at lit-Tiba'at wa an-Nashr, Beirut: 1974) p 160.

60 Sab', *Sa'adat wa 'Aflaq fii al-Fikr as-Siyasi al-Orthothuksiy*, p 320.

61 'Aflaq, *Fi sabil al-ba'ath*, p 161.

62 Ibid., p 160.

63 Ibid., p 46.

place even in the veneration of the Almighty. It is also a remarkable marriage of Marxist interpretations of history, which rely on a deterministic linearity tied to economic sophistication,[64] with religious concepts of divine election usually reserved for nationalist historiography. Islam, according to Aflaq, was revealed to Muhammad because of the level of socio-economic development attained by the Arabs of the Hijaz at that particular historical juncture. Thus Islam contains the eternal and essential *jawhar* of the Arab people – a calque on common nationalist tropes of essentialism and timelessness[65] – but its revelation was historical and the national consciousness to which it led was constructed through experience.[66] In Aflaq's reasoning, then, the Arab sense of nationhood is both essential and material, timeless and historical. Such inconsistencies might have been conceived as a means of countering – or appealing to – both Marxists and traditionalists, two groups subjected to considerable criticism in Aflaq's writing; or they might simply represent sloppy reasoning on the part of Aflaq.

Regardless of errors or tricks of dogma, it is difficult to dilute Aflaq's estimation of the symbolic importance of the religion imparted to Muhammad. Aflaq called Islam the 'genius of the Arab nation'.[67] This was a position that put him in direct opposition to the view held by a radicalised segment of Lebanese Christians, who had allegedly rejected Arabism because of its esteem for Islam.[68] Aflaq's view of Islam's place in Arabism, and its importance for Arabists, is most evident in his rebuttal of Lebanese 'fanatical Christian elements'. They discounted Arab nationalism because they believed its meaning to be 'Islam's reign as religion, legislation, tradition and civilization.'[69] If this view is erroneous, it is because Arabism – or rather Aflaq's Arabism – believes Islam to be not all of these phenomena. Islam is obviously a religion, and it likely can fit into the category of tradition, at least for those whose families became Muslims in the removed past. The categorization of Islam as civilisational or

---

64 Helmut Fleischer, *Marxism and History*, (transl.) Eric Mosbacher (Suhrkamp Verlag, Frankfurt am Main: 1973) p 107.

65 J. Breuilly, 'Nationalism and Historians: Some Reflections. The Formation of National(ist) Historiographical Discourse', in Claire Norton (ed), *Nationalism, Historiography and the (Re) construction of the Past* (New Academia Publishing, Washington D.C.: 2007) pp 14–15.

66 'Aflaq, *Fi sabil al-ba'ath*, p 44.

67 Ibid., p 119.

68 Ibid., p 170.

69 Ibid.

a basis for legislation, however, is where the fissures between Christian Lebanese nationalists and Aflaq began to appear, and it is exactly in these fissures
that the parallels with Gökalp's philosophy become evident.

Islam is not proscribed to the Arab nation, but it is an Arab product. As
such, Aflaq sees in Islam a source of pride and celebration for the Arabs. The
organic nature in which Islam arose from Arab culture distinguishes the Arabs
from the Europeans, who adopted a foreign religion (Christianity), divorced
from their national characteristics, and who were able to just as easily separate their religion from nationalism in the modern period. The complicated
means by which Islam has been interwoven into Arab culture makes this an
impossible proposition for the Arabs to carry out without destroying the Arab
character.[70] For Gökalp, this same conceptualisation was possible through
discussion of the Turkish-Islamic culture, which embodied the unique qualities and independent spirit of the Turkish nation.[71] In his view, those cultures
which are not moribund, namely the Turkish and Islamic cultures, must be
preserved as a means of providing a common link between all members of
the nation as it adopts modern civilisation.[72] Similarly, for Aflaq, Islam was a
means of providing security for the unity of the Arab nation during troubled
times,[73] despite the fact that it was in political and economic nationalism that
the path towards future glory is to be sought.[74]

The parallel approaches to religion go much deeper in both ideologies.
For both men, Islam was important for its effects on the individual as well as
on the collectivity. Neither Gökalp nor Aflaq espoused or endorsed atheism.
Both were explicit in their recognition of religion – particularly Islam – as
a source of personal direction and discipline for the individual. Heyd has
pointed to Gökalp's reliance on Durkheim to reinterpret Islam as an attempt
by humanity to constrain or eliminate 'individualistic' and animalistic desires
and proclivities while strengthening collective identification through positive
religious rites and ceremonies.[75] For Gökalp, therefore, Islam was a useful
tool in elevating the mentality of people from that of individual existence to

---

70 'Aflaq, *Mukhtarat min Aqwal mu'assis al-Ba'th*, pp 52–53.

71 Parla, *Ziya Gökalp, Kemalizm ve Türkiye'de Korporatizm*, p 77.

72 Gökalp, *Turkish Nationalism and Western Civilization*, p 265.

73 'Aflaq, *Mukhtarat min Aqwal mu'assis al-Ba'ath*, p 57.

74 'Aflaq, *Fi sabil al-ba'ath*, p 160.

75 Heyd, *The Foundations of Turkish Nationalism: The Life and Teachings of Ziya Gökalp*, p 84.

participation in and belonging to a collectivity, identified as the nation in the modern period. Aflaq, too, linked religious practice with personal discipline. Islam provided a means of combatting the laxity and decadence of modern existence by steeling members of the Arab *umma* for the construction of a strong and independent nation. Here, Aflaq was not as concerned with man's baser instincts as Gökalp was, but rather with Islam's 'strength of patience and resistance to the trends of a sick reality'.[76] Gökalp's rendering might be closer to the philosophical tenets of the Islamic faith – betterment through devotion to God – but the end effect is much the same. Both men saw religion as a convenient means for the creation of national consciousness and preparation of their respective co-nationals for transition to a modernity of nation-states.

Faith – particularly Islam – was thus to be harnessed by nationalism and the nationalist State, rather than to remain outside its grasp. Religion was not, however, the only potentially independent force that would be subjugated to the national will in future Turkish and Arab states. Personal liberty and individual agency, too, were to take second place to the will of the nation as distilled and articulated by the State.

For both Gökalp and Aflaq, the concept of liberty was an important one, but it had limitations and qualifications. As a follower of Durkheim, Gökalp believed that the group, and specifically the nation, was a more important and more efficient means of social organisation than the individual. For Aflaq, an avowed nationalist, only God came above the nation in a ranking of interests.[77] These bounds placed on the freedom and agency of the individual were paramount in the writings of both men, and they affected both their economic and their political views.

Despite Gökalp's support for solidarism as conceived in European circles, he rejected the social views of the communalists, preferring a form of exceptionalism based on the uniqueness of Turkish culture.[78] This line of thinking worked through the link between Turkish-Islamic culture and solidarism. As traditional Turkish culture was communal and egalitarian in nature,[79] it naturally rejected the rampant individualism of the Liberal thinkers of the 19th century.[80] Instead, collective actions and identities were more in tune with traditional culture, and

---

76 'Aflaq, *Fi sabil al-ba'ath*, p 143.
77 'Aflaq, *Mukhtarat min Aqwal mu'assis al-Ba'th*, pp 64–65.
78 Parla, *Ziya Gökalp, Kemalizm ve Türkiye'de Korporatizm*, p 67.
79 Gökalp, *Türkçülüğün esasları*, p 180.
80 Parla, *Ziya Gökalp, Kemalizm ve Türkiye'de Korporatizm*, p 77.

thus would provide a more stable and lasting basis for the regeneration of the Turkish nation. In normal periods, parliamentary activity would be founded upon the corporation-based interest groups that would represent the people or advise the powers that be. These corporate structures would obviate the intense competition of lobby groups based on individual interests, a characteristic of the Liberal system.[81] During times of crisis, however, the identity and interests of the nation would subsume completely those of individuals and subgroups. The survival of the nation being the most important goal of all national groupings, this aim would subordinate all individual interests until such time as the preservation of national unity and independence was assured.[82]

The result of this conceptualisation of state-individual and nation-individual relations is not limited to mutually beneficial interactions and forms of representation. Rather, in the quest for social and cultural development, it is the nation – acting through the state – that educates the individual. Gökalp was particularly critical of élites (especially Ottoman élites) who saw it as their duty to educate the masses. The élite is alienated from the masses, and thus cannot bring national culture to them, as it is the masses who produce this. The élites can only go to the masses to learn about national culture or to bring civilisation, in the form of technological advances.[83] Individual members of the masses, however, are not much better. In Heyd's interpretation of Gökalp's writings, the individual is incapable of forming a 'moral ideal', as it is her ego and not the national interest that is at the centre of her identity. As identity 'can only attain honour and respect for representing and reflecting society, that is the nation', it must be imposed from above by a benevolent state.[84] This is not to say that Gökalp held a totalitarian view of the state's role in socialising the individual to the new national society. Rather, he believed that state education could change individuals and thus society, but that tolerance and pluralism should still be respected. In effect, Gökalp was interested not in the homogenisation of individuals but their socialisation, which, of course, would still involve restrictive actions by the state.[85]

This mistrust of the individual's ability to formulate a beneficial construct of her own interest is mirrored in the writings of Aflaq. As a movement emerging

---

81 Ibid., p 110.
82 Ibid., pp 126–127.
83 Ibid., p 149.
84 Ibid., p 141.
85 Parla, *The Social and Political Thought of Ziya Gökalp: 1876–1924*, pp 66–67.

in the 1940s, the Ba'thists employed language much closer to contemporary terminology regarding the relationship between the individual and the state than did the Turkists of the CUP. For Aflaq, the individual's freedom is a crucial component of the revitalisation of the Arab nation, but her right to live as she chooses is proscribed by the harmonisation of this desire with the national interest.[86] Similarly, the yearning for Arabist revolution, in the words of Aflaq, comes 'from the very depths of the Arab masses.'[87] Yet, despite rhetoric about this innate desire of the masses for revolution and change, education of the masses of their wishes and needs was to be in the hands of the Ba'th party. The people had yet to achieve the social and educational levels requisite for full participation in the national renaissance and thus would have to be guided by the Party. As this education was necessary for the betterment of the Arab nation, the interests of the Arab nation would be paramount and dominant until those of individuals could be aligned with them.[88] Even when members of the favoured classes, particularly the workers, sinned against the interests of the Arab *umma*, they were to be forgiven their transgressions because of their lack of enlightenment; the ignorant masses were robbed even of their agency in the commission of errors against Ba'thism.[89]

Even more so than in Gökalp's writings, Aflaq's ideology afforded scant freedom of choice to the people with respect to culture and self-identification once they had aligned themselves with the interest of the Arab nation. Of particular concern for Aflaq was the development of independent identities of national groups not considered to be Arabs. In Aflaq's idealised nation, the Armenians, Kurds, Berbers, Assyrians and other ethnic minorities enjoyed equal opportunities in their pursuit of prosperity and happiness, as all members of the masses shared equally in the good fortune of the Arab people.[90] These opportunities, of course, were contingent on the abandonment of secessionist nationalisms, which were doomed to failure in any case.[91] Any attempt to counter this inevitability – particularly in the Kurdish regions of Iraq – was

---

86 Al-Aysami, *Hizb al-Ba'ath al-'Arabiy al-Ishtiraki: (1) MarHala Al-Arba'inat At-Ta'asissiya 1940–1949*, p 114.

87 'Aflaq, *Mukhtarat min Aqwal mu'assis al-Ba'ath*, pp 9–10.

88 Devlin, *The Ba'ath Party: A History from its Origins to 1966*, pp 28–29.

89 *Al-Ba'ath... Wa NiDal at-Tabaqat Al-'Amila*, p 75.

90 'Aflaq, *Fi sabil al-ba'ath*, p 172.

91 Ibid., p 171.

interpreted as exploitation and manipulation by foreign colonisers.[92] Once again, the deviant subgroup is deprived of agency in its fight against the dominant discourse of Arab nationalism, as it is the state and not the individual or the masses who determines the content of culture and identity. In turn, the only solution offered to those who dissent is working together with other collectives towards the betterment of a fatherland that they refuse to recognise as such.[93]

Thus, for both Gökalp and Aflaq, the individual is of greatest importance as an abstract component of the mass, rather than a person ultimately endowed with agency and free will. While it might be expected that nationalists of one colour or another would consistently exalt the nation over the citizen, the particularities of both men's reaction towards the role of the individual in governance and the determination of identity is indicative of parallel processes within their respective societies. For Gökalp, the fragmentation of the collective (in the form of the Empire) into components (nations) required direct intervention to harness the transformation and mould the end product. For Aflaq, a member of that product, stymying that same process when it was in danger of escaping state control was paramount. Both men, in the end, saw the individual as a medium towards the regeneration and rejuvenation of the nation; a medium, the use of which was to be left exclusively in the hands of an enlightened and benevolent ruling cadre.

Throughout this chapter, I have demonstrated that strong congruencies exist between the writings of the ideologue of the Young Turk and early Turkish Republican period, Ziya Gökalp, and those of one of the founders of the Ba'th movement, Michel Aflaq. These similarities are most evident in three particular aspects of these men's rhetoric: their espousal of solidarist elements in economic policy; the particular role they assigned to Islam in the construction of modern nations; and their mistrust of unfettered personal liberties and individual agency. The establishment of a direct influence of Gökalp on Aflaq may prove impossible to establish. Nevertheless, the parallels examined in this paper point to common reactions to a monumental paradigm shift in a turbulent part of the Periphery exhibited by both men during their most productive periods of writing.

The legacy of both men, unfortunately, has suffered the same fate. Ziya Gökalp's works are, in the words of the Turkish historian Niyazi Berkes,

92 Michel 'Aflaq, NaqTat al-Bidayat: Ahadith ba'd al-Khamis min Haziran (Al-Mu'asissat Al-'Arabiya lid-Dirasat wa an-Nashr, Beirut: 1971) p 105.
93 Ibid., p 107.

largely 'unknown and unread'. This has allowed his ideas to be twisted in order to suit the most disparate of political ideologies.[94] The same is very much true of Aflaq's works, largely because of the history of the Ba'th Party. As early as 1947, when the Party held its first congress, serious rifts had developed between leading personalities. While all members agreed on the importance of Arabism, they were divided on issues of land reform, nationalisation, secularism and social reform.[95] These divisions were only exacerbated by an increased emphasis on class struggle as a means of broadening the Party's appeal. Social conflict began to overshadow the belief in liberal democracy within the Ba'th,[96] and heavy recruitment among young officers in the Syrian Army presaged the Party's future entanglement with military interventions.[97] Army backing was not enough, however, for even the core principle of Arab unity to withstand internecine struggles, particularly over the 1958 union of Syria and Egypt. The Party split into four factions, and Aflaq's cadre lost out when an anti-UAR faction led by the military took power in Syria in 1963.[98] The end of a brief period of Ba'thist rule in Iraq in 1963 alienated the Party's left wing, to Aflaq's advantage, but this did not last long.[99] A new coup in Syria in 1966 brought neo-Ba'thist military cadres to power, effectively ending Aflaq's influence over the Syrian party and establishing a dominant Alawite, leftist and rural presence among its ranks.[100] The centrist Ba'thists returned to power in Iraq in 1968, with Saddam Hussein al-Tikriti ascending to the Presidency in 1979.[101] A slightly more moderate Ba'thist government also took Syria in 1970, when Minister of Defence Hafez al-Assad seized power in a coup d'état.[102] Although Ba'thist régimes persisted in Iraq until 2003[103] and in Syria until the present day (in a limited fashion), the turbulent period of the mid-1960s truly marked the

---

94 Gökalp, *Turkish Nationalism and Western Civilization*, pp 14–15.

95 Hinnebusch, *Authoritarian Power and State Formation in Ba'thist Syria*, p 90.

96 Ibid., p 92.

97 Ibid., p 97.

98 Torrey, "The Ba'th: Ideology and Practice", pp 456–458.

99 Baram, 'Broken Promises', p 43.

100 Hinnebusch, *Authoritarian Power and State Formation in Ba'thist Syria*, p 130.

101 Baram, 'Broken Promises', p 43.

102 Olson, "The Ba'th in Syria 1947–1979: An Interpretative Historical Essay (Part Two)", p 461.

103 Baram, 'Broken Promises', p 41.

end of the ideological and intellectual influence of the Party's founding members.[104]

Under this fog of deliberate misinterpretations, political machinations and amnesia, there are undoubtedly other similarities between Gökalp and Aflaq to be discovered, as well as obvious differences between the two men and their ideologies. Despite this, the analysis of parallelisms discussed in this paper provides an important challenge to received wisdom on 20th century Middle Eastern history: that Turkey and her Arab neighbours share more than just geography, and that Arab states might have retained more than just a sense of historical grievance from four centuries of Ottoman rule.

---

104 Ibid., p 50. See also: Olson, "The Ba'th in Syria 1947–1979: An Interpretative Historical Essay (Part Two)", p 445; Hinnebusch, *Authoritarian Power and State Formation in Ba'thist Syria*, p 122–123; El-Attrache, "The Political Philosophy of Michel Aflaq and The Ba'ath Party in Syria", p 35.

14

Women, war and the foundations of the Turkish Republic: the vision of New Womanhood in Halide Edib Adıvar's *The Shirt of Flame* (1922)

Sevinç Elaman-Garner

One of the consequences of the First World War was the defeat of the Ottoman Empire and the Allied occupation of Istanbul, leading to the Turkish 'war of independence' and ultimately the foundation of the Turkish Republic in 1923. This process of the birth of the new Turkish nation-state also required the birth of a new Turkish subjectivity, one which fitted with the visions of the new modernising nationalist elite and the search for a break from a 'backward' past. A major part of this nation-building process was a growing attention to the position of women. The question of what role women should play in public life, and how to create a new female identity fit for a modern Turkey, became a central subject of debate.[1] The image of the 'New Woman', which was often linked to positive aspects of modernity and socially progressive

---

1 Prior to the First World War, Ottoman reformers had implemented several reform projects taking the 'West' as a model to improve the economic and political situation of the empire. After the fall of the Ottoman Empire, the Westernisation process was also followed by the elite reformers of the Turkish Republic, promoting 'rapid modernisation and secularisation of daily life as a means to establish Turkey's legitimacy, both domestically and internationally.' Kathryn Libal, 'Staging Turkish Women's Emancipation: Istanbul, 1935', *Journal of Middle East Women's Studies*, 1 (2008) p 34.

ideals, was considered an integral part of the visions of Republican reformers and was constructed as a quintessential symbol of the Turkish nation itself. In the public life and literature of early twentieth century Turkey, she appeared as 'the emancipated ...(chaste) nationalist woman',[2] often associated with the image of the 'modern but modest" woman'[3]: that is, 'respect for the community over the individual, faith in education (in order to perform her "duties" as a "good" wife), being patriotic (in order to educate her children – and thus nation – as a "good" mother) and a careful exercise of her sexuality.'[4]

The focus of this chapter is on the depiction of this particular image of Turkish womanhood as it appears in *The Shirt of Flame* (1922), one of the most famous Turkish nationalist novels. The novel gives us a detailed picture of the period between the First World War and the foundation of the Turkish Republic in 1923. Thus, analysing a novel such as *The Shirt of Flame* helps us to develop insights into the Turkish experience of the War of Independence and, in particular, into the role that women were expected to play in the visions of new nationhood. The central argument of this chapter is that Ayşe, the heroine in the novel, is represented as the image of the New Woman and as a symbol of nation through which collective unity among male characters is generated, leading to the emergence of national sentiments in the nascent Turkish Republic.

The novel is written by Halide Edib Adıvar, one of the leading figures of the Turkish nationalist movement and a prominent figure of the canon of Turkish nationalist literature. During the formative years of the Turkish Republic, Adıvar played an important role ingenerating the discourse concerning 'national identity' and the image of the New Turkish Woman not only through her image as a model of 'ideal' Turkish womanhood but also through her

---

2 Deniz Kandiyoti, *Cariyeler, Fettan Kadinlar ve Yoldaşlar* (*Slave Girls, Temptresses and Comrades*) (Metis Yayinlari, Istanbul: 1996) p 150.

3 For a full discussion of the New Turkish Woman, see, for example, Şirin Tekeli, 'Emergence of the feminist movement in Turkey', in Drude Dahlerup (ed), *The New Women's Movement*, (Sage, London: 1986); Zehra F. Arat. (ed), *Deconstructing Images of "The Turkish Woman"*, (Macmillan Press, Basingstoke: 1998); Deniz Kandiyoti, 'Emancipated but Unliberated? Reflections on the Turkish Case', *Feminist Studies*, 13 (1987) pp 317–338; Jenny. B. White, 'State Feminism, Modernization, and the Turkish Republican Woman', *NWSA Journal*, 3 (2003), pp 145–159.

4 Sevinç Elaman-Garner, 'The New Turkish Woman and Her Discontents: Contradictory Depictions of the (A)sexual Zeyno in Halide Edib Adıvar's *Kalp Ağrısı(Heartache)*', *Journal Of Turkish Literature*, 10 (2013) p 22.

novels. As a writer, public speaker, parliamentarian and cosmopolitan intellectual, she was also active in shaping the cultural, ideological and political discourse of twentieth century Turkey. Her contribution to the national movement and her engagement with national causes and ideological debates on 'Turkishness' was so significant that she came to be regarded as 'the Mother of the Turks'.[5] Her works remain as popular as ever today and are relevant not only to understand her as a historical figure but also to allow us to gain insight into the construction and role of New Womanhood as an integral part of the project of modernisation and Turkish nation-building.

The chapter will include two sections: The first section will address the significance of the image of Turkish womanhood as part of the formation of Turkish nationalism and the attempt to foster a new national and cultural identity in postwar Turkey. The second section will explore the novel, *The Shirt of Flame*, focusing on the portrayal of the heroine, Ayşe, as a symbol of the nation and representation of 'ideal' Turkish womanhood, a vehicle that provides insights into the role that women were being envisaged to play in these embryonic visions of a new nation. This section will also look at how the novel addresses the way that the Turkish people – in particular women – engage in a new battle (the Turkish War of Independence) after the trauma of the First World War.

Women's involvement in public and political life had begun before the First World War through the Tanzimat reforms (1839).[6] The period leading up

---

5 In the aftermath of the Balkan Wars and during the First World War, she delivered a number of public lectures, most famously in the heart of Istanbul in Sultanahmet in 1919, where she called upon Turkish women to join the Turkish national movement and urged them to fight against the occupying forces. Adıvar later noted that the Turkish Independence War could not have been fought without the support of women and indeed she herself joined the Turkish Independence War and was given the rank of corporal by the war's leader – and later the founder of Turkish Republic – Mustafa Kemal. For a full detailed discussion on Adıvar, see, for example, Ayse Durakbasa, *Halide Edib: Türk Modernlesmesi ve Feminizm* (*Halide Edib: Turkish Modernisation and Feminism*), (IletisimYayınları, Istanbul: 2007); 'Hülya Adak, 'National Myths and Self-Na(rra)tions: Mustafa Kemal's *Nutuk* and Halide Edib's *Memoirs* and *Turkish Ordeal'*, in *The South Atlantic Quarterly* 2/3 (102), 2003, pp 509–527.

6 The Tanzimat (Reorganisation) reforms are regarded as the beginning of the modernisation process in the Ottoman Empire in the 19th century. These reforms sought some important changes in Ottoman society such as the equality of all persons of all religions, security of the subject's life, honour and property, fair and public trial, and so on. For a succinct discussion of the Tanzimat period and its reforms, see Bernard Lewis, *The Emergence of Modern Turkey*

to and during the First World War saw gains for Turkish women in education, work and family life, as well as leading to greater visibility and participation in cultural and social spaces.[7] During the Balkan War (1912–1913), women were actively involved in social welfare activities, attending to wounded soldiers and helping war orphans; meanwhile in 1911, the first lycée for women had been established and, in 1914, Istanbul University opened to women.[8] In 1917, the Family Law brought advances regarding divorce and marriage, and men and women's mutual responsibilities. Although Ottoman women demanded education not only to contribute to their domestic duties but also 'to capture the sense of self-confidence that they had been lacking',[9] the education they received was 'mainly religious in orientation, with the aim of creating good Muslim wives and mothers.'[10] The official view of the teachers' training college was as follows:

> Women should be educated in the same way as men with a view toward enabling them to help and comfort their husbands, on whose shoulders rest the responsibility of earning a living for their families. Moreover, education will greatly help women towards a better understanding of religious and secular considerations and encourage them to obey their husbands, to refrain from going against their wishes, and above all, to protect their honour.[11]

(Oxford University Press, London: 1968); as well as other contemporary historians such as Şerif Mardin, *The Genesis of Young Ottoman Thought* (University Press, Syracuse, N.Y.: 2000); Sibel Bozdoğan, *Modernism and Nation Building: Turkish Architectural Culture in the Early Republic* (University of Washington Press., Washington: 2002); Fatma Müge Göçek, *The Transformation of Turkey: Redefining State and Society from the Ottoman Empire to the Modern Era* (Tauris Academic Studies, London: 2011).

7 For more discussion on the status of Turkish women before and during WWI see, for example, Deniz Kandiyoti, 'End of Empire: Islam, Nationalism and Women in Turkey', in Deniz Kandiyoti (ed), *Women, Islam & State*, (Temple University Press, Philadelphia: 1991), pp 1–20.

8 Nikki R. Keddie, *Women in the Middle East: past and present* (Princeton University Press, Princeton: 2007) p 81.

9 Aynur Demirdirek, 'In Pursuit of the Ottoman Women's Movement' in Zehra F. Arat (ed), *Deconstructing Images of the "Turkish Woman"* (Macmillan Press, Hampshire: 1998) p 68.

10 Kumari Jayawardena, *Feminism and Nationalism in the Third World* (Zed Books Ltd., London and New Jersey: 1986) p 28.

11 Emel Sönmez, 'Turkish women in Turkish literature of the nineteenth century', in *Die Welt des Islams* (Leiden) 12, (1969) p 25.

In this way, the implementation of educational reforms reflected the concern of the Ottoman reformists to strike a balance between Islam and modernisation in the creation of the New Turkish Woman. Such reforms and advances for women were given added momentum by the wave of patriotism and national feeling which played a major role in driving Turkish women to join the cause and take up active roles behind the lines, where they worked often with great sacrifice. Regarding the role women played during the First World War, Halide Edib Adıvar said:

> The pressure of the Great War urged women forward to many
> indispensable services and sacrifices…From end to end the only
> producers were women…Without the activity and enormous service of
> women, Turkey would have collapsed internally during the Great War.[12]

During the formative years of the Turkish Republic, women's images and their role became central to the Turkish nation-building project. The image of the New Woman, both in fiction and the wider social discourse of politics, newspapers and magazines, was generally associated with a vision of 'ideal' – modern but modest – Turkish womanhood and was considered an integral part of the nationalist project to forge a new national and cultural identity. As Ayşe Durakbaşa aptly observes, for the new Turkish Republic, "the image of the 'new woman' was a marker not only of cultural authenticity but also of being 'civilized' as a nation."[13] Several legal and constitutional reforms were undertaken to become this 'civilised' nation and improve the status of women, such as the introduction of a secular civil code as a replacement of Islamic law, abolishing polygamous marriage, granting women the right to choose their spouses and to initiate divorce, preventing child marriage by imposing a minimum age for marriage. Women were encouraged to unveil, enter the universities and professions and granted the right to vote in local elections in 1930 and in national elections in 1934. These new rights granted to women sought primarily to strengthen the sense of a new official national identity as being based on a break from a 'backward' Islamic past. Alongside these advances for women in the public and civic spheres, however, is the emphasis

---

12 Halide Edib Adıvar, *Conflict of East and West in Turkey* (S.M. Ashraf, Lahore: 1935)
pp 195–96.
13 Ayşe Durakbaşa, 'Kemalism as Identity Politics in Turkey', in Zehra F. Arat (ed),
Deconstructing Images of the Turkish Woman (Macmillan Press, Hampshire: 1998) p 139.

on traditional roles in line with the Kemalist vision, where the New Turkish Woman is also associated with the role of a dutiful mother and wife. In one of his speeches, Mustafa Kemal Ataturk – the founder of the Turkish Republic – emphasises this aspect of New Turkish Womanhood:

> The [New] Turkish woman should be the most enlightened, most virtuous, and most reserved woman of the world...The duty of the Turkish woman is to raise generations that are capable of preserving and protecting the Turk with his mentality, strength and determination. The woman who is the source and social foundation of the nation can fulfil her duty only if she is virtuous.[14]

By referring to the duty of women as 'good' mothers and wives, Mustafa Kemal here draws attention to the importance of marriage and sexual virtue for the New Woman who was encouraged to 'avoid any possibility of arousing sexual excitement which was an essential condition for symbolizing the virtue of the Turkish Republic.'[15] This idea was expressed in the 'asexual' ideal of the New Turkish Woman, a female figure who is required to repress her sexual identity in order to fulfil her private and public roles. In this way, women and their virtue are also constructed as symbols of the Turkish nation's "honour".

Adıvar's view of the New Woman and her emphasis on the domestic roles of women to raise the future generation of the Turkish nation resonates with the Kemalist vision of 'ideal' womanhood, emphasising the link between nation and woman. This is explicitly outlined the following statement, where Adıvar reminds Turkish women to be mindful of their national duties:

> Women need to learn about everything as much as men do. In this case, women are no different than men...Yet, these needs should not distract women from their household duties such as mothering. No matter how high the knowledge that women possess, this should be in harmony with their womanly responsibilities...The right of the nation is a thousand times more important and sacred than a woman's right; for that reason, when women raise their voice (for their rights) today, they should remember

---

14 Mustafa Kemal Ataturk, *Atatürk'ün Söylev ve Demeçleri* [Atatürk's statements and speeches], 2 (1989), p 242 (as cited and translated by Arat's *Deconstructing Images of "the Turkish Woman"*).

15 Elaman-Garner, 'The New Turkish Woman', p. 20.

that this is not for themselves but to be able to raise generations for their nation...[16]

In harnessing domestic values to civic duty in such ways, Adıvar reproduces the concept of New Womanhood and expresses a nationalist disposition in her view ofthe 'ideal' woman as a patriotic citizen who is expected to serve her country not only by being actively involved in public life but also by being a 'good' wife and mother with the mission of producing children as the future citizens of the nation. From this, we can see that Adıvar underlines the importance of women's roles as critical agents in the making of the Turkish nation-state, in a way which is suggestive of an allegorical relationship between nation and woman.

Such an allegorical relationship between nation and woman has been emphasised in a number of studies of nation-building processes.They have shown us that in nationalist discourses, women have often been constructed as symbols of nations' identities and "honour". In her *Gender and Nation*, Nira Yuval-Davis explores this relationship between nation and woman and argues that 'it is women...who produce nations, biologically culturally and symbolically.'[17] She also stresses the role – and importance – of women in nationalist discourse during war. Yuval-Davis eloquently articulates that,

When discussing war and its aftermath, it is important to remember what a gendered...experience this usually is...But it is not just experiences of war which are different between men and women...militarized images of femininity at war – whether they call women to stay at home and be good wives and mothers, or to volunteer to the military industry...are highly necessary for the militarized images of masculinity...Wars are seen to be fought for the sake of 'womenandchildren' and the fighting men are comforted and reassured by the knowledge that 'their women' are keeping the hearth fires going and are waiting for them to come home.[18]

---

16 Halide Edib Adıvar, 'Mehasini Okuyan Kardeşlerime [To My Sisters Who Read Mehasin]', *Mehasin*, 6 (1908) pp 418–421, as cited in Aynur Demirdirek's *Osmanlı Kadınlarının Hayat Hakkı Arayışının Bir Hikayesi [A Story of Ottoman Women's Demands for the Right to Life]* (Imge Kitabevi Yayınları, Ankara: 1993) pp 39–40.
17 Nira Yuval-Davis, *Gender & Nation* (Sage Publications Ltd., London: 1997) p 2.
18 Ibid., pp 110–11.

Yuval-Davis's discussion of the notion of 'womenandchildren' for whom wars 'are fought' re-emphasises the link between the significance of the images of femininity 'which has been so necessary for war discourse' (Yuval-Davis, p 111), and the notion of nation that has been central to the construction of 'masculinised' male bonding charged with protecting the 'feminine' homeland/ nation. (Yuval-Davis, p 111). In a similar vein, in an attempt to illustrate the link between woman and nation and explore how male bonding is mediated through the figure of woman, Afsaneh Najmabadi asks: 'How can an idea [nationalism] so philosophically deficient evoke such politically (and emotive) power that men...are willing to kill and die for it?'[19] She contends that homeland 'was... envisaged as the outlines of a female body: A body to love and be devoted, to possess and protect, to kill and die for.[20] In other words, by appealing to men's sense of honour, nationalist discourses equate the purity and vulnerability of the nation with that of women. These passages, quoted from Yuval-Davis and Najmabadi, represent the central themes that will be dealt with in the analysis of *The Shirt of Flame* in the following section of this chapter. It aims to show that Ayşe is represented as the symbol of nation through which male bonding among the male characters is mediated. It will also explore the extent to which the novel reflects the nationalist reformers' vision of the New Woman.

The Shirt of Flame takes place during the Allied occupation of Istanbul (1918–1923) and is written in the form of a diary of the narrator, Peyami, a former diplomat, who has lost both of his legs during the war. The focus of Peyami's story is his cousin, Ayşe. The first indication of Ayşe as a symbol of national trauma appears when she arrives in Istanbul after her husband and son are killed during the Greek invasion of Izmir. Covered in her black *charsaf* (the veil worn by Turkish women) with her bandaged, broken arm and suffering from the loss of her husband and son, Ayşe comes to represent a victim of military violence, an icon of 'the violated, injured and invaded motherland.'[21] When Peyami sees her for the first time, he says 'here comes Izmir!' (26): the city which is also known as 'Guzel Izmir' ('beautiful Smyrna') andis now embodied in Ayşe as a violated and beautiful woman.[22]

---

19 Afsaneh Najmabadi, 'The Erotic *Vatan*[Homeland] as Beloved and Mother: To Love, To Possess, and To Protect', in *Comparative Studies in Society and History*, 3 (1997) p 443.
20 Ibid., p 445.
21 Azade Seyhan, *Tales of Crossed Destinies* (MLA, New York: 2008) p 52.
22 Ibid. As Seyhan points out, 'Izmir is famous for its surrounding fertile lands, its harbour, its significance as a center of sea commerce, and its Turkish-Greek culture'.

Ayşe's symbolic value as national honour is most obvious in her meeting with Mr Cook, an English correspondent who is described as 'an abominable example of the cruel colonialist British Empire' (37). Mr Cook says 'This is useless madam, England will never forgive you. You've killed sixty thousand British in Canakkale...How dare you resist such a big nation like the British? All this time, you have wasted Britain's money, blood, time...' (38). Mr. Cook believes that all Turkish people 'must ask for English protection' (38) and believes in colonialism as the best solution for the defeated Ottoman Empire. By giving England's colonialism in India as an example, he says, 'Look at India, how happy [the country is]! They always pray: "May God never separate us from the white man". If you show a sincere repent [then] perhaps England will forgive you...' (38).

Of all those present in the room, including the military officers, it is Ayşe who resists Mr. Cook. She says: 'Let England forgive those who ask for forgiveness ... Pardon is given by the oppressed, not by the oppressor. In Canakkale we were neither rebel nor slaves. We fought, died and killed like an honourable nation.' (39) By presenting Ayşe as the voice of Turkey who silences Mr Cook, the voice of the occupying forces, Adıvari idealises her heroine as a brave, patriotic New Woman; a woman who refuses to be the object of pity and can restore the pride of the Turkish nation.

The same scene – where Ayşe meets the British journalist – also dramatises the birth of national resistance through the figure of woman; in other words, national unity and male bonding are mediated through the figure of woman. Najmabadi astutely argues that, 'representing homeland as a female body has often been used to construct a national identity based on male bonding among a nation of brothers.'[23] Similarly, the army officers in the room are so moved by Ayşe's voice of resistance and her 'honourable' response to the British journalist that they gather around her chair and vow to fight for national resistance until they liberate Izmir from the Greek invasion. It is for the honour of Ayşe, symbol of the nation, that the male characters are motivated to fight for the national resistance during the War of Independence, a war that will contribute not only to the construction of a new identity for women but also to the 'militarisation' of the men of the period. Ayşe Saraçgil analyses the relation of the War of Independence to militarisation as follows:

---

23 Najmabadi, "The Erotic Vatan[Homeland] as Beloved and Mother" , p 442.

[The] War of Independence not only formed the ground for national liberation and the improvement of republican ideas but also paved the way to reconstruct social gender and create new identities for women and men. The National Independence War both glorified manhood by exalting the soldier figure and in public discourse propagated the idea that woman belongs not only to the family but also to the whole nation.[24]

Similarly, male characters begin to perceive Ayşe as belonging to the (Turkish) nation, although in different female roles: as a beloved, as a sister, as a mother. In short, they all see her as a woman who needs 'protection', a woman for whom they would kill and die. Once nation is imagined as a woman, then woman is given a body that would produce 'the soldier figure', 'new patriot' Turks, and nourish her children with love of nation. For example, after meeting Ayşe, Ihsan describes himself as a different man: 'I became a different man, a man that Ayşe reshaped, a new creation of Ayşe' (151). 'I wanted to be crushed under the foot of her who was a symbol of love, strength and pity, a symbol of my suffering country, in the midst of fire and blood' (136).

Peyami is also depicted as one of the 'soldier figures(s)': a 'new' patriotic Turkish man that Ayşe-the-nation creates. At the beginning of the novel, he is depicted as a lazy, weak and 'not yet militarised' male who lives with his mother and works as a plain, lifeless bureaucrat in his office. However, after he meets Ayşe, he gradually becomes one of her new creations, a man who is ready to fight for Ayşe [and nation]. After the defeat of the Ottoman Empire in the First World War and the invasion of Izmir and Istanbul by the Allied forces, he leaves his affluent lifestyle in Istanbul and joins Ayşe, her brother Cemal and Cemal's friend, Major Ihsan, to fight for the national resistance in Anatolia. Ayşe becomes the inspiration in his transformation from a 'weak' to a brave 'nationalist', 'masculinised' soldier. Towards the end of the novel, there is no fear in Peyami, he even likes the war (201), shouting in the middle of the battlefield and cursing enemies (204), and feeling very proud to sacrifice his legs [and later his life] for his motherland. As worshippers of Ayşe, who is described as having the power to create the 'new' men of the Turkish nation, both Ihsan and Peyami are transformed from 'cosmopolitan Ottomans' to 'nationalist Turks'.

As Deniz Kandiyoti convincingly argues, in nationalist discourses, women's

---

24 Ayse Saraçgil, *Bukalemun Erkek (Chameleon Man)* (Iletisim, Istanbul: 2005) p 211.

sexuality is also central to national processes.[25] Thus, the virtue of the New Woman was presented as a sign of female modesty. Similarly, as well as Ayşe's portrayal as beloved and mother, her 'asexuality' also influences male characters to perceive her as representative of the nation's honour: although Ayşe is depicted as an object of male desire, their feelings are aroused not by any erotic qualities but by her sacred/consecrated image as a holy/patriotic figure that feeds the passion of men to defend their nation and homeland. Ihsan kisses her hands 'in a religious and excited way' (25) and describes her 'with no womanhood, no gender, or a mortal weakness [but with] a strength and silence that nothing can ever touch' (172). In such ways, Adıvar reproduces a nationalist discourse that uses the image of an 'asexual' New Woman figure to construct an image of Turkey as a nation of honour, virtue and morality.

Deniz Kandiyoti, in 'Identity and its Discontents: Women and the Nation', argues that in nationalist projects, women were portrayed as the 'symbols of the nation's newly found vigour and modernity.'[26] Studying a novel such as *The Shirt of Flame* helps us see how the image of the New Turkish Woman was vital to the vision of a new national identity: not only as a symbol of 'modern' nationhood but also of the nation's honour in a way which could generate bonds and evoke patriotic sentiments among citizen-soldiers in the nascent Turkish Republic. Ayşe in the novel is cast in the image of a dignified and brave New Turkish Woman with whom Adıvar found inspiration: a socially active, patriotic and asexual woman whose honour is represented as the honour of the national collectivity for which the male characters are driven to protect, to kill and die, 'to set the political injustice right and to reconstitute their manhood in one act of justified revolt.'[27] Reading Ayşe's depiction as a symbol of nation allows us to study the allegorical relationship between the Turkish nation and woman and the roles that they have played in serving the nationalists' need to create a sense of relatedness and unity among people.

---

25 Deniz Kandiyoti, 'Identity and its Discontents: Women and the Nation', *Millennium: Journal of international Studies,* 3 (1991) p 429.

26 Ibid., p 440.

27 Najmabadi, 'The Erotic *Vatan* [Homeland] as Beloved and Mother', pp 65, 445.

15

The limits of soft power: why Kurdish nationalism failed in the French Mandate of Syria

Laila McQuade and Nabil Al-Tikriti[1]

By 1943 and 1946, Lebanon and Syria, respectively, had gained their independence from the French Mandate of Syria. However, this split of the original mandatory state into two sovereign states had been mapped out well before their official independence. From the inception of the Mandate, Lebanon was to be carved from Syria for independence, due to the Maronites' special relationship with France. The fate of the remaining state of Syria, though, was less concrete. France favoured Syria's minorities, and the Mandate evolved in the shadow of Woodrow Wilson's Fourteen Points and his advocacy of self-determination. For these reasons, several groups aspired to autonomy or independence from Syria. One of the most prominent of these groups was the Kurds. However, by 1936, the borders of Syria were set by the Franco-Syrian Treaty. Though never fully implemented, it did establish the borders granted to Syria upon independence. Under the treaty, Syria remained unified, with the exception of Lebanon, and with no provision for Kurdish autonomy. While some have argued that this resulted from the lack of a viable Kurdish

1 This submission originated from Ms. McQuade's thesis project, supervised by Prof. Nabil Al-Tikriti. The authors would like to thank the Dean of the College of Arts and Sciences at the University of Mary Washington for providing financial support for McQuade's research in the French Foreign Ministry Archives in Nantes, France.

independence movement or unity among the Kurds, the Kurds in Syria appear to have actually had a structured and cohesive nationalist movement.[2] Rather, Kurdish nationalists failed to achieve their primary goal due to their friendly relations with the French, and the consequences of that relationship in light of France's shifting priorities in the 1920s and 1930s. Specifically, the entrenchment of Kurds in the mandatory establishment limited their hard power and put them at odds with key players when the time came to set borders. As their relationship with France was based on a marriage of interests rather than affinity or ideals, when their interests were no longer aligned, the Kurdish nationalists were ill-equipped to promote their goals through the soft power they had accrued, and lacked the hard power they desperately needed to forcibly achieve them.

The attendance of a Kurdish delegation at the 1919 Paris Peace Conference demonstrates both the presence of a Kurdish national consciousness, and its international recognition at that time. This presence was further confirmed by the Conference's granting a Kurdish state under the 1920 Treaty of Sèvres.[3] However, during negotiations for the Treaty of Sèvres, Lloyd George of Great Britain remarked:

> He himself had tried to find out what the feelings of the Kurds were.
> After inquiries in Constantinople, Baghdad and elsewhere, he had found
> it impossible to discover any representative Kurd. No Kurd appeared to
> represent anything more than his own particular clan...[4]

This quote is both indicative of, and predictive of, the main criticism of Kurdish nationalism, namely that it failed to offer a united front. Further, while negotiating the Treaty, Kurdish nationalists could not decide on boundaries. For example, Sharif Pasha, who represented the 'Society for the Ascension of Kurdistan' [Kurdistan Teali Cemiyeti], excluded the Van region. Amin Ali Bedir Khan, of the elite Kurdish Bedir Khan family, proposed a Kurdistan that

---

2 For one example of this trend, see Jordi Tejel, *Syria's Kurds: History, Politics and Society* (Routledge, New York, NY: 2009).

3 Hakan Özoğlu, "'Nationalism' and Kurdish Notables in the Late Ottoman-Early Republic Era", in *International Journal of Middle East Studies* 33, No 3 (August, 2001) pp 383.

4 Paul C. Helmreich, *From Paris to Sevres: the Partition of the Ottoman Empire at the Peace Conference of 1919–1920* (Ohio State University Press, Columbus: 1974) p 301.

included Van, but dropped claims to Erzerum and Sassoun.[5] Sèvres ended up allocating to a Kurdish state only territories present within modern Turkey. However, Sèvres was never ratified because the Turkish War of Independence changed realities on the ground. During this conflict, most Kurdish clans supported the French. However, the Jazira tribes were heavily penetrated by pan-Islamic propaganda from Turkey, and fought mostly on the Turkish nationalist side. They were persuaded by the promise of a Turkish-Kurdish federated state, which was not to be.[6]

The end of the Turkish War of Independence culminated in the Treaty of Lausanne, signed on 24 July 1923, which made no allowance for a Kurdish state. By this time, a French Mandate had already been established by a League of Nations charter that placed the Kurds in Syria under French administration.[7] However, due to border disputes, it was not put into effect until the conclusion of the conflict. Border disputes between the mandatory officials and Turkey were not officially settled for over a decade later.[8]

After the First World War, the League of Nations established Mandates to deal with transferred territories, divided into Class A, Class B, and Class C Mandates. Each class was based on whom the territory was taken from, and the assessment by the European powers of their development and oversight needs. Along with other former Ottoman territories, Syria was classified as a Class A Mandate.[9] For Class A Mandates, the League of Nations stated that the territories had:

> reached a stage of development where their existence as independent
> nations can be provisionally recognized subject to the rendering of
> administrative advice and assistance by a Mandatory until such time as
> they are able to stand alone. The wishes of these communities must be a
> principal consideration in the selection of the Mandatory.[10]

---

5 Hakan Özoğlu, *Kurdish Notables and the Ottoman State: Evolving Identities, Competing Loyalties, and Shifting Boundaries* (State University of New York Press, Albany: 2004) p 40.
6 Tejel, *Syria's Kurds*, p 12.
7 Kerim Yıldız, *The Kurds in Syria: the Forgotten People* (Pluto Press, Ann Arbor, MI: 2005) p 15.
8 Keith Watenpaugh, 'Creating Phantoms: Zaki al-Arsuzi, the Alexandretta Crisis and the Formation of Modern Arab Nationalism in Syria', *International Journal of Middle East Studies* 28, No 3 (August, 1996) p 364.
9 'League of Nations Mandate', from http://www.princeton.edu/~achaney/tmve/wiki100k/docs/League_of_Nations_mandate.html (last accessed 3 February 2015).
10 Ibid.

The designation of Syria under the Class A Mandate fit with the conclusions of the King-Crane Commission, which had reported its findings in July
1919. The Commission was comprised of Americans, engaged by the major
powers to investigate local views on identity and governance.[11] It concluded
that Syria should be put under a mandatory power until its infrastructure had
been reformed and it had become a stable state. King-Crane also emphasised
that Syria was not to be broken up, but that particular recommendation was
disregarded by France upon the creation of Lebanon.[12]

Minority rights protection was a major component of the Mandate. France's
main interest was in continuing its role as protector of the Christians in the territory, specifically the Maronites. However, they reached out to other minority groups as well.[13] The French used minorities to legitimate their rule, as
they were easier to control. As a corollary, under the French, minority groups
enjoyed special privileges otherwise denied to the majority.

In addition to thus encouraging and exploiting religious and ethnic divides
within Syria, French authorities also exploited Syria's agro-cities social structure.[14] Agro-cities were the major method of communal organisation in Syria.
As much of the economy was based on agriculture, city centres relied on surrounding villages to produce agricultural products and sell them in the city to
support the economy. Similarly, surrounding villages relied on the city centres
to provide a central location to sell and trade agricultural products, as well as
for protection. The millet system under the Ottomans, which allowed for a great
degree of local autonomy, only strengthened agro-city identities. However,
religious and ethnic differences did affect agro-city identities, because mixed
areas tended to identify their city centre based on the closest one sharing their
religious or ethnic composition, as opposed to the city actually closest to them.
The agro-city identity, therefore, helped to further strengthen ethnic identity
in areas with a strong presence of a particular ethnic group. The Kurds proved

11 David W. Lesch, *The Middle East and the United States: a Historical and Political
Reassessment*, 4th ed. (Westview Press, Boulder, CO: 2007) p 14.
12 'Recommendations of the King-Crane Commission with Regard to Syria-Palestine and
Iraq (August 29, 1919)', from http://unispal.un.org/UNISPAL.NSF/0/392AD7EB00902A0C8525
70C000795153 (last accessed 9 February 2015).
13 M B and H L, 'Syria and Lebanon: The States of the Levant under French Mandate', in
Bulletin of International News 17, No 14 (13 July 1940) p 844.
14 Michael Van Dusen, 'Political Integration and Regionalism in Syria', in *Middle East Journal*
6, No 2 (Spring, 1972) pp 124–125.

no exception to the agro-city effect. During the French Mandate, the Kurds could be found in high concentrations within several areas. Kurd Dagh / Jabal al-Akrad, Kobani / 'Ayn al-Arab, al-Hasaka / al-Jazira, and Damascus all have significant Kurdish populations. Kurd Dagh, located at the foot of the Taurus Mountains, has a dense population, settled for thousands of years.[15] Kobani lies directly on the Turkish border, and is the smallest Kurdish area. Surrounding areas comprise mixed Kurdish and Arab villages.[16] Located between the Tigris and Euphrates, the Jazira is historically pastoral land. However, it was settled by Kurdish nomads by the time that borders formed in the region. Its population grew in the 1920s, with an influx of Kurdish refugees from Turkey.[17] The Kurdish population of Damascus had been well-established since the 11th century, when Kurds fought alongside other Muslims and established cantons in and around the city, which were divided along ethnic lines. Eventually, these cantons became permanent, establishing a Kurdish quarter of Damascus. Unlike in the rest of Syria, however, this area's Kurds became more assimilated into Arab society.[18] Kurds in Damascus also ended up more Arabised due to the city's strong affiliation with Arab nationalism. However, Kurds in other agro-cities maintained a stronger Kurdish identity[19] France recognised the importance of the agro-cities and kept administrative systems within Syria similar to how they had operated under the Ottomans, in that they organised local governments according to the agro-city system, and tended to allow them to handle issues locally. Continuing the agro-city structure simultaneously divided the Kurdish populations and reinforced their ethnic identity. Kurds in the Jazira underwent different experiences than the Kurds in Kobani, and it created a certain degree of political fragmentation. This fragmentation according to agro-cities in turn facilitated French control.[20]

French officials faced several challenges within the Mandate. First, the borders with Turkey were precarious, as Turkey still wanted to recover more formerly Ottoman territory. Second, Arab nationalism was on the rise and becoming a highly disruptive force.[21] Arab nationalists had helped the Entente

---

15 Yıldız, *The Kurds in Syria*, pp 24–26.
16 Ibid, p 24.
17 Ibid, p 25.
18 Ibid, p 26.
19 Van Dusen, *Political Integration and Regionalism in Syria*, pp 124–125.
20 Ibid., pp 124–125.
21 MB and HGL, *Syria and Lebanon*, p 847.

Powers win the territory and felt entitled to run their own affairs, resenting French administration. France's solution was to reach out to minorities in order to maintain stability through divide and rule.[22] Mandatory authorities recognised that religious and ethnic minorities together in the region were nearly comparable in population to Sunni Arabs, and figured they would be easier to control because some feared losing power within an Arab nationalist state. They could also be more easily divided, and France, like most external powers, favoured the divide and rule method of governance. This strategy also helped lay the groundwork for the federated Syria envisioned by the French authorities at the time, which consisted of Alawite, Sunni, and Druze states.[23] The Kurdish populations were to serve as a buffer in the frontier between Turkey and Syria, as long as the French administered the Mandate.[24]

The French allowed the Kurdish elite to hold positions of power, as they did with all minorities. However, they also used them to curb growing Arab nationalist sentiments throughout the mandate. Not all Kurds were helpful, though. The agro-cities structure had helped foster divisions among Kurds based on geographic location. Some supported the movement for an independent Syria, while others saw the French administration as beneficial to their positions and supported it fully.[25]

France created *Les Troupes Speciales du Levant* in its Levantine Mandates, a force comprised mostly of minorities. When an Arab nationalist revolt broke out in 1925, *Les Troupes Speciales du Levant* crushed it. As these troops were drawn primarily from minority groups, and Sunni Arabs were mostly excluded from service, it became integral in controlling Arab nationalist stirrings. It also drove a wedge between the Kurdish and Arab nationalists.[26]

In 1924, predating the rebellion, the chiefs of the Kurdish tribes in the Jazira wrote a letter to the Haute-Commissaire. In this letter, they expressed a fear of being absorbed into Arab society despite having a distinct history. At the centre of their concern was the fact that the French administration had placed Jerablous district, with over 400 Kurdish villages, under Arab and

---

22 Tejel, *Syria's Kurds,* p 16.

23 Yıldız *The Kurds in Syria*, p 28.

24 Jordi Tejel Gorgas, 'The Terrier Plan and the Emergence of a Kurdish Policy under the French Mandate in Syria, 1926–1936', *International Journal of Kurdish Studies* 21, No 2 (June, 2007) p 97.

25 Yıldız, *The Kurds in Syria,* p 28.

26 Ibid., p 29.

Turkish functionaries. The administration had also developed more contacts with Arab populations in the area, which they felt degraded Kurdish interests. To entice the French to help, they pointed out that they buffered the border between Turkey and Syria, and could do so more effectively if independent. Specifically, they stated:

> Les Kurdes sont les gardiens courageux des portes de la Syrie du Nord. Ils sont prets, sur un signe de vous, a faire preuve de leur fidelite en se sacrifiant. Nous ne connaissons aucun peuple Syrien de vous faire une pareille promesse. Vos honnetes et fideles amis Kurdes peuvent vous etre utile. Un Kurdestan Independent a Nord de la Syrie constituerait une assez puissante barriere entre les turcs et les arabs.

Translation:

> The Kurds are courageous guardians of Syria's northern borders. They are prepared, at your signal, to prove their loyalty through self-sacrifice. We know of no Syrian people to make you such a promise. Your honest and loyal Kurdish friends can be useful. An independent Kurdistan in the North of Syria would constitute a powerful barrier between the Turks and Arabs.[27]

Kurdish leaders knew that their main value to France at this time was to serve as a buffer between Turkey and Syria, and they used this advantage as a bargaining tool. Jordi Tejel has dismissed the value of this document to demonstrate early nationalism, by stating that it 'revealed more the wish of its signatories to become the local support for the French administration than a desire to obtain specific cultural or political rights that would be to the benefit of the Kurdish population.'[28] However, it is apparent that the Kurds were offering support to the French administration in order to retain cultural and political rights. It also signals an early strategy of attempting to gain rights through cooperation with the French mandatory power.

Within the same letter, Kurdish leaders specifically mentioned that they did not want to be administered by or mixed together with Turks or Arabs, because they considered themselves distinct. This suggests both a sense of

---

27 BEY 569, 1926–1941.Cabinet Politique. CADN. Nantes, France.
28 Tejel, *Syria's Kurds*, p 28.

national identity and a will to preserve it. The Kurdish tribal chiefs nominated Bozan Bey, also known as Shahin Beyzade, as head of the Jerablous administration. This was done unanimously, and the letter contained the signatures of all the tribal chiefs of the Jazira.[29] Not only does this document show that Kurdish nationalism had its roots in Syria before the 1925 influx of Kurdish refugees from Turkey, but that it was a united front with a solid sense of identity and leadership. The front was civil in nature, not an armed resistance movement as in other areas with high Kurdish populations. Their civil orientation coincided with the mandatory policy of favouring minorities. As France's Mandate in Syria did not threaten Kurdish identity, there was no need for a hostile relationship between Kurdish leaders and France. Kurdish populations living under other authorities, however, had more confrontational relationships with those in charge, triggering armed resistance by the Kurds in those areas. One of those areas was Turkey.

In 1925 the nascent Turkish state crushed the first of several Kurdish rebellions, the Sheikh Said revolt, which led to an influx into northern Syria of Kurdish refugees. Due to the rebellion's focus and ideology, most of those expelled proved to be staunch Kurdish nationalists, and they soon merged their interests with the pre-existing nationalist foundation. Upon their arrival to Syria, these newcomers established a Kurdish political party known as 'Khoybun'.[30] Khoybun, meaning 'Independence', not only breathed life into Kurdish nationalism in the French Mandate of Syria, but its cross-border activity signaled that Kurdish nationalism was not to be limited to one part of Kurdish majority territory.[31] Jaladet Bedir Khan, of the prominent Kurdish Bedir Khan family, served as the head of Khoybun. This new party not only established diplomatic relations with Iran, France, Great Britain, Italy and the Soviet Union, but it also established Kurdish committees and associations throughout Syria. Mainly comprised of elites, membership included tribal leaders, intellectuals, and former military officers.[32] However, Kurds outside the elite circles were not yet extremely active in Kurdish nationalist activities within the French mandate. Members were obliged to swear the following oath to the Kurdish cause:

---

29 BEY 569 , 1926–1941.Cabinet Politique. CADN. Nantes, France.
30 Tejel, *Syria's Kurds,* p 29.
31 Wadie Jwaideh, *The Kurdish National Movement: Its Origins and Development* (Syracuse University Press, Syracuse, N.Y.: 2006) p 145.
32 Tejel, *Syria's Kurds,* p 17.

I do hereby swear on my honor and religion that from the date of my signing this promise, for a period of two years, I will not use arms against any Kurd unless an attack is made by him on my life and honor or upon the lives and honor of those for whose safety I am responsible by family or national obligation. I will postpone, until the expiration of these two years, all blood feuds and other disputes, and do my utmost to prevent bloodshed among two Kurds on private matters. Any Kurd who attempts to contravene this undertaking is regarded a traitor of his nation, and the murder of every traitor is a duty.[33]

This oath suggests that Kurdish leaders were striving to resolve any outstanding lack of unity among the Kurdish population. Because of Khoybun's founding members' exile from Turkey, they were firmly anti-Kemalist and used mandatory Syria as a staging ground from which to attack Turkey. Kurdish nationalists thus proved a willing and valuable asset to France in its ongoing border dispute with Turkey. Accordingly, from 1927 to 1930, Khoybun attempted to assist several Kurdish uprisings in Turkey.[34]

Khoybun also allied with the Armenian Dashnak Party, forming an Armenian-Kurdish coalition. The first congress of this coalition was held in 1927 in Bihamdoun, Lebanon, with Vahan Papazian representing the Dashnak. It was held again the following year, but with Ador Levonian heading the Dashnak delegation. This Armenian-Kurdish coalition strengthened Khoybun's foothold in the Levant.[35] However, they had less success in other Kurdish areas, as their influence mainly extended to Sunni Kurds who spoke the Kurmanji dialect. For example, when they attempted to expand into Suleymaniya, a Sorani speaking Kurdish region in Iraq, they met with little success.[36] A member of the Bedir Khan family even tried to rally support among Kurds in Detroit, Michigan, for the revolts in Turkey.[37] Such partnerships showed an attempt to strengthen the cause through internationalisation. By building such coalitions, the Kurdish

---

33 Ibid., p 18.
34 Jwaideh, p 145.
35 Tejel, *Syria's Kurds*, p 18.
36 The Kurmanji and Sorani dialects are the primary dialects of Kurdish. Kurmanji is more prevalent in northern, western and eastern areas of Kurdistan, while Sorani is commonly spoken in the southern areas. Kurmanji is more common than Sorani. (Yıldız, *The Kurds in Syria*, p 8).
37 Tejel, *Syria's Kurds*, p 18.

nationalists hoped to construct a widespread base from which to draw support when necessary. However, such partnerships did not prove long lasting.

French officials tolerated Khoybun, despite their full awareness of the party's activities. French intelligence services not only monitored Khoybun, but even utilised Jaladet Bedir Khan as one of their informants, which exemplifies the entanglements of the Kurdish nationalist leadership with the mandatory authority. When dealing with Turkey in border disputes, French officials found Khoybun useful as a threat to Turkish stability.[38] At the same time, they did not want Khoybun to grow too successful or powerful, so they backed Ankara whenever direct conflicts flared up. In 1928, to appease Turkey, France even closed the Khoybun headquarters in Aleppo. Not wanting to give up their 'Kurdish Card' entirely, they continued to allow Khoybun to operate elsewhere throughout the Mandate.[39]

Khoybun disseminated its ideas primarily through brochures. While its main focus was Kurdish nationalism, it did not always demand Kurdish independence. For example, Jaladet Bedir Khan once wrote an open letter to Atatürk showing a willingness to be incorporated into countries' territories as long as there was a degree of autonomy for Kurdish inhabited provinces.[40]

After the failure of the 1930 Mount Ararat revolt, Khoybun gave up on its militant activities in the Turkish provinces. Instead, the Bedir Khan family began to concentrate on fortifying Kurdish identity. In 1932, a charity to help poor Kurds in the Jazira was launched. In the same year, Jaladet Bedir Khan started publishing a Kurdish journal called *Hawar*, or *'Calling'*.[41] *Hawar* focused on enhancing Kurdish culture through its writings, publishing studies on Kurdish dialects, grammar, poetry, history, music, and folklore. Jaladet Bedir Khan emphasised that he thought language was key to the success of Kurdish nationalism, which is why *Hawar* was published in Kurdish and placed so much emphasis on Kurdish grammar.[42] The importance of the Kurdish language's proliferation did not escape the Salah al-Din club

---

38 Ibid., p 19.

39 Yıldız, *The Kurds in Syria*, p 29.

40 Jordi Tejel Gorgas, *Le Mouvement Kurde de Turquie en Exil: Continuités et Discontinuités du Nationalisme Kurde sous le Mandat Français en Syrie et au Liban (1925–1946)* (Peter Lang International Academic Publishers, Berne: 2006) p 18.

41 *Hawar* was published in Kurmanji using the Roman alphabet, in an attempt to standardise written Kurdish (Yıldız, *The Kurds in Syria*, p 8).

42 Özoğlu, *Kurdish Notables and the Ottoman State*, p 101.

in Damascus, which began to teach Kurdish following the example set by Jaladet Bedir Khan.[43]

The Bedir Khans were not the only ones to push for Kurdish nationalism in Syria. Certain French administrators took an interest in the Kurds and helped guide the Bedir Khans in creating a national identity. Such support amongst officials within the French Mandate probably served to reinforce the idea that Kurdish objectives could best be achieved through strong relations with the French. Pierre Rondot, Pierre Terrier, and Roger Lescot were the most prominent French supporters, with Pierre Terrier perhaps the most active contributor to the Kurdish cause, due to his Terrier Plan.[44]

Captain Terrier was stationed in the Jazira in 1924, and upon leaving in 1927 was placed in the Political Cabinet of the Haute-Commissaire as an attaché to deal with Franco-Kurdish relations.[45] Seeing a demand for independence from multiple Kurdish districts, he devised a solution. Terrier did not consider liberation of all Kurdish majority territories to be feasible. Instead, he urged Kurdish leaders to press for just the independence of the Jazira. The Terrier Plan allowed for Kurdish independence movements to establish themselves in the capital of the Jazira, al-Hasaka. It also suggested other steps towards autonomy that came to fruition in the 1930s. These included the French forcing the Syrians to grant identity cards to Kurdish refugees, offering Kurdish language classes in a Damascus university, supporting Kurdish courses in Beirut, creating a Kurdish battalion in Les Troupes Speciales du Levant, and employing Kurdish administrators in the Jazira.[46]

Rondot and Lescot provided less direct assistance to Kurdish nationalism. Their contact with Kurdish nationalists helped the Bedir Khans navigate how to present their case and people to the outside world in order to gain the most sympathy and support.[47] They appealed towards Europe's love of the 'noble savage', and framed Kurdish identity to the outside world via its supposed primitiveness. Roger Lescot researched topics that would contribute to a stronger Kurdish identity and sent his findings, mainly proverbs and legends, to Kurdish publications. However, these proverbs and stories were then used by the Kurds to render themselves more marketable to a Western audience.

---

43 Gorgas, *The Terrier Plan,* p 4.
44 Tejel, *Scholarship on the Kurds in Syria,* pp 1–2.
45 Gorgas, *The Terrier Plan,* p 6.
46 Ibid., p 7.
47 Tejel, *Syria's Kurds,* p 23.

Pierre Rondot was especially helpful in promoting Kurdish proverbs, in order
to demonstrate their distinct nature.[48] This 'noble savage' campaign was relatively successful in Europe, and left a lasting impact. Its success is shown by
a 1966 *Middle East Journal* article by Israel T. Naamani, a professor at the
University of Louisville, in which he stated:

> Some Kurds are as primitive today as their ancestors were at the dawn
> of civilization. But it has been emphasized by many who know them
> that they learn swiftly enough, given the opportunity. A Kurd pursuing
> knowledge is as purposeful as a Kurd pursuing an adversary. The region
> he inhabits is rugged, mountainous, not given much to cultivation or
> commerce, so he was driven to horse and rifle. He became a scourge to
> everyone. But if his manners are bad, they are the manners of one who
> has been incessantly kicked around, without an opportunity for creative
> self-expression.[49]

Clearly, the Kurds benefitted from soft power through such assistance.
However, soft power proved insufficient to give birth to a Kurdish state. In
1936, the French moved towards a Syrian Arab nationalist state with the
Franco-Syrian Treaty, and an Arab nationalist government was installed. It is
apparent that under the French Mandate, the nationalism of the Kurds of Syria
increased dramatically and reached the point of a tangible movement. Due
to this, it seems illogical that by 1936 the Kurds would have been supportive
of a unified Syria that made no provisions for Kurdish autonomy. However,
it is important to note that during this time there was no armed movement
for Kurdish autonomy within the French mandate of Syria. Furthermore, they
carried little weight in terms of economic impact. The significance of the 1936
treaty is that it set the template for Syria's final borders, so its construction
provides insight into why the Kurds did not get a state.

Kurds are conspicuously absent from archival documents addressing the
1936 Treaty. The Druze leadership sent multiple requests for a state, as did the
Alawites'. Christian leaders asked for some degree of protection.[50] At certain
points the idea of a confederation was floated, but specific groups were not

48 Ibid., p 24.
49 Israel Naamani, 'The Kurdish Drive for Self Determination', in *The Middle East Journal* 20,
No 3 (Summer, 1966) p 280.
50 BEY 490, 1926–1941, Cabinet Politique. CADN. Nantes, France.

mentioned, and Lebanon was to be part of that confederation.[51] However, there are no documents from Kurdish leaders or advocates during this period. Nothing explains this absence, as Kurdish publications and schools were opening up, thereby solidifying Kurdish identity. The Kurdish leadership did not favour the 1936 Franco-Syrian Treaty, which is why they formed a bloc with the Christian leadership before it could be ratified. This bloc then led a revolt in 1937 in the Jazira, with Hajo Agha leading the Kurdish tribes.[52] From this, it is reasonable to infer that the lack of petitioning by the Kurds for autonomy in the treaty did not stem from a lack of desire on their part.

To understand why the French would not include Kurdistan, or at least an autonomous region for the Kurds, in the 1936 Franco-Syrian Treaty, the motivations of the treaty must be examined. During the early 1930s, the French began to worry about an ambitious Germany. Defence planning started to examine whether the French could win against the German army in case of war.[53]

At this time, France was a major naval power. France's navy was ranked fourth in capability, which made Italy its prime competitor. Its air power was weak. However, its army was its main strength. The French army was subdivided into three main portions: Metropolitan (domestic), Armée d'Afrique (French North Africa), and the Colonial Army (specialist regiments and indigenous units with French officers, charged with overseeing French territory globally). During times of war, the Armée d'Afrique and Colonial Army would be expected to help protect France. This means that they would abandon their posts to aid the Metropolitan army in Europe.[54] By December 1934, France began training Africans *en masse* for the Armée d'Afrique, with the anticipation that they could be shipped to Europe in the event of war. The estimate was that shipments of troops from North Africa would arrive in numbers of 45,000 per month. Within a few years, France began mobilising its Colonial and Armée d'Afrique troops to aid France. This meant that many were pulled from Syria. Even so, the Armée d'Afrique remained the easiest to mobilise. Therefore, in French defence planning, securing the western Mediterranean

---

51 Ibid.

52 Tejel, *Syria's Kurds,* pp 30–31.

53 Martin Thomas. 'At the Heart of Things? French Imperial Defense Planning in the Late 1930s.' *French Historical Studies* 21, no. 2 (Spring 1998) p 331.

54 Ibid., pp 331–332.

became the top priority, and the Levant began to hold less strategic value.[55] In order to safely redistribute troops away from the Levant, and to ensure that the Armée d'Afrique did not have to reinforce it, France needed to minimise conflict in the area.

As mentioned, a major flashpoint and security concern in the French Mandate of Syria was the border dispute with Turkey.[56] The Syria mandatory authority originally included Alexandretta Province following the First World World War. Alexandretta is demographically mixed, with both Arab and Turkish populations. In the course of the Turkish War of Independence, this status was renegotiated. Alexandretta became autonomous for a few years thereafter, but was soon re-incorporated into the French Mandate of Syria. At this time, Turkish nationalism was growing more powerful under Atatürk's leadership. He felt strongly that Alexandretta should be part of Turkey due to its Turkish population. This border dispute kept relations between France and Turkey tense.[57] Due to the Kurdish position along Turkey's border, however, this dispute is also what maintained Kurdish value for the French. As previously mentioned, they could serve as a buffer. Further, they could be used to threaten Turkey. As French defence planning picked up momentum, however, the need for cordial relations with Turkey became apparent.

Italy and Turkey had cooperative relations throughout the late 1920s and early 1930s.[58] During this period, Italy supplied Turkey with naval ships. Much of this was due to their common hostility against France, and because Italy was attempting to expand its influence. France's defence planning indicated that a neutral Italy was key to its success in a war.[59] However, if Italian power expanded into Turkey, it could potentially provide them with enough confidence to leave aside their neutrality. This prompted France to begin resolving its border issues with Turkey.

Without the dispute, France's need for the Kurds diminished. Furthermore, with Turkey becoming more valuable to France, France had to consider their concerns and interests. The Kurds were highly problematic to Turkey, who

---

55 Ibid., p 334.

56 Montagne, p 35.

57 Ibid., p 41.

58 Lek Barlas and Serhat Güvenç, 'To Build a Navy with the Help of an Adversary: Italian-Turkish Naval Arms Trade, 1929–1932', *Middle Eastern Studies*, Vol. 38, No. 4 (Oct., 2002) pp 143.

59 Ibid.

had its own Kurdish population to deal with. The high visibility of the Kurdish refugees from Turkey in the Syrian Kurdish nationalist movement could only give Turkey greater anxiety if they were to gain any autonomous recognition. Creating an independent Kurdistan in the 1936 Franco-Syrian Treaty would have seriously harmed relations with Turkey. Not only would it provide a completely unchecked base for Turkey's own Kurds to attack the Turkish state, but it would also give them hope and a sense of legitimacy.[60] At that point, the Turkish state was assiduously pursuing Turkification. Minority identities were in the course of being erased through a policy of forceful assimilation. Kurds were no longer 'Kurds', but were now designated as 'mountain Turks'.[61] Such a policy would have been far less likely to succeed if a Kurdistan had been established for the Kurds of Syria. Therefore, ironically, the Kurds were denied autonomy in part because of the same factors that had once rendered them valuable to France.

Not only did Turkey not favour the Kurdish nationalists, but the Arab nationalists of Syria were not friendly towards them either. In 1925, there was also an Arab nationalist rebellion in Syria.[62] As stated, the French favoured minorities, and used them to control the majority population. This was because minorities were less likely to reject French rule, knowing that they would do better under it than under majority rule. Further, it would be easier to divide populations in such a situation should their loyalties ever change.[63] Accordingly, when the French created Les Troupes Speciales du Levant, they filled it with minority populations, to crush the 1925 rebellion and subsequently maintain order within the Mandate. This left the Kurdish nationalists fundamentally at odds with the Arab nationalists.[64]

Arab nationalism was growing stronger during the 1930s, with the National Bloc gaining strength and beginning to demonstrate their power. In January of 1936, a commemoration for Ibrahim Hanano was held by the National Bloc. Interestingly, Hanano was of Kurdish origin.[65] However, identity tended to be

---

60 Philip Robins, 'The Overlord State: Turkish Policy and the Kurdish Issue', *International Affairs* 69, No 4 (October, 1993) p 660.

61 Ibid, p 661.

62 Yıldız, *the Kurds in Syria*, p 29.

63 Ibid., p 27.

64 Ibid., p 29.

65 Sami M. Moubayed, *Steel and Silk: Men and Women Who Shaped Syria 1900–2000* (Cune, Seattle, WA: 2006) pp 376–377.

dictated by the agro-city structure of Syria, and he was no exception to this rule.[66] Hanano, who appears to have prioritised his Muslim identity over his ethnic identity, supported several variant sides in the chaotic decades before and after the First World War. He was from Aleppo, and educated in Istanbul. During Ottoman times he had been a member of the Committee of Union and Progress. Later, he joined the 1916 Arab revolt. During the early 1920s, he fought in the Turkish War of Independence, for the Turkish side. In 1927 he helped found the National Bloc. During the 1930s, he refused to negotiate with France, instead demanding a pledge of complete independence for Syria. Hanano died in November 1935.[67] During his commemoration, a number of speakers continuously derided and condemned French rule. France retaliated by arresting National Bloc officers and closing their office in Damascus.[68] Angered by France's moves, the National Bloc called for a general strike throughout Syria. Student protests and work stoppages spread across the country, bringing the economy to a complete halt. France attempted to squash the protests by exiling National Bloc leaders and firing into protesters, which spread the protests to other Arab countries. This was a vigorous display of hard power.

Domestic French politics were also shifting. As the Popular Front party made gains, a shift in policy in the Levant grew increasingly manifest. This shift pushed France into negotiating with the National Bloc for the Franco-Syrian Treaty.[69] It is important to note that during this time, the National Bloc had few stated goals or ideology beyond wanting independence from France for Syria. However, due to the ethnic and religious composition of Syria, it has come to be viewed as an exclusively Arab nationalist movement. Its rhetoric was also steeped in Arab nationalism and its connection to the greater Arab world strengthened it.[70] By demonstrating its ability to control events so forcefully, it became important for the French to meet their demands. Uprisings from Kurds, Alawites, or Druze could be contained. They tended to be concentrated in specific areas and made up a much smaller portion of the population. However, the 1936 general strike demonstrated the strength of Arab nationalism across the country and region. Due to France's defensive

---

66 Van Dusen, *Political Integration and Regionalism in Syria*, pp 124–125.

67 Moubayed, *Steel and Silk*, pp 376–377.

68 Raghid Sulh, *Lebanon and Arabism: National Identity and State Formation* (I.B. Tauris, London: 2004) pp 20–21.

69 Ibid.

70 BEY 490, 1926–1941. Cabinet Politique. CADN. Nantes, France.

planning, it could not afford to use the Colonial troops or Armée d'Afrique to suppress a major rebellion. This is what pushed them into negotiations for the treaty. It became clear that in time of war, the French Mandate of Syria could become a distraction if the Arab nationalists did not get their way. Kurds lacked that bargaining power.

The power differential between the Arab nationalists and other minorities in Syria is clearly shown in the archival file documenting minority petitions filed during the negotiations leading up to the 1936 Franco-Syrian Treaty. All of the minority groups sent diplomatic appeals to France to insert minority protections or autonomy for their communities into the treaty. A willingness to work with the established Mandate structure had been demonstrated in the earlier Kurdish appeals, such as the previously mentioned 1924 Jerablous petition. While the Kurds were noticeably absent in this file, it can be inferred from their previous interactions that they were also trying to work with the mandatory authority to achieve their desired outcome.

Arab nationalists, however, did not petition, since they were controlling the negotiations with France. However, they did contribute a document in the file, an article in the newspaper *al-Taqaddum*. The article is a transcript of a speech given by an Arab nationalist in the Grand Mosque of Aleppo, and its translation was forwarded from local officials in Aleppo to the mandatory authorities. This speech offered no room for diplomacy, only demands. France was clearly the enemy, and independence was called for with the phrase 'independence or death', underscoring a clear willingness to turn to armed struggle. Furthermore, the speaker affirmed the movement's status as linked to the greater Arab struggle by referencing links to other independence movements in the mandatory system. Likewise, the speaker articulated the centrality of Arab identity to their vision of Syria by insisting it fly an Arab flag. Finally, the speech confirmed that the Arab nationalist vision for Syria would not permit a reduction in its size to accommodate minorities, stating that they would not accept an Alawite or Druze state carved out from Syria's territories.[71] The speech was threatening, directly hostile, and completely inflexible. It suggested that the Arab nationalists were in control of the treaty negotiations, and why. Unlike the other groups, they were willing to fight France for independence, at a time when France could not spare military resources.

The terms of the treaty indicate clearly France's concern over its security. While Syria was given independence, Syria was obligated to pledge itself to

---

71 BEY 490, 1926–1941. Cabinet Politique. CADN. Nantes, France.

France in times of war. Alexandretta was ceded to Turkey (which renamed it Hatay) to minimise that dispute and improve relations with Turkey. French troops in the region were to be reduced. All of this was done at the expense of the previously autonomous Alawite and Druze areas, which were incorporated into Greater Syria, along with the Kurds.

The Kurds were passed over during the 1936 Franco-Syrian Treaty because it went against French interests to grant them a state. Though France had previously been committed to minority protection, their strategic interests in the changing political environment of Europe did not allow them to follow through in this instance. Lebanon was granted autonomy due to France's deep rooted historical relationship with the Maronites. However, they did not have such a commitment to other minorities, which is why the Alawites and Druze were also excluded from gaining states. France could not engage militarily in the Levant in the event of a war in Europe. Therefore, it needed to appease the biggest threats to their control over the mandate, the National Bloc and Turkey. Neither wanted an independent Kurdistan. Ironically, relationships between the Kurds of Syria and the other two groups were strained, in part, due to the Kurdish nationalists' strong relationship with France, and the means by which they had solidified that relationship. This decision appeared safe due to the lack of an armed Kurdish movement against the Syrian mandate. In other words, since Kurdish nationalists in Syria were not engaging in armed struggle, it made it easier for the French officials to deny them a state. Furthermore, the concentration of Kurds into smaller geographic areas also helped mitigate the risk to France, as any potential rebellions would be more localised and therefore easier to suppress. The Kurdish leadership also lacked the ability to disrupt the economy as the 1936 general strike had.

The Kurdish nationalists were not deprived of statehood for lack of desire. They had both a strong nationalist movement at the time of the 1936 treaty, and a viable leadership. Rather, their nationalism was not as threatening as Arab nationalism to the stability of the Mandate, or to France's foreign policy objectives. It was their close relationship with France that harmed them, by allowing the growth of a nationalist movement with neither hard power nor strong allies beyond the French administration itself. They relied heavily on their relationship with France, without realising the risk of betting on a relationship built on mutable interests, rather than permanent affinity or ideals. In the end, the ideal of Kurdish self-determination, which French officials promoted aggressively in the 1920s, lost out to French realist objectives in the 1930s.

16

The other jihad: Enver Pasha, Bolsheviks, and politics of anticolonial Muslim nationalism during the Baku Congress 1920

Alp Yenen

'May the holy war of the peoples of the East and of the toilers of the entire world against imperialist Britain burn with unquenchable fire!'[1] With these words, the Communist International (Comintern) appealed to the anti-imperialist sentiments of Muslim delegates attending the First Congress of the Peoples of East in Baku (in short Baku Congress) in September 1920. Like many lost and forgotten moments and movements during the aftermath of the First World War, the Baku Congress and the ideological climate of anticolonial Muslim nationalism were long dismissed by teleological narratives as marginal and obscure. Even an eyewitness has prominently concluded: 'I cannot take this Baku Conference very seriously. It was an excursion, a pageant, a Beano. As a meeting of Asiatic proletarians it was preposterous.'[2] Several scholars underlined the importance of the Baku Congress in demonstrating the complex

---

[1] John Riddell (ed), *To See the Dawn: Baku 1920 – First Congress of the Peoples of the East* (Pathfinder, New York: 1993) p 263.
[2] Herbert G. Wells, *Russia in the Shadows* (George H. Doran Company, New York: 1921) p 99.

intentions and actions of the Bolsheviks regarding national and colonial questions during the eventful years of the Russian Civil War.[3]

     This chapter places the Baku Congress within the global moment of the aftermath of the First World War. This global moment is generally depicted as conditioned by Lenin's declaration on the rights of nations and President Wilson's fourteen point programme which opened up framing strategies for national self-determination.[4] Although the declarations by Lenin and Wilson are important in framing the national struggles of this era, this approach might reproduce a certain West vs. East conflict before the actual Cold War.[5] We

---

3   The most influential work on Baku Congress is still Stephen White, 'Communism and the East: The Baku Congress, 1920', in *Slavic Review* 33, No 3 (1974). See also: Cosroe Chaqueri, 'The Baku Congress', *Central Asian Survey* 2, No 2 (1983); Edith Ybert-Chabrier, *Le premier congrès des peuples de l'Orient (Bakou, 1–8 Septembre 1920)* (EHESS, Paris: 1984); Edith Ybert-Chabrier, 'Les délégués au Premier Congrès des Peuples d'Orient, Bakou (1er-8 Septembre 1920)', *Cahiers du monde russe et soviétique* 26, No 1 (1985); Nermin Menemencioğlu, 'Congress of the Peoples of the East, Baku, September 1920', in *XI. Türk Tarih Kongresi: Ankara, 5–9 Eylül 1990. Kongreye Sunulan Bildiriler*, Vol 6 of 6 Vols. (Türk Tarih Kurumu Yayınları, Ankara: 1994) pp 2223–33; Solmaz Rustamova-Towhidi, 'The First Congress of the Peoples of the East: Aims, Tasks, Results', in Mikhail Narinsky and Jürgen Rojahn (eds), *Centre and Periphery: The History of the Comintern in the Light of New Documents* (International Institute of Social History, Amsterdam: 1996) pp 74–80; Pezhmann Dailami, 'The First Congress of Peoples of the East and the Iranian Soviet Republic of Gilan, 1920–21', in Stephanie Cronin (ed) *Reformers and Revolutionaries in Modern Iran: New Perspectives on the Iranian Left* (Routledge Curzon, London: 2004) pp 85–117. For a Soviet account see: G. Z. Sorkin, *Pervyi s"ezd Narodov Vostoka* (Nauka, Moscow: 1961).

4   Sebastian Conrad and Dominic Sachsenmaier, 'Introduction: Competing Visions of World Order: Global Moments and Movements, 1880s-1930s', in Sebastian Conrad and Dominic Sachsenmaier (eds), *Competing Visions of World Order: Global Moments and Movements, 1880s – 1930s* (Palgrave Macmillan, New York: 2007) pp 1–25, 15–16.

5   Erez Manila rightly notes the fallacies of a Wilson vs. Lenin approach, but rather to underline Wilson's superior impact in the colonial debates of early post-war years: 'It may be tempting, for example, to construe the ideological essence of 1919 as a clash between Wilsonian and communist internationalism; "Wilson vs. Lenin" is the influential phrase that Arno Mayer coined some decades ago. But while the Wilson versus Lenin framework is helpful, as Mayer used it, for understanding the struggle over the European Left at the time, it cannot be extended to the colonial world in 1919. Socialist ideas were influential among some colonial intellectuals at the time, and the Russian Bolsheviks also used the language of self-determination, but until late 1919 Wilson's words carried far greater weight in the colonial world than Lenin's.' Erez Manela, *The Wilsonian Moment: Self-Determination and the International Origins of Anticolonial Nationalism* (Oxford University Press, Oxford: 2009) pp

need to see this global moment also within the context of the peak of colonial penetration of the Muslim world as manifested in the Sykes-Picot agreeement, Balfour, and Sèvres documents and in the numerous local declarations and claims made against these colonial and imperial machinations by local Muslim insurgents.

Within this global moment of the aftermath of the First World War, a global movement of anticolonial Muslim nationalism emerged. Different movements -without being united under one umbrella or led by a 'hidden hand' – were entangled with each other in a complex network of interrelations and shared the same 'Young Turk zeitgeist' of Muslim nationalism, political culture of par-tisanship, and anticolonial mobilisation.[6] Even though diplomatic history of the peace talks in Paris and London has brought light on imperialist and colonial-ist schemes, one needs to regard only the emergence of several new Muslim states and republics in the aftermath of the First World War, to appreciate the many (and mostly failed) bottom-up struggles of Muslim insurgents.[7] Beyond national and diplomatic narratives, transnational approaches are necessary in understanding the contentious interaction of local non-state actors in shaping the modern Middle East.[8] This transnational movement of anticolonial Muslim nationalism was ideologically framed by growing ideas of Muslim nationalism, people's sovereignty, and political anti-Westernism. In the Middle East, this moment was long built up in cultural memories during the era of the Great Game and the Eastern Question and found its emotional tipping point with

6–7. See also: Arno Joseph Mayer, *Wilson vs. Lenin: Political Origins of the New Diplomacy, 1917–1918* (The World Publishing Company, Cleveland: 1969).

6 Alp Yenen, 'The "Young Turk Zeitgeist" among the Middle Eastern Uprisings in the Aftermath of World War I', in M. Hakan Yavuz and Feroz Ahmad (eds), *War and Collapse: World War I and the Ottoman State* (University of Utah Press, Salt Lake City: forthcoming in 2015).

7 For a great overview of Muslim-national attempts of state-formation after the Russian Revolution and the end of the First World World War see: Stefan Reichmuth, 'Der Erste Weltkrieg und die muslimischen Republiken der Nachkriegszeit', in *Geschichte und Gesellschaft* 40 (2014).

8 Alp Yenen, 'Approaching Transnational Political History: The Role of Non-State Actors in Post-Ottoman State-Formation' in Steffi Marung and Matthias Middell (eds), *Transnational Actors – Crossing Borders: Transnational History Studies* (Leipziger Universitätsverlag, Leipzig: 2015) pp 261–70. See also: Michael Provence, 'Ottoman Modernity, Colonialism, and Insurgency in the Interwar Arab East', in *International Journal of Middle East Studies* 43, No 2 (2011).

the colonial partition of the Muslim world after the First World War. Different revolts, rebellions, revolutions, wars of independence in Libya, Egypt, Syria, Palestine, Iraq, Anatolia, Iran, Afghanistan, and India between 1918 and 1922 were all framed within the same discursive template of anticolonial Muslim nationalism regardless of their different local cleavages and complex diversities. As the Comintern called for holy war in Baku 1920, spirits of jihad were already bedeviling the colonial powers.

In this chapter, I will showcase one of the most symbolic events trying to embark this transnational movement of Muslim anticolonialism, namely the Bolshevik call for jihad during the Baku Congress in 1920. Two of the major political actors who tried to steal the show from each other at this eventful congress were Enver Pasha and the Bolsheviks. Their story tells the greater story of anticolonial Muslim nationalism during this 'jihad' of 1920.

The chapter will, first, illustrate the approach of Comintern and Soviet Russia towards the Baku Congress. Second, it will dwell on the Bolshevik call for jihad and discuss their problematic approach to Islam in mobilising Muslim anticolonialism. Third, it will contextualise the Baku Congress from the British perspective, which delivered fancy conspiracy theories in trying to make sense out of the anticolonial uprisings in the Middle East. Lastly, it will discuss the role of Enver Pasha in Baku and argue that his struggle needs to be read within movement of anticolonial Muslim nationalism. Louise Bryant, who witnessed the revolutionary days in Soviet Russia, evaluates the contention between Enver Pasha and Zinoviev, the chairman of the Comintern, at the Baku Congress as follows:

> The Communists understood perfectly well that Enver Pasha was
> not at the Oriental Conference as a sudden and sincere convert to
> Internationalism, and he knew that they knew. Both Zinoviev and Enver
> were actors taking the lead rôles in a significant historical pageant. The
> results are really all that matter, since the motives will soon be forgotten.[9]

The First (and last) Congress of the Peoples of the East was held in Baku, from 1 to 8 September 1920. It was the first and most famous result of Comintern's new Eastern policy. During the Second Congress of the Third (Communist) International in the early summer of 1920, Lenin presented his preliminary

9 Louise Bryant, *Mirrors of Moscow*, Reprint (Hyperion Press, Westport, Conn.: 1973) pp 157–58.

draft of his 'Theses on the National and Colonial Questions'.[10] Lenin was thereby in favour of supporting revolutionary movements in the colonial world regardless of their stance towards communist ideals.[11] In article six of the theses on the national and colonial questions, adopted by the Second Congress of the Comintern, this idea was manifested as follows:

> Consequently, we cannot limit ourselves at this time merely to recognizing or proclaiming the friendship of the toilers of various nations. Rather we must pursue a policy of implementing the closest possible alliance of all national and colonial liberation movements with Soviet Russia. The forms of this alliance will be determined by the level of development of the Communist movement within the proletariat of each country or of the revolutionary liberation movement in the backward countries and among the backward nationalities.[12]

The idea was to organise a conference for this new Eastern policy following the conference model of the Communist International.[13] The Baku Conference was subordinated to the Comintern and it was, according to Zinoviev, even

---

10 For the final draft of these theses see: Vladimir I. Lenin, 'Theses on the National and Colonial Questions: Adopted by the Second Congress of the Communist International (July 28, 1920)', in John Riddell (ed), *To See the Dawn: Baku 1920 – First Congress of the Peoples of the East* (Pathfinder, New York: 1993) pp 300–307; John Riddell (ed), *Workers of the World and Oppressed Peoples, Unite! Proceedings and Documents of the Second Congress of the Communist International, 1920,* 2 Vols., The Communist International in Lenin's Time 1 (Pathfinder Press, New York: 1991) pp 283–90.

11 Rudolf Schlesinger, *Die Kolonialfrage in der Kommunistischen Internationale* (Europäische Verlagsanstalt, Frankfurt am Main: 1970) p 32; White, 'Communism and the East', p 495. The main objection to Lenin's proposal came from M. N. Roy, the Indian communist revolutionary. Due to Roy's objection, Lenin changed the term 'bourgeois-democratic' to 'national-revolutionary' in order to distinguish between different national struggles. Manabendra Nath Roy, *Memoirs* (Allied Publishers, Bombay: 1964) p 392. See also: Dailami, 'The First Congress of Peoples of the East and the Iranian Soviet Republic of Gilan, 1920–21', p 103; White, 'Communism and the East', p 497; Schlesinger, *Die Kolonialfrage in der Kommunistischen Internationale,* p 45.

12 Riddell, *To See the Dawn,* p 302

13 Ahmed Zeki Velidi Togan, *Memoirs: National Existence and Cultural Struggles of Turkistan and other Muslim Eastern Turks,* (transl.) H. B. Paksoy (CreateSpace, North Charleston: 2012) p 263. See also: Bülent Gökay, *A Clash of Empires: Turkey Between Russian Bolshevism and British Imperialism, 1918 – 1923* (Tauris Academic Studies, London: 1997) p 99.

the 'complement, the second part, the second half' of the Second Comintern Congress.[14] Later M. N. Pavlovich announced the general euphoria in the Comintern as follows: 'All Communists – Russian, French, Italian, and so on – have now become Asians and are resolved to help every revolutionary movement in the East and in Africa.'[15]

As one eyewitness concluded, the Bolshevik motivation behind the Baku Congress was presumably not much more 'than a vague idea of hitting back at the British Government through Mesopotamia and India, because it has been hitting them through Kolchak, Deniken, Wrangel, and the Poles'.[16] The Cominterns's world revolution plans were usually exposed to dominance of Soviet state interests.[17] Trotsky wrote at the eve of the Baku Congress in a letter to Chicherin that 'a potential Soviet revolution in the East is now advantageous for us chiefly as a major item of diplomatic barter with England.'[18] The strategic momentum should not dismiss the Baku Congress to a mere instrument of Soviet foreign affairs.[19] For many Bolsheviks the world revolution was more than a lip service, although they were rather unsure how to deal with it.

Around 2,000 attendees were present at the Baku Congress.[20] The majority of the delegates were Russian Muslims from Caucasus and Central Asia and Asian political émigrés living in Soviet Russia.[21] The major part of the delegates were, nonetheless, not members of a communist party, and were in many cases even members of a petty-bourgeois movement.[22] The contradiction of Soviet

---

14 Riddell, *To See the Dawn*, p 71.

15 M. N. Pavlovich's speech at the Baku Congress, 5th session, 5 September 1920, in ibid., pp 164–65.

16 Wells, *Russia in the Shadows*, pp 97–98.

17 Ben Fowkes and Bülent Gökay, 'Unholy Alliance: Muslims and Communists: An Introduction', in *Journal of Communist Studies and Transition Politics* 25, No 1 (2009) p 9. See also: Rustamova-Towhidi, 'The First Congress of the Peoples of the East', p 74.

18 L. Trotsky, letter to Chicherin, 4 June 1920, in Jan M. Meijer (ed), *The Trotsky papers, 1917–1922*, Vol 2 of 2 Vols (Mouton, The Hague: 1971) p 209. See also White, 'Communism and the East', p 503.

19 White, 'Communism and the East', p 493.

20 For the statistics see Sorkin, *Pervyi s"ezd Narodov Vostoka*, pp 21–22; White, 'Communism and the East', p 499; Chaqueri, 'The Baku Congress', p 92.

21 White, 'Communism and the East', pp 506–7. See also the critical remarks about the election of the delegates in: Chaqueri, 'The Baku Congress', p 93.

22 Schlesinger, *Die Kolonialfrage in der Kommunistischen Internationale*, p 49; White, 'Communism and the East', p 507.

support for nationalist forces in Turkey, Iran, India, and China remained a disputed issue within the Comintern and needed to be justified again and again. In his opening speech of the Baku Congress, Zinoviev argued once again:

> And so I say that we patiently support groups that are not yet with us and even against us on some questions. For example, in Turkey, comrades, you know that the Soviet government supports Kemal. We do not forget for one moment that the movement headed by Kemal is not a Communist movement. [...] It is not out of some mercenary calculation that we support national movements like those in Turkey, Persia, India, and China. Rather we support them because a conscious worker will tell himself that the Turks who today do not yet understand where all their interests lie will understand this tomorrow. We must support this Turk and help him, and wait for a real people's revolution to arise in Turkey, when veneration for sultans and other obsolete notions will vanish from his mind.[23]

Nevertheless, the Baku Congress was convened with typical Soviet-style parades and Internationalist ceremonies. For instance, one of the major topics was, why the Third (Communist) International was superior to the Second (Socialist) International. This was an unnecessary concern in Baku, since the major part of the participants were non-party delegates. To entertain the delegates the anthem 'International' was playing repeatedly by an orchestra during ovations. On 3 September 1920, there were no sessions out of respect to Friday prayers, but a military parade of the Red Army took place. Also a huge statue of Karl Marx was unveiled by Comintern leaders in the city centre with a great ceremony.[24] One of the propaganda highlights was a public trial, at which effigies of Lloyd George, Alexandre Millerand, and Woodrow Wilson were show-trialed and set on fire.[25] At the end of the

---

23 Riddell, *To See the Dawn*, pp 82, 84.

24 White, 'Communism and the East', pp 500–501. There is a photograph of this event in Riddell, *To See the Dawn*.

25 Secret Political Report, 25 October 1920, The National Archives, London, Foreign Office correspondence and files (hereafter FO), FO 371/5178/E13412, quoted in White, 'Communism and the East', p 501. The Constantinople correspondent of *The Times* describes the same incident remarkably similarly to British intelligence report. *The Times*, 'Communist Congress at Baku: Its "Asiatic" Policy', 1 October 1920. This event is confirmed also by eye-witness accounts: Wells, *Russia in the Shadows*, pp 96–97.

congress sessions, there was a ceremony for 26 Baku commissars, killed by the British.[26]

Despite all the sincere efforts for world revolution, there was also a certain Orientalism in Comintern's approach to the 'backward nationalities' at the Baku Congress. John Reed, who made his last journey to the Baku Congress before his sudden death, was strongly disappointed by Zinoviev's and Radek's insincerity and cynical rhetoric.[27] But tropes of Orientalism were even stronger on the part of the critics of the Baku Congress. Despite his alleged insincerity, as Zinoviev was defending the Baku Congress to his European comrades, he made pains-taking efforts to counter Rudolf Hilferding's Orientalist criticism of '"mullahs of Chiva", whom the demagogues, the Bolsheviks, were trying to draw into the Comminist international.'[28] British Intelligence ridiculed the competence of the delegates as well: 'The majority of the delegates seem to have been illiterate and to have taken far more interest in each other's weapons and in selling the produce, which they had brought with them from their native countries, than in the proceedings of the Conference.'[29] Also Şevket Süreyya (Aydemir) who was a delegate in Baku recalls as a later leftist-Kemalist dismissively that:

> the first sessions of the congress passed by with parades, screams, roars and cheers. The swords were drawn out without ceasing. Besides these, a few program meetings took place, but since it was necessary to listen to the speeches there, rather than drawing out the sword and yelling, these didn't get the attention of the honorable delegates.[30]

The Times mocked the Bolshevik approach and the mentality of the Oriental delegates: 'In view of the fact that the Soviet gave free meals to the delegates at the expense of the Baku population, the following Russian *mot*

26 Alfred Rosmer, *Moscou sous Lénine* (Maspéro, Paris: 1970) pp 145–46.

27 Warren Lerner, *Karl Radek: The Last Internationalist* (Stanford University Press, Stanford: 1970) p 104.

28 Ben Lewis and Lars T. Lih, *Martov and Zinoviev: Head to Head in Halle* (November Publications, London: 2011) pp 69, 88, 136–140.

29 Weekly Summary of Intelligence Reports (Constantinople Branch), 30 September 1920, FO 371/5171 E13451/262/44, quoted in Richard H. Ullman, *The Anglo-Soviet Accord*, Anglo-Soviet Relations, 1917–1921, Vol 3 of 3 Vols (Princeton University Press, Princeton, NJ: 1972) p 319.

30 Şevket Süreyya Aydemir, *Suyu Arayan Adam*, 7th Ed. (Remzi Kitabevi, Istanbul: 1979) p 189.

seems to be a good summing-up of this sorry farce: – "The Eastern Communists Congress has simply shown that Orientals like pilaff [a rice meal] and that our Communists have not understood the Moslem mentality".'[31]

The very highlight of Baku Congress was not very much communist or internationalist. Zinoviev finished his long speech at the first session of the congress with the following appeal to Eastern delegates:

> Comrades! Brothers! The time has come when you can set about
> organizing a true people's holy war against the robbers and oppressors.
> The Communist International turns today to the peoples of the East and
> says to them "Brothers, we summon you to a holy war, above all against
> British Imperialism!" (Loud applause. Prolonged shouts of "Hurrah!"
> Members of the congress stand up, brandishing their weapons. The
> speaker is unable to continue for some time. All the delegates stand up
> and applaud. Shouts: "We swear it!")[32]

Also in the Manifesto of Peoples of the East, which was accepted by the Baku Congress, 'holy war' was one of the signal words, which was frequently repeated. Why would the Bolsheviks call for holy war? According to general assumptions, the notorious First World War jihad of 1914 was nothing but hot air as a general revolution did not take place in the Muslim lands of Ottoman Empire's enemies. However, the picture differs severely when one looks past 1918. In the aftermath of the First World War, there were Muslim uprisings everywhere from North Africa over Middle East and Central Asia to South Asia. One could argue that the jihad of 1914 only catalysed in 1919 reaching its peak in the summer of 1920. In these anticolonial Muslim-nationalist struggles, jihad was not only in the eye of the colonialist beholder, but also on the lips – and probably in the hearts and minds – of those who rallied against colonial rule. Thus, Zinoviev did not need to seek far in looking for ways to mobilise anticolonial Muslim nationalism. But ever since the overtly vocal role the Germans played in the jihad of 1914, 'infidel' calls for jihad were broadly suspicious, especially by atheist Bolsheviks.

The Bolshevik approach that 'religion is the opium of the people' bedeviled the jihad of Baku 1920 from the beginning on. It is remarkable that 'Islam' was never directly mentioned by name in this Bolshevik call for holy war. Even

---

31 *The Times*,'Pilaff and Palaver: Communist Farce at Baku', 6 October 1920.
32 Riddell, *To See the Dawn*, p 88.

within the whole of the conference proceedings Islam is mentioned only on few occasions.[33] Nevertheless, while Zinoviev's call for a holy war was translated into Turkish, Azeri, and Persian, it was probably translated as *jihād*. Even a direct translation as *ḥarb-i muḳaddes*,[34] which one can find in some documents, does refer only to the concept of jihad.[35]

At the Baku Congress, some speakers were going long distances in emphasising that 'the Muslim religion is rooted in principles of religious communism'.[36] The Bolshevik delegates were stressing the revolutionary potential of the East for the struggle against imperialism to disappointed delegates coming from Soviet Central Asia where Russian colonialist overtones were still very much present.[37] Whereas Islam was barely mentioned by name, there was a repeating and derogative discourse about Pan-Islamism. Zinoviev, for instance, said that 'Pan-Islamism, Musavatism, all these trends are not ours. We have a different policy.'[38] Already in Lenin's theses, the article 11, c) made a similar objection regarding Pan-Islamism:

> It is necessary to struggle against the pan-Islamic and pan-Asian movements and similar currents that try to link the liberation struggle against European and American imperialism with strengthening the power of Turkish and Japanese imperialism and of the nobles, large landowners, clergy, and so forth.[39]

---

33 Ibid., pp 95, 159.

34 Report on Baku Congress, 24 September 1920, General Staff Military History and Strategic Studies Directorate Archives, Ankara (Genelkurmay Başkanlığı Askeri Tarih ve Stratejik Etüd Daire Başkanlığı Arşivi, hereafter ATASE), ATASE, İSH-11, sıra no. 3115, kutu no. 717, gömlek no. 83.

35 Even before the proclamation of jihad and Ottoman entry to the First World World War, Enver Pasha was convinced, for instance, that the coming war with England 'would be a holy war [böyle bir harb mukaddes olacağına]' and 'it will definitely be pertinent to rally the Muslim population [...] in [neighbouring] Iran under Russian and English rule to revolution.' Enver to Cavid, 24/25 Temmuz 330 [7/8 August 1914], ATASE, BDH, klasör 68, yeni dosya 337, fihrist 1 and 1–1, quoted in Mustafa Aksakal, '"Holy War Made in Germany"? Ottoman Origins of the 1914 Jihad', War in History 18, No 2 (2011) p 196.

36 Riddell, To See the Dawn, p 209. See also: Fowkes and Gökay, 'Unholy Alliance: Muslims and Communists', p 11.

37 Hélène Carrère d'Encausse and Stuart R. Schram, Marxism and Asia: An Introduction with Readings (Lane, London: 1969) pp 33–34.

38 Riddell, To See the Dawn, p 84.

39 Riddell, To See the Dawn, p 305.

This was not a single remark. The attitude towards Pan-Islam was clear and harsh, but not necessarily smart.[40] On the one hand, some true communists were displeased, since 'there was hardly anything Socialistic about Zinoviev's appeal for a "holy war."'[41] On the other hand, for Muslim delegates, this was contradictory. British Intelligence was proudly reporting that 'the Congress has been a failure. From the point of view of those Muslims, who sincerely expected to further the cause of Islam, it is certainly a failure.'[42] Later it was confirmed by Muslim communists that by rejecting Pan-Islam, the Comintern terribly damaged its relation to Muslim masses.[43]

Also other sources reveal the existence of a certain Muslim spirit during the days of Baku Congress which needs to be appreciated. In Aydemir's account, there is a certain cynicism towards his own romanticism in his young days. These romantic sentiments need further attention, because it delivers a certain insight to Baku Congress through the eyes of a passionate Muslim delegate. Aydemir strongly emphasises the general euphoria and solidarity among the Muslims, who were fraternising with each other, even though they could not speak or understand each other's language. Everywhere, everybody was celebrating the so-called 'awakening of the East': the end of the long-lasting oppression of Asia. It was felt like a 'judgement day' as Aydemir remembers. The sleeping nations of the East were now waking up from their centuries old sleep of death to finally overthrow their oppressors and besiegers.[44] The official maxim was that '[a] new world [was] awakening to the life and struggle: the world of the oppressed nationalities.'[45] Naciye Hanım, a young lady delegate from Turkey, was saying that 'in order to see the dawn one has to pass through the dark night.'[46] This idea of the 'awakening of the East' was probably at least since the Japanese victory over Russia in 1905 slowly but surely spreading among the intellectuals of the East.[47] This trope of the 'awakening

---

40 Fowkes and Gökay, 'Unholy Alliance: Muslims and Communists', p 11.

41 Bryant, *Mirrors of Moscow*, p 158.

42 Weekly Summary of Intelligence Reports (Constantinople Branch), 30 September 1920, FO 371/5171 E13451/262/44, quoted in Ullman, *The Anglo-Soviet Accord*, p 319.

43 Carrère d'Encausse and Schram, *Marxism and Asia*, pp 188–189.

44 Aydemir, *Suyu Arayan Adam*, p 187.

45 'A New World: Declaration Delivered at the Baku Congress by the Baku City Executive Committee, Communist Party of Azerbaijan', in John Riddell (ed), *To See the Dawn: Baku 1920 – First Congress of the Peoples of the East* (Pathfinder, New York: 1993) pp 308–11, 308.

46 Riddell, *To See the Dawn*, pp 234.

47 For the effect of the victory of 1905 in the Islamic world see: Cemil Aydın, *The Politics*

of the East' was simultaneously supported by the imagination and anxiety of European Orientalists.

In British intelligence and news coverage, the Baku Congress was interpreted in common tropes of conspiracy theories. For instance, in an article about the Baku Congress, *The Times* reporter was illustrating the Comintern leaders as criminal Jewish conspirators: 'Apfelbaum [Zinoviev] is a Jew, like his associate Bela Kun, or Cohen, from Budapest, who was also at Baku; and of all the strange things which have happened in the last few years, none has been stranger than this spectacle of two Jews, one of them a convicted pickpocket, summoning the world of Islam to a new Jehad.'[48] From the beginning on, the Russian Revolution was seen as a Jewish conspiracy, thus also Zinoviev's call for jihad.[49] The British Baku delegate Wells confirms that this tradition of conspiracy theories in the British press: 'According to the crazier section of the British Press they [the Bolshevists] are the agents of a mysterious racial plot, a secret society in which Jews, Jesuits, Freemasons, and Germans are all jumbled together in the maddest fashion.' Further, he explains that in England there is 'a peculiar style of thinking, so impervious to any general ideas that it must needs fall back upon the notion of a conspiracy to explain the simplest reactions of the human mind.'[50] David Fromkin describes these British conspiracy theories within the broader context of Middle Eastern uprisings:

> When the uprisings in the Middle East after the war occurred, it was natural for British officials to explain that they formed part of a sinister design woven by the long-time conspirators. Bolshevism and international finance, pan-Arabs and pan-Turks, Islam and Russia were pictured by British Intelligence as agents of international Jewry and Prussian Germany, the managing partners of the great conspiracy.[51]

---

of Anti-Westernism in Asia: Visions of World Order in Pan-Islamic and Pan-Asian Thought (Columbia University Press, New York, NY: 2007); Renée Worringer, Ottomans Imagining Japan: East, Middle East, and Non-Western Modernity at the Turn of the Twentieth Century (Palgrave Macmillan, New York: 2014).

48 The Times,'The Red Flag in the East', 23 September 1920.

49 On the British perception of the Russian Revolution as a Jewish conspiracy see: Sharman Kadish, Bolsheviks and British Jews: The Anglo-Jewish Community, Britain and the Russian Revolution (Cass, London: 1992) pp 10–55.

50 Wells, Russia in the Shadows, p 79.

51 David Fromkin, A Peace to End All Peace: The Fall of the Ottoman Empire and the Creation of the Modern Middle East, 20th anniversary ed. (Henry Holt & Co., New York, NY: 2009) p 466.

At the end of the war in November 1918, Sir Eyre Crowe from the Foreign
Office was suspecting that 'the heart and soul of all revolutionary and terror-
istic movements have invariably been the Jews, the Bolsheviks and the Turkish
Committee of Union and Progress' (in short CUP).[52] Other senior officials
claimed even that 'there is or ever has been any dividing line between the
CUP and bolshevism. The force behind all these movements is the same.'[53]
There was a 'far more dangerous party, that of Enver & Talaat & the CUP-Jew-
German-Bolshevik combination' which was said to be occupied 'with the
Pan-Islamic offensive of Bolshevism throughout the East, primarily directed
against Great Britain'.[54] Even in the lack of facts and proofs, the paranoid style
was delivering creative visions:

> I do not think we can say Bolshevism does not exist because we can
> certify that no *Bolshevist organization* exists [emphasis in original]. We
> are looking for something far more elusive and intangible than that, viz:
> tendencies and sympathies on the part of the Turks or any of the peoples
> of Turkey, which foreshadows a fusion with Bolshevism or may end
> directly or indirectly, morally or materially, in aiding the Bolshevik cause
> to our detriment ... There have in fact been a number of incidents relevant
> to the subject, which, with the concomitant evil of Pan-Islamism, seem
> to fill the near horizon day by day with greater power of disturbing the
> British world.[55]

---

52 Eyre Crowe, Minute to Foreign Office, 18 November 1918, F0.371.4369.513, quoted
in John Fisher, 'British Responses to Mahdist and Other Unrest in North and West Africa,
1919–1930', in *Australian Journal of Politics and History* 52, No 3 (2006) p 348; John Ferris,
'The British Empire vs. The Hidden Hand: British Intelligence and Strategy and 'The CUP-Jew-
German-Bolshevik combination', 1918–1924', in Keith Neilson and Greg Kennedy (eds) *The
British Way in Warfare: Power and the International System, 1856–1956: Essays in Honour of
David French* (Ashgate, Farnham: 2010) pp 325–45, 337.
53 George Kidston from Foreign Office, quoted in Priya Satia, *Spies in Arabia: The Great War
and the Cultural Foundations of Britain's Covert Empire in the Middle East* (Oxford University
Press, Oxford, New York: 2008) p 224.
54 D. G. Osbourne, Minute, 23 September 1920, F0.371.4946.E11702, quoted in Ferris, 'The
British Empire vs. The Hidden Hand', p 342.
55 SIS chief in Constantinople, Political Report, 5 May 5, 1920, F0.371.5178.E.4689, quoted
in John Ferris, '"The Internationalism of Islam": The British Perception of a Muslim Menace,
1840–1951', in *Intelligence and National Security* 24, No 1 (2009) p 65.

Paranoid thinking or not, the events of the aftermath of the First World War caused a shift in the strategic perception of British officials. Suddenly, it was the 'Russian menace in the East', which threatened the British Empire "incomparably greater than anything else'.[56] Priya Satia writes in her brilliant study of cultural foundations of British colonialism in the Middle East: 'Bolshevism and Islam were both giant secret societies in the British official mind, their members following party decrees and clerical fatwas, respectively.'[57]

Accordingly, the British high officials were highly concerned about the Baku Congress. British occupation forces in Turkey and Persia did everything to prevent the arrival of delegates to Baku – as in the case of some unfortunate Persian delegates even by using deadly force.[58] Meanwhile, British newspapers were reporting about the anti-British propaganda, which the Baku Congress set out.[59] According to *The Times* '[t]he real danger in Middle Asia, as elsewhere' was not the Red Army nor "Enver's stage army", but rather the "Bolshevist propaganda."'[60] As Ullman summarises, among the British officials the term of 'propaganda' became by then 'the shorthand term which increasingly came to stand for the whole complex of Soviet revolutionary activities against British interests, especially in Asia.'[61]

In echoing many concerned voices in the British officialdom, *The Times* was propagandising that 'Bolshevism and Islam can no more mix than oil and water; but Enver is no Moslem.'[62] Enver Pasha, on the other side, saw this quite differently. Before he went to the 'Islam conference' as he referred to the Baku Congress, he wrote to Cemal Pasha:

Here [in Moscow] I got in touch with all the Muslim delegations. Either they be communist or not, they all support from their heart a military enterprise for the Muslims. From the mufti of Kazan to Sultan Galiev.

---

56 Lord Curzon, quoted in Fromkin, *A Peace to End All Peace*, p 461.
57 Satia, *Spies in Arabia*, p 211.
58 White, 'Communism and the East', pp 501–2.
59 'At this gathering it is proposed that, among other things, lectures should be given and pamphlets issued on the question of freeing India from "British tyranny".' *The Times*,'"Oriental Congress" at Baku: Bolshevists Pulling the Strings', 8 September 1920.
60 *The Times*, 'The Red Flag in the East', 23 September 1920.
61 Ullman, *The Anglo-Soviet Accord*, p 318.
62 *The Times*, 'The Red Flag in the East', 23 September 1920.

Accordingly, I am sure that great services will be done for the Islamic world when the general spirit is as such.[63]

Kazım Karabekir, one of the leaders of the Turkish national struggle, wrote to Enver Pasha after learning that the latter will go to the Baku Congress: 'It is a very important matter that you will be present at the Baku Conference where the fate of the Islamic world and all nations of the East will certainly be discussed [...].' Kazım Karabekir referred to general Muslim solidarity and that 'delegations coming to Ankara from India, Syria and Iraq declared that they all recognize the Anatolian government and that they are ready to make any sacrifice and will not abstain from any expenditure to save Turkey, but need our help and trained personnel to build up an organization.'[64]

Enver Pasha travelled from Moscow to the Baku Congress in the same train as Zinoviev and other Comintern leaders, but rather as a special guest, not a delegate.[65] But Zinoviev seemed to have open misgivings towards Enver's presence at the conference.[66] The Bolsheviks had every reason to fear that Enver could cast a shadow on the Comintern leaders in Baku. For instance, as Enver Pasha entered the congress hall during Zinoviev's opening speech. His sudden appearance caused a great curiosity and excitement among the Muslim delegates during the session.[67] Enver was not necessarily hiding his self-promoting schemes either. During the military parade on 3 September, Enver Pasha galloped on a near-by hill and saluted the crowds on his reared horse, which strongly displeased the Comintern leaders.[68]

At the end, Enver was not even allowed to read his own declaration. His

---

63 Enver Pasha, letter (Moscow) to Cemal Pasha (Afghanistan), 25 August 1920 in Hüseyin Cahit Yalçın and Osman Selim Kocahanoğlu (eds) İttihatçı Liderlerin Gizli Mektupları: Bir Devri Aydınlatan Tarihî Mektuplar 40–41 (Istanbul: Temel Yayınları, 2002) pp 41.

64 Kazım Karabekir, letter to Enver Pasha, 7 September 1920, ATASE, İSH-10, sıra no. 4345, kutu no. 570, gömlek no. 50. For the same letter see also Archive of the Turkish Historical Society, Ankara (Türk Tarih Kurumu Arşivi, hereafter TTK), TTK, EP, 1–70.

65 Enver Pasha, letter (Baku) to Cemal Pasha (Afghanistan), [around 8 September 1920], in Yalçın and Kocahanoğlu, İttihatçı Liderlerin Gizli Mektupları, p 42; Aydemir, Suyu Arayan Adam, p 194.

66 Chaqueri, 'The Baku Congress', p 94.

67 Şevket Süreyya Aydemir, Enver Paşa: Makedonya'dan Orta Asya'ya, Vol 3 of 3 Vols. (Remzi Kitabevi, Istanbul: 1972) p 543; Aydemir, Suyu Arayan Adam, p 190; Kurt Okay, Enver Pascha, der große Freund Deutschlands (Verlag für Kulturpolitik, Berlin: 1935) pp 311–12.

68 Rosmer, Moscou sous Lénine, p 147.

anti-imperialist declaration was read out on the fourth session (4 September 1920). Strangely enough, Enver Pasha claimed to represent the Union of the Revolutionary Organizations of Morocco, Algeria, Tunisia, Tripoli, Egypt, Arabia and India.[69] Masayuki Yamauchi carefully compared Enver Pasha's hand-written declaration in Ottoman-Turkish with the Russian stenographic record. He found out that expressions, like 'Allah's rule', 'Islam warriors', 'sacredness of the people' and 'victory by the grace of Allah' are changed in favour of Bolshevik terminology in the Russian text.[70]

The following harsh resolution, which was adopted in reaction to his declaration, demonstrate the Comintern's disillusionment about exploiting Enver Pasha for the mobilisation of anticolonial Muslim nationalism, but also how much defamation Enver Pasha's name would bring along in European minds due to his association with warmongering, self-enrichment, and Armenian massacres. Later during the Labour Conference in Halle, Zinoviev had to explain the presence of Enver Pasha at the Baku Conference against his European comrades:

> I have to say that comrade Crispien really has taken in with this Enver Pasha business. Such outrageous flimflam has been written on the question of nationalities. But it is not only in Germany that people are talking of this 'spectre Enver', but in Switzerland too. I just received a letter from the Swiss comrade Rose Bloch, in which she asks: 'Well comrade, tell me, is Enver really your ally? Tell me, is the terrible Enver Pasha your

69 According to Yamauchi, this Union, which Enver was claiming to represent, 'was obviously invented for the purpose at Baku and for his own depiction of his ties with various Muslim leaders of local movements, mainly in Arabic-speaking areas, with whom he had conversations in Berlin.' Especially, it was Emir Shakib Arslan and his friends, with whom Enver Pasha was indeed in contact in Berlin. Masayuki Yamauchi, *The Green Crescent under the Red Star: Enver Pasha in Soviet Russia, 1919–1922* (Institute for the Study of Languages and Cultures of Asia and Africa, Tokio: 1991) p 32.

70 Ibid., p 33. For the Russian original see: *Pervyy s"ezd narodov vostoka: Baku 1–8 sent. 1920g.* (Communist International Publishing House, Petrograd: 1920) pp 108–12; Türkkaya Ataöv, '1–7 Eylül 1920 Doğu Halkları Birinci Kongresinde (Bakü) Enver Paşa'nın Konuşma Metni ve Bununla İlgili Kongre Kararı', in *Ankara Üniversitesi Siyasal Bilgiler Fakültesi Dergisi* 29, No 1 (1974) pp 46–47. For the English translation of the Russian text: Riddell, *To See the Dawn*, pp 138–42. For the transcription of the original Ottoman-Turkish manuscript see: Enver Pasha, Original Text of the Speech Delivered at the Baku Congress, [ca. August – September 1920], TTK, EP, 1–77, in Yamauchi, *The Green Crescent under the Red Star*, pp 318–21.

ally?' And I have a pamphlet from Frankfurt, signed by Gütler and Kohl, which cries that Enver Pasha, the executioner of the Armenian people, is admitted into the Third International, but Ledebour the old revolutionary fighter is refused admittance.

Allow me to tell you how things really stand [Heckles. Unrest] Enver Pasha was present at the Baku congress, he was not a delegate. He requested that we give him the opportunity to issue a statement. [...] So, we did not allow him to speak, indeed this was at my instigation as president of the congress. Then he asked us to read out a statement. We agreed to do that. [...]

So that is what the Enver Pasha story looks like. [Unrest] Enver Pasha was not a delegate, and there was even a resolution against him. Of course, Enver Pasha was the leading butcher of the Armenians, and we also told him that to his face.[71]

Although the European public was more or less suspicious about Enver, what all accounts agree on is that Enver Pasha indeed had a great reputation among the Muslim delegates and caused great excitement during the Baku Congress. Aydemir says for instance that 'his fame was in the Muslim Orient like a fairy tale or a legend. According to the belief of these peoples, he was not of humankind from this earth. Everywhere, where he appeared, the sky had to open up, the ground had to split up, and great and magnificent things had to occur. He was over everything and over everyone.'[72] A British Intelligence report confirms that he 'exercised great influence over the Moslem delegates from the various districts of Central Asia', and he was 'looked upon by them as heroic figure and the representative of Moslem hostility to the Western powers and particularly England.' Furthermore, many senior Muslim representatives 'insisted on rendering Oriental obeisance to Enver Pasha when presented to him'.[73] Even Zinoviev himself remarked later in Halle that

---

71 Grigory Zinoviev, *Die Weltrevolution und die III. Kommunistische Internationale: Rede auf dem Parteitag der USPD in Halle am 14. Oktober 1920* (Verlag der Kommunistischen Internationale, Hamburg: 1920), quoted here from the English translation in Lewis and Lih, *Martov and Zinoviev*, pp 135–36.

72 Aydemir, *Suyu Arayan Adam*, pp 190–91.

73 Report of British High Commissioner (Constantinople) about the Baku Congress, 5 November 1920, FO 371/5439/N2539, quoted in White, 'Communism and the East', p 509.

In Baku, the influence of Enver over a large part of the Muslim population is so great that people on the streets kiss his hands and feet. Of course, this is regrettable. I will not hide that. But I do not want to hear that the whole Muslim population is totally different compared to us. This is what we must understand. We must be able to respond to and remove such local difficulties which the working class in the Orient always comes across.[74]

Enver definitely enjoyed the respect and love of the Muslim delegates and was fully aware that this was disturbing the Bolsheviks. In a letter Enver Pasha wrote to Mustafa Kemal Pasha, Enver emphasised the 'revival of Islam' and the lack of understanding on part of the Bolsheviks that there is a Muslim 'force' at stake which is beyond the grasp of communism:

Nevertheless, at the [Baku] congress I talked to many Muslim delegates, either they be communists or not, from "Turkestan", Afghanistan, Kirgizstan, Dagestan, and Caucasus and Chechenia. They have demonstrated by their spirit and acclamations that they are allied to Turkey and possess an indescribable degree of attachment to the Turks with strong ties. As far as I understood, as a result of a general revival of Islam, they came to the conclusion that any war taking place against Turkey will bring a greater degree of attention to them. Some of these ovations out of this position made the communists concerned. For some reason, I think that the Russian communist executive committee which considers Turkey as aspiring to communist rule, did neither understand that this Muslim union is a force nor that this force cannot be obtained by communism.[75]

Although in the literature there is strong tendency to associate Enver Pasha with Pan-Turkism from his Caucasus campaign in the First World War to his post-war exile adventures leading to his death in Central Asia in 1922, his private correspondence and public statements feature rather stronger senti-ments for the cause of Islam and Muslims in a global anticolonial struggle. In a private letter, after returning from the Baku Congress, he wrote: 'Let's see,

74 Zinoviev, *Die Weltrevolution und die III. Kommunistische Internationale,* quoted from the English translation in Lewis and Lih, *Martov and Zinoviev,* p 140.
75 Enver Pasha, letter to Mustafa Kemal Pasha, late September 1920, ATASE, İSH-10, sıra no. 5774, kutu no. 570, gömlek no. 51.

what Allah will bring upon us. Is there hope for the future? The World War did not end yet. No matter what happens, I am sure it will end with the redemption of Islam.'[76] In an internal note on the results of the Baku Congress, Enver Pasha made clear: 'Since we have the opinion that in the Islamic world only by operating as Muslims we can mobilize them against our enemies and only then they can move towards progress, no other ways of operation need to be considered.'[77] One year later, at the third conference of the Communist International, Enver Pasha – still a 'special guest' of the Comintern – opened and finished his speech with references to the global struggle of Muslims:

It is now almost a year since the Baku Congress of the Eastern Nations. With great pleasure, we observe the struggle towards freedom of a people of five hundred millions of Muslims making the four-fifth of the people from the Atlantic Ocean over Nord Africa reaching into the Great Chinese Ocean who are thirsty for freedom.

Those independence struggles in Morocco, Algeria, Tunisia, Tripoli, Egypt, Albania, Yemen, Syria, Iraq, Iran, and India which has joined the Union of Islamic Revolutionary Societies and the results achieved so far are rapidly encouraging our hopes. [...]

Like we said last year, the war between the imperialists which started in 1914 still continues. These monsters whose rapacity cannot be satisfied will long quarrel over the body of oppressed nations they knocked down.

Let us continue to prepare for the world revolution so that when the time is ripe let us all free ourselves by working together as hand in glove. Time is working for our benefit. Let us not sleep, but move with courage. Definitely, the last triumph will be ours. Because we are the oppressed, we are the rightful.[78]

Zinoviev had declared in his opening speech of the Baku Congress that '[t] he enormous significance of the revolution that is beginning in the East does

76 Enver Pasha, letter to Kazım (Özalp), 23 September 1920, ATASE, İSH-10, sıra no. 5826, kutu no. 570, gömlek no. 57.
77 Enver Pasha, Remarks on the Baku Congress and the Domestic Situations of Russia, [September or October 1920], TTK, EP, 7–6, in Yamauchi, *The Green Crescent under the Red Star*, pp 321–22.
78 Enver Pasha's speech at the Third Conference of the Communist International, 2 June -12 July 1921, Moscow, published in *Liwa-el-Islam* 1, No 11–12 (1921), pp 113, 118–120.

not consist in requesting the British imperialist gentlemen to take their feet off the table, only to then permit the Turkish rich to stretch their feet comfortably on the table.'[79] Soon Zinoviev would discover that even as a fallen hero and fugitive war-criminal, Enver Pasha was still too strong to be left alone in Baku.[80] At the end of the Baku Congress, as Zinoviev returned to Moscow, he took Enver Pasha with him in the armoured train of the Communist International.[81] As disappointed as Zinoviev might possibly have been, Enver Pasha wrote to Kazım Karabekir: 'I arrived to Moscow from Baku. Anyway, I am greatly satisfied with the result of the conference.'[82]

The Comintern leaders practically did not really know how to deal with the situation in Baku: an uneducated crowd largely uninterested about class-struggle and Internationalist ceremonies, a dangerous but alluring rise of anti-colonial Muslim nationalism, and the celebration of dubious men like Enver. Although the Baku Congress was directed against the rest of the world as an asset to Soviet foreign policy, the large participation of Russian Muslim delegates and the impact of Enver Pasha on Russian Muslims coupled the Baku Congress unintendedly with the Soviet internal affairs in the Caucasus and Central Asia. At the Baku Congress, one of its most prominent delegates, the leader of the nonparty fraction Narbutabekov from Tashkent, for instance, harshly criticised 'the local authorities, whose policy is alienating the working masses from the Soviet government.' He called upon the communist leaders to pull back their 'colonizers who are now working behind the mask of communism!' He even did not hesitate to say that only when 'that is done, I am sure, not a single Muslim will venture to raise his hand against Soviet power.'[83] But the Soviets soon began an anti-Islamic campaign in Central Asia.[84] The representative of the Ankara Government İbrahim Tali was also fully aware of

---

79 Riddell, *To See the Dawn*, p 74.

80 Yamauchi argues that Enver Pasha was in touch with leading Muslim delegates, and the Bolshevik feared a possible coup d'état against themselves. Yamauchi, *The Green Crescent under the Red Star*, pp 33–34.

81 Aydemir, *Suyu Arayan Adam*, p 194; *The Times*, 'Pilaff and Palaver'.

82 Enver Pasha, letter to Kazım Karabekir, October 1920, ATASE, ATAZB, sıra no. 4262, kutu no. 38, gömlek no. 13.

83 Riddell, *To See the Dawn*, pp 116–23. Okay especially emphasises Narbutabekov's speech. Okay, *Enver Pascha, der große Freund Deutschlands*, pp 317–20.

84 For more details on the anti-Islamic campaign in Soviet Central Asia see: Shoshana Keller, *To Moscow, Not Mecca: The Soviet Campaign against Islam in Central Asia, 1917 – 1941* (Praeger, Westport: 2001).

the inconsistencies in the Bolshevik schemes in his report on the Baku congress: 'My mind doesn't grasp the Bolsheviks' depiction and perspective of a world federation. What I heard from Khiva and Turkestan and what I saw in Azerbaijan has opened my eyes to this mentality.'[85]

At the end, in May 1922 as the jihad cries were slowly fading away and the Muslim world was getting finally parcelled by the British, French, and Soviet colonisers and only few successful local struggles in Turkey, Iran, Saudi Arabia, and Afghanistan could stand their ground, one British observer rightly concluded that

> the fundamental cause of unrest in Eastern Countries is an intense nationalism, which may be briefly described as the attempt on the various Eastern peoples to emancipate themselves from any form of control by Europeans. Consequently it is not surprising to find an anti-European fanaticism prevalent throughout the East. [...] Pan-Islamic intrigue is more apparent in local fanaticism than in any world-wide combination [...] [but it] does provide an added and dangerous element in Eastern unrest [...].[86]

---

85 İbrahim Tali, report on the Baku Congress, 1 October, 1920, ATASE, İSH-10, sıra no. 5822, kutu no. 570, gömlek no. 53.

86 Inter-Departmental Committee on Eastern Unrest, Interim report, 24 May 1922, FO.371.7790, quoted in Ferris, 'The British Empire vs. The Hidden Hand', pp 343–44.

17

A point of order: [illegible] in the First Legislative Council of Transjordan

Harrison [illegible]

At all times during the [illegible] between [illegible] ly controlled the [illegible] over [illegible] Jordanian government [illegible] The creation of the [illegible] Abdullah's monarch[illegible] however, the [illegible] the population [illegible] played out in Transjordan [illegible]

The history of the Leg[illegible] nation between [illegible] Legislative Council [illegible] chants, and landowners [illegible] interact with the [illegible] mandate and the British [illegible] ment. The level of [illegible] ary, one group [illegible] Transjordan [illegible] These political [illegible]

17

A point of order: a battle for autonomy in the First Legislative Council of Transjordan

Harrison Guthorn

At all times during the Transjordan Mandate, the power of the state was divided between its monarch and its colonial overseers. These two poles of authority controlled the development of Transjordan's institutions and jockeyed for control over its future. These competing forces shaped the development of Jordanian governance and the enduring legacy of the Anglo-Hashemite state. The creation of the Hashemite Kingdom of Jordan was the synthesis of Amir Abdullah's monarchical machinations tempered by British colonial oversight. However, the Transjordan state could only be successful if it involved the local elite population as well. The ensuing competition for influence and control played out in Transjordan's first political arena, the Legislative Council.

The history of the Legislative Council, created in 1929, is the story of negotiation between the central government and the elites of Transjordan. The Legislative Council gathered leading elites (urban notables, tribal sheikhs, merchants, and landowners) from throughout Transjordan and made them directly interact with the Anglo-Hashemite state (as represented by the Executive Committee and the British Resident). Sectarian differences did not define these men. The levels of power and political intrigue in the Council transcended any one group or region. The Legislative Council forced the traditional elites of Transjordan to respond to the realities of the new centralising state in Amman. These political jousts reinforced Amman's centrality as the home of politics and governmental might in Transjordan. This artificially manufactured Emirate survived because it incorporated local elites into the Anglo-Hashemite state to bolster its authority while simultaneously trumpeting the importance of its Sherifian Amir, Abdullah Ibn Husayn.

This chapter will explore the battle over the 1928 Anglo-Transjordan Agreement's ratification in the Legislative Council. The opening of political space necessitated by the League of Nations Mandates Charter forced the Anglo-Hashemite government to accommodate the dissident elites of Transjordan, at least temporarily. The 1928 Agreement ratification battle transformed Amman into both the home of legislative authority and political opposition in Transjordan. The nascent Transjordanian state needed to incorporate the elites of Transjordan into the government if it hoped to survive. These exchanges in the Legislative Council incorporated formerly autonomous tribal sheikhs and urban notables into the machinery of the state. In Transjordan, the British adopted a similar model of elite manipulation as they had earlier enacted in neighboring Hashemite Iraq. Both states had early defining moments in which the local, previously autonomous, established elites attempted to delineate and protect their spheres of influence and privileges.[1] Although the efforts of the Council representatives to safeguard their autonomy and institutional control were eventually defeated, these proceedings marked a clear battle over power and control in the new Hashemite state.

From its inception, the Mandate of Transjordan, and its capital Amman, held conflicting levels of importance for the British. Transjordan was the least important of the British imperial holdings in the Middle East. At the same time, despite its lack of natural resources or historical pedigree, Transjordan and Amman were vital for British imperial interests in the region. Britain needed to control Transjordan in order to protect its interests in neighboring Palestine and Iraq. The British approached the maintenance of regional security through the development of the Transjordan state. Initially, the British allowed Amir Abdullah a relatively free hand in Transjordan. However, after a series of revolts and budgetary mishaps between 1921 and 1924, the British issued an ultimatum to Abdullah – either submit to tighter British colonial control, or,

---

1 For more on the development of Iraq's representative assembly see Toby Dodge, 'International Obligation, Domestic Pressure and Colonial Nationalism; The Birth of the Iraqi State Under the Mandate System', in Nadine Méouchy and Peter Sluglett (eds), *The British and French Mandates in Comparative Perspectives* (Brill, Boston: 2004) pp 143–164; Charles Tripp, *A History of Iraq* (Cambridge University Press, New York: 2000) pp 36–53.

be ousted as the Amir of Transjordan.[2] Thereafter, Amir Abdullah submitted to more pervasive colonial administration under British Resident Henry Cox.[3] In an effort to reinforce the validity and legality of British colonial control in Transjordan, the British created the 1928 Anglo-Transjordanian Agreement.

The 1928 Anglo-Transjordanian Agreement was unmistakably a document that originated from the British with minimal, if any, Transjordanian input. It is clear from the reaction and reception the terms of the agreement received that the inhabitants disliked it. However, Amir Abdullah staunchly argued for the treaty's ratification in Transjordan. High Commissioner Field Marshal Herbert Plumer noted that Amir Abdullah was 'prepared to accept [the treaty] and indeed anxious to bring it into force' as of March 1926.[4] The British intended the Agreement to normalise their position within Transjordan and to create the legal precedent for a permanent state. In an effort to satisfy the spirt of the League of Nations Mandate, Britain stipulated that the local population must acquiesce in the Mandate terms in the form of a treaty. The ratification of the 1928 Agreement by an elected constituent assembly would symbolise the acceptance of the local population of the mandatory arrangement.[5] However, stipulating the need for local approval of the Agreement opened a political space in Transjordan in which an open and vocal opposition could exist.[6]

---

2 Two notable revolts took place in the early years of the Mandate, the Kura Revolts from 1921–1922 and the Adwan Rebellion in 1923. For more on these revolts see Yoav Alon, *The Making of Jordan: Tribes, Colonialism and the Modern State* (I.B. Tauris, New York: 2007) pp 43–60.

3 For more on the early period of the Transjordan Mandate see Mary C. Wilson, *King Abdullah, Britain, and the Making of Jordan* (Cambridge University Press, New York: 1987) pp 60–90; Philip Robins, *A History of Jordan* (Cambridge University Press, New York: 2004) pp 29–31. Text of the ultimatum found in Clayton to Abdullah, August 14, 1924, FO 371/10102, The National Archives, Kew, London (hereafter, TNA).

4 LOC, Secret Report on the Middle East No. 9, *Transjordan Constitutional Arrangements: Draft Agreement and Draft Organic Law 1926–1927*, High Commissioner (HC) to Secretary of State (SoS), 22 April 1926.

5 The British employed bilateral treaties in both Iraq and Transjordan to reinforce the validity and legitimacy of British Mandatory rule.

6 My conception of political space is the allocation of room in which discrete political actors may jockey for political control, authority, and sovereignty. This understanding of political competition is similar to Sami Zubaida's 'political field' in which various actors compete over resources and influence operating in the fields of nationalism, nationality, popular sovereignty, library, legality, representation, and parliamentary instutions. According to Zubaida, an entire opposition may be forced under ground by the monopolization of the 'political field' by the

The British did not need to enter into an additional agreement to solidify their position as the mandatory power. Instead of ruling purely through force of will, the Anglo-Transjordanian Agreement gave Britain the cloak of local acceptance and participation. The Agreement was a public relations gambit on an international stage.

The Executive Committee (also referred to as the Cabinet) saw a draft of the agreement in June of 1927.[7] The Executive Committee members rebuffed the Agreement from the onset, but the Amir preferred to push forward despite the advice of the Chief Secretary 'Aref al-'Aref.[8] The Amir contended that it would be easier to amend the treaty once it had passed rather than contest its ratification.[9] The open discussion and debate presented by 'Aref in his diary challenges the position of previous historians, such as Naseer H. Aruri and Madi and Musa, that the Cabinet blindly accepted the treaty at face value.[10] Although the Amir and his Executive Committee eventually approved the treaty, these discussions demonstrate that the individuals involved were very much aware of both the benefits and the potential costs that the treaty presented. These were not the actions of people who were politically unaware or naïve. Plenipotentiaries signed the Agreement in Jerusalem on February 20, 1928 and published it on 26 March 1928.

The public reaction to the treaty was swift, vocal, and negative. The

---

dominant government. It is unclear at the onset of the Legislative Council deliberations what the political order was, and over time, the representatives do actively attempt to change the political role attributed to them by the 1928 Agreement. Sami Zubaida, *Islam, the People and the State*, 3rd ed. (I.B. Tauris, London: 2009) pp 145–162.

7 The Executive Committee or council was Abdullah's cabinet, which had a number of different names throughout the Mandate Period.

8 According to *'Aref el-'Aref: A biographical sketch 1892–1964* (Al Ma'aref Press, Jerusalem: no publishing date), 'Aref el-'Aref was born in Jerusalem in 1892. 'Aref, a vocal opponent to British actions in both Palestine and Transjordan, would remain an active political entity throughout most of his life. After his tenure as Chief Secretary of Transjordan from 1926 to 1929, he worked in the Palestine civil service. He was appointed mayor of Jerusalem by Abdullah in 1950. He was elected to the same mayoral post in 1951 and re-elected in 1955.

9 Middle East Centre Archive St Antony's, Oxford , England (hereafter MECA), *'Aref el-'Aref Diary Amman 1926–1929*, 1 June 1927.

10 Naseer H. Aruri, *Jordan: A Study in Political Development (1921–1965)* (Martinus Nijhoff, Netherlands: 1972) pp 37, 74–78, and Munib Madi and Sulayman Musa, *Tarikh al-Urdun Fi al-Qarn al-'Ishrin* (History of Jordan in the Twentieth Century 1900–1959) (al-Matba'a al-Wataniyya, Amman: 1959) p 279.

general rejection of the agreement surprised the British. British Resident Henry Cox reported that the agreement was 'met with a considerable amount of adverse criticism and in the Northern district [where] some demonstrations were held.'[11] By April, there were widespread protests against the treaty. A telegraph sent from northern tribal elders to the Amir proclaimed that they 'strongly protest against the treaty and [we] inform you that the nation does not accept absolute treaties that are used as instruments of slavery.'[12] The animosity that the treaty met shocked Amir Abdullah. He resented the opposition to the treaty as a personal attack against himself, and his legitimacy. Early on, the Amir brought 'the prominent amongst the agitators and other influential persons' to Amman to discuss the treaty's terms in person. These meetings generally dispelled fears that article ten, which dealt with Great Britain's ability to raise and maintain a force in Transjordan, might mean conscription.[13]

In the face of this opposition, 'Aref tried to counsel Abdullah that now was the time to seek amendment of the treaty to appease the populace. 'Aref argued with the Amir that the treaty was, 'one sided, [with] all obligations on Jordan, all restrictions on her independence.'[14] The Chief Minister, Hassan Pasha Khalid Abu al-Huda, argued that this was not possible because the Amir 'is the one who insisted on the treaty to the British.'[15] Hassan Pasha bluntly stated that the Amir was arrogant and never consulted with any of his men if seeking a treaty was in the best interests of the state. The Chief Minister admitted that he had no power to negotiate the terms of the treaty in Jerusalem. His only function was to represent the Amir in his signature. The 1928 Agreement would legally install him and his family as the rulers of the Emirate and reinforce their place in the country. Similar to his brother Faysal in Iraq, Abdullah knew the limitations of his office and his need to reinforce it if he was to survive in Transjordan. Both Hashemites depended on British power to become sovereign over states in which they had no inherent sovereignty.[16]

---

11 BR Cox to HC JR Chancellor, 'Report on the Situation in TJ for period 1/1/28–31/3/28', CO 831/1/2, (TNA).

12 'Aref el-'Aref Diary, 9 April 1928.

13 British Resident (BR) Cox to HC Chancellor, 'Report on Situation in TJ for Period 1/1/1928 – 31/3/1928', CO 831/1/2, (TNA).

14 MECA, 'Aref el-'Aref Diary Amman 1926–1929, 20–21 February 1928.

15 'Aref el-'Aref Diary, 9 April 1928.

16 Tripp, A History of Iraq, pp 49–50.

The 1928 Agreement called for the creation of a representative body to satisfy the developmental aspects of the Mandate itself.[17] The British hoped that this new legislative body would create a class of clients who depended upon the British for their position.[18] The first order of business of the Legislative Council, once convened, would be to ratify the 1928 Agreement. The 1928 Electoral Law started the process of Agreement's ratification. In essence, the first thing the representatives would have to do would be to affirm the terms of their involvement in the Hashemite regime. The new law dictated how the elections for the new assembly would take place. The law called for indirect elections where primary electors selected a secondary elector, who in turn, would vote for the fourteen actual members of the assembly.[19] The elections selected a set number of representatives from each of the three major regions of Transjordan: Ajlun (4), Balqa (6), and Karak (4). These elections were for the settled population of Transjordan only.[20] For the Bedouin representatives, the Amir selected two ten-member committees of sheikhs who would in turn selected a Northern and Southern Bedouin representative for the Legislative Council.[21] This system acknowledged the prevailing tribal system throughout Transjordan and the logistical difficulties in having Bedouin participate in a normal election.[22]

Generally, electoral competition in Transjordan focused on the 'nationality' of the prospective representatives and the degree to which the nominees opposed the British. The Transjordanian population was mainly Sunni Muslim with small minority enclaves of Arab Christians and Circassians making up less than 11% of the total population. The demographic allocations for the

17 "The Covenant of the League of Nations" Article 22 and "The Palestine Mandate" London, 24 July 24 1922. http://avalon.law.yale.edu/20th_century/palmanda.asp#art22 (last accessed 10 January 2015).
18 Peter Sluglett, 'The Mandates: Some Reflections on the Nature of the British Presence in Iraq (1914–1932) and the French Presence in Syria (1918–1946)' in Nadine Méouchy and Peter Sluglett (eds), The British and French Mandates in Comparative Perspectives (Brill, Boston: 2004) p 120.
19 Tripp, A History of Iraq, p 58.
20 Ma'an Abu Nowar, The History of the Hashemite Kingdom of Jordan Volume 1: The Creation and Development of Transjordan; 1920–1929 (Ithaca Press, Oxford: 1989) pp 232–233.
21 The Mandatory government arbitrarily divided the tribes of Transjordan into a Northern and Southern group for the purpose of the Legislative Council elections.
22 Alon, The Making of Jordan, pp 70–71.

Legislative Council did not match the population distribution of Transjordan. Roughly speaking about half of the population of Transjordan lived in 'Ajlun, thirty percent in Balqa, and the remaining twenty percent in Karak and Ma'an.[23] The electoral law allocated nine Muslim Arab seats, three Christian Arab seats and two Circassian seats. This allocation drastically increased the representation of both the Christian and Circassian community on the Council. It is likely that these representative figures were assigned by the British to stack the Legislative Council with more pro-government members. Both the Circassians and the Christians had been Ottoman supporters and both groups understood the necessity of a centralised state. The Circassian population, in particular, remained closely associated with the Hashemite Monarchy with Abdullah's personal guard being composed solely of Circassians. Despite the over-representation of Christians and Circassians on the Council, there were no sectarian issues whatsoever during the Mandate period. Unlike neighbouring Iraq, Palestine, Syria, and Lebanon, Transjordan's opposition was solely focused against the scope of British control during the Mandate. Confessional seats existed throughout the Mandate and apparently never raised any ire among its populace.

Regardless of the Council's composition, the elections were set to occur without the prospective representatives knowing the actual powers of the Legislative Council itself. Beyond being an elected representative body, the degree of autonomy and influence the representatives would have was unclear. As a result, the potential representatives were running for newly created, ill-defined positions of power in the new state. This level of ambiguity worked to the advantage of the Amir and the British because it gave them greater flexibility in dictating the function of the Council.

The publication of the new election law on 15 August 1928, spurred the growing resistance to the 1928 Agreement. The clearest illustration of the popular rejection of the 1928 Agreement was the formation of the National Congress. The main opposition party, Hizb al-Sha'b (The People's Party),

---

23 A. Konikoff, *Transjordan: An Economic Survey* (Economic Research Institute of the Jewish Agency of Palestine, Jerusalem: 1946) p 19. There were no censuses taken during the Mandate period so all of the above demographic figures are estimates taken from voter registration during the Ottoman period and food ration cards during World War II. The total population of Transjordan in 1944 was approximately 340,000 with 300,000 Arab Muslims, 30,000 Arab Christian and 10,000 Circassians.

organised a convention to oppose the 1928 Agreement.[24] The National Congress, composed of roughly 150 'notables, sheikhs and intellectuals' convened for the first time on 25 July 1928 in Amman at Hamdan coffee house.[25] The coffee house was located in the heart of downtown Amman (al-balad) adjacent to the central square, Faysal Square. This downtown corridor, which included Amman's major mosque, Husseini Mosque, was the nexus of exchange in the young capital city. By 1928, Faysal Square had become the political and cultural heart of the state. The location of the opposition's congress demonstrates the open and free nature of the opposition. It would have been impossible to select a more public and prominent location to hold a political meeting in Transjordan in 1928. These meetings are indicative of a strong open opposition, not a cowed assemblage of elite puppets.

The National Congress, which elected Hussein al-Tarawnah, a notable from Karak as its president, questioned the terms of the 1928 Agreement and the Organic Law in reference to how Transjordan should be ruled.[26] The National Congress sent a letter composed by Tarawnah, to Amir Abdullah and British Resident Cox arguing against the scope of power that the Amir and the Executive Committee were afforded by the Agreement. The Congress believed it was unjust and contrary to the purpose of the Legislative Council to allow cabinet members to sit on the Council as ex-officio members. To do so would be in violation to the basic law of 1923. The Legislative Council must have primacy over the appointed Executive Committee, not vice versa.[27]

British Resident Cox's reply was inadequate in the eyes of the National Congress. Cox reasserted that Transjordan was under the domain of His Majesty's Government but went no further in addressing the actual terms of the 1928 Agreement or the Organic Law. Undeterred, the National Congress published the National Pact at their next meeting on 11 March 1929, and sent it, along with petitions from notables in Karak and Ajlun, to the League of

24 Joseph A. Massad, Colonial Effects: The Making of National Identity in Jordan (Columbia University Press, New York: 2001) p 30.

25 Munib Madi and Sulayman Musa, Tarikh al Urdun Fi al-Qarn al- 'Ishrin [History of Jordan in the Twentieth Century 1900–1959] (al-Matba'a al-Wataniyya, Amman: 1959) p 289. For English translation see: Kamel Abu Jaber, 'The Legislature of the Hashemite Kingdom of Jordan: A Study in Political Development', in The Muslim World 59, Nos 3–4 (July 1969) p 224.

26 Tarawaneh would act as president for the entire duration of the National Congress' existence (1928–1933).

27 'Aref el-'Aref Diary, 23 August 1928.

Nations Permanent Mandates Commission. The National Pact's language was much stronger than initial attempts to appeal to Amir Abdullah and British Resident Cox. The National Pact called on the League of Nations to recognise Transjordan's right to self-determination. In an eleven-point doctrine, it stated the need for the establishment of a constitutional monarchy under the Amir. It also argued that that the electoral process should be changed, and that the indirect electoral system of the 1928 Electoral Law should be replaced with direct elections and representation determined by population demographics. Finally, it demanded complete independence for Transjordan from Great Britain.[28] The League of Nations in their official response to the petitions stated that 'the commission was of [the] opinion that the complaints submitted by the petitioners were not of such a nature as to call for any action' because few of the petitioners were 'men of standing.'[29]

Despite the petitions and protests, the Legislative Council election proceeded on schedule but in the face of 'strong opposition.' The opposition was a reaction from 'a considerable body of opinion [which] was not satisfied with the form of government proposed and desired that the government should be fully responsible to the electorate.'[30] While it is unclear from the British records the exact scope of the election boycott that took place, the boycott was strong enough to prevent elections in the province of Ma'an. In response, Karak and Ma'an, with their combined population of roughly 60,000 people, were counted as a single region for this election. This southern opposition was a subtle nod to Ottoman continuity. During the late 19th century, the Ottoman Empire had reasserted its control over the 'Ajlun and most of the Balqa. However, Ottoman authority never travelled further south than Salt. Karak and Ma'an had no legacy of centralised state control.[31] Much of the opposition to the 1928 Agreement and centralised state authority came from these southern provinces. It is clear that the British anticipated opposition from the southern portion of Transjordan because of the reduced number of

---

28 Betty S. Anderson, *Nationalist Voices in Jordan: The Street and the State* (University of Texas Press, Austin, TX: 2005) p 51.

29 'League of Nations Mandates Commission to Secretary of State for the Colonies Lewis Vernon Harcourt' 28 September 1929, FO 371/13748, (TNA).

30 BR Cox to HC JR Chancellor, 'Report on the Administration of Transjordan for the year 1929', 6 February 1930, CO 831/8/5, (TNA).

31 For more on Ottoman Transjordan see Eugene Rogan, *Frontiers of the State in the Late Ottoman Empire: Transjordan 1850–1921* (Cambridge University Press, New York: 1999).

southern seats, four, opposed to 'Ajlun or Balqa's combined ten seats. Despite the omission of Ma'an, the British maintained in November 1929 when asked by the League of Nations Mandates Commission about the election that the boycotts had not affected the validity or legality of the election results.[32]

Regardless of the scope of the boycott, five signers of the National Pact were elected to the Legislative Council. The election of Shaikh Hamd Ibn Jazi (Premier Sheikh of Huwaitat and Southern Bedouin representative), Sheikh Mithqal al-Fayiz (Premier Sheikh of Bani Sakhr and Northern Bedouin representative), 'Atallah al-Suhaimat (notable of Karak), Sa'id al-Mufti (Circassian notable from Amman), and Shams al-Din Sami (Circassian notable from Balqa) demonstrated a level of disorganisation amongst the opposition. It is curious that some members of the opposition ran for council seats while its leader, Hussein al-Tarawnah, was not elected. These mixed election results are also indicative of a weak sense of political solidarity. The members of the opposition agreed on the need to limit the powers of the British and the Amir in Transjordan but it is doubtful that they agreed on much else. Personal interest and the protection of regional prestige remained the guiding influence for the elected Legislative Council representatives. Beyond the five signers of the National Pact, the remaining representatives did not belong to any political organisations. Fourteen out of the sixteen members were sheikhs or notables supported by large tribes or tribal federations. The new representatives were not political neophytes.[33] They all were involved in local politics, many had held government positions, and the ex-officio cabinet members of the council would not easily sway them. In no way was it clear at the time of the election that the members of the Legislative Council would be subservient to the British or the Amir.

The first extraordinary session of the First Legislative Council opened without incident on 2 April 1929. The Council was comprised of nine Muslim Arabs, three Christian Arabs, two Circassians, and two Bedouin sheikhs. Six ex-officio members of the Executive Committee joined the sixteen elected representatives.[34] This newly formed body was comprised of the 'important

---

32 British response to petition (Monteagle) to League of Nations, 29 November 1929, FO 371/13748, (TNA).

33 Ma'an Abu Nowar, *The History of the Hashemite Kingdom of Jordan Volume 1: The Creation and Development of Transjordan; 1920–1929* (Ithaca Press, Oxford: 1989) pp 232–234.

34 BR Cox to HC JR Chancellor, 6 February 1930, BNA, CO 831/8/5, (TNA).

notables of Jordan' but was not yet a 'powerless body' as Kamel Abu Jaber asserts.[35] The Legislative Council would have its authority and influence neutered over time but that eventuality was far from a foregone conclusion at the beginning. The government needed the Council to ratify the Agreement and could not be aggressive with the Council's members at the onset. An atmosphere of apprehension and competition almost immediately set in between the elected representatives and the ex-officio Executive Committee members.[36] From the start, members were jockeying for position and influence in the Council. It is exactly this anxiety that informed the proceedings of the First Legislative Council. These newly minted Transjordanian elites had to work out exactly what their new positions would afford them and how their new elected office would affect their formerly autonomous positions in their home districts. The Legislative Council did not have clearly defined powers at the onset of the Council's proceedings. The ambiguity of the powers and responsibilities of the Council temporarily increased its authority and influence.

The first order of business was the drafting the Internal Regulations of the Council to define the powers of the Legislative Council. These regulations were to define the parliamentary procedures of the council and the exact scope of the powers and the limitations of the Council. The passage of articles 19, 24, 25, and 26, dealing with if the Council could draft laws, became the first contest in the Council for power and authority. According to article 19 of the proposed Internal Legislative Council Regulations, only the Chief Minister or the head of a department could introduce legislation because they were 'competent' and 'experts.'[37] In the sixth session, representative Shams al-Din Sami (Circassian from the Balqa and member of the National Congress) suggested the revision of this provision so that members of the Council could introduce legislation. Representative Najib Abu Sha'r (Christian representative from Husn in Ajlun) asserted, 'We are not minors and we are eager to work for independence.'[38] At stake for Abu Sha'r and Shams al-Din was their ability to institute real change though the Council. Without the ability to introduce bills, the Council would be subject to the whims of British and the Amir. Eventually,

---

35 Abu Jaber, 'The Legislature of the Hashemite Kingdom of Jordan', p 223.

36 'Report on the administration of TJ for the year 1929', 6 February 1930, CO 831/8/5, (TNA).

37 The Organic Law was the partner document of the 1928 Agreement. It presented the legal regulations of Transjordan and functioned as its first constitution.

38 Jordan Parliamentary Library, Amman Jordan (JPL), Legislative Council Minutes, 6th session 17 April 1929.

due to the absences of a number of pro-Amir members, the opposition was able to pass the revised versions of articles 24, 25 and 26.[39]

This opposition victory was short lived when the Amir's *Iradah* (executive order) rejected the revised versions of articles 24, 25, and 26 because they were in opposition to article 37 of the Organic Law. Despite the efforts of the opposition, the Legislative Council passed the original versions of articles 24, 25, and 26 during the tenth session on 25 April. In the end, the internal regulations specified that only heads of departments might introduce laws.[40] The Internal Regulations had an enormous impact on the powers afforded to the representatives of the Council. For example, the members of the Transjordanian Legislative Council held far less sway than their Iraqi counterparts. In Iraq, 'any deputy could propose legislation, provided he had the support of ten others.'[41] The Iraqi constituent assembly was far from all-powerful, but their ability to introduce their own legislation gave them a far higher degree of autonomy than their Transjordanian brethren.[42] In contrast, the Transjordanian representatives could only vote up or down on legislation. The government now controlled the terms of the engagement; all the Council could do was react. The representatives had lost the ability to shape the trajectory of Transjordan independently. These abridged responsibilities represent the first true curtailment of the influence of the elites who sat on the Council. The shift away from autonomous tribal elites had begun. The political space in which the Legislative Council existed and operated had begun to close. The limitations set forth in the Internal Regulations handicapped the abilities of this elected body throughout the history of the Mandate.

After the conclusion of this opening bout, the real fight over the ratification of the 1928 Anglo-Transjordanian Agreement could begin. The Legislative Council became a battleground. The terms of the 1928 Agreement and the nature of Transjordan's future relationship with the British hung in the balance. Beyond the five signers of the National Pact, the majority of the remaining eleven unaffiliated representatives also vocally opposed the language of the

---

39 The president, al Majali, al fayiz, ibn Jazi, and Adib Wahbah were absent from the council session which proceeded with only 14 total members.

40 JPL, Legislative Council Minutes, 10th session, 25 April 25 1929.

41 Tripp, *A History of Iraq*, p 58.

42 *Miscellaneous No. 9 (1928) League of Nations Fifty-First and Fifty-Second Sessions of the Council: Reported by the Right Hon. Lord Cushendun*, August 30 to September 8, 1928, Library of Congress, Washington DC (LOC), pp 5–7.

1928 Agreement.[43] The major source of opposition to the treaty resulted from the British creation of the 1928 Anglo-Transjordanian Agreement without Transjordanian input. The demands and related rhetorical flourishes of the members differed widely, but they were united in their opposition to a treaty that was foreign to them. Only one representative of the Legislative Council advocated for the ratification of the 1928 Agreement in tandem with the ex-officio members of the cabinet: 'Audah al-Qusus.

Representatives used a number of tactics to attack the British and the Agreement but all of the opposition boils down to one point of contention: just because the British drafted the Agreement without Transjordanians did not mean the Transjordanians had to accept it. Najib Abu Sha'r argued 'this agreement is not a verse from heaven and difficult to amend. There is no justification for obliging us to ratify it, simply because it was signed.' In these comments Najib Abu Sha'r never questioned the good intentions of the British. Instead, he reinforced his understanding of their benevolent nature by asking the question 'What is the meaning of Mandate except to train for self-government not colonialism or slavery? We are not asking for anything contrary to the main British interest and its international obligations in our country?' These comments further reinforced that the members of the Legislative Council were well versed in political and diplomatic negotiations. Najib Abu Sha'r knew what principles and ideals the British lauded and only asked that they be consistent in their treatment of Transjordan.[44]

Despite their reservations, most members of the Council understood the need for some form of treaty. Mohammed Bey al-Unsi (Muslim from the Balqa and former chief of the Royal Diwan) and 'Ala' al-Din Tuqan (Muslim from Salt in the Balqa) acknowledged that the future of the nation depended on the ratification of a treaty to give the country legality. However, such a treaty would only be acceptable if three conditions were satisfied: the ability to send ambassadors and consuls to other countries, the ability to raise an army and declare war, and the right to negotiate and conclude treaties independently. They cited articles ten and eleven and argued, 'That the army is the true appearance of independence' and the only way to protect the dignity of the nation. Al-Unsi was adamant that this was a reasonable request. If these three limitations were left unresolved, it amounted to a near complete loss of sovereignty to the British. Furthermore, the representatives saw these stipulations

---

43 The five signers of the National Pact were Shams al-Din Sami, Sa'id al-Mufti, 'Atallah al-Suhaimat, Shaikh Mithqal Ibn Fayiz and Shaikh Hamd Ibn Jazi.
44 JPL, Legislative Council Minutes, 14th session, 11 May 1929.

as particularly egregious because they were not applied to Palestine, Iraq, or Syria. However, despite these limitations, neither al-Unsi nor Tuqan advocated for the outright rejection of the treaty.

Only Shams al-Din Sami rejected the idea that Transjordan needed the agreement at all. 'The acceptance of this agreement won't change any current position of us. Of course, it is said to us that acceptance of this agreement would render our temporary constitutional government a permanent one, but where is that constitutional government and, what is the meaning of consti-tution if we accepted this agreement that would otherwise dispossess us of the right of life.'[45] Shams al-Din completely dismissed the idea that the Tran-sjordanian government needed the 1928 Agreement to validate, legalise, or perpetuate its existence. He saw the Agreement as nothing more there a litany of abuses against the sovereignty of the Transjordanian people.

'Audah al-Qusus (Christian from Karak) was the only elected member of the Legislative Council who advocated for the 1928 Agreement's ratification. Rep-resentative al-Qusus understood the goal of independence in broader terms. He, like the ex-officio members of the Executive Committee, argued that the Agreement was necessary to establish the Legislative Council as a legal admin-istrative body.[46] 'Either we take in our hands the right of free action in our resources or otherwise surrender to the mandated government to enforce the mandate act literally and then no one of us will be able to raise his head and ask about what is going on.'[47] In essence, al-Qusus reminded the council that Transjordan could not afford the risk inherent in rejecting the 1928 Agreement.

The opposition covered a wide spectrum of opinions from minor changes to its complete rejection. None of the representatives blindly followed a singu-lar ideology. Council members were informed individuals who advocated for themselves pragmatically to ensure the preservation of their rights and author-ity. These men needed to protect their own authority in their patrimonial networks in their home regions. These varied approaches reject the binary competition described by historian Maan Abu Nowar as 'the opposition' against 'the government' which acted out British interests indiscriminately.[48] It

---

45 JPL, Legislative Council Minutes, 16th session, 14 May 1929.

46 The most vocal members of the EC during these deliberations were the Prime Minister Hassan Khalid Abu al-Huda, Chief Justice Ibrahim Hashim and Secretary General Tawfiq Abu al-Huda.

47 JPL, Legislative Council Minutes, 16th session, 14 May 1929.

48 Abu Nowar, The History of Jordan, pp 247–51.

becomes clearer that the competition for lasting influence and power within Transjordan was not only a competition between foreign and national interests, but of diverging local interests of domestic actors. These sessions represent competition amongst Arabs and Circassians, between northern and southern tribesmen, between native Transjordanians and Arab Palestinians. This was no simple rhetorical clash.

Finally, during the eighteenth session of the first Legislative Council things came to a head. Najib al-Shraidah (representative from Madaba) presented a motion signed by fourteen representatives. This proposal demanded that articles 1, 2, 5, 6, 7, 10, 11, 14 and 16 be amended. Every member of the Legislative Council, except for the two Bedouin representatives, signed the motion.[49] In the following session Tawfiq Abu al-Huda (the Secretary General of the Executive Committee and future Prime Minister) read both a letter he had written to British Resident Cox and Cox's reply. In the letter to Cox, Tawfiq Abu al-Huda included a copy of the petition signed by the fourteen representatives and had asked for a date to negotiate the 1928 Agreement's terms. British Resident Cox replied stating that the Legislative Council has had sufficient time to study the Agreement and that it was now necessary for the representatives to 'take their decision without delay.'

After reading British Resident Cox's reply, Tawfiq Abu al-Huda warned the Council that this response was dangerous and that inaction would weaken the Legislative Council. Representative Sa'id al-Mufti (Circassian representative from Amman and member of the National Congress) referred to Cox's veiled threat as if a 'bomb [were] thrown into the council.'[50] The next day opened with the Speaker reading a motion signed by fifteen members, including the five ex-officio members, in which they decided to ratify the 1928 Agreement. Sa'id al-Mufti, Shams al-Din Sami, Najib Abu Sha'r, Bakhit al-Ibrahim (Christian representative from Salt who lived in Amman), Najib al-Shraidah, and Mithqal al-Fayiz did not sign the petition. Although Cox's letter never concretely threatened to dissolve the Legislative Council, the members of the Council understood that to be his message. Rather than risk the stability

---

49 JPL, Legislative Council Minutes, 18th session, 30 May 1929. It is odd that the Bedouin members, both of whom signed the National Pact, did not sign the motion for amendment. Perhaps, since the Amir played a more direct role in the selection of the Bedouin representatives Mithqal al-Fayiz and Hamd ibn Jazi were afraid to vocally and openly oppose the will of Abdullah.

50 JPL, Legislative Council Minutes, 19th session, 1 June 1929.

and the integrity of the Council itself, the representatives decided to pass the Agreement. In essence, they decided to live to fight another day.[51] The Amir formally ratified the Agreement on 29 June 1929, and then closed the first sessions of the First Legislative Council the next day.[52]

The Agreement's ratification did not lead to the immediate dissolution of the opposition. On the contrary, President of the National Congress Hussein al-Tarawnah wrote a personal letter to the League of Nations Permanent Mandates Commission asserting that the 1928 Agreement amounted to 'the nightmare of arbitrary colonization and military occupation of our weak country.'[53] The opposition changed their tactics in response to the Agreement's passage. It became more important to be a part of the government, rather than simply criticise from the outside. The rules of engagement began to change. It appeared better, to work within the system than to challenge it and risk losing their positions of influence and power.

The opposition continued their resistance towards the 1928 Agreement and the new political status quo in Transjordan. The British blamed these 'propagandists' for circulating falsehoods and fomenting unrest. The propagandists included former members of the government including 'a number of notables who had lost their power in proportion as law and order were established.'[54] Even after the completion of the 1928 Agreement ratification, opposition figures struggled to protect a degree of autonomy and authority. These notables had lost power in proportion to the centralisation efforts of the new government in Amman. This push and pull, the competing efforts of consolidation and decentralisation, would define the events of the first Legislative Council. By 1929, Amman had become both the seat of the government and the centre of all political intrigue in Transjordan. Cox described Amman as 'the centre of all politics...There would scarcely be any serious trouble in Transjordan, which was not organised, and ordered from Amman.'[55]

---

51 JPL, Legislative Council Minutes, 20th session, 4 June 1929.

52 BR Cox to HC Chancellor, Transjordan: political reports for second quarter, 1929 (1 April 1929–30 June 1929), FO 864/4, (TNA).

53 Husain al-Tarawaneh to League of Nations Mandates Commission Secretary, 21 June 1929, FO 371/13748, (TNA).

54 The British records do not specifically name any members of the opposition. They simply lump them together as 'troublemakers', 'propagandists' or 'the opposition'.

55 BR Cox to HC JR Chancellor, 'Situation Report' 17 November 1929, CO 831/5/9, (TNA).

The 1928 Agreement ratification battle illustrates the nuanced power dynamics of Transjordan in the late 1920s. The contesting of power and the political intrigue that accompanied it transcended any one group or region. At the onset, there was internal opposition in Abdullah's cabinet where the Amir pushed for the Agreement's acceptance while others, most notably 'Aref al-'Aref, advised caution and reconsideration. The Agreement's publication generated opposition from the National Congress and other regional elites. Numerous opposition figures were elected to the First Legislative Council. However, the proceedings of the Legislative Council show that the political clash was far more than simply 'us' vs. 'them.' It was a competition for power, influence, and authority between the new and old elites of Transjordan. Every member of the Legislative Council attempted to protect his own privileged status in Transjordan. The 1928 Agreement's ratification marked a shift away from tribal hegemony in favor of centralised state control. This contest was particularly acute because of Amman's recent reestablishment and its growing political gravity in Transjordan.

Despite the defeat of the Council in the ratification debate, the opposition parties would continue to hamstring the efforts of the Amir and the British for years to come. The shadow of the opposition was even felt during the formal celebration of the Agreement's ratification on 5 November 1929 when 'some 200 riff raff and children paraded the town with flags and shouts against the Balfour Declaration.'[56] These demonstrations were indicative of the continuing efforts of the opposition, including notables whose authority and influence were being trivialised, to continue fighting. This opposition existed in the political space opened by the British when they stipulated that the representatives must ratify the 1928 Agreement. Throughout the remainder of the Mandate, the Anglo-Hashemite government attempted to close this political space while the opposition struggled to keep it open. This political tug-of-war continued throughout the Mandate, with the Legislative Council giving up more ground with every passing year and every subsequent Council. The lure of prestige, government positions, and financial incentives slowly muted the strength of oppositional voices. It became more important for Transjordanian elites to be a part of the Council than vocally oppose the government. The prize became the Council seats themselves, as opposed to any actual legislative authority exercised by the elected representatives. By the end of the Mandate, the

---

56 BR Cox to HC JR Chancellor, description of opening of Legislative Council, 5 November 1929, CO 831/5/9, (TNA).

political machinery of the centralised Transjordanian state absorbed formerly autonomous elites. Over time, the Hashemite state's shadow engulfed and overtook the halls of the Legislative Council.

18

Drawing the line: Calouste Gulbenkian and the Red Line Agreement of 1928

Jonathan Conlin

Every map has its legend. The map attached to the Red Line Agreement of 31 July 1928 is no exception. The Agreement was signed by an international consortium of oil companies who together owned 95% of the Turkish Petroleum Company (TPC). Bloodied as they were by previous price wars, the TPC shareholders now undertook to work together. Within the line they would prospect and produce solely through their joint-venture, TPC. In March 1914 TPC partners had met at the Foreign Office and agreed that their collaboration would extend, not only over the oil-rich Ottoman provinces of Mosul and Baghdad, but the entire 'Ottoman Empire in Asia'.[1] According to the legend, the parties who met at Ostend that day in 1928 were unable to agree on the borders of this vanished Empire. In 1914 several parts of the empire had recently declared independence or fallen under the control of neighbouring powers – in some cases, both at the same time. All was confusion until the owner of the remaining 5% of TPC, Calouste Gulbenkian, intervened:

---

1 For the origins and early history of Turkish Petroleum Company see Stephen H. Longrigg, *The Origins and Early History of the Iraq Petroleum Company* (Privately Published, London: 1969); Marian Kent, *Oil and Empire: British Policy and Mesopotamian Oil, 1900–1920* (Macmillan, Basingstoke: 1976); Helmut Mejcher, *Imperial Quest for Oil: Iraq, 1910–1928* (Ithica Press, London: 1976); Geoffrey Jones, *The State and the Emergence of the British Oil Industry* (Macmillan, London: 1981).

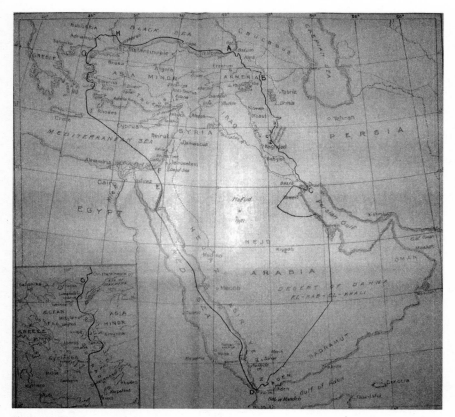

Figure 1: APOC proposal

Source: Total Archives, 812X916–66

When the conference looked like foundering, he again produced one of his brainwaves. He called for a large map of the Middle East, took a thick red pencil and slowly drew a red line round the central area.

'That was the Ottoman Empire which I knew in 1914,' he said. 'And I ought to know. I was born in it, lived in it and served it. If anybody knows better, carry on....'

Gulbenkian's TPC partners inspected the map, and it was good. This account, taken from Ralph Hewins' 1957 biography, continues: 'Gulbenkian had built a framework for Middle East oil development which lasted until 1948:

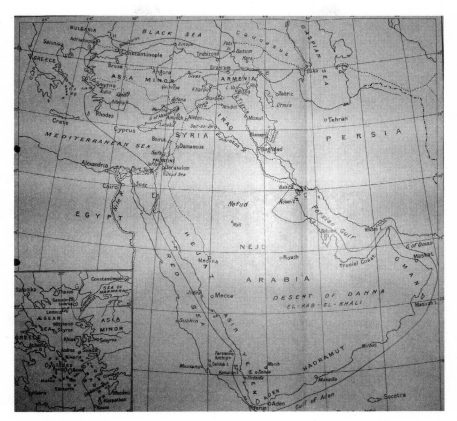

Figure 2: Final version

Source: Total Archives, 812X916–66

another fantastic one-man feat, unsurpassed in international big business.'[2]

A 1927 article in *Political Science Quarterly* referred to Gulbenkian as 'the Talleyrand of oil', and the Red Line legend does indeed smack of nineteenth-century high diplomacy.[3] The 1916 Sykes-Picot agreement had seen woefully

---

2 Ralph Hewins, *Mr Five Per Cent. The Biography of Calouste Gulbenkian* (Hutchinson, London: 1957) p 141.

3 *Political Science Quarterly* 39 (June 1924) p 267. Associates of Gulbenkian including Ramsay Macdonald's PPS regularly addressed him as 'Talleyrand'. Col. Sir. Ronald D. Waterhouse to CSG, 7 July, 1924, LDN00570. Fundação Calouste Gulbenkian, Lisbon (hereafter, FCG).

ill-informed British and French proconsuls carve out 'spheres of influence' using a series of straight lines, lines which paid scant regard to physical or human geography. Perhaps the most notorious example is 'Churchill's Sneeze', the triangular indent in Jordan's southern border that supposedly resulted from the statesman's momentary distraction while drawing the Jordanian-Saudi Arabian border. In Hewins' account Gulbenkian's gesture is more sprezzatura than sneeze, and is accompanied by claims to an expertise the others around the map table lack, expertise born of personal and professional experience. The tone and the narrator's portentiousness, however, lend Gulbenkian a statesman's authority to determine the fate of millions with the stroke of a pen.

If Calouste Gulbenkian is recognised today, it is as the man who drew the Red Line, a milestone in the history of the oil industry and the Middle East. With one exception, Hewins' account has been widely accepted.[4] Although he was not yet known as 'Mr Five Percent', the 1928 agreement embodied Gulbenkian's personal claim to five percent of Middle East oil, a claim which he later vested in a firm, Partex, which continues to this day. The episode encouraged observers to hail Gulbenkian in regal terms, as 'the uncrowned king of the oil trade in much of Europe and the Middle East.'[5] Yet on closer inspection the legend falls apart. Although the map was certainly left until the final phase of the four-year slog which culminated at Ostend, Calouste had little input in the map and did not even bother to attend meetings himself. The episode does not feature in the memoirs Gulbenkian dictated for private circulation in 1945.[6]

---

4 Anthony Sampson, *The Seven Sisters: the Great Oil Companies and the World They Made* (Hodder & Stoughton, New York: 1978); George Sweet Gibb and Evelyn H. Knowlton, *The Resurgent Years, 1911–27: History of the Standard Oil Company of New Jersey* (Business History Foundation, New York: 1956) p 291; Daniel Yergin, *The Prize: the Epic Quest for Oil, Money and Power* (Free Press, New York: 2009) p 188 (with a note of scepticism, but with an inaccurate map). The exception is William Stivers, 'A Note on the Red Line Agreement' in *Diplomatic History* 7.1 (1983) pp 23–34.

5 Joost Jonker and Jan Luiten van Zanden, *A History of Royal Dutch Shell* Vol 10f 3 Vols, *From Challenger to Joint Industry Leader, 1890–1939* (Oxford University Press, Oxford: 2007) p 95

6 Stivers is thus incorrect when he suggests that Hewins' story is 'derived from Gulbenkian's confidential memoir.' Stivers, 'A note', 24. Gulbenkian's memoirs were drafted in 1945 as part of his attempts to retain his interests during the renegotiation of the Red Line Agreement, and should be read in that context. Copies can be found in several archives, including British Petroleum Archive, University of Warwick (hereafter BP), 070229; National Archives and Records Administration, Washington. RG59, 890G.6363/7729/3–448. Total Archives, Paris (hereafter Total). 89ZY521–21, 89.14/21

Nor does it feature in his son Nubar's autobiography.[7] This is odd, as the legend and the quotation were probably made up by Nubar in the course of Hewins' interviews for the book. The grand gesture smacks more of the prodigal son than of the reticent father. Although he was much less significant, in the folk memory of the oil industry Nubar outshines his less demonstrative father. Nubar's habit of being chauffeured around in a black cab with a monocle in his eye and an orchid in his buttonhole made him a conspicuous sight on the streets of London's West End in the 1950s and 1960s. His massive beard, gourmandising, serial marriages, and car- and plane-crashes always made for good copy, encouraging the press to present him as a sort of bearded Mr Toad, a role he happily grew into. In the absence of such cooperation the press had little to work with in the case of Calouste Gulbenkian, painting him as an enigmatic, isolated and lonely figure. Hewins was a reporter for the *Daily Mail*, and he and Nubar may have held that 'Mr Five Percent's life story could benefit from some myth-making.

In so far as the Red Line Agreement was an interpretation of the earlier 1914 Foreign Office agreement, a more detailed account serves to outline the shifts in power which shaped the inter-war era, the period in which Gulbenkian was at the peak of his powers. The other actors with whom he competed and collaborated were powerful empires, nation-states, multi-national companies, staffed by hundreds of employees, backed by armies of soldiers and sailors as well as taxpayers and shareholders. Gulbenkian was one man. That one man could not only survive but flourish on a stage populated with such heavyweights is remarkable. It was an achievement built as a backroom fixer, someone very different from the Gulbenkian who would draw on maps and strike dramatic poses.

In drawing the line the TPC partners were not only shaping the future of the Middle East, they were also conferring on its past. The Ottoman Empire had originally emerged from the early sixteenth-century conquests of Arabia and Egypt, and reached its fullest extent in the late seventeenth century. To the west it embraced all of the Balkans, latter-day Hungary and Romania and even threatened the Austrian capital, Vienna. To the east the 'Ottoman Empire in Asia' was vast, extending over most of North Africa, including Egypt, the Arabian peninsula, the Levant and Caucasus as well as Asia Minor itself. Over the following centuries the Sultan's realms failed to hold the line against expanding European empires, however, beginning in the eighteenth century with the Russians to the north and the Austrians to the west.

---

7 Nubar Gulbenkian, *Portrait in Oil* (Simon & Schuster, New York: 1965).

A shifting palimpsest of protectorates and dependencies expressing different degrees of fealty to the Sultan, even at the best of times the Ottoman Empire struggled to marshal the financial and military resources nominally at its command. Taxes were farmed rather than centrally collected. Military service was restricted to an introspective, self-serving warrior caste. Training in tactics and the associated sciences of war largely ignored advances being made elsewhere in Europe. By the time of the Congress of Berlin in 1878 it was clear to Britain, France, Italy, Germany, Austro-Hungary and Russia that the collapse of the Ottoman Empire was both inevitable and potentially disastrous for European harmony. The following fifty years saw these powers prescribe a series of fiscal and other reforms, in an attempt to manage decline and discourage any one power from grabbing cherished bits of the Empire. These efforts were challenged by both nationalist movements springing up within the Ottoman domains as well as periodic attempts by the Ottoman regime itself to reassert sovereignty, with or without the agenda of reforms demanded by the nations to whom it was heavily indebted.

Drawing the boundary of the 'Ottoman Empire in Asia' as of March 1914 was far from straightforward, therefore. Empires by their very nature tend to be blurry around the edges. The Ottoman view of empire accepted this fact. Its view of *hitta* was very different from the cartographic lens traditional among the western powers, denoting a territory with vague boundaries.[8] This was a contrast to the western powers, which saw the world as a jigsaw puzzle made up of closely-fitting blocks of subject territory. The Sultan did not need accurate maps of his realms to feel that he controlled them, whereas to the western powers, maps were themselves a form of control. This explains the care taken to draw them up and the precautions taken to control access to them. Even in 1928, when one might have thought pre-1914 maps were of purely historical interest, gaining sight of the detailed maps the TPC partners needed to draw the line was not easy. Nor was it easy to reach consensus on the precise significance of the line being drawn. Depending on the language used to describe the course of the line in the legend attached to the map the Agreement could be construed as a diplomatic or commercial agreement, or both at the same time.

TPC partners needed consensus, therefore, both on where to draw the line and on what status should be accorded to the line itself. Broadly speaking they

---

8 M. Sükrü Hanioglu, *A Brief History of the Late Ottoman Empire* (Princeton University Press, Princeton: 2008) p 9.

were divided between the French view, which saw the line as having something approaching the authority of an international treaty, and the view of the
Anglo-Persian Oil Company (APOC, later known as Anglo-Iranian, and finally
BP), which held that the line was purely a matter of business. The French map
had its line embracing a greater area than the APOC map [Figs 1- 2]. The disa-
greement soon drew in both the British and French foreign ministries, as well
as the other TPC partners and the US State Department. It did not, however,
draw in the Turks, even though they certainly had a view on the position of
their eastern border with the new state of Iraq, as well as residual claims to
some of the proceeds from the oil to be extracted from Mosul. The Turks, like
the Iraqis, were entirely excluded.

Although the *Compagnie Française des Pétroles* was viewed by its TPC
partners as a branch of the Quai d'Orsay (the French Foreign Ministry), the
Compagnie appears to have drawn up its map independently in late September 1927. They then showed it to Lefroy, one of APOC's negotiators, who
passed it on to Gulbenkian in early October. Lefroy doubted that the Foreign
Office would agree that Aden, Socotra and other areas included within the
line had in fact been Ottoman in 1914.[9] Even before the opening of the Suez
Canal in 1869, Aden had been identified as a key way station on the way
to India. The East India Company landed troops there in 1839, and Aden
was administered from India until it became a Crown Colony in 1937. Lefroy
ensured that map page in the first print of the draft agreement prepared later
that month was left blank.

On 4 January 1928 Nubar Gulbenkian met with Montagu Piesse, the lawyer
representing the American oil firms who had agreed to come together in a
consortium (Near East Development Corporation) to take their quarter share
in TPC. Piesse felt the map question had been shirked for far too long. During
a recent trip to consult with his superiors at the New York headquarters of
the mighty Standard Oil of New Jersey, Piesse had been informed that Royal
Dutch Shell were already busy chipping away at the western edges of the
would-be Red Line area. In addition to a concession on the Farasan Islands,
Royal Dutch had 'a whole bunch of geologists on the Arabian coast at Assir',
looking for oil on the western edge of the Arabian peninsula.[10]

In defining the area to be controlled by the TPC the 1914 Foreign Office
Agreement had specifically excluded two de facto British protectorates which

9 Lefroy to Calouste Gulbenkian, 3 October 1927, LDN00881, (FCG).
10 Nubar Gulbenkian, Memo 56, 4 January 1928, LDN02938, (FCG).

might otherwise have been considered Ottoman: Kuwait, which had signed a treaty with Britain in 1899, and Egypt, which had achieved semi-autonomous status under the Khedive only to fall under British control after 1882, eventually becoming a British protectorate in 1914. The British seem to have seen the Farasan islands as Egyptian, or at least as lying within their sphere of interest. When the Idrissi princes of Yemen occupied the archipelago in 1914, they were first driven off by British arms, and then offered a Kuwait-style treaty, guaranteeing the Idrissi protection in return for keeping out non-British concessionaires. Among the latter were the Italians, who had grabbed the remaining pieces of Ottoman North Africa in the Tripolitanian War of 1911–2, and were moving aggressively into the horn of Africa.

Royal Dutch was the first oil major to exploit Egyptian oil, and in 1913 managed to secure the Farasan concession from the authorities in Istanbul.[11] By 1927 Ottoman claims seem to have been lapsed, and Royal Dutch secured a new concession from the Idrissi princes on the mainland. According to French foreign ministry sources the concession was paid for partly in two boatloads of weapons.[12] The Idrissi had urgent need of them to fight the Italian-backed Imam Yahya. Like the Americans, the French saw Royal Dutch's actions as contrary to the spirit of the Foreign Office Agreement, and cited the Farasan concession as grounds for legal proceedings they had started against Royal Dutch. Negotiations over the map along with all the other terms of the Red Line Agreement proceeded under a constant barrage of such suits and counter-suits.

In addition to consulting with Nubar, Piesse had also approached Royal Dutch's lawyer, Pirrie, to ask if they approved of the French map. Pirrie replied that they did not, which set Piesse 'furiously thinking'. Piesse saw the Chairman of APOC, John Cadman, who argued that the map could be left until everything else had been agreed. In view of rumours that APOC were angling to divert the Red Line from that traced by the Iraqi-Persian border, Piesse was not reassured.[13] Cadman had prepared his own map, which differed from the French in excluding much of the eastern Gulf and Arabian Peninsula. Given the climate of suspicion fuelled by Farasan and French court proceedings,

---

11 F0195/2453/2338, The National Archives, Kew, London, (hereafter, TNA).

12 French consular official, Jeddah, cited in Pineau to Mercier, 21 February 1927. Mercier had asked the Quai d'Orsay to inform them of the islands' status and the concession in November 1926, 81ZX916–43, (Total).

13 Nubar Gulbenkian, Memo 56, 4 January 1928, LDN02938, (FCG).

APOC's partners in the TPC can be excused for assuming that Cadman left these areas out because he wished to exploit them on his own, without having to share them with Royal Dutch, the French or the Americans.

For their part Near East Development preferred the French map. Jersey Standard counsel Guy Wellman sent a draft of the Red Line Agreement together with the French map to the State Department in early December 1927, asking for their view of the Sultan's claims in 1914. In his reply the Department's Near East Division chief, G. Howland Shaw included copies of plates from a British and French atlas of 1915 and 1912 respectively. 'Although not in any sense official', Shaw wrote, 'they represent, respectively, recognizedly trustworthy British and French sources of information.' Ottoman Turkish suzerainty in the Arabian peninsula had been limited to enclaves at Hejaz, Asir and Yemen, El Hasa, 'and, though not included on either map, the peninsula of El Qatar (where, in accordance with offical British publications, a Turkish garrison had been maintained since 1882).' Even in these areas, however, Shaw noted that Ottoman sovereignty was 'but nominally recognized by the native tribal chieftains' outside the towns.[14]

Rather than make waves, however, the Department was happy to approve the Agreement. For them the main issue had not been the map, but the need for the Agreement to pay lip-service to that 'formula' (never clearly defined) known as 'the Open Door', under which no exclusive or monopolistic commercial arrangements were to be tolerated. American diplomats had been embarrassed by the failure of the 1923 attempt to revive the Chester Concession in Turkey. Although Rear-Admiral Colby Chester's pre-war claim on a vast Anatolian railway and petroleum concession was weak, during the Lausanne conference it had seemed as if American interests might ally with Kemal, supporting the Turkish claim to Mosul in return for Turkish support of this American claim on Mosul's oil. Rather than representing serious financial interests, however, management of this Concession had fallen into the hands of a group of quarrelsome and incompetent shysters whose antics threatened to harm American prestige in the whole region.[15] By 1924 the State Department was

14 These were plate 4 of *The Statesman's Year-Book* (1915) and plate 44 of the *Atlas Universel de Geographie* (Paris: Vivien de St. Martin et Schrader, 1912). Wellman to G. H. Shaw, 7 December, 1927; G. H. Shaw to Wellman, 22 December 1927, RG59, 890G.6363/T84/292, National Archives and Records Administration, College Park, Maryland, [hereafter, NARA].
15 For their antics and State Department unease see Grew to State, 23 May 1923, RG59 867.6020T81/9891/329. (NARA); A. W. Dulles, memo, 26 July 1923; G. H. Shaw to Dulles,

ready to draw its own line under years of tough rhetoric, agreeing with Jersey Standard that TPC was the best chance for leading American oil companies to get into Middle East oil. There was no other chance 'at this late hour to obtain [an] independent concession if such chance ever existed in view of political situation of Iraq.'[16]

On 17 January 1928 the parties met in London to discuss the two maps. Cadman argued that the area excluded from his map had been surveyed by his geologists and was unlikely to contain oil. There was no commercial value, therefore, in including Bahrain, Qatar, Abu Dhabi and Oman. Nor had these territories ever been claimed by the Ottomans (unlike the Persians), so there was no historical or diplomatic rationale, either. Though with hindsight the former argument was to prove inaccurate, on the latter point Cadman was on solid ground. It does indeed seem as if the so-called Trucial States, identified by their 1853 Kuwaiti-style treaties of (exclusive) friendship with Britain were far too remote to have been considered dependencies by the Sultan. Indeed, a 1917 search of the Ottoman archives undertaken to bolster claims to the Arabian peninsula had to be abandoned. In lieu of documentation recourse was had to *Encyclopaedia Britannica*.[17]

Cadman's line was not drawn freely, but followed the 'violet line' established under an Anglo-Ottoman convention negotiated in early 1914 and ratified by the Sultan in June.[18] This addressed a potential source of Anglo-Ottoman friction over the Gulf and the hinterland of Aden, but may have sown a seed of Anglo-Saudi dissension, by seeming to see Britain leave Ibn Sa'ud to strike his own bargain with the Sublime Porte, which he did in May 1914, becoming hereditary governor of the Nejd, what we know as Saudi Arabia. Though Cadman thus had his justifications for a smaller Red Line area, he told the January 1928 meeting that he was happy to go along with the French map, provided it was shown, as a 'courtesy', to the Foreign Office.[19] He duly reported

---

11 June 1923; Durbin to State, 11 April 1923; Thomas Owens to State, 10 May 1923; S. K. Hornbeck, memo, 2 December 1922; RG59 867.6020T81/9891/390, /378, /322, /333 and /338, (NARA).

16 Walter Teagle (quoting Wellman) to A. W. Dulles, 11 November 1924, RG59 890G.6363/ T84/178, (NARA).

17 Hanioglu, *Late Ottoman Empire*, p 13.

18 Strictly speaking this convention was not in force at the time of the Foreign Office Agreement, signed in March 1914, but the point is probably moot.

19 Nubar Gulbenkian, Memo 64, 17 January 1928, LDN02938, (FCG).

on the TPC consensus, adding the unfounded accusation that the *Compagnie Française des Pétroles* 'attach to the decision an ultra-commercial and international importance, in which attitude we have every reason to suppose they are acting under specific instructions from their Government.'[20] In fact the head of the French Office *Nationale des Carburants Liquides* (ONCL), Pineau, only saw the map after the meeting, and was told that French state intervention would only be necessary if the Foreign Office objected to the French map.[21]

At the Foreign Office a librarian named John W. Field set to work, carefully noting the treaties and conventions governing the various sections of the French line.[22] The Black and Red Sea sections simply followed standard definitions of territorial waters. The northeastern, Russo-Ottoman section dated back to the 1870s, to the era of the Congress of Berlin. Otherwise, however, the French line reflected a bevy of agreements reached much more recently, either as a result of Ottoman defeats at the hands of former dependencies such as Greece and Bulgaria, or as the result of conventions with the British, such as that which produced the 'violet line'. The Gulbenkian Red Line myth harked back to some golden age in which the Ottoman Empire's borders had remained static long enough to become indelibly fixed in the memory of every loyal subject. The Red Line negotiations reflect a very different reality: an empire which was shrinking faster than the cartographers could update their maps.

The situation was so fluid that Under-Secretary of State William Tyrrell feared getting bogged down in discussions of, say, the precise borders of Kuwait, discussions which might end up having unintended diplomatic consequences. Even if the Foreign Office could not accept the French map, Tyrrell wrote to his opposite number at the Quai d'Orsay, Philippe Berthelot, was it so important to the TPC that their Red Line be accepted by the Foreign Office as a representation of the extent of the Ottoman Empire in March 1914? Berthelot's response was to suggest that the red line map legend be removed. Stripped of the legend *'Empire Turc en 1914'* the map would not longer be yoked to this messy raft of international conventions, many of which had not in fact been ratified by the Ottomans.[23]

---

20 Cadman to FO, 18 January 1928, F0371/13028 (E330/94/65), (TNA).

21 Tronchère to Pineau, 19 January 1928, 81ZX916–65, (Total).

22 John W. Field, 'Boundaries of the Turkish Empire in March 1914', 24 January 1928, F0371/13028 (E330/94/65), (TNA).

23 Tyrrell to Berthelot, 2 February 1928; Berthelot to Tyrrell, 18 February 1928, 81ZX916–65, (Total).

Robert Cayrol of the *Compagnie* was insisting that the map should document the limit, not of the actual run of the Sultan's writ, but the 'limits of his pretensions' to sovereignty. They should include the Tripolitaine, therefore, as the Sultan still claimed it in 1914, even though this part of Libya had been lost to the Italians in the aforementioned war of 1911–12. Nay, Cayrol continued, it was ultimately down to the TPC partners to determine how widely the red line net could be cast. 'Only conflicts between the partners' interests can determine its limits', he argued, concluding that it was in the interest of all TPC partners to make the area as wide as possible.[24] This was easy for CFP to say, as the French had no interests outside the area, having been latecomers to the diplomacy of oil and having failed to find oil in exploitable quantities among its colonies.

By March 1928 APOC had produced a third map which followed the French line with the exception of Kuwait, where it adopted the 'green line' defined under the unratified Anglo-Turkish Convention of 29 July 1913. This agreement provided that the Sheikh of Kuwait should enjoy complete administrative autonomy within a certain area, demarcated by a red line. Meanwhile within a larger area encompassed by a green line, 'an area occupied by tribes dependent upon him' the Sheikh was to levy the tribute due to the Ottoman sultan. Needless to say, the Ottomans were not to interfere in either area.[25] The convention demonstrated the difficulty of imposing western map-centred ways of representing territory on the Ottoman realms, where sovereignty was attached as much to groups of people (many of them nomadic, or practising transhumance) as it was to plots of ground, and which could be anything but exclusive, with different kinds of sovereignty being exercised upon the same people or territory by different masters at the same time. In Persia, for example, APOC paid royalties both to the state (represented by the Shah in Tehran) as well to the local Bakhtiari khans, a system which relied on all parties signing up to conflicting fictions as to who in fact controlled southern Persia.

Far from learning from this experience Anglo-Persian's Chairman, Cadman, attempted to take the western map-centred model to a logical, if ludicrous conclusion. If the French wanted to take away the title *'Empire Turc en 1914'*, he reasoned, why not go all the way and strip the map of any legend that might invite diplomatic cavilling? The red line should not follow the course of

---

24 Cayrol minute, 11 February 1928, 81ZX916–65, (Total).
25 Seymour memo, 12 March 1928, F0371/13028 (E1219/94/65), (TNA).

this or that prior treaty, but stand on its own. Tyrrell relayed this suggestion to Berthelot in mid-March, urging the removal of 'all the definitions and political explanations relating to the position of the red line.'[26] The *Compagnie* greeted this as an 'infantile manoeuvre', intended to help Anglo-Persian grab more oil-producing land in the Transferred Territories, an ill-defined patch of terri-tory on the Iraqi-Persian border, which would remain one of the most fought over frontiers in the Middle East. Berthelot pointed out to Tyrrell the obvious problem: 'The line cannot possibly be considered in isolation: on a map of so small a scale a deviation of a millimeter might represent an error of several kilometers.'[27]

For the time being, however, the *Compagnie* was outnumbered, as the other TPC partners declared themselves in favour of a map with a red line and no legend at all, while conceding that such a map would have to be drawn on a much larger scale. Cadman seemed to have succeeded in iso-lating the *Compagnie* even from the Quai d'Orsay, while making it seem as if it had been the Foreign Office's idea to suppress the legend.[28] Yet it proved surprisingly difficult to come up with a large-scale red line map. When Cadman asked to use their map collection the Foreign Office informed him that tracing the line would involve consulting no less than nineteen maps, some of which were secret and could not be borrowed. An Anglo-Persian representative duly visited the map room in early May, and Cadman insisted to Cayrol that a line-only map was the best option.[29] Meanwhile Berthelot cabled the French Ambassador in London, de Fleuriau, twice asking him to get a clear statement on the map from the Foreign Office in time to stop Cadman (or rather, *les groupes anglo-saxons*) presenting the *Compagnie Française* with a fait d'accompli at the TPC meeting scheduled for 5 June.[30]

That the second Anglo-Persian map was carried with the French text citing various diplomatic accords, albeit without the title referring to the '*Empire Turc*

---

26 Tyrrell to Berthelot, 15 March 1928, 81ZX916–65, (Total).

27 Tronchère to Ministère des Affaires Etrangères, 21 March 1928 (territories); Tronchère to Burgin ('infantile'), 30 March 1928, 81ZX916–65, (Total). Berthelot to Tyrrell, 3 April 1928, 81ZX916–66, (Total).

28 Burgin to Tronchere, 24 May 1928; 'Contrat Principal – La Carte', memo [before 3 June, 1928], 81ZX916–66, (Total).

29 Cadman to Cayrol, 25 May 1928, F0371/13028 (E2836/94/65), (TNA).

30 Berthelot to de Fleuriau, 24 and 30 May 1928, 19RC/61, 62 and 69, *Ministère des Affaires Etrangères Archives*, Paris (hereafter, MAE).

en 1914', was partly a result of the challenge of producing a map that did not depend on the foundations laid by previous treaties. News came on 29 May that two Iraqi wells at Baba Gurgur and Al Qayyarah had struck oil. Though the TPC still lacked a pipeline and terminal needed to realise these assets, this must nonetheless have served to remind the partners of the cost of further delay. On the eve of the June TPC meeting the chairman of the CFP Mercier told a meeting of French state and company officials that speed was now of the essence: the map should be agreed and the Transferred Territories border defined as the Wilson-Minorsky Line, the border defined by a 1913–14 border commission led by a Briton, Arnold Wilson, and the Russian Vladimir Minorsky.[31]

Over a further three days of meetings language was found to skate over the problems with the Wilson-Minorsky line (whose own map did not tally with the written definition) and agree on an arbitrator for disputes. Cadman eventually agreed to include Bahrain, Qatar, Oman and the other territories included within the French line. As Cadman wrote to Gulbenkian, he did so 'with the reservation that in our opinion that position of the red line is without historical or political basis.'[32] In late June a version (the tenth print) of the Red Line Agreement finally appeared complete with a map. On the 11 July a copy sailed for New York on the *Île de France*.

In March 1928, in the midst of the map negotiations the Iraqi ambassador to Britain, Muzahim Beg Ali Pachachi (who had helped negotiate TPC's 1925 concession agreement) had reassured Cadman that although he would adopt 'ultra nationalist' rhetoric on his return to Baghdad, this was merely window dressing: he would stick by TPC. TPC responded by indulging in some window-dressing of his own, sending Pachachi back with a letter offering to give TPC 'a more Irak sounding name, such as Irak Petroleum, or Mossoul Petroleum, or something like that.'[33] The name was, indeed, changed the following year, to Iraq Petroleum.[34] Meanwhile news of the Red Line Agreement reached Baghdad, even before the final signatures were appended (and court

---

31 'Note pour Monsieur Berthelot', 4 June 1928, 19RC/61, (MAE), p 74.

32 Cadman to Calouste Gulbenkian, 15 June 1928, LDN00881, (FCG). The same phrase appears in Cadman to CFP, 15 June 1928, 81ZX916–66, (Total).

33 Nubar Gulbenkian, TPC memo, 3 March 1928. LDN02938, (FCG). TPC's H. E. Nichols had proposed dropping the 'Turkish' moniker in 1924, but Calouste Gulbenkian had felt it premature, as the Turkish-Iraqi border had yet to be settled. Nichols to Calouste Gulbenkian, 2 January 1924, LDN00565, (FCG).

34 To prevent confusion, however, I refer to TPC throughout.

proceedings stopped) on 31 July. The Iraqi government asked the TPC for a copy of the Red Line Agreement. The TPC partners consulted with each other, agreeing that they would refuse to share this information.[35]

Where was Gulbenkian amidst all this? There is little evidence that he had much input. This was not because he was uninterested in maps. Indeed, the maps guarded by the Foreign Office may well have included items Gulbenkian had donated to the War Office in 1915. As Lord Kitchener's Private Secretary had noted at the time 'we have no such maps on quite so complete a scale.'[36] Ten years later, when a League of Nations delegation led by a Hungarian, Count Teleki, was deputised to settle the Turkish-Iraqi border, Gulbenkian offered to help get the maps drawn in such a way that any oil-producing areas the TPC might want ended up on the Iraqi side. Teleki's cartographer, Gulbenkian explained, a certain Khanzadian, was the old Ottoman cartographer, knew of Gulbenkian's interest in TPC and had approached Gulbenkian through a mutual school friend, Aram Djevhirdjian:

Khanzadian knows all the crooks [sic] and corners of the place, and as the other members are not cartographers, it remains for him to make up the map according to certain instructions regarding topographical positions; I am given to understand that he can turn this as he likes, and so Khanzadian desires to get into personal and confidential touch with me, relying on my position and name to keep the whole thing a dead letter. He is desirous of knowing which are the points that our company would like to remain on the side of Iraq.[37]

Why bother with international conventions, delegations, protocols and treaties, Gulbenkian argued, when borders could be fixed your way, for just £2,000? Others might go to the starting line. Gulbenkian went straight to the finish. It was all about contacts, and contacts were rarely made at board meetings or around a table in the Geneva headquarters of the League of Nations.

It was entirely characteristic, therefore, that while the Red Line negotiations were held in London, Calouste Gulbenkian spent most of the four years

35 Tronchère to Calouste Gulbenkian, 22 July, 1928; Essayan to Tronchère, 22 July 1928, LDN02937, (FCG).
36 H.J. Creedy (PS to Kitchener) to Calouste Gulbenkian, 26 April 1915, LDN00514, (FCG).
37 Calouste Gulbenkian, 'Memorandum to be read to Mr Nichols', 20 June 1925, LDN00866, (FCG).

of negotiations (1924–8) in France, either at the Ritz in Paris or in one of the resorts he frequented throughout his life: Cannes, Deauville, Aix-Les-Bains. Nubar attended the London meetings for him, assisted by his brother-in-law, Kevork Essayan. In late May 1928 Nubar mentioned the map in one of his regular memos to his father. Nubar assumed Calouste would be happy to go along with his fellow TPC partners. A long phone conversation with Cadman had left Nubar persuaded that the French were simply seeking to make trouble with their map, and trying unsuccessfully to claim that they had Gulbenkian's support.[38]

Gulbenkian's aloof stance contrasted with the sense of occasion his son brought to the final signature of the Agreement in Ostend. Nubar chartered a plane from a friend who was a pilot and arranged for the various lawyers as well as the crew to regale themselves before returning. According to the lively account given in Nubar's autobiography, the party was lucky to make it back in one piece.[39] The squabble over the map was something of a sideshow compared to the negotiations over the various agreements which accompanied it, negotiations which had taken up four years and in which Gulbenkian had taken a conspicuous, if sometimes obstreperous part – again, largely working through intermediaries.

The difficulties surrounding the drawing of the Red Line in turn reflected the challenges faced by the oil majors and the various foreign ministries as they staked their claims to Middle Eastern oil in post-imperial world. Although transport infrastructure was extremely poor in most of the Red Line area, making oil exploration and production expensive and time consuming, the difficulties the TPC and its sponsors faced in conceiving the former Ottoman Empire mentally were arguably just as great. Sovereignties and territories had often overlapped in the Ottoman realms, and the treaties struck between the Ottoman Empire and western powers (Britain above all) only added another layer to the confusing palimpsest.

As the exchange with Pachachi shows, in 1928 the TPC partners had hardly begun to conceive of 'Iraq', which reached formal independence in 1932. Many observers held that Iraqi policy was set by Britain, which had received the League's Mandate in 1920, in the same way that France had for Syria. Alongside the Red Line negotiations the TPC was also negotiating for an oil concession in Iraq, which was signed on 14 March 1925. But who exactly were they negotiating with? The Hashemite monarch the Britain had imported

---

38 Nubar Gulbenkian memo, 31 May 1928, LDN02938, (FCG).
39 Nubar Gulbenkian, *Selfportrait*, pp 98–9.

and put on a new Iraqi throne (Faysal) in August 1921, his ministers (drawn from local elites) or the British Civil Commissioner (Sir Percy Cox)? Though these negotiations form a distinct story, here again the question 'whose oil?' was far from clear.

In November 1946 one of the negotiators of the Red Line Agreement, Lefroy, was asked by colleagues at BP to provide information on how it was drawn up. Another epic round of TPC negotiations was now under way, which would culminate in the so-called Group Agreement of 1948, which saw (among other things) Gulbenkian alloted extra 'liftings' of oil in compensation for his American colleagues' having taken advantage of the Second World War and the discovery of oil in Saudi Arabia to leave the 1928 agreement. The map came up again. Lefroy's reply gives a sense of the corporate memory of an oil company, which in this case dates back to the era of D'Arcy Exploration, the predecessor of APOC/BP. It also gives a sense of the gruelling nature of TPC negotiations: a game of skill and tactics fought, with four 'partners', in board-rooms, courtrooms, chancelleries and back-room meetings:

> As for the 1928 Red Line I have told you the story many times (CFP/alias
> Quai d'Orsay) were anxous for the most extended application of the FO.
> Ag[reemen]t. reference to the 'Turkish Empire', and produced the first draft
> of a map to be attached to the hoped for Group Agreement. It appeared
> to me fantastic to claim such places as Bahrain, Muscat and Aden as parts
> of the Turkish Empire and of no service to A[P]OC to tie in these lands
> unnecessarily in the Gulf, tho' in those days all scientists attached v[er]
> y little importance to Saudi Arabia, Kuwait, Bahrain or the Trucial Coast
> incl. Qatar. It took a good deal of pains to discover any maps of service
> in regard to the Turkish areas of Arabia and eventually found in W.O. the
> (then) secret map of 1912 or thereabouts and based thereupon the D'Arcy
> proposal for a red line – by March 1928 the attempt to secure agreement
> among the group had succeeded up to the map stage but broken me and
> I had 3 months sick leave, in which I went with my wife to Persia at our
> own costs, and on return found J[ohn] C[adman] had conceded the Red
> line in Arabia, on which others were indifferent, in exchange for some
> concession of the French, I forget what. JC told me specifically that it was
> in the belief that retention of liberty of action in the area enclosed by the
> "Darcy" line was valueless to us, viz. Bahrain, Qatar and Trucial Coast.[40]

---

40 Lefroy to Taylor, 6 November 1946, 126859, (BP).

Rather than being a coup de main by Calouste Gulbenkian, the process of delineating the red line was drawn out. The negotiations over the map came as a surprise to TPC partners, who had previously assumed that drawing the line would be a matter of dotting the 'i's and crossing the 't's of the Agreement, over which directors and teams of highly-paid lawyers had toiled for several years. That it were not so was partly down to history. Ottoman conceptions of sovereignty over peoples was difficult to accommodate within a European 'jigsaw' model based on geography. The way in which the Ottoman Empire's decline had been managed by and for the benefit of Britain, France and other powers ensured that it would be difficult for them to agree on even a historical 'snapshot' of how the 'Turkish Empire in Asia' had looked in March 1914.

The French were also partly to blame, for seeking the widest possible interpretation of 'the Turkish Empire in Asia', as a means of compensating for their woefully unsuccessful attempts to secure their own oil supplies in the years after 1916, when the French war effort had almost come to a standstill for want of liquid fuels. A sense of the French debt to Gulbenkian for helping France out of that perilous situation may explain CFP's tendency to ally with Gulbenkian. It more likely reflected a desire for solidarity against the aforementioned *groupes anglo-saxons*. Despite his British citizenship, Gulbenkian's close relationship with Royal Dutch-Shell had ruptured in 1926, facilitating this. As it happens, the map negotiations saw CFP pulling away from Gulbenkian. They would subsequently receive their own reward for accepting the Americans' grab for Saudi Arabia.

For all APOC's claims that for CFP one should read 'Quai d'Orsay', the map episode shows that the relationship between 'national champions' and their governments was far from a question of puppet and puppet-master. The 'French' map originated as a CFP map, not a Quai d'Orsay map. CFP was more eager to involve French diplomats than vice versa. As for the British Foreign Office, Tyrrell seems to have been eager to let APOC get on with it; like CFP, APOC seems to have invited the meddling of 'their' government, which was also a major shareholder. Such moves may have helped both firms play games of 'Good Cop'/'Bad Cop' with each other, claiming that their own demands had in fact been imposed on them by pesky chancelleries. When it came to Iraq, having a hegemon to call on was reassuring as well as tactically useful. Iraq without her mandatory power was *terra incognita*, one few within TPC were curious to explore.

A year later, in October 1929 Nubar Gulbenkian was busy organising characteristically lavish entertainments with a geo-political purpose: to prepare for the British exit from Iraq by establishing friendly relations with 'the various Iraq notabilities.' Although in 1928 they had supported the decision not to share the Red Line Agreement with the Iraqis, over the following years Nubar and his father were lone voices within TPC in favour of greater transparency. By taking the effort to inform and educate such 'notabilities' about the risks, technology and massive capital necessary to tap 'their' oil reserves one could forestall calls for nationalisation, calls later driven by the very rhetoric of western exploitation Muzahim Beg cheerfully admitted stoking. At a dinner hosted by Nubar and his sister Rita Essayan, John Cadman and other oil directors as well as General Nouri Pasha al-Said (Iraqi Minister of War, later Prime Minister) and the Persian Ambassador to Britain listened as Ja'far Pasha al-Askari (former Iraqi Prime Minister) explained how he saw the TPC/Iraq relationship. 'He said it was like a woman married to four husbands and that was very difficult for the woman and for Iraq. I asked him where Gulbenkian comes in that simile and he told me that Iraq considers Gulbenkian the 'Amant'.'[41]

Iraq's apparent willingness to sit by while the Red Line carve-up went on in London seems of a piece with its negotiations in Baghdad between 1923 and 1925, which saw it advance a demand for a shareholding in TPC, only to drop it. As R. W. Ferrier has suggested, this may simply reflect a desire to trade 'later expectations' for the 'immediate benefits' of allowing TPC to push on to production, which would in turn provide royalty funds urgently needed as Iraq (like Britain) sought a swift exit from Mandate status (achieved in 1932).[42] Granting the Iraqi state a shareholding would have roused slumbering Turkish hopes of receiving shares (or some other form of compensation) for tolerating the drawing of the Turkey-Iraq border in 1926 in such a way that the oil-rich lands ended up on the non-Turkish side.[43]

At the end of the day, one had to draw the line somewhere.

---

41 Nubar Gulbenkian to Calouste Gulbenkian, 7 October 1929, LDN00812, (FCG).

42 R. W. Ferrier and James Bamberg, *The History of the British Petroleum Company* Vol 1 of 2, *The Developing Years* (Cambridge University Press, Cambridge: 1982–94) p 585.

43 Curzon as well as the British Colonial Office had hinted at this possibility at Lausanne in 1923. Mejcher, *Imperial Quest*, pp 133, 140.

Acknowledgements

'To everything there is a season.' With this quote from the Book of Ecclesiastes Johann Wolfgang von Goethe opens the scholarly essay part of his *West-Eastern Divan*, his homage to the Persian poet Hafez and to Islamic culture. The Persian-Arabic word *divan* means assembly, and in the *West-Eastern Divan* Goethe assembled lyrical and scholarly texts about the East. This study of the Other was Goethe's personal attempt to broaden the minds of his readers who were fearful of the Islamic world. Today once again the Western world feels threatened; the debate all too often framed as a clash of civilisations. Werner Mark Linz, the founder of Continuum and later Director of the American University in Cairo Press, believed that the time had come for a new *divan*, and towards the end of his life envisaged this project of academic conferences and publications by scholars from both the West and the MENA region. I would not have dared set about realizing his dream without the initial and continued encouragement of El Hassan bin Talal and David Owen, both of whom knew Mark and shared his vision of fostering understanding between East and West through dialogue based on mutual respect. The Gingko Library is named after the best known poem in the *West-Eastern Divan*, an ode to friendship and symbol of the union between old and young, man and woman, the human and the Divine, literature and scholarship, East and West.

To hold the first of the annual dialogues within months of the Gingko Library's registration as a charity in England and Wales was an ambitious plan. It was realised only with the advice and support of many people. Those who selflessly gave of their time and expertise include Tessa Boteler and Melanie Gibson, who guided the team through the maze of organising an academic conference, and Max Weiss and Eugene Rogan, who commented on countless draft schedules and were at hand to chair sessions.

The conference would never have come together without the hard work and long planning meetings of a core team headed by Stephen Brown, Aran Byrne and Harry Hall, supported by Farhanah Mamoojee and Daniel El-Gamry.

Anthony Grayling pledged his support, along with that of the New College of the Humanities, from the outset and welcomed the delegates as co-host on the opening morning of the conference. In her keynote address Leila Tarazi Fawaz brilliantly set the scene for a conference on the impact and aftermath of the First World War on the Middle East.

The conference had particular focus on how the period began a long process of reshaping the identities of the peoples of the Middle East. It asked how our understanding of this history has changed in both Western and Middle-Eastern scholarship. What is the relevance of this history to the self-understanding of the people and politics of the region today? What were the implications in terms of the concept of nation state and national boundaries? And how did it influence the legitimacy and governance in the region? This volume includes a selection of papers presented at the conference and reflects the wide variety of participants from universities in North America, Europe and the Middle East, including Egypt, Israel and the Gulf. It also includes contributions from scholars who could not join the proceedings in person but whose views make this an even more wide-ranging study, covering the histories of present-day Egypt, Iran, Iraq, Jordan, Lebanon, Libya, Syria and Turkey on topics ranging from oil, the Kurds, the Caliphate and Jihad. I owe huge debt of gratitude to the editorial team headed by Tom Fraser and Alan Sharp. Matthew Eastwood and Stephen Chumbley worked tirelessly to get this volume ready for publication at the Gingko Library Conference of 2015.

I also want to thank Luc Ferier, President of the Forgotten Heroes 14–19 Foundation, for his support and providing the photograph on the jacket of this volume. His foundation has become a driving force in creating international awareness of the fact that soldiers from countries like Algeria, Egypt, Morocco and Tunisia contributed tremendously in the fiercest battles during the First World War and paid a huge price with the loss of hundreds of thousand lives. 'In these extremely difficult times for the Muslim and Arab community, in which the media seem to link every aspect of their culture, philosophy and religion with evil, bloodshed and fear, I believe it is my duty to bring forward this beautiful story about their ancestors,' Luc Ferier said. 'It is an important part of their history and identity they are looking for. Telling this positive story, that remained forgotten far too long, will help them reclaim their dignity and confidence, no matter the continent or country they currently live in.' The

Gingko Library shares the Foundation's hopes that this will be 'a good start to reach out to this community and to create the possibility to build an everlasting bridge, founded on strong pillars of mutual respect.'

Barbara Haus Schwepcke
July 2015
Trustee of the Gingko Library

Contributors

T.G. Fraser MBE is Emeritus Professor of History at Ulster University, former Provost of its Magee campus, and Fulbright Scholar-in-Residence Indiana University at South Bend. He has written extensively on the modern history of the Middle East, India and American foreign policy, including, with Andrew Mango and Robert McNamara, *The Makers of the Modern Middle East* (Gingko Library, London: 2015, revised and updated); *The Arab-Israeli Conflict* (Palgrave, London: 2015, 4th edition); edited, with John Hume and Leonie Murray *Peacemaking in the twenty-first century* (Manchester University Press, Manchester: 2013). He is a Fellow of the Royal Asiatic Society.

Amany Soliman is a Lecturer in Modern History and International Relations in the Mediterranean Studies Institute at the Faculty of Arts – Alexandria University in Egypt. Her latest published work is Amany Soliman and Gulcin Coskun (ed.) *Guardians or opressors: Civil Military relations and democratization in the Mediterranean Region* by Cambridge Scholars Publishing. In 2010, she obtained her PhD in the political and social history of the Mediterranean. She was a fellow of the International Centre for the Study of Radicalization and Political Violence in King's College London during 2011. Soliman's research interests includes: nationalism, ethnic and regional disputes, democratisation, the Great War and its impact on the Middle East, The EuroMed relations and history of modern Egyptian nationalism and feminism. She was awarded the first Gingko Scholarship which enabled her to participate in the Inaugural Gingko Library Conference the proceedings of which are published in this volume.

Jason Pack is President of Libya-Analysis® and a doctoral candidate at the University of Cambridge. His thesis will appear in book form as *Britain's Informal*

Empire in Libya? The Anglo-Sanussi Relationship, 1889–1969 (Hurst, London: 2017). Mr Pack is the editor of The 2011 Libyan Uprisings and the Struggle for the Post-Qadhafi Future (Palgrave Macmillan, London: June 2013), lead author of Libya's Faustian Bargains: Breaking the Appeasement Cycle (Atlantic Council, May 2014), and author of frequently-updated Libya: Situation Report for the Tony Blair Faith Foundation. His articles have appeared in *The New York Times, The Wall Street Journal, The Spectator, Foreign Affairs,* and *Foreign Policy.*

Steven Wagner completed his doctorate in history from the University of Oxford in 2014. His dissertation examined matters of intelligence and policy in Anglo-Arab-Zionist relations during the British Mandate of Palestine. Currently, he is converting his dissertation into a book, and will begin a postdoctoral fellowship at McGill University in August 2015. His new research focuses on British intelligence and policy in the Middle East during 1915–42, a period of continuous Arab revolt.

Noga Efrati is Senior Lecturer at the Department of History, Philosophy, and Judaic Studies, The Open University of Israel. She is the author of *Women in Iraq: Past Meets Present* (Columbia University Press, New York: 2012).

Mark Farha (PhD Harvard, 2007) is an Assistant Professor of Government at the School of Foreign Service in Doha, Qatar. Since 2008, he has taught courses at Georgetown on the history and politics of the modern Middle East, with a special focus on secularism and sectarianism. His publications include: 'Demographic Dilemmas' in *Lebanon: Liberation, Conflict and Crisis,* ed. Barry Rubin, (New York: 2009); 'From Beirut Spring to Regional Winter?' in *Breaking the Cycle: Civil Wars in Lebanon* (London: 2007), 'Historical Legacy and Political Implications of State and Sectarian Schools in Lebanon' in *Rethinking Education for Social Cohesion,* ed. by Maha Shuayb, (London: 2012); 'Global Gradations of Secularism', *Comparative Sociology.* 11:3 (2012); *'The Arab Revolts: Local, Regional and Global Catalysts and Consequences.'* in *Conceptualizing the Arab Uprisings: Origins, Experiences and Trajectories,* edited by Michael Hudson & Fahad al Sumait, (Rowen and Littlefield, London: 2014); 'Stumbling Blocks to the Secularization of Personal Status Laws in the Lebanese Republic (1926–2012)', *Arab Law Quarterly,* v01.29, Jan. 2015. 'Secular Autocracy vs. Sectarian Democracy? The Minority Malaise in Egypt and Syria.' Coauthored with Salma Mousa. Lorenzo Kamel. (ed.) *Mediterranean Politics,*

2015, Vol 2. 'Secularism in a Sectarian Society: The divisive drafting of the Lebanese Constitution of 1926' in *Constitution Writing, Religion and Democracy,* ed. Bali and Lerner (Cambridge University Press, Cambridge: 2016).

Najwa al-Qattan is Associate Professor of Middle East History at Loyola Marymount University in Los Angeles. She received her PhD from Harvard University in 1996. She has written on the history of Syria and Lebanon in the First World War, as well as the Jews and Christians in the Ottoman Empire, in books and journals, including *International Journal of Middle East Studies (IJMES) and Comparative Studies in Society and History (CSSH).*

Andrew Arsan is University Lecturer in Modern Middle Eastern History in the Faculty of History, Cambridge, and a Fellow of St John's College. His publications include *Interlopers of Empire: The Lebanese Diaspora in Colonial West Africa* (Hurst, London: 2014).

Ms Louise Pyne-Jones is a current PhD candidate at the University of Leeds, where her research is a comparative study that focuses on the ideologies of the British and French military in the Middle East Campaigns of the First World War. Her MA in International Relations, alongside many years spent in the Middle East, led her to historical research of the region. She has recently been teaching Academic English courses at UK universities.

Aaron Y. Zelin is the Richard Borow Fellow at the Washington Institute for Near East Policy and Rena and Sami David Fellow at the International Centre for the Study of Radicalisation and Political Violence. He is also a PhD candidate at King's College London where his dissertation is on the history of the Tunisian jihadi movement. Zelin is also the founder of the widely acclaimed and cited website Jihadology.net.

John McHugo is the author of *A Concise History of the Arabs* and *Syria: A Recent History.* He is a Senior Fellow at the Centre for Syrian Studies at St Andrews University and a former honorary Visiting Fellow at the Scottish Centre for International Law at Edinburgh University. After studying Arabic and Islamic studies at Oxford and the American University in Cairo, he qualified as a solicitor and practised law in relation to Arab countries during the period 1981–2007 with the City of London law firm Trowers & Hamlins, after which he retired to devote himself to writing and research. www.johnmchugo.com.

Kaveh Ehsani is Assistant Professor of International Studies at DePaul University. His current research investigates the historical impact of the oil industry on society and politics. He is completing a book manuscript titled 'The Urban Life of Oil: Abadan and the Making of Modern Iran'.

Bruno Ronfard lived and worked for thirteen years in Cairo. He co-edited, together with Zina Weygand, Suzanne Taha Hussein's manuscript *Avec toi – De la France à l'Égypte : « Un extraordinaire amour » Suzanne et Taha Hussein (1915–1973)* (Cerf, Paris: 2011). He is the author of several works including a biography of Taha Hussein. He is currently Director of the Center for e-Learning at the Faculty of Continuing Education – University of Montreal (Quebec, Canada).

Michael Erdman is a PhD candidate in the Near and Middle East Studies Programme at the School of Oriental and African Studies. Michael's doctoral project is a comparative analysis of Soviet and Turkish historiographies of pre-Islamic Central Asia between 1921 and 1947. His research interests also include late Ottoman history, Middle Eastern ideologies and left-wing extremist movements in the Middle East.

Dr Sevinç Elaman-Garner is a Lecturer in the Middle Eastern Department at the University of Manchester. Her research interests are in gender, sexuality, ethnicity, nationalism and women and war, women's movement (in particular in Ottoman/Turkish society and literature). She has taught courses including Modern Turkish Literature, Contemporary Middle Eastern Cinema and Middle Eastern Studies. Her PhD thesis was a comparative study of literary depictions of New Womanhood in Turkey and the USA in the late 19th and 20th centuries.

Laila McQuade graduated from the University of Mary Washington in May 2014 with a Bachelor's degree in Political Science and International Affairs.

An expert on the modern Middle East, **Nabil Al-Tikriti** earned a Bachelor's degree in Arab Studies from Georgetown University, a Master's degree in International Affairs from Columbia University, and a Doctorate in Ottoman History from the University of Chicago in 2004. He has also studied at Boğaziçi Üniversitesi in Istanbul, the Center for Arabic Studies Abroad in Cairo, and the American University in Cairo. He is the recipient of several grants and scholarships, including two Fulbrights, a U.S. Institute of Peace Fellowship, and a NEH/American Research Institute in Turkey grant. Dr. Al-Tikriti is currently Associate Professor of Middle East History at the University of Mary Washington, and a member of the MSF/Doctors Without Borders USA Board of Directors.

Alp Yenen is a PhD candidate and an Assistant Lecturer in Middle Eastern Studies at the University of Basel. He graduated from a combined undergraduate and graduate programme at the University of Munich in History and Culture of the Middle East and Political Science. For his PhD dissertation Alp Yenen is working on Muslim revolutionary networks during the aftermath of World War I. His recent publications are 'Approaching Transnational Political History: The Role of Non-State Actors in the Post-Ottoman State-Formation', in Steffi Marung and Matthias Middell (eds.), *Transnational Actors – Crossing Borders: Transnational History Studies* (Leipziger Universitätsverlag, Leipzig: 2015) and 'The "Young Turk Zeitgeist" among the Middle Eastern Uprisings during the Aftermath of World War I' in M. Hakan Yavuz and Feroz Ahmad (eds.), *War and Collapse: World War I and the Ottoman State* (University of Utah Press, Salt Lake City: forthcoming in 2015). Alp Yenen's research interests focus on contentious politics of state formation and reformation, actors and networks of parapolitics, and history of political ideas in the modern Middle East.

Harrison B. Guthorn recently completed his Ph.D. at the University of Maryland and is now a Lecturer at the University of Virginia. His dissertation 'Capital Development: Mandate Era Amman and the Construction of the Hashemite State' focused on how Amman became the nexus of power in Jordan while still allowing for the development of a hybridised city that incorporated Ottoman, Arab, and British heritage.

Dr Jonathan Conlin teaches modern British history at the University of Southampton. His books include *The Nation's Mantelpiece, a history of the National Gallery, Evolution and the Victorians* and most recently *Tales of Two Cities: Paris, London and the Birth of the Modern City.* Since 2013 he has been leading a five-year project researching the life and career of Calouste Gulbenkian. Supported by the Calouste Gulbenkian Foundation, this project aims to produce the definitive biography of this pre-eminent business architect.

Index

Index

Mustafa Kemal (Ataturk) 1, 12, 35,
104, 131, 182, 228, 248, 290

N
Nasser, President 20
Nasser al-Din Shah 194
Nucaima, Mikhail 117–19, 120

O
Odian, Yervent 33
oil 5, 14, 60
Anglo-Persian Oil Company
(APOC), the 5, 191–3, 195–7,
199, 202–3, 205–8, 210–11,
319, 320–1, 324, 329, 330
Compagnie Française des Pétroles
(CFP) 319, 323–4, 328, 329,
330
Iran, and 191–212
Red Line Agreement, the 313–31
Royal Dutch Shell 319–21, 330
Turkish Petroleum Company
(TPC), the 313–14, 317, 318–19,
321–31
Oman 322, 326
Ottoman Empire, the 2–3, 25, 31,
32, 64, 65–7, 94, 114, 148, 151,
154, 187–8, 225, 227, 230–1,
233–4, 243, 303, 313–14, 317–18,
323, 328

P
Pachachi, Muzahim Beg Ali 326,
328
Palestine 3, 5–6, 7, 9–10, 11, 22,
64, 70, 71–2, 92, 132, 158, 175–6,
179, 180, 181–2, 186, 187, 276,
296, 301, 308

pan-Islamism 47, 54, 64–5, 68–9,
73–5, 97, 104, 132, 257, 282
Paris Peace Conference, the 8,
127–45, 267
Hijaz delegation to 128–35,
139–40, 144
Lebanese delegations 105,
129–31, 134, 140–1, 143–4
Pavlovich, M. N. 278
Pichon, Stephen 141
Piesse, Montagu 319–20
Plumer, Field Marshal Herbert 297
Poincaré, President 105

Q
Qadhafi, Colonel 60, 61
Qassab, Kamil al- 66, 67, 72, 74–5
Qassam, Izz al-Din 186
Qatar 321, 322, 326, 329
Qutb, Sayyid 160, 163–4, 166, 169,
189
Quzma, Amīn 95

R
Radek, Karl 280
Red Line Agreement (1928), the, *see
under* oil
Reed, John 280
Reuter, G. Talbot Julius 194
Reza Khan 197, 209–10, 211, 212
Rida, Rashid 65–8, 70, 72, 73, 75,
94, 216, 218
Rihāni, Amin al- 103
Rondot, Pierre 265–6
Rothschild, Lord 7
Royal Dutch Shell 319–21, 330
Royle, Captain Leopold 52
Rusafi, Ma'ruf al- 81–2